ADVANCE PRAISE FOR *THE FIRST SCIENTIFIC AMERICAN*

"This delightful portrait of Benjamin Franklin is unlike any recent study of the original American 'genius.' In contrast to other biographers, the historian Joyce Chaplin rightfully portrays Franklin first and foremost as a man of science, curious not only about electricity but about ocean currents, winds, and maps—indeed, about virtually all the phenomena of heaven and earth. In convincing detail, she demonstrates how the ambitious printer and natural philosopher from Philadelphia parlayed his scientific fame into an internationally acclaimed career as a gentleman and statesman."

> —Ronald L. Numbers, Hilldale and William Coleman Professor
> of the History of Science and Medicine,
> University of Wisconsin–Madison

"This is a brilliant and compelling book that restores science to its rightful centrality in Benjamin Franklin's thought and career, and that makes us think anew about the changing nature of scientific genius."

> —Linda Colley, Shelby M. C. Davis 1958 Professor
> of History, Princeton University

"*The First Scientific American* shows how Benjamin Franklin became a statesman because of his science and offers a fresh perspective on one of America's founding fathers in a brilliant analysis of the seesaw between science and politics two centuries ago. Joyce Chaplin takes us back to an era when science was in society's mainstream, when there were no specialists. She has written an engaging, literate portrait of Franklin that changes traditional perceptions of this remarkable genius. This is an important, ground-breaking work which places the history of early American science on a new footing."

> —Brian Fagan, Emeritus Professor of Anthropology,
> University of California, and author of
> *Fish on Friday: Feasting, Fasting, and the Discovery of North America*

The
First Scientific
American

THE
First Scientific American

BENJAMIN FRANKLIN

AND THE

PURSUIT *of* GENIUS

JOYCE E. CHAPLIN

BASIC

BOOKS

A Member of the Perseus Books Group

NEW YORK

FOR CLINT
"A Brother's a Treasure"
—Poor Richard

Published by Basic Books
A Member of the Perseus Books Group

Design by Jane Raese
Text set in 11-point New Baskerville

Library of Congress Cataloging-in-Publication Data
Chaplin, Joyce E.
The first scientific American : Benjamin Franklin and the pursuit of
genius / Joyce E. Chaplin.
p. cm.
ISBN-10: 0-465-00955-7
ISBN-13: 978-0-465-00955-8 (hardcover)
1. Franklin, Benjamin, 1706–1790. 2. Scientists—United States—
Biography. 3. Statesman—United States—Biography. I. Title.
Q143.F8C47
2006
509'.2—dc22
2006000125

06 07 08 09 / 10 9 8 7 6 5 4 3 2 1

CONTENTS

ILLUSTRATIONS

Chapter 1

GENIUS

F AMOUS, fascinating Benjamin Franklin—he would be neither without his accomplishments in natural science. Yet science, his life's central feature, is also its most mysterious aspect, the one least understood now and a part of a world we have lost. In his lifetime, science illuminated him with a brilliant electrical flash. We seem to have been blinded by that light. Not so Franklin's contemporaries, who saw at its burning center something, and someone: a unique and remarkable man—the first scientific American.

By the end of his life, Benjamin Franklin (1706–1790) was one of the most recognized people in the Western Hemisphere. The youngest son of a Boston candle- and soap-maker, Franklin won fame through printing, writing, politics, and especially the sciences. Once he was famous, his likeness proliferated in nearly every medium imaginable. Franklin could admire himself printed on paper, carved in marble, transferred onto china, modeled in wax, fired in clay, painted onto canvas, cast in metal, and, perhaps most appropriately, electrically burned into silk. In 1779, he chuckled to his daughter that his face had become "as well known as that of the moon."[1]

He had become an international "pop" icon in his own lifetime. Only one other individual who worked in the sciences has ever achieved this status: Albert Einstein. So here they are, the pair of celebrities in modern science, the Founding Father who invented the lightning rod and the Swiss physicist who claimed that $E = mc^2$. Indeed, each man's array of icons is uncannily like the other's, showing just how extensively they entered homes, lives, and consciousnesses. Choose your poison: take snuff from a box topped with Franklin's face or drink coffee from a mug bearing Einstein's image. Decorate your interior with a mezzotint of the "Master Electrician" or a thumbtacked poster of the master of relativity. Wear your hero with a cameo brooch of the eighteenth-century American or a T-shirt of the twentieth-century European.

Why have only Franklin and Einstein attained this status? Other people who labored at science enjoyed celebrity (Marie Curie adorns posters, too), though none to the same degree, not even the man who started it all, Isaac Newton. Newton was the first modern figure in the sciences who had a cult following. His acolytes claimed that in his ability to divine the secrets of the cosmos, he seemed second only to God. Newton cultivated his image by making sure that his work was printed and reprinted and that he himself was painted and commemorated. And he exercised political power through a position at the Royal Mint. But he largely avoided public life.

Franklin was not so shy. He recognized Newton's achievements in the sciences and followed suit, if on a smaller scale. But he then parlayed his fame in natural science into a reputation for political influence, until he managed to shoot past his role model and become as recognized as the moon. A lull would follow before Einstein would occupy a similar cultural position; he would become internationally celebrated for an uncanny gift in science and was therefore believed to have extraordinary wisdom that might help to solve the problems of the day.

A commonplace explanation for Franklin's fame and Einstein's eminence is that each man was a genius. A genius is above the norm, whatever his or her field, so much so that he or she appears to have been born, not made—possessed of an innate gift. Such is the genius's intelligence that, though perhaps strongest in one area, it cannot be contained and instead spills over into others. By these standards, Franklin was a genius, and so was Einstein, hence the huge presence of each man in his own day and in ours. Geniuses transcend geography and time—their brilliance illuminates all. Of course Franklin and Einstein became icons.

But there is no "of course" in this story. The word *genius* itself has a history and a recent one. Before the eighteenth century, no one used the term in the way we do now. In earlier eras, it implied a specific disposition or aptitude, not an inherent and universal quality of mind. No one *was* a genius, though one might *possess* a particular genius or be ingenious in a given field. But during the eighteenth century, the old idea of *genius* as an aptitude faded. Genius became a noun applied to humans. It emerged just in time to describe Franklin, an early example. In fact, the shifting meanings of the word revealed themselves over the course of his career. In 1729, Franklin himself used *genius* in its older sense—"different Men have

Genius's adapted to Variety of different Arts and Manufactures"; by 1771, he was described as "the distinguish'd genius of America."[2]

So Franklin and Einstein were categorized as geniuses, but why were they *iconic* geniuses? In this regard, historical context matters. Both men worked in areas of physics that were, for their times, astonishingly new. Each man redefined the very fabric of material reality, Franklin by using electricity to reexamine the nature of matter and Einstein by using mathematics to redefine time and space. Each man worked, moreover, during a period of tremendous transformation in the human order. Franklin lived during the rise and fall of the first British empire, Einstein during the collapse of Europe into war and genocide. In consequence, each man would be strongly associated with a conflict that had global dimensions—Franklin with the Seven Years' War and its aftermath, the American Revolution, and Einstein with World War II. At each historical moment—the end of the eighteenth century, the beginning of the twentieth—onlookers wanted and needed to see someone wise enough to make sense of all that was happening in their world.

Franklin was celebrated for another reason as well. Science, too, has a history, and Franklin was born at a critical moment in that history. People have always struggled to understand the natural world. But only at the end of the seventeenth century did some Europeans begin to think that their ways of explaining nature were uniquely truthful. Men of science, including Newton, argued that their means of comprehending nature, particularly their experiments, were definitive. Much contested at the time (and since), this idea of science nevertheless stuck.

Franklin had an important place in this story, but it is now a surprisingly misunderstood one. Consider the following illustration. It is probably what most people think of when they see or hear the words "Benjamin Franklin" and "science": a stout colonial character flies a kite in a Philadelphia thunderstorm. This image, which Nathaniel Currier and James Ives produced in 1876, even has a caption to explain that "Franklin's Experiment" demonstrated "the identity of Lightning and Electricity," from which "he invented the Lightning Rod."

The illustration is charming, but it is wrong in many ways. Indeed, its very caption is inaccurate. Franklin's kite experiment did not identify lighting with electricity. An earlier experiment of his had already done so—the kite verified the finding. And Franklin

American science—Child's play. Engraving by Currier and Ives, *Franklin's Experiment, June 1752* (1876). LIBRARY OF CONGRESS.

was trying to gauge whether clouds were electrified and, if so, whether with a positive or a negative charge. He wanted to determine the presence of a particular kind of matter, electricity, within nature and to use it to investigate the characteristics of other kinds of matter. He was doing far more than playing with a kite, and it reduces his efforts considerably to describe them as resulting only in a clever device, the lightning rod.

The characters in the illustration, moreover, are not quite right. In this and many of the kite pictures that include Franklin's son, William, the younger Franklin is depicted as a child, even though he was in his twenties at the time of the kite experiment. That he was often portrayed as a child may reflect a post-eighteenth-century suspicion that the only thing more ridiculous than a grown man flying a kite in the rain is two grown men doing so. Nor is it very helpful to think of Franklin as firmly planted in America, let alone as quintessentially American. That notion gives too local a view of him. Certainly, he was born, lived, and did his important electrical experiments in America. But he lived almost a third of his life abroad, in Europe. He published his account of his experiments in London, and the first important verification of the experiments came from Paris. Franklin was not situated in one place—he ended up everywhere, on both sides of the Atlantic. Throughout his life, he looked to Europe (or went to Europe) for his education, books, ideas, and friends. Franklin deliberately chose to work in natural science—a decision intended to make himself part of a cosmopolitan, enlightened culture, one that impressed him at an early age as encompassing everything America did not.

Yet we still retain an image of Franklin that is suspiciously like the Currier and Ives illustration. He is currently celebrated as an American statesman or a Founder, a politician who happened to do a little science on the side. But that description puts the cart before the horse. Franklin was not a statesman who did science. He became a statesman because he had done science. And he was able to do so because, in the eighteenth century, science became part of public culture. That was how someone who excelled in the sciences could become a public figure or even a celebrity. Franklin's contemporaries recognized that this had been his route to prominence. A famous tag proposed that Franklin had snatched lightning from the sky and the scepter from the tyrants—in that order.

At some point, each of these two accomplishments—the study of electricity and the defiance of tyrants—attracted the attention of distinct sets of historians. That division of labor may explain why we now misunderstand Franklin. A very small group of specialists has seriously examined Franklin's work in science. But most people who are interested in eighteenth-century science tend to look at Europe and therefore miss Franklin; most people who are interested in Benjamin Franklin tend to look at America and therefore miss the science. The fuller biographies of Franklin, which offer catalogs of his life, do list all his accomplishments, but they do not make sense of the connections between the public life and the life in science. Moreover, most biographies of Franklin stress his American qualities, even though his devotion to science made it clear that he identified with a cosmopolitan culture that stretched across the Atlantic Ocean and united the hemispheres.[3]

So rather astonishingly, there has never been a biography that examines Franklin's scientific pursuits as an intrinsic part of his life's story—as an important guide to his early education, his career as a printer, his entry into political life, his triumphs and failures, his celebrity throughout Europe, and his later fame as an American Revolutionary. Science did indeed become part of public knowledge in the eighteenth century, and Benjamin Franklin is the ultimate proof of that. His life had the shape and texture that it did because of his abiding curiosity about nature and his interest in science.

And what a vast, unsettling, breathtaking enterprise science was in the eighteenth century—no wonder Franklin found it irresistible. Eighteenth-century science was enormous in scope. In Franklin's era, the term *science* meant simply "wisdom." Only at the end of the century would it begin to specify knowledge about nature, and only at that point, toward the end of Franklin's life, would people begin to use the term *scientific* in the way we do now. The best way to describe Franklin's pursuits is in the plural, as the *sciences*. These pursuits were not specialized practices cut off from other aspects of learning or indeed everyday life. They took up all manner of questions, including topics we would now assign to medicine, engineering, travel writing, or even ethnography.[4]

Science was welcoming. Everyone who could do so read about the sciences. Experiments and demonstrations were public events. Members of the clergy preached the new philosophy of nature. Newspapers, even provincial ones, regularly published accounts of experiments, new technologies, and medical news. Much more of science was in the mainstream. Someone like Franklin, who pursued science, did not even think of himself as particularly different from anyone else. The word *scientist* would not be coined until well into the nineteenth century, when a few people finally did earn a living through specialized scientific work. The eighteenth century's so-called men of science did not specialize in this way. They had other occupations or careers. They were clergymen, members of Parliament, farmers, tax administrators, ships' captains, noblewomen, and even printers.[5]

Science was demanding and even dangerous. People were not flocking to the sciences because they were easily pursued. Experiments involved complex equipment, terminology, and logic: "Take two Vials," Franklin instructed in 1753, "charge one of them with Lightning from the Iron Rod, and give the other an equal Charge by the electric Glass Globe thro' the prime Conductor." Does this sound easy—or safe? In fact, the pursuit of science had a casualty rate. Some of the pioneers of ballooning died quite horribly. Seafaring explorers also died; others returned in such poor health that they nearly succumbed, which happened to Franklin twice. Electrical and chemical experimenters were stunned, burned, blinded, or killed.[6]

But science was exciting. It explored the world and opened up hidden worlds. In the forty years before the American Revolution,

the number of North American plants introduced to Britain doubled—in large part due to the handiwork of one of Franklin's
friends, John Bartram. Franklin witnessed the introduction of inoculation against smallpox, the first meaningful calculations of the distance between earth and sun, the early definitions of oxygen, and
the first manned aerial flight. He himself made a signal contribution when he defined electricity, for the first time, as a particular
form of matter.

This science was, however, different. In fact, we would not recognize a great deal of its practices or central assumptions. Franklin believed that nude air baths hastened bodily circulation. He thought
that water would pile up on one side of the Atlantic and then seek
its level by flowing back across to the other side. He argued that a
human body should be heated evenly, lest ill health result, particularly colds. He maintained that overeating slowed mental functioning. Many histories of early America try to make us feel as if "we are
there." Meet eighteenth-century Americans, we are told—hear their
racking coughs, see their ships tossed by Atlantic tempests, feel the
warmth from their roaring fires, and smell their sizzling fried fish or
their hot apple pie. But this approach gives a false sense of identifi-
cation. Clearly, Franklin's ideas about health, weather, heat, and nu-
trition—about matter itself—were not like ours. We understand
Franklin best when we comprehend what he thought he was sensing, not when we pretend we can sense what he did. Nor should we
compare his sciences to our science. True, some of his beliefs and
practices seem uncannily familiar, but others seem bizarre. To
Franklin, however, they all made sense in relation to each other.

Science was argumentative. Nothing was settled—things were being decided—and that is what made it so exciting. The fruitful indecision pertained, above all, to knowledge. What was knowledge?
Could it be distinguished from mere opinion or supported by facts
or numbers? What kind of knowledge could be established about
the natural world? What knowledge did the mind have? What
knowledge might sensuously flow into and through the body? And
who possessed knowledge? Which parts of it should have been public? Which parts should have been secret, open only to a few? Who
had the power to define knowledge—the elite or ordinary working
people?

Finally, science was powerful. People used it to argue for universal
truths. They based their decisions about religion and law on science.

They created important naturalistic metaphors. Franklin adopted one of these in the form of the concept of circulation, which he used to explore natural phenomena (weather, heat, electricity, ocean currents) but which he then also deployed to explain social phenomena—the circulation of money, news, letters, people, and ideas.

Science is knowledge of things; politics is power over people. During the eighteenth century, the two enterprises overlapped in fascinating ways. Franklin entered both realms but flourished especially in the territory they held in common. A man of science, he became a political leader—indeed, the personification of a nation with an unprecedented history. A single book could not do justice to either one of these enormous topics, either Franklin's science or his political career. Instead, this book examines the most important ways in which Franklin made his pursuits in the sciences and in public affairs inform and support each other.

Benjamin Franklin was the first scientific American. He was the first person born in the Americas who became internationally celebrated (not just known and respected) for work in physical science. Put it another way. Franklin, an American, was the first person to be internationally celebrated for work in the physical sciences. A mere colonial of ordinary birth managed to achieve this stature. Several stories are embedded here, about America, about science, and about Benjamin Franklin. And ultimately, they are—conveniently, marvelously—all the same story.

Chapter 2

HEAD AND HANDS

W HERE TO BEGIN? The question stumped even Franklin. In
1771, when he set out to write his autobiography, he considered two beginnings. The outline for his memoir began with "My
writing." But the narrative itself began with "my Ancestors," the
humble working folk whose "Poverty and Obscurity" Franklin had
escaped precisely because of his writing. And just as the story of his
life had two possible beginnings, so did the life itself. The first two
things Franklin ever wanted to do were to go to sea or to go to college, to become either a sailor or a learned divine. Head or hands—
mental exertion or manual labor—these were his options. In the
end, he combined them, which was possible during his lifetime because old boundaries between the unwritten knowledge of manual
trades and the knowledge contained in books had begun to blur.[1]

Even the two starts that Franklin proposed for his life simplify the
story. Though highly self-disciplined as an adult, he meandered during his youth. At various points, Franklin contemplated careers as a
puritan minister, a Boston chandler, a sea captain, a philosopher of
metaphysics, a swimming master to the London gentry, and a
Philadelphia merchant. Then he chose to become a printer.

Printing proved to be the activity—and the medium—that connected all the options Franklin had considered in his youth. Printing
united head with hands. It required both manual labor and careful
thought about words and their meanings. It allowed Franklin to
write for an audience under his own name and under many pseudonyms. He would become one character by becoming a printer, but
he inhabited many more characters precisely because print could
represent them. (At that time, *character* meant one of the lead letters
or other symbols used to set type, but it also signified a certain kind
of person or personality.) To see all the people Franklin might have
become is to understand the one person that he did become, as a
printer, a published author, and a philosopher of nature.

———————

WORK, BOOKS, AND THE SEA—Boston would be known for many things, but these were the three aspects of that puritan port city that strongly marked Franklin's start in life.

As far as most people in Europe were concerned, Boston was on the edge of nowhere. The original puritan settlers of the Massachusetts Bay Colony had wanted it that way. They had fled to a New England where they could practice their faith far from English authorities. Franklin's maternal grandfather was one of the earliest colonists of Massachusetts; his father emigrated slightly later, in 1683. In remembering his pious ancestors in his autobiography, Franklin noted their early conversion to Protestantism and their consequent persecution during the Catholic reign of Queen Mary. They hid their banned English Bible "under and within the Frame of a Joint Stool" so that if the authorities approached while they read the scriptures cradled in the upturned stool, they could quickly flip everything over and "the Bible remain'd conceal'd." Not for the last time would a Franklin invent a clever device, but Benjamin's English ancestors preferred, he stressed, "to enjoy their Mode of Religion with Freedom" and so emigrated to New England, the edge of nowhere.[2]

Most English people took little interest in their colonial cousins or in the ocean they had crossed. Indeed, they did not even think of the vast water as a single body. Until the latter part of the eighteenth century, the ocean we now call the Atlantic carried several names, including Atlantic but also Western Ocean or North Sea. The North Sea was considered an ocean unto itself—what we now refer to as the South Atlantic was then commonly referred to as the Ethiopian Sea. Europe was always the point of geographic orientation: the different parts of the Atlantic designated western and southern boundaries to the world of Europeans. Although Europeans had colonized the Western and Southern Hemispheres, they thought of those regions as forbiddingly remote.[3]

Born in 1706, Franklin was the fifteenth of his twice-married father's seventeen children and the eighth of his mother's ten children. Even in Josiah and Abiah Franklin's teeming family, their youngest son stood out. He remembered such an "early Readiness in learning to read" that he could not recall a time when he was unable to do so. For that reason, he recalled, his father intended "to devote me as the Tithe of his Sons to the Service of the Church." At the age of eight, he began to attend a Latin grammar school in Boston, from which he could proceed to Harvard College.[4]

In pious New England, college was the gateway to social and intellectual prominence. The Franklins would have known the Reverend Cotton Mather, whose monumental career dominated public life in New England during Benjamin's youth. A college-educated divine who owned about 3,000 books, which was then, as now, a substantial private library, Mather was widely recognized as the towering figure in American learning. His influential publications included *Bonifacius: Essays to Do Good* (1710), which recommended the formation of small self-improvement societies in New England and urged greater civic responsibility among ordinary New Englanders.[5]

By linking learning to Christian leadership, New England's puritans followed a tradition that stretched back to medieval monasteries. Sequestered from the world, monks mastered Latin texts that were incomprehensible even to those literate in vernacular languages. They took religious vows (including celibacy), a sign of the unworldly nature of their wisdom. Universities were offshoots of monasteries and were similarly populated with dark-garbed men who knew Latin and were celibate "professors" of the faith. Puritan colonists likewise founded Harvard College to train their religious leaders. They drew on the monastic tradition but protestantized it. Harvard graduates, for instance, were expected to marry.[6]

Grammar schools sprang up in New England in order to prepare bright boys, such as Franklin, for college. Franklin excelled at his school. Within a year of his enrollment, he rose to the head of the class and was promoted to the next. Latin, learning, college—a career as a minister would surely follow. But Josiah Franklin had a large family. At a moment of instability in Boston's economy, he was straining his income by spending so much on one son. The money ran out, and Benjamin had to transfer to a lesser "School for Writing and Arithmetic." The Reverend Mr. Benjamin Franklin, A.B. Harvard, would never exist. Instead, at ten, when he had learned to write (arithmetic defeated him), Benjamin returned home to assist his father.[7]

Franklin's father was a craftsman. He had been a cloth dyer in England, and then, after emigrating, he was a Boston tallow chandler who made soap and candles from animal fat. Various Franklin sons were also craftsmen—blacksmith, printer, soap-maker. Craftsmen such as Josiah Franklin worked independently in small workshops that were near or even within households. They had far greater autonomy than their descendants would have as they labored under central control in factories. But household workshops could be dangerous, not least to small children exposed to fire, sharp tools, or heavily shod work animals. Before Benjamin was born, his brother Ebenezer had, at sixteen months, accidentally "drown'd in a Tub of Suds," presumably one of his father's soap vats.[8]

As a chandler and soap-maker, Josiah Franklin was in the middle rank of society. Men of higher rank, such as gentlemen and members of the professions, did not work with their hands. Yet men such as Josiah were respected for their economic independence. With the labor of their wives and older children, they supported their families without recourse to charity. They could acquire property—and if they accumulated enough, they could vote. The boundary between skilled working people and the gentry was permeable, as evidenced by Josiah's desire to send a son to grammar school and college.

Craftspeople kept the world going—from building its ships to delivering its babies—because they possessed crucial skills or knew trade secrets. So prized was craftsmanship that some people even described nature as an amazing piece of artifice, as if God were a master artisan. Knowledge was, in this way, an important attainment even for ordinary people who worked with their hands. Valuable trade secrets were not usually written down; masters communicated them orally to apprentices. The word *mystery* was, at that time, a synonym for *craft* or *guild*; the indentures that bound an apprentice to a master specified an initiation into the "mystery" of a trade. In Europe, apprentices had to pay fees, take oaths, and participate in rituals, all of which separated the skilled from the unskilled. Secrecy protected craft artisans from economic competition, guaranteed the quality of products or services, and instilled solidarity among workers.[9]

Guild structure was weak or absent in the colonies, however, and craftspeople of Josiah Franklin's generation were, in any case, losing some control over the mysteries of their trades as those secrets—and many others—made their way into books.

This development had religious roots. During the Reformation, religious reformers had protested that monks and clergymen monopolized knowledge of God's word. They encouraged the publication of scripture and the spread of literacy—hence the Bible that the English Franklins had hidden in a stool. To some extent, the printing press helped in this transformation. A literate person could now learn about religious controversy, or anything else, simply by reading. But printed knowledge was contested; books did not always inspire confidence. When printed books of trade knowledge began to appear, they were aptly called books of secrets. Some of these texts managed to convey a sense of mystery by using metaphor, code, and partial formulas in order to fool readers. The boundary between secret knowledge and published knowledge still existed, if haphazardly. If control of knowledge had given craftspeople power, they stood to lose that power.[10]

Josiah Franklin could, however, control the labor of his younger children and of other unfree persons, such as slaves. Like other Boston craftsmen, he was engaged in a small way in the slave trade; in 1713, he advertised (on behalf of another party) that six slaves could be examined and purchased at his house. He could also raise a son to inherit his trade, thereby avoiding the expense of apprenticing him and gaining his labor. This was precisely what Josiah Franklin was doing when he took Benjamin from school and set him to cutting wicks and dipping candles.[11]

But the younger Franklin soon rebelled and later emphasized that he "dislik'd the Trade and had a strong Inclination for the Sea." The inclination would linger throughout Franklin's life and indeed reflected very well the world in which he lived. Any alert child in Boston, one of the British empire's port cities, would have noticed that seafaring was fairly exciting. Unlike their puritan forebears, who saw the Atlantic as a barrier against English meddling, colonists now saw the ocean as a place of opportunity. Sailors managed the ships that brought wealth to the nation; they connected colonies to the home country; and they manned the naval vessels that fought Britain's enemies.[12]

The supply of ships and sailors expanded as the empire did. And as colonial populations grew, young men from big families or in crowded port cities had to look seaward for their livelihood. During Franklin's lifetime, the Royal Navy became the most powerful branch of the British state and drew many men into its service. (Franklin had two in-laws who were Royal Naval captains.) Oceans connected people and places—and they were doing so more readily than ever before. This trend was above all apparent in the establishment, in 1714 (when Franklin was eight), of a parliamentary prize for solving the problem of determining longitude at sea. Without accurate knowledge of a ship's east-west position, navigation was a dangerous and inefficient business.[13]

The maritime trades ran deep in Franklin's family, particularly on his mother's side. Franklin's mother, née Abiah Folger, came from Nantucket, a small island that supported little land-based activity. Many of the Folgers went to sea, including one Peleg Folger, who was a whaler. Via the prolific Folgers, Franklin was related to several Nantucket clans, including the still-extant Coffins. One of his cousins, Keziah Folger Coffin, was a Quaker who was notable on the island. The Folgers also intermarried with Nantucket's Starbucks.[14]

These names are familiar to anyone who has read Herman Melville's *Moby Dick*. That novel features a Captain Peleg, a Peter Coffin, and a Starbuck. Melville was not idly raiding Nantucket's small stock of names—he knew very well the significance of its lineages: "They have something better than royal blood there. The grandmother of Benjamin Franklin was Mary Morrel; afterwards, by marriage, Mary Folger, one of the old settlers of Nantucket, and the ancestress to a long line of Folgers and harpooneers—all kith and kin to noble Benjamin."[15]

"Noble Benjamin" was himself fascinated by his maternal genealogy and fond of his Nantucket kin, who would always seem to be visiting or writing him later in his life. The Folgers mattered to Franklin. In an era when ordinary people generally lacked middle names, Franklin bestowed one on his first legitimate child: Francis Folger Franklin. In 1747, he would report to his mother that "our family" in Philadelphia included "two Folgers, all well." If anything, Franklin strengthened these ties after his mother's death. When he traced his genealogy, "Loving Cousin" Keziah Folger Coffin evidently helped him sort out the Nantucket cousins. In 1773, Franklin reported seeing two Nantucket relatives at his house in London, and he would also entertain a Folger while he lived in Paris.[16]

Many Franklins had joined the Folgers at sea. Franklin recalled a remarkable family "Entertainment" when the entire Boston family gathered "all at one Table" to celebrate the return of the oldest child, Benjamin's half brother Josiah, who had "been absent in the East-Indies, and unheard of for nine Years." This prodigal son was without a doubt the most exotic member of the Franklin family, filled as he would have been with stories of East Indian marvels, tempests, and spices. What a lesson he must have provided for his goggling little brother, who likely saw in Josiah's example a way either to be the center of attention at home or to leave home—or both.[17]

Other Franklins rose in the nautical trades. Benjamin's full brother, Peter, was master of a ship out of Newport in his youth and apparently remained a family expert on maritime concerns. In February 1765, Peter would write that he had not looked for Benjamin's letters from London because, "Being Aquaintd with Sea affairs," he knew that the packet service could not guarantee correspondence to Philadelphia in that stormy season. Franklin also had several maritime in-laws, including a brother-in-law who was master of a sloop and a nephew by marriage who was a ship's captain and based in Newport. Seafaring was dangerous, however, and at least two family members were lost at sea, presumed drowned. This was the fate of Josiah Franklin and of Benjamin's nephew, John, another sailor. On a genealogical chart Franklin constructed in 1758, he would carefully note both of these losses, as well as tiny Ebenezer's demise in a tub at home. It is no wonder that he became an ardent swimmer early in life.[18]

Between the ages of ten and twelve, Franklin was keen on everything about the sea. "Living near the Water," he confessed, "I was much in and about it, learnt early to swim well, and to manage Boats." He might have been especially attracted to the military aspect of seafaring. (This attraction had caused his uncle to warn his four-year-old nephew, "Beleeve me Ben. It is a Dangerous Trade.") A naval career was a classic way for a man to make his name and fortune. News of Queen Anne's War (1702–1713) would have reminded Bostonians of the exploits of naval commanders.[19]

Seafaring held additional allure because mariners maintained a particularly rich tradition of trade customs and secrets. Because they were isolated from the rest of society, sailors (like monks) may have belonged to one of the more exclusive crafts in early modern Europe. Many features of shipboard life reinforced this sense of exclusivity. For instance, all seafarers endured a ritual humiliation when they crossed the equator for the first time—sailors, including officers, had to pay a fee (often in the form of alcoholic drink) or be dunked overboard or soaked on deck. Even on land, sailors looked distinctive, with their rocking gait, sunburned skin, outlandish clothing, and, eventually, tattoos. They sounded odd, as well. Their unusual diction and vocabulary resulted in speech that—deliberately—baffled outsiders. Consequently, sailors could fascinate a boy such as Benjamin Franklin yet simultaneously appall his father.[20]

Franklin's swimming and boating alarmed his father, who suspected that his son meant to "break away" and somehow "get to Sea." Josiah Franklin expressed "Vexation" that his namesake had already run off in this manner. But his earlier failure might have taught him a more subtle kind of parenting. He escorted his younger son to different workshops in Boston, nudging the twelve-year-old Benjamin toward a safer, land-based trade. Together, they visited "Joiners, Bricklayers, Turners, Braziers," and others. Josiah won the battle of wills, and Benjamin realized that some land trades were in fact quite interesting. "It has ever since been a Pleasure to me to see good Workmen handle their Tools," Franklin noted later in life.[21]

IN THE END, Benjamin chose printing, which offered a unique blend of manual and mental labor. The job required considerable physical stamina and manual dexterity. A printer arranged "characters" or "sorts" of lead type into lines guided by a composing stick, fit the lines into a square form, inked the type, levered down the "press" that compacted the inked type against a sheet of paper, hung the printed sheets to dry, and then folded and sewed the pages together. (Binding was done to order.) In bigger printshops, these tasks were divided among specialized workers. Printers' bodies announced their trade and sometimes their specialities within it. A pressman, for instance, had a crooked walk, the result of building up muscles on one side of the body. And all printers tended to be ink-stained, particularly on their hands. Some printers even ate ink, believing it warded off the devil.[22]

But printers also worked with their heads. They had to be able to read the language or languages in which they set type—and they had to read them upside down and backward, the way the pieces of type lay in the press. We still use the expression *out of sorts,* a reminder of how irritating it was for a printer to run out of a crucial character at a crucial point. Good compositors were hyperliterate, able to scan words, sentences, and paragraphs in order to prevent error. Not surprisingly, printers were connoisseurs of verbal wit, economy, and force. (They were known to improve authors whose texts they found wanting.) They also were critical aesthetes of the printed page; a good printer would automatically recognize a book's typeface and feel the quality of its paper even before the words began to register.[23]

Printing was an exacting trade, but it was safer than seamanship. By making his son a printer, Josiah Franklin saved him from a harsh life and possible death at sea—and thus saved him for us. Yet Benjamin could not get maritime adventure out of his head. He was apprenticed to his older brother, James, in 1718 and shortly thereafter wrote a pair of ballads, his first published works. These ballads told in verse the story of a shipwreck (yet more drowning) and the exploits of Edward Teach, alias Blackbeard, the pirate. Sensing a possible profit, James Franklin printed these "Grubstreet" verses, and Benjamin hawked them around Boston. He would later remember that although the ballads were "wretched Stuff," one of them "sold wonderfully." Again, his father worried. Benjamin recalled him "telling me Verse-makers were generally Beggars; so I escap'd being a Poet." Yet Franklin's rudimentary schooling was beginning to pay off. Ever after, he followed the pattern he had set as a twelve-year-old ballad-seller: write something you know readers will want, and if you can, charge them for it.[24]

Ink, paper, imagination—Franklin did not see the world by going to sea but instead by entering the infinite worlds that the printed page can present. In his brother's printshop, Benjamin learned three ways to engage with printed material: to physically produce it, to read it, and to write it. Between the ages of twelve and sixteen, he tackled all three. Later, in his autobiography, he produced a dense account of this five-year period. Except when he slept, Franklin seemed never to be without some reminder of the written or printed word. His inky fingers laid out type, turned pages of books, and pushed a quill over paper.

Franklin wanted not only to write but also to improve his writing. He took as his models the essays in Joseph Addison and Richard Steele's *Spectator* (1711–1712). Although that London journal had lasted less than two years, it had become one of the most influential pieces of prose writing in the English-speaking world. Franklin used the essays in the third volume of the *Spectator* as lessons. He tore them apart and then rewrote them—in both prose and verse—in order to learn "Method in the Arrangement of Thoughts."[25]

James Franklin kept a bound set of the *Spectator* in his printing office, and the journal gave his younger brother a crash course in eighteenth-century social theory. The journal's very title, *Spectator*, showed that to see and to be seen were new social goals. Humans were social animals, Addison and Steele assumed, creatures endowed with language and sympathies that compelled them to create social networks and institutions. Conversation or even debate was essential to social life. The *Spectator* was part of an explosion of popular publications, including journals and newspapers, that brought general readers into the conversation. The journal reviewed nearly everything that was being printed or discussed—plays, essays, gossip, foreign news, the sciences. From this, Franklin would learn that the sciences were part of public culture, which any cultivated person should be able to discuss.[26]

Indeed, Addison and Steele endorsed an even bigger claim: the sciences were the hallmark of modern knowledge. The claim was a bit unfair to people in the Middle Ages, but it was part of a long campaign to portray the eighteenth century as an improved era. No one yet used the term *Enlightenment*, but people in the eighteenth century did talk about themselves as being enlightened, able to see things in a new and better light. In this highly partisan interpretation of history, they argued that natural science trumped the medieval forms of learning that had failed to explain nature. Locked up in monasteries, medieval knowledge had been bookish, authoritarian, and disengaged with the world; modern knowledge examined vivid nature rather than arid texts, was sociable, and was engaged with the larger debates and events of the age. As Addison wrote, "I have brought Philosophy out of Closets and Libraries, Schools and Colleges, to dwell in Clubs and Assemblies, at Tea-Tables and in Coffee Houses."[27]

Addison and Steele also made the standard patriotic claim that their nation had been the first to become enlightened. Modern science had an English pedigree. The *Spectator* extolled Francis Bacon, from the previous century, as "one of the most extensive and improved Genius's we have had any Instance of in our own Nation," a pioneer who "began to strike out new Tracks of Science." "The Excellent Mr. [Robert] *Boyle*" then "filled up those Plans and Out-Lines of Science" in his "Pursuit of Nature." Next came Isaac Newton, still alive when Addison and Steele praised him and "such a Genius" that he seemed almost "like one of another Species!" "The vast Machine, we inhabit, lies open to him," and "he seems not unacquainted with the general Laws that govern it." "Pursuit of Nature," nature's "general Laws," "Genius"—the *Spectator* taught Franklin that the sciences were essential to knowledge and a route to fame.[28]

During his intense period of reading, Franklin for the first time confronted philosophy and "became a real Doubter" of religion. Not yet sixteen, he read John Locke's germinal *Essay Concerning Human Understanding* (1690), with its shattering contention that humans knew what they did not from innate ideas God had planted within them but because of their sensory experience and their capacity to reason about the experience. Revealed religion and faith were the obvious targets of this profoundly skeptical work. Franklin's exposure to the work is our first evidence that he was questioning the piety of his puritan forebears and the Christian knowledge taught at places such as Harvard College.[29]

Around the same time, Franklin read some of the lectures that natural philosopher Robert Boyle had endowed in order to combat irreligion. (Perhaps Franklin's father knew his son was absorbing dangerous philosophies and gave him the Boyle lectures as antidote.) Boyle, a man of science, worried that his contemporaries were turning away from religion. The lectures given in his name decried deism, a doctrine that challenged the orthodox view of God as all-powerful and all-intervening. Boyle would have been dismayed at their impact on the young Bostonian. "They wrought an Effect on me," Franklin later remembered, "quite contrary to what was intended by them: For the Arguments of the Deists which were quoted to be refuted, appeared to me much stronger than the Refutations." He became "a thorough Deist." He believed that divine power was remote and that humans could understand its effects through sense and reason. For him, God was demoted and humans promoted.[30]

As he educated himself, Franklin also remedied his early failure to master numbers. He found that he could do arithmetic "with great Ease" and moved on to geometry, a field that took him back to the sea. In his day, geometry was a practical skill left mostly to craftspeople who needed to measure space in order to construct buildings or to divide land for planting. It was essential to sailors because it allowed them to navigate ships.[31]

Nautical texts had multiplied just in time for Franklin to begin to consult them. Navigation was no longer the exclusive province of mariners. Instead, it was of interest to the state and to the individuals in state employ. When the English empire had expanded in the late seventeenth century, navigational knowledge had become part of its official apparatus—a means to control the high seas. And the navy needed more skilled men. So in 1677, it instituted an examination for the rank of lieutenant. A successful candidate had to certify that he had spent at least three years at sea as a midshipman and prove that he had learned the crafts of navigation and gunnery. Books on mathematics, geometry, and navigation allowed highborn men to claim the skills of sailors. Some ordinary seamen, or "tarpaulins," could also study these books and advance into the officer ranks. Such reforms established the navy as a state-controlled profession, even as they eroded the internally based craft ethic of seamanship.[32]

The British state also took advantage of ordinary sailors' reduced status. In wartime, for example, any man who had any nautical skill could be forcibly "impressed" into naval service. To be sure, many people respected sailors for their experience at sea. And they remained fairly literate as a group. But sailors' swearing, rough speech, and defiantly plebian culture distanced them from the gentility of officers and land folk. They were becoming mere hands, unthinking workers who were commanded by others. For this reason, they would always be a good test of Franklin's respect—or lack of respect—for working people.[33]

Franklin learned about navigation from two late seventeenth-century authors, John Seller and Samuel Sturmy, who wrote in the wake of the navy's post-1660 reforms. Unfortunately, Franklin did not state the titles of the works he consulted. One of Sturmy's works, *The Mariner's Magazine*, must serve as a possible and representative example of what he read. Sturmy defended ordinary sailors from the scorn of the learned and proclaimed that navigation was "more necessary for the well being and honour of our Nation, than any other Art or Science Mathematical, which is more carefully kept in the Universities." But, he contended, maritime knowledge should be available to the public. At the start of the book, an admirer offered an acrostic that used Sturmy's first and last names to celebrate the publication of mariners' secrets. It began:

> S-ome men, when they this MAGAZINE shall spy,
> A-nd note the Author, presently will cry,
> M-any such Captains will undo the Trade:
> U-nlock these Secrets, all are Captains made.
> E-nvy thus, Devil-like, would keep men blind,
> L-et Noble Sons of Art be free and kind.[34]

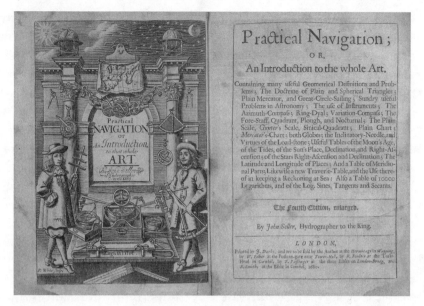

Geometry, a how-to guide. John Seller, *Practical Navigation* . . . (1680).
JOHN CARTER BROWN LIBRARY AT BROWN UNIVERSITY.

Franklin might have learned more from Sturmy (and Seller) about the controversy over publicizing trade secrets than he did about navigation. (He later confessed that he "never proceeded far" in the "Science" of geometry.) The issue was certainly relevant to his own craft: printers were the very tradespeople who published secrets.[35]

Printers were contradictory creatures. They had their own trade secrets, but their business was to make things public by printing and circulating them. They revered words yet were often irreverent toward authors and authorities. Indeed, they used words to challenge authority. James Franklin seemed to encourage a general irreverence in his younger brother. Once Benjamin was apprenticed, he confessed his lack of "Attendance on publick Worship." He could not bear to forego time for reading—and he read books that challenged religious doctrine. Josiah Franklin may have regretted putting one impressionable son in the hands of another who was determined to challenge Boston's religious establishment.[36]

James Franklin was hell-bent on defiance. At one time or another, his paper, *The New-England Courant,* mocked everyone, from ministers to magistrates, who held power in Boston. James had his reasons. His paper was Boston's third newspaper, so it needed to stand out to attract readers. And as it was the only Boston paper printed without the approval of the government, James had a free hand.[37]

In the spring of 1721, three years into Benjamin's apprenticeship, James outdid himself. An opportunity to stir up controversy arrived in the form of a ship from the West Indies. The *Seahorse* reintroduced smallpox to Boston and set off an epidemic. Within nine months, 6,000 people out of Boston's population of 10,500 had suffered or were recovering from the disease, and 900 had died.

Cotton Mather proposed a solution. Mather was a newly designated Fellow of the Royal Society of London, England's first learned organization devoted to natural science. He recalled an essay on inoculation published in the society's *Philosophical Transactions*. Inoculation was practiced in the Near East; pus from smallpox sores was inserted under the skin of a healthy person, who then (usually) suffered a mild case of the disease but gained future resistance to it. Mather had also asked his West African slave Onesimus if he had suffered smallpox. Onesimus gave an interesting answer—yes and no—meaning he had been inoculated. Citing the *Philosophical Transactions* and Onesimus, the minister pled inoculation's case. Zabdiel Boylston, who had been trained in medicine by his father and by another local doctor, began to perform it on others, including Mather's son. It was a gamble. Inoculation sometimes produced a form of smallpox as virulent as the naturally occurring kind. Some inoculated people died, and some (including Boylston's son) suffered horrendously before they recovered.

William Douglass, the colony's only university-trained doctor, was enraged. He believed that when they intervened in medical affairs, men such as Mather and Boylston ignorantly meddled in matters of life and death. Who were they to stick pus in people who might never have caught smallpox anyway? James Franklin was not much interested in whether inoculation worked, but he thought that a controversy over it would interest readers as the epidemic raged around them. And so, he was eager to print Douglass's denunciations of Mather and Boylston.

What followed was a debate over knowledge. Nonphysicians, Douglass maintained in the *Courant*'s first issue, should not promote dangerous medical therapies. Inoculation was "the Practice of Greek old Women" and "not in the least vouched or recommended (being meerly published, in the Philosophick Transactions by way of

Amusement)." By equating Mather and Boylston with old foreign women who lacked formal training, Douglass was trumpeting his own medical knowledge. By contrast, he suggested, the Reverend Mather (university educated but not in medicine), the slave Onesimus, and Boylston (merely apprenticed to doctors) were all unqualified. Douglass even questioned whether the Royal Society, established as an alternative to the universities, promulgated any useful knowledge.[38]

James Franklin had wanted attention, and he got it—but soon regretted it. The *Courant* continued to criticize inoculation until Mather ran into James on the street and reproached him. Franklin then published a lengthy defense of his responsibility as a printer to publish material that might interest the public, however much it offended the great and the good. "To anathematize a Printer for publishing the different Opinions of Men," he protested in November 1721, "is as injudicious as it is wicked." But the *Courant*'s editorials and letters on inoculation gradually dropped off, and the controversy died.[39]

There is no evidence that James Franklin's tactic had improved circulation. But the voluble exchange surely impressed Benjamin. He had followed the controversy, meaning he helped print his brother's side of it. From the whole affair, he learned about debates in the sciences and about printers' ability to manipulate them. James could label different views of inoculation as mere "Opinions" because they did not elicit agreement; inoculation's efficacy was not yet a fact (which required near-universal agreement) or even a recognized form of knowledge (which required agreement among experts).

It is telling that Benjamin Franklin never gave his opinion on the controversy. Indeed, we do not even know when and whether he had smallpox. He was born after Boston's previous outbreak of 1702. Had he picked up a case in the meantime? Was he one of the 6,000 who caught and survived it in 1721? What about his two younger siblings? James Franklin may have decried Mather, but Josiah Franklin would never have done so. Did the father quietly have his three youngest children, including Benjamin, inoculated, and did James decline to publicize the different opinions within his own family? However it had happened, Benjamin survived smallpox and now wanted to enter the public fray, meaning publish writing that people followed as avidly as they had the inoculation controversy.

Fearful that James would scoff at his ambition, he wrote fourteen letters under a female alias, Silence Dogood, and left them for his brother to find. James could not resist publishing them, even though they might have been his younger brother's anonymous digs at him. The name Dogood echoed Cotton Mather's *Bonifacius: Essays to Do Good.* But because the character who bore that name was so comical, the younger Franklin might also have intended a rebuke of Mather. In this efficient and arresting way, Benjamin Franklin was able to establish his independence from his master and his master's adversary.

"Silence" belied her first name in order to do good, meaning give Boston the benefit of her tart opinions and lively personal history. She related (in the letter in which the anonymous Franklin introduced her) that she was born at sea. Her parents had been passing "from London to N. England" when she was born below decks. Meanwhile, her father died above, swept away by "a merciless Wave" as he was "rejoycing at my Birth." Any competent writer could have made this scene either profound or comic; the sixteen-year-old Franklin made it both. Dogood irrationally explained her father's death: "Tho' I was not then capable of knowing, I shall never be able to forget."[40]

She advised lovesick bachelors. She scolded religious hypocrites. She mocked dim-witted Harvard students. She reproached Boston fashion victims. Dogood was a hit. When she stopped sending letters, one reader wrote her, via James Franklin, begging that she break her silence: "Is your Common-Place Wit all Exhausted, your stock of matter all spent?" James Franklin had probably guessed that Dogood was an alias (but did not suspect his brother's hand). He too wanted to keep the joke going—and paying—so he placed an advertisement in his paper. He asked for any "Account of Mrs. Silence Dogood, whether Dead or alive, Married or unmarried, in Town or Countrey" and for a way "she may be spoke with, or Letters convey'd to her."[41]

It is amazing that Franklin's family did not at once spot Dogood as their kin. Yet Josiah Franklin did not see Dogood's drowned father as himself, a migrant from England to New England, consigned to a watery death in the fantasy of a scribbling boy whose father had thwarted his desire to go to sea. Nor did James Franklin recognize Dogood as the same author who had versified, four years earlier, on shipwreck and piracy. Yet Dogood kept returning to nautical topics, as with her birth and when, on an evening stroll in Boston, she met "a Crowd of *Tarpolins* and their Doxies, link'd to each other by the Arms, who ran (by their own Account) after the Rate of *Six Knots an Hour*" until two of them fell over their own feet and "the Company were call'd upon to *bring to*, for that Jack and Betty were *founder'd*," as if a ship foundered on rocks.[42]

A published author at sixteen, recognized around town (albeit anonymously) for his wit and wisdom, Franklin hoped that he might have a scribbling future. He would, but not with his brother. James Franklin overstepped his bounds in 1722 when he derided Massachusetts officials' faltering attempts to crack down on pirates. The criticism "gave Offence to the Assembly," the representative house in Massachusetts. That body ordered James Franklin jailed. James hid. Loyalty to master and craft dictated that the younger brother not give up the older. Indeed, the authorities questioned him but then dismissed Benjamin from their inquiries, "considering me perhaps as an Apprentice who was bound to keep his Master's Secrets," including his place of hiding.[43]

Forbidden in 1723 to publish the *New-England Courant* under his own name, James ordered it "printed for the future under the Name of *Benjamin Franklin*." This solution required him to release Benjamin from his "Indenture," or contractual apprenticeship. An apprentice was the creature of his master; a Benjamin Franklin apprenticed to a banned James Franklin could not have published anything. Though Benjamin was legally emancipated, James continued to run the printshop. The arrangement was, Benjamin recalled, a "very flimsy Scheme." It must have irked him that while his brother jibed at all kinds of authority, he insisted on his own. He "had often beaten me," the younger brother complained, "which I took extreamly amiss."[44]

After the next squabble with his brother, Benjamin quit the printshop at age seventeen, four years short of becoming a qualified journeyman. Already, a lifetime preference was clear: he hated working for others, and he even had trouble working *with* others. Not for the last time would he separate himself from a collaborator, which he had been, however oddly and briefly, with his brother.

Benjamin had to leave Boston: the town was not big enough for two printing Franklins, the assembly regarded both brothers as "a little obnoxious to the governing Party," and Benjamin had acquired a reputation as an "Infidel or Atheist." His scoffing about religion, he himself confessed, "began to make me pointed at with Horror by good People." He seized the opportunity in the fall of 1723 to run away from home—finally.[45]

In search of another printshop, Franklin went first to New York. He had discovered that his "Inclinations for the Sea, were by this time worne out." He now had "a Trade" to keep him busy on land. It was nevertheless quickest to get from Boston to New York by sea, and fittingly, printed matter funded Franklin's long-awaited first sea voyage: "I sold some of my Books to raise a little Money" for the ship's passage. Not finding employment in New York, Franklin headed to Philadelphia, taking boat passage via New Jersey. Coastal seafaring had the hazards, if not the excitement, of oceanic voyaging. Franklin's boat to New Jersey "met with a Squall that tore our rotten Sails to pieces" and was driven to Long Island, where it could not land. Instead, the passengers stayed offshore until morning, tossed by the wind and soaked by the spray. (Franklin's bad luck would continue. When he returned home from Philadelphia to Boston in 1724, he took a ship that "sprung a Leak" and all aboard "were oblig'd to pump almost continually, at which I took my Turn.")[46]

On Philadephia's dry land, Franklin found employment but not independence. He was desperate for work. Tired, dirty, and ravenous when he finally walked into the city, he spent some of his little remaining money on bread and gobbled it in the street, to the amusement of a young woman standing in a doorway. (She would later overlook his initial "awkward ridiculous Appearance" and marry him.)[47]

Philadelphia was about thirty years younger than Boston and much smaller—it boasted fewer than 3,000 residents. In a town short on cultural amenities, an underage runaway was welcome if he knew a valuable trade. On Franklin's arrival, one printer quizzed him with "a few Questions" and handed him "a Composing Stick" to see if he could lay out type. He could, and he was hired. But Franklin was not keen to work for another master in another printshop, the fate he thought he had averted when he escaped from his brother.[48]

He was flattered when no less than the governor, William Keith, suggested that he open his own printshop. He went home to Boston to consult his father. Josiah Franklin marveled that Pennsylvania's governor "must be of small Discretion, to think of setting a Boy up in Business who wanted yet 3 Years of being at Man's Estate." It was indeed suspicious—Philadelphia was obviously small enough for the governor to know all of the city's printers, but his interest in the youngest among them hinted that he hoped to make Franklin his tool. Josiah Franklin declined to help his son with the scheme. But Keith kept discussing the plan with the younger Franklin and offered to send him to London to buy equipment and to meet the major printers and booksellers who would become essential business contacts. (James Franklin had done the same early in his career.) So in the same year he arrived in Philadelphia, Franklin headed to London.[49]

IT SEEMS too good to be true that Franklin took passage on a ship named the *London Hope*, and we can only hope the name was a consolation for more seaborne suffering. Franklin enjoyed the ship's "sociable Company" and became friends with a Quaker merchant, fellow passenger Thomas Denham, who would help him in the future. But Franklin's first Atlantic voyage "was otherwise not a pleasant one," for they had "a great deal of bad Weather."[50]

Even worse, he learned on disembarking that his seeming patron, Governor Keith, was as untrustworthy as Josiah Franklin had suspected. Keith had lied to him, failing to furnish the promised letters of introduction and credit to ease his entry into London. Franklin had to fall back on his eminently portable skill of printing, which proved an unintended boon. By practicing his trade in London, the heart of the English book trade, he would learn more about books and printing than he would have been able to do in the colonies, where small and scattered artisanal populations sustained only pale imitations of guild life.[51]

Franklin must have already been a good printer when he arrived in London. Underage and without letters of introduction, he was nonetheless hired at two successive printing establishments. The discipline of guild life seemed to settle him down, at least a bit. At a large printer's establishment, "Watt's near Lincoln's Inn Fields," Franklin had to pay an entry fee to the press room, where the pressmen squeezed together frames of inked type and sheets of paper. Promoted to the composing room, where more-skilled workers laid out the pages, he refused to pay "a new *Bienvenu* or Sum for Drink" to his fellow compositors. They punished him "by mixing my Sorts,

transposing my Pages, breaking my Matter," and then blandly ascrib-
ing the mischief "to the Chapel Ghost." (Franklin added that "A
Printing House is always called a Chappel by the Workmen.") The
compositors also pretended he was not even there, rendering him
"an Excommunicate" from their work order. He gave up and paid
up.[52]

Once Franklin had ingratiated himself, his fellows gave him an
extraordinary education in books and their making. They esteemed
him as "a pretty good Riggite, that is a jocular verbal Satyrist"—and
we thank them for encouraging the lightning wit that ever after
flashed through Franklin's writing. They warned him to protect
hands as well as head. Four years before he died, Franklin would recall "an old Workman" in a London printing house warning him
against handling lead type when it was warm, lest he absorb the lead
and "lose the Use of my Hands by it," the world's worst prospect for
a working man. Franklin eventually became valuable to his master
and his fellow workers and enjoyed his "Consequence in the Society" they formed.[53]

Even better were the societies of greater London. The city's dirty
streets, raucous playhouses, disputatious coffeehouses, and busy
dockyards—and indeed printshops—all contributed to the metropolis's intense creativity and productivity. Human energy poured in
from the countryside and the empire, not least in the form of young
colonists such as Franklin. London had just overtaken Paris as the
largest city in Europe, but more people died than were bred there;
consequently, migrants were needed for the city's sustained growth.
It was not a place for a timid youth. Londoners were aggressively sociable and thrust themselves into places where they could display
their wit and conversation, just as Franklin had learned from the
Spectator, whose very title yanked readers from their armchairs and
flung them before the public eye.[54]

Franklin, who had fled Boston when "good" people stared at him
for his religious unorthodoxy, wanted to become someone Londoners would stare at. He became both spectator and spectacle. He later
admitted that he spent so much of his "Earnings in going to Plays
and other Places of Amusement" that he just barely "rubb'd on from
hand to mouth." He also found a bookseller, with "an immense Collection of second-hand Books," who, for a small fee, let him borrow
and read whatever he pleased—a much broader range of materials
than he could have found even in bookish Boston.[55]

Franklin also tried out a new voice as a philosopher. He helped set type for an edition of William Wollaston's *The Religion of Nature Delineated* and, reading as he composed, realized that he disagreed with the author. So Franklin wrote and had printed one hundred copies of a rebuttal, *A Dissertation on Liberty and Necessity, Pleasure and Pain* (1725). The work went well beyond the timid queries and deist pronouncements that Franklin had made earlier. Contemporaries would have recognized it as libertine, meaning that it renounced conventional religion. Franklin argued that human nature could be explained in secular and deterministic terms, as pursuit of pleasure and avoidance of pain. He did not directly deny God but refused to accept that humanity contained anything mysterious or even especially spiritual; morality was a matter of physical sensation.[56]

Even in a city crammed with ambition and argument, Franklin's deliberate provocation attracted notice. His master, Samuel Palmer, thought the work's principles "abominable." Franklin later regretted his foray into "metaphysical" matters that, as with his irreligion in Boston, made him a spectacle for the wrong reasons. But one admirer, Franklin boasted, "introduc'd me to Dr. [Bernard] Mandevil[l]e," who had written *The Fable of the Bees, or Private Vices Public Benefits* (1714), a book as cynical as Franklin's own but rendered in verse and far more influential. His notoriety earned Franklin a brief entry into Mandeville's social club at a tavern called the Horns. His admirer, surgeon Henry Pemberton, also introduced him to a doctor at Batson's Coffee House near the Royal Exchange, which was frequented by physicians and men of science. Pemberton, who promised to introduce Franklin to none other than Isaac Newton, would edit the third edition of Newton's masterwork, *Principia* (1687), and produce a popular guide to Newton's natural philosophy.[57]

Plays, coffeehouses, clever pamphlets—no renegade puritan and runaway youth could resist them. Franklin never lost his taste for the urban life that had dazzled him during his eighteen months in London, in the course of which he celebrated his nineteenth and twentieth birthdays. And his passing comment about falling in with doctors and men of science revealed a new interest. It is a frustratingly casual notation of an important intellectual shift. We know little about what Franklin was reading in London—he neglected to mention any of the titles he borrowed from his obliging bookseller—but he left a few clues we can follow.

If he had not already, Franklin could have learned from Ovid's *Metamorphoses* the ancient understanding of nature. His first London master, Samuel Palmer, produced a two-volume edition of Ovid in 1724, Franklin's first year in London. In Ovid's great poem, anything could change into something else. Women, for instance, grew into shrubs or hardened into rocks. This transformation was possible because material things all shared the same elementary composition. Four basic elements—earth, air, fire, and water—constituted all matter and gave it four qualities—cold, dry, hot, and wet. Although the heavens were perfect and unchanging, everything on earth constantly altered—Ovid's examples were just particularly dramatic. Analogical connections existed among all things. Thus, the human body was a microcosm of the whole cosmos or macrocosm. Bounded by its thin skin, each body was a leaky, unstable bag containing four fluids, or humors (blood, phlegm, choler, and bile), associated with the four elements and subject to cosmic forces, such as the position of the planets overhead.[58]

Franklin's reference to Newton indicated that he had, by 1726, realized that the old philosophy of nature was subject to dispute, as the *Spectator* had asserted, without giving much detail. It did not matter that Franklin had not read Newton's *Principia* and never did—the *Principia* was one of the most talked-about unread books of all time. Published in Latin and crammed with mathematics, the work was celebrated—and debated—much more than it was read. In it, Newton attacked the ancient ideas that had been second nature to Ovid. He assumed that heaven and earth operated not analogically (the latter as an imperfect example of the former) but similarly. Newton regarded the planets as physical bodies whose motion explained the construction of the cosmos. He portrayed that construction mathematically, as a set of functions and connections that could be represented by numbers. Above all, Newton proposed a way to understand the unseen connections between objects distant from each other: his theory of universal gravitation represented bodies as suspended in a network of interactive forces that kept heavenly planets in their orbits and earthly objects from flying off into space.[59]

Newton made nature seem regular and rational, more accessible to human comprehension. It was self-evident. By designating mathematically defined laws that predicted physical action in all parts of the cosmos, he set new standards for the sciences: observation (as with telescopes), calculation, and reexamination of old principles.

Newton, premier natural
philosopher. Charles Jervas,
Isaac Newton (1717).
THE ROYAL SOCIETY.

These practices had an amazing impact on the reading public's
ideas of nature. Popularized versions of Newton existed for everyone. John Newbury, under the pseudonym "Tom Telescope," wrote
*The Newtonian System of Philosophy, Adapted to the Capacities of Young
Gentlemen and Ladies,* meaning children. There were accounts of
upper-class women who refused to marry or even get dressed in the
morning lest they lose time for their astronomy and mathematics.
Newton became a public figure, a near celebrity. When he died,
Alexander Pope composed an epitaph: "Nature and nature's Laws
lay hid in Night: / GOD said, *Let Newton be!* and all was Light." God
had created the natural world; Newton had decoded it—the epitaph
was endlessly reused.[60]

No wonder that an ambitious young man such as Franklin gravi-
tated toward Newton. Franklin eagerly noted the prospect "of seeing Sir Isaac Newton, of which I was extreamly desirous; but this
never happened," much to his regret (and that of his biographers).
Would he have had anything to say to Newton? Was Franklin, a
provincial youth just shy of his twentieth birthday, overreaching? In
fact, all but the most abstract sciences were supposed to be accessible to anyone who could read and took an interest in the affairs of
the day—precisely people such as Franklin who hung around coffeehouses reading newspapers, absorbing gossip, and hoping to give
Newton a polite bow.[61]

Having failed to meet the great man, Franklin laid siege to the learned organization, the Royal Society, of which Newton was president. Franklin had known about the Royal Society at least since Boston's inoculation controversy. The society was formally closed to Franklin; its fellows were elected only if they were deemed to have made some significant contribution to knowledge. Moreover, it was a gentleman's club. Tradesmen, even if they had made discoveries, never became fellows. But the society's journal of record, the *Philosophical Transactions*, was available to the reading public, and events at the society and reports of its fellows were published in newspapers and elsewhere. Most promising for Franklin, the society solicited information. Its members studied some of the trade-based knowledge that working people had to offer, and they welcomed news from foreign and colonial correspondents.[62]

That was how Franklin wedged his foot in the Royal Society's door. Just before he left London in 1726, he wrote to Hans Sloane, the society's secretary (and then, succeeding Newton in 1727, its president). Franklin probably knew that Sloane had visited and described the natural history of the West Indies; he could be expected to take an interest in colonial specimens. In his studiously offhand letter to Sloane, Franklin tried to pass himself off as a gentleman traveler, Sloane's equal. "Having lately been in the No[r]thern Parts of America," he began, "I have brought from thence" several items made of asbestos, "call'd by the Inhabitants, Salamander Cotton." Franklin evidently wanted Sloane to think he had merely visited the "Inhabitants" of the northern colonies. Moreover, he implied that he had an English country residence or friends who did. In a grand postscript, he added, "I expect to be out of Town in 2 or 3 Days, and therefore beg an immediate Answer." It was a nice try, but Franklin was unable to sustain the conceit. He faltered by offering Sloane the chance to "purchase" his asbestos items, making himself sound more like a tradesman selling wares than one gentleman showing his "Curiosities" to another.[63]

Sloane met Franklin and obligingly purchased a small purse woven from "Salamander Cotton." It is now held in the British Museum, part of the collection Sloane *donated*, as a gentleman was expected to do, without payment. Franklin must have realized that he had played his part in this drama somewhat shabbily because he remembered it differently when he wrote his autobiography. There, he asserted that he had indeed brought over "Curiosities," including the asbestos purse, but that "Sir Hans Sloane heard of it, came to see me, and invited me to his House in Bloomsbury Square, where he show'd me all his Curiosities, and persuaded me to let him add that to the Number, for which he paid me handsomely." In this version, Franklin was Sloane's social equal—which was true when he wrote the account but not when he had had the encounter.[64]

Whatever the transaction was like, it carried Franklin a step further on the path of science. He had learned to make money from books, both as a printer and as a bookseller, as when he had needed cash to leave Boston. Now, specimens allowed him to raise money when he needed it and to gain access to one of the most highly esteemed naturalists of his age. And the asbestos, a substance that resists fire, is the first indication of his long-lasting interest in heat and its effects.

Franklin also considered making money by turning himself into a curiosity, an American as waterproof as asbestos was fireproof. He had astonished Londoners with his ability to swim well. At one point, he had stripped down and swum in the Thames for a distance of three and a half miles, "performing on the Way many Feats of Activity both upon and under Water." An eminent political figure, Sir William Wyndham, heard of the demonstration and summoned Franklin. Wyndham advised him to open a "Swimming School," which would make him "a good deal of Money." Had he stayed in London, Franklin thought, this school would have been his best prospect. Money was clearly on his mind. He had saved none in London and believed that if he returned to Philadelphia, he would have to take "Leave of Printing" and enter trade. Thomas Denham, the Quaker merchant he had met on the way to London, had offered to take him on as a clerk.[65]

BALLAD-SELLER, irreligious printshop worker, runaway, Londoner, pamphleteer, and playgoer—Franklin feared that all his endeavors and adventures were leading him nowhere. He resolved to reform himself and return to Philadelphia, which still needed printers. He left London in July 1726. He must have calculated that he would soon turn twenty-one (in January 1727) and could expect to be his own master at last.

His new sense of seriousness was apparent in "the *Plan*" he "formed at Sea, for regulating my future Conduct in Life." In the plan, he confessed that he had "never fixed a regular design in life;

by which means it has been a confused variety of different scenes."
Henceforth, Franklin resolved on a plan of frugality, truth, industry,
and goodwill toward others. At the end of his life, he congratulated
himself that the plan was all "the more remarkable, as being form'd
when I was so young, and yet being pretty faithfully adhered to quite
thro' to old Age." Like the entertainingly censorious Silence Dogood, the earnest and improvement-minded Benjamin Franklin was
born at sea.[66]

The journal that he kept during his 1726 voyage on the *Berkshire*,
on the way back to Philadelphia, revealed his new solemnity and in-
dustriousness. He made forays into different areas of learning and
experimented with different types of writing. The text contained
sentimental prose that Franklin would wisely abjure in his adult writing. ("Albion, farewell!" he penned when his ship set out, and, even
worse, "my eyes were dimmed with the suffusion of two small drops
of joy" at the sight of America.) To a remarkable extent, however,
the journal was the progenitor of all Franklin's work in the sciences.
It was his first extended inquiry into the natural world—indeed, the
first sign that he thought he had something to say about it.[67]

He began modestly, with descriptions of nature. His daily entries
followed the conventions of sea logs: "Wednesday, August 10 / Wind
N. W. Course S. W. about four knots. By observation in latitude 48°
50'. Nothing remarkable happened"—a dull day for science and
perhaps for the passengers. Franklin also studied the weather and
the heavens: "Saturday, October 1 / These South-Wests are hot
damp winds, and bring abundance of rain and dirty weather." Two
eclipses, one solar and one lunar, enlivened the voyage. The lunar
eclipse, predicted in London almanacs, encouraged Franklin to stay
on deck all night to see when it would begin "with us" at sea and
how it would help determine longitude, which was still a problem
for navigators.[68]

Franklin also observed marine life. He noted the dolphins and
sharks around the ship; the sharks discouraged his own swimming.
He pitied "a poor little bird" that came aboard "almost tired to
death." The ship was about 200 leagues from land, and the bird was
desperate to put down somewhere. (The ship's cat had "destroyed"
an earlier refugee.) Even better was a "*Tropic bird*" that must have
been, like the weary temperate birds, blown off course by the winds.
Franklin was therefore interested not only in the presence of animals at sea but also in the question of whether they belonged where

he saw them. How did climate and weather patterns indicate the proper places for different creatures?[69]

His interest in what we might call habitat led him to investigate the crabs and seaweed that coexisted in the North Atlantic. On September 28, he wrote: "This afternoon we took up several branches of gulf weed (with which the sea is spread all over from the Western Isles to the coast of America); but one of these branches had something peculiar in it." The peculiarity was "a small shell-fish like a heart," appearing as "embrios" and as fully formed crabs. From these fragments—weed, embryo, adult crab—Franklin postulated a small, interconnected world. The crab was "a native of the branch" of the seaweed and had perhaps just developed out of "the same condition with the rest of those little embrios." To prove this "conjecture," he "resolved to keep the weed in salt water . . . by this experiment to see whether any more crabs will be produced or not in this manner." Two days later, Franklin gathered more gulfweed with the boat hook. This sample had more crabs, "each less than the nail of my little finger," and one with a vestigial piece of embryonic shell that supported his idea that the crabs must grow while latched onto the marine plant.[70]

He decided to save some of the seaweed and the partly developed crab in a glass container "to preserve the curiosity till I come on shore." Just as his asbestos items indicated an emerging interest in heat, so the crabs hinted at his similarly long-lived fascination with reproduction. The gulf-related phenomena were, as well, the start of Franklin's investigations into the circulation of the Atlantic waters.[71]

It is interesting that Franklin thought the crab in the gulfweed was the curiosity, not the weed itself. Indeed, using the term *gulf* to describe Atlantic phenomena had become a commonplace. The word had first described maritime things in and around the Gulf of Mexico and was undoubtedly derived from Spanish use, which might have started as early as the sixteenth century. Much later, the word began to describe Atlantic things more generally. The first printed evidence in English of this broader usage appeared in 1674, when John Josselyn traveled from England to New England and referred to the "gulf weed" that spread over certain parts of the Atlantic, presumably from the warmer waters of the Gulf of Mexico. Franklin had made his first encounter with the Gulf Stream, though that phrase would not be used in print until the 1740s.[72]

His journal notations may be juvenilia, but they are remarkable ones. Franklin had clearly absorbed the plain style of writing and the focus on visible evidence that characterized the era's sciences. And he had taken up some of the sciences' most important topics: astronomy, climate, and the generation of life. This kind of narrative description of nature would become common, but it was not in the 1720s—certainly not for a self-trained man in his twenties. Franklin's determination to "preserve a curiosity" bespeaks his ambition, a desire to retain specimens to impress fellow naturalists. He had also learned about the collaborative nature of the sciences—he used plural pronouns to describe his activities: "we see Tropic birds every day," the sun was "hid from our eyes," "we took up several branches of gulf weed," the eclipse "began with us," "we have had abundance of dolphins." Indeed, he must have had collaborators aboard the ship; he would have needed permission to use the boat hook to collect seaweed.[73]

What kind of collaboration was it? It is all too easy to imagine the young Franklin bouncing about the ship, generally getting in the way, and assuming that he, veteran of one earlier Atlantic crossing, had opinions worth the notice of mariners. But he and the sailors needed desperately, if for rather different reasons, to keep busy.

The voyage took much longer than Franklin's journey to England had, an agonizing eighty-three days. His eastward passage had been, in contrast, roughly forty-nine days. Franklin was painfully aware that the winds were "westerly," that is, coming from the west, where the ship was trying to go. The command would invariably have been "helm's a lee," to point the ship ahead of any promising wind, so the crew swiveled their craft around and around. "The word *helm-a-lee* is become," he complained, "almost as disagreeable to our ears as the sentence of a judge to a convicted malefactor." Food stores ran low. On September 20, after two months at sea, ship biscuit was rationed; the next day, the steward was flogged "for making an extravagant use of flour in the puddings."[74]

It is no wonder that Franklin was busy looking at crabs—he was certainly bored and possibly anxious. He had reveled in big, talkative London and was now, for almost three months, reduced to a small audience of twenty-one people. As when his London coworkers had made him an "excommunicate," social isolation frightened Franklin. He noted that a fellow passenger on the *Berkshire* who had cheated at cards was likewise excommunicated—denied any company until he paid a fine. "Man is a sociable being," Franklin commented; being "excluded from society" was "the worst of punishments." He was elated when, at the end of September, the *Berkshire* encountered a ship bound for New York from Dublin. "There is really something strangely cheering to the spirits," he confessed to his journal, "in the meeting of a ship at sea, containing a society of creatures of the same species and in the same circumstances with ourselves." "My heart fluttered in my breast with joy," he continued (with some of that awful sentimentality he was still trying out), "when I saw so many human countenances."[75]

After a few days, the other ship fell off, and the *Berkshire* was again alone. At that point, Franklin and the others must not only have been bored at sea but also fearful they might not spot land before their stores gave out. Franklin admitted that all the conversation was now focused on the destination, Philadelphia. On September 27, he laid a bet, "a bowl of punch," that they would arrive a week from the upcoming Saturday.[76]

He was desperate to confirm the ship's proximity to land. The gulfweed and the eclipse were probably his attempts to determine a rough position. And on Sunday, October 2, he wrote, "I cannot help fancying the water is changed a little as is usual when a ship comes within soundings," meaning over shallow ground, sign of coastline. Still, he wondered whether appearances were deceiving: "'Tis probable I am mistaken; for there is but one besides myself of my opinion." Precisely because only one other person saw what Franklin did, he labeled his perception a mere "opinion," something that fell short of universal acceptance. But the next day, he emphatically noted that "the water is now very visibly changed to the eyes of all except the Captain and Mate, and they will by no means allow it; I suppose because they did not see it first."[77]

One senses that the officers might have been a bit tired of Franklin and his curiosity—and that he recognized their annoyance with him. Still, his relationships with the crew had not broken down completely. For the rest of the voyage, he continued to write down observations that he could not have obtained alone. He noted, for instance, the depth of the water and the distance of the ship from land during the last four days of the journey. Obviously, the crew had not entirely excommunicated Franklin—someone was still talking to him.[78]

The 1726 journal offers an excellent record of Franklin's early engagement with the sciences. In it, he revealed his interest in a broad range of phenomena. He had learned that inquiry into the natural world was a sociable and collaborative endeavor. And he consulted relevant trade groups about their knowledge.

Above all, Franklin recorded his ambition: he wanted to discover new things that would get noticed and get him noticed—hence his curiosity about the timing of eclipses at sea and about the way in which animal life was generated. The same ambition surfaced in Franklin's assessment of what he had accomplished during his year and a half in London. "I had by no means improv'd my Fortune," he wrote, "but I had pick'd up some very ingenious Acquaintance whose Conversation was of great Advantage to me, and I had read considerably." Franklin remained penniless, but he had gained capital in the form of knowledge and could, as a printer, disseminate both his opinions and his knowledge. Head and hands were serving him well. His encounter with Hans Sloane and his near encounter with Isaac Newton were especially promising. Franklin had discovered that some forms of knowledge could blur the boundary between a workingman and a gentleman, even if the worker lacked formal education.[79]

Chapter 3

MAN of LETTERS

O N HIS RETURN to Philadelphia, Franklin began his new life quite dramatically—by nearly dying. He arrived in America in poor health. "The voyage had [so] much weakened us," he noted, that he and some other passengers did not have the strength to get off at Chester, Pennsylvania, the first port, and continue overland. Instead, they lingered aboard the *Berkshire* until it made Philadelphia in October 1726. Franklin then began clerking for merchant Thomas Denham, part owner of the *Berkshire*, who had advanced Franklin the cost of his passage against future wages.[1]

The excruciating ship's passage, the work, and the onset of winter all took a toll on Franklin. Shortly after his twenty-first birthday, in February 1727, both he and Denham became ill. "My Distemper was a Pleurisy, which very nearly carried me off," Franklin recounted many years later: "I suffered a good deal, gave up the Point in my own mind, and was rather disappointed when I found my Self recovering; regretting in some degree that I must now some time or other have all that disagreable Work to do over again." Denham was not so fortunate; he died that winter. His will specified that Franklin was to be forgiven the cost of his passage. Rather incredibly, Franklin later would not remember what felled his sponsor—"I forget what his Distemper was"—even though Denham's death "left [him] once more to the wide World."[2]

The experience was Franklin's first brush with death. Indeed, it was the first time he admitted any physical weakness. His body had survived the 1721 smallpox epidemic in Boston, had carried him to Philadelphia as a runaway, and had astonished Londoners with its feats of swimming. Now, however, mortality haunted Franklin. Around 1728, he wrote himself an epitaph, which was never used and never published. Franklin kept and privately circulated it as a lifelong memento mori:[3]

The Body of
B. Franklin,
Printer;
Like the Cover of an old Book,
Its Contents torn out,
And stript of its Lettering and Gilding,
Lies here, Food for Worms.
But the Work shall not be wholly lost:
For it will, as he believ'd, appear once more,
In a new & more perfect Edition,
Corrected and amended
By the Author.
He was born Jan. 6. 1706.
Died 17

What would the terminal date be? As if fearful it might come soon, Franklin was anxious to follow the "Plan of Conduct" he had written on the *Berkshire*. He became maniacally productive. He founded a club, took over a newspaper, established a public library, became a Freemason, married and acquired property, published an almanac, gained political office, and proposed a learned society and academy for his adopted city—all within six years.

He became a man of letters, in several senses. He was a printer, whose successes derived from arranging small lead letters and other "sorts" to form words on a page. He wrote a variety of letters (signed with his own name or a variety of pseudonyms) in which he offered his opinions on every topic of contemporary interest. He continued the reading and discussion he had enjoyed in London, making himself into a person of letters, someone conversant with topics of current learning, including natural science. And he aspired to join the international republic of letters, a sociable network of learned men and women.

————————

FRANKLIN missed the garrulous, disputatious life of London. So he worked to re-create it in Philadelphia. The city lacked clubs—its taverns and coffeehouses, whatever their sturdy contributions to civic life, were not known for their witty conversation. And the colonies still lacked Masonic lodges, the new clubs that were spreading over Europe. (An infant lodge was rumored in Philadelphia in the early 1720s, but Franklin was not part of it.) If he was going to continue the talking and reading he regarded as his most important activities in London, he would have to create a venue for them.

His first accomplishment on returning to Philadelphia was to help found a club. In 1727, Franklin and other young Philadelphia tradesmen organized themselves to read and debate the ideas of the day. The club might have been partially based on the colonial self-improvement associations Cotton Mather had advocated in his *Essays to Do Good,* as well as on learned societies such as the Royal Society of London. The ideal of human sociability that was drifting around the Atlantic had found a berth in Philadelphia.

Franklin's group initially bore two names: the Junto and the Leather Apron Club. The latter name was a problem because it emphasized its members' status as craftworkers. So did the rumor that the group was a political cabal in the pocket of the governor, Sir William Keith. The implication was that workingmen could not possibly have time to read, let alone think, unless they were bankrolled by a patron; that individual's patronage made them his fawning creatures, and they merely parroted his opinions. The allegation represented quite well the contemporary assumption that reading, reflection, and debate belonged to propertied men, the only people capable of forming ideas that were not beholden to the support of others. That seems to have been precisely the prejudice that Franklin and his friends were trying to escape. They read to improve themselves and make themselves into independent gentlemen. So, at some point before 1731, the name Junto edged out that of the Leather Apron Club.[4]

The early members of the Junto nevertheless rejected the gentlemanly atmosphere of the Royal Society and of London's grander clubs. The original club contained many craftsmen who, like printers, worked with head and hands; these included a mathematical instrument maker, a graduate of Balliol College, Oxford (who had been reduced to indentured servitude), and two surveyors, all of whom were presumably as eager as Franklin to exercise their wits. Franklin would maintain a friendship with one cofounder, William Coleman, for forty years. He claimed Coleman had "the coolest clearest Head, the best Heart, and the exactest Morals, of almost any

Man I ever met with." Franklin also grew close to Philip Syng, a silversmith and, along with Franklin, one of the last three surviving members of the original Junto.[5]

The club was organized on one principle: devotion to truth. Reading and discussion were intended to make constant and critical distinctions between true knowledge and mere opinion (which varied between individuals, sects, and factions). Religious and political differences were never to affect club relations or conversation. No one was admitted to the Junto unless he agreed to these stipulations. Any prospective member was required—"hand on his breast"—to state four things, affirming: first, that he bore no ill will to any current member; second, to "sincerely declare that you love mankind in general; of what profession or religion soever"; third, to reject any penalty for anyone holding "mere speculative opinions" or unorthodox "way of worship"; and fourth, that he "love[d] truth for truth's sake."[6]

The philosophy was part of a broader commitment to self-improvement. For Franklin and the other Junto members, learning and social advancement were linked goals. The first of the club's "Standing Queries" asked that members relate whether they had "met with any thing in the author you last read, remarkable, or suitable to be communicated to the Junto." Further questions followed, for a total of twenty-four, many of which addressed issues that concerned young men eager, as Franklin was, to rise in the world. ("Hath any body attacked your reputation lately?" "Have you any weighty affair in hand, in which you think the advice of the Junto may be of service?") Franklin and his friends were not, however, tedious sobersides—consider a slightly later proposal that the queries be "read distinctly each Meeting" with a "Pause between each while one might fill and drink a Glass of Wine." The club, after all, met in a tavern.[7]

Franklin had created a forum for mental stimulation and amusement—now, he had to make money. In 1728, he formed a printers' partnership with Hugh Meredith, a fellow Junto founder. Franklin and Meredith planned to begin a newspaper. But they unwisely revealed their intention to a potential employee. This journeyman leaked the news, which encouraged a rival printer, Samuel Keimer (Franklin's former employer), to inaugurate, in December 1728, his *Universal Instructor in All Arts and Sciences: and Pennsylvania Gazette.* "I resented this," Franklin later said, with some understatement. Philadelphia now had two newspapers, and Franklin was in the same position his brother had been in when he had to ram the *New-England Courant* into an already crowded newspaper market.[8]

Keimer's presumption that he was Pennsylvania's universal instructor of all arts and sciences must have particularly galled Franklin, fresh from London and busy keeping up with current ideas in the Junto. The only solution for Franklin was to wreck Keimer's project, a task from which he did not shrink. He used the town's other newspaper, Andrew Bradford's *American Weekly Mercury*, to launch another series of anonymous essays, this one written (as fair warning to Keimer) by "the Busy-Body."

The Busy-Body took it on himself to be "a Kind of *Censor Morum,*" or arbiter of manners, for Philadelphia. He adopted Silence Dogood's seemingly artless yet self-promoting sanctimony: "*What is every Body's Business is no Body's Business,* and the Business is done accordingly. I, therefore, upon mature Deliberation, think fit to take *no Body's Business* wholly into my own Hands." The Busy-Body worried particularly that his neighbors suffered from scarcity of "good Books"; "good Conversation is still more scarce." Thus, there was a need for a qualified commentator to "deliver Lectures of Morality or Philosophy." In short, the Busy-Body would supply the true wisdom and enlightening conversation that Keimer only thought his ostentatiously named paper was delivering.[9]

The ongoing debate over publication of "secrets" offered the perfect opening for an attack on Keimer. Keimer had been padding his *Universal Instructor* with excerpts from Ephraim Chambers's *Cyclopedia*, an alphabetically organized compendium of knowledge. By January 21, 1729, he had reached the entry on abortion, which he incautiously printed.

Franklin had learned a thing or two from his brother's strategic assault on inoculation. He was probably the author of two essays, ostensibly by "Martha Careful" and "Caelia Shortface," that denounced Keimer's decision to print knowledge once restricted to doctors and married women. Careful and Shortface offered scathing letters to the *American Weekly Mercury;* each claimed to speak for others in Philadelphia. Shortface's phrasing hinted that she was Quaker and represented those exacting matrons: "If thou proceed any further in that *Scandalous manner,*" she told Keimer, "we intend very soon to have thy right Ear for it." Careful added that "the Secrets of our Sex" should not be "read in all *Taverns* and *Coffee-Houses,* and by the Vulgar." Such matters might be revealed to men only as part of "the Repositary of the Learned," a tenet Franklin probably did not hold but found useful to claim against Keimer.[10]

Altogether, the contributions of the Busy-Body and Mesdames Careful and Shortface made the *American Weekly Mercury* far more interesting to read than the dutiful *Universal Instructor* ever was. On October 2, 1729, less than a year after Keimer had begun his newspaper, he gave up and sold it to Franklin, who would maintain a connection with it until 1766. Franklin used the subtitle of Keimer's paper for his paper's name—the *Pennsylvania Gazette*. And the Busy-Body vanished. Franklin had won his first trade battle. Pity poor Keimer, who would die in 1742. He would have needed to survive another decade to be able to console himself that he had, after all, been outwitted by no less than the famous Benjamin Franklin.

The *Pennsylvania Gazette* would help Franklin make himself into Philadelphia's paramount man of letters. The newspaper gave him his first successes as a printer-publisher, led him into political discussions (unavoidable for a newspaperman), and allowed him to continue Keimer's discussion of learning, as with extracts from Chambers's *Cyclopedia*, to which Franklin no longer objected now that Keimer was out of the way.

The *Pennsylvania Gazette* was, in many ways, a typical colonial paper, much more so than James Franklin's argumentative *Courant*. The *Gazette* jumbled together news from the metropolis, the empire, and the rest of the world, along with local headlines. And the paper was a tool for the editors' political ambitions and preferences— readers expected this. Reporting news of Britain's peace with Spain in 1729, the *Gazette* offered four paragraphs, "from four different London Papers": two related the government's opinions; one leaned toward the Whig party, which was critical of the current administration; and the fourth came from "a Tory Paper" that was critical of both administration and Whigs. "When the Reader has allowed for these Distinctions," the *Gazette* editors warned, "he will be better able to form his Judgment on the Affair."[11]

Pennsylvania's politics likewise required careful treatment. The colony was a proprietary one, meaning it was privately owned. It had been founded by Quaker William Penn, and his descendants retained title to it; Quakers dominated the House of Assembly and government offices. But Penn had thrown his colony open to settlers of all religions and nations, thus guaranteeing a diversity of people and ideas. By the 1720s, some residents had begun to criticize the proprietors (and Quakers generally) and to press for their own power. The result was a set of factions whose different interests would forever enliven Franklin's political awareness and activities.[12]

Franklin and Meredith were extremely careful to remain on the good side of Pennsylvania's authorities. For example, when Burlington officials restricted access to their town fair in order to prevent Philadelphia's smallpox from invading their area, Franklin and Meredith did not merely describe the town order but also warned that any who did not obey "will answer for their Contempt at their Perils." Their deference paid off. At the end of January 1730, a mere four months after Keimer had consigned the *Pennsylvania Gazette* to them, they became the official printers to the Pennsylvania Assembly—a great boost to their visibility and business.[13]

His new visibility made Franklin even more cautious. He made sure that he and his printing business avoided partisan positions. And he was extremely careful not to give offense on the subject of religion. Pennsylvania was an example of a society based on religious toleration; Franklin had to respect all its faiths while favoring none. He knew that his actions were now matters of record, not youthful foibles. He could no longer afford to publish irreligious philosophical works. In fact, he bought up and burned as many copies as he could of his *Dissertation on Liberty and Necessity, Pleasure and Pain*, the libertine text he had published in London. He later described the work as an "Erratum," a printer's term for an error in composition. Only four copies of the offending work survive. However much Franklin would become known for his free dissemination of knowledge, he took great care to restrict the circulation of information that put him in a bad light.[14]

Franklin now accepted a new theory, derived from the sciences, which softened his antipathy to religion. In the late seventeenth century, naturalists who were Christian believers (and sometimes even ministers) had defined an "argument from design." This theory specified that the material creation was too vast and complicated to be anything but the work of a divine power; hence God must exist. The argument from design drew on an older tradition of an emblematic nature—natural things were emblems of spiritual meaning. These doctrines united science and religion, and they unified a range of people, from deists (who saw God as a remote creator but not an intervener) to traditional churchgoers (who regarded everything in nature as evidence of God's constantly present and providential authority).[15]

Several of Franklin's writings from the late 1720s and early 1730s endorsed the argument from design. His 1728 "Articles of Belief and Acts of Religion," a private liturgy, thus offered nature as proof of God: "Thy Wisdom, thy Power, and thy GOODNESS are every where clearly seen; in the Air and in the Water, in the Heavens and on the Earth. . . . Thou givest Cold and Heat, Rain and Sunshine in their Season, and to the Fruits of the Earth Increase. Praised be thy Name for ever." Franklin evidently recited these and similar invocations, then reminded himself to read not scripture but modern writings that likewise addressed God as "O Creator, O Father." His point was that humans could appreciate divine power if they used their reason to scan nature; books, clerics, and organized religion were not essential. Thus, in a 1732 statement of his beliefs, Franklin emphasized his use of "plain Reasoning, devoid of Art and Ornament; unsupported by the Authority of any Books or Men how sacred soever." This convention did not mean he mocked religion, merely that he sought new proof for it within the Creation.[16]

Franklin made clear, in 1731, that he was not intimidated by religious orthodoxies. That year, he published his celebrated "Apology for Printers" in the *Pennsylvania Gazette*. The piece rebutted critics who had attacked him for printing an advertisement soliciting passengers for a ship heading to Barbados. The advertiser had specified that the ship would not carry any "*Black Gowns*"—clergy—"*on any Terms*." In his "Apology," Franklin emphasized that he himself was not anticlerical and that he regretted any offense the advertisement may have caused. He then elaborated beyond the case at hand. He could not, he explained, make a policy of never printing things that some people would "say ought not to be printed." He argued that a printer had to reflect a world in which "the Opinions of Men are almost as various as their Faces." After all, "the Business of Printing has chiefly to do with Mens Opinions." If printers decided never to print anything offensive, he pointed out, "there would be very little printed." Regrettable though prejudice against the clergy might be, Franklin did not consider it his business to censor it.[17]

Clearly, he modeled his "Apology" on James Franklin's similar defense against the Reverend Cotton Mather's criticism. Franklin's apology reminded readers that public life required toleration of varied beliefs. Religious differences did not have to disturb the peace unless people were determined that they should. Yet rather subversively, Franklin had reiterated his conviction that most religious beliefs were mere "opinions" that could never be vindicated as universal truths.

On other matters, he was far less tolerant—as he reminded his readers. He rejected anything that resembled "Party or Personal Reflections" and was particularly wary of anything potentially slanderous. A foolish public greatly needed his caution. He wryly observed that a printed collection of songs about Robin Hood was currently outselling a volume of the Psalms. He avoided items that would "countenance Vice, or promote Immorality." Throughout his "apology," Franklin put himself forward as a cautious *censor morum*—a reincarnation of the moralizing "Busy-Body" who had insinuated himself into Philadelphia's public life at Samuel Keimer's expense.[18]

Franklin would reiterate his beliefs about the press a few years later when he defended a fellow newspaperman, John Peter Zenger. Unlike Benjamin Franklin (but much like James Franklin), Zenger had, in his *New-York Weekly Journal*, attacked members of his colony's government. Zenger was accused of seditious libel and taken to trial in 1735. Whatever he might privately have thought of Zenger's lack of caution, Franklin used his *Pennsylvania Gazette* to protest the man's persecution, to reprint pro-Zenger material from London newspapers, and to advertise the sale of Zenger's own 1736 *Narrative* of his trial.[19]

Most of the *Pennsylvania Gazette* was, however, uncontroversial. Its primary subject was commerce. Philadelphia was no longer the backward town Franklin had first entered in 1723, nine years before he and Meredith gained their newspaper. The town was well on its way to becoming the second-largest city in the British empire and the most important North American port.[20]

Accounts of shipbuilding, trade, transportation, maritime accidents, and warfare all appeared in Franklin's newspaper. In 1732, for example, the paper recounted the progress of a "Mast Ship" in Casco Bay, New England, which had just loaded "large, fair, and fine Trees for the Supply of his Majesty's Navy." In 1741, the *Rubie* advertised its imports of manufactured goods, including linens, hats, greatcoats, and cutlery, available for "ready Money" or flour, Philadelphia's main export. Those who wished in turn to ship goods or embark on the *Rubie* for its run to the West Indies were invited to approach the ship's master "on board said ship." In 1748, the paper reported that the *Griffin* of Philadelphia had been struck by lightning on its way to Jamaica. The next year, the paper carried a notice that the *Success*, with twenty guns, was stationed in Boston, an ominous portent as Anglo-French conflict mounted.[21]

The newspaper was awash in advertisements, Franklin's most substantial source of revenue. People paid him to place ads for everything imaginable. They wanted to sell goods or laborers, to advertise their services, to solicit customers for their businesses, to request assistance for various projects, to demand that debtors pay up, to plead for the return of lost items, to threaten legal action, to notify the public about runaway slaves or servants or kinfolk, or simply to declare something about themselves. In the pages of the *Pennsylvania Gazette*, husbands demanded the return of runaway wives, wives retorted that their husbands' abuse had made them flee, merchants listed imported wares, gentlemen wondered where their pocketwatches had gone to, widows advertised their peerless medical remedies, tutors solicited students, and masters complained that escaped slaves had packed up several sets of clothing as disguises and as easily shed capital. These fragments of lives—happy, despairing, prosperous, boring, inventive, or about to end badly—were bread and butter for their printer.[22]

The advertisements, more to the point, tell us a great deal about Franklin's willingness to conform to his neighbors' expectations. That he profited from slavery is abundantly clear in the many *Pennsylvania Gazette* notices about the sale of human laborers or rewards for the recapture of runaways. Thus, the former bonded apprentice and runaway who had freed himself because he knew how to set type now used that skill to secure the bondage of others. At this stage of his life, Franklin comfortably accepted this aspect of his world.[23]

To increase his profits, he also sold a variety of goods at his printing office—he had become a merchant after all. He showcased his own printed items but would also, over the course of his career as printer, sell everything from linseed oil to "Very Good COFFEE." He even sold "superfine CROWN SOAP," the Franklin family's characteristic green soap stamped with a crown to indicate its quality. "It is cut in exact and equal Cakes, neatly put up, and sold at the New Printing-Office," declared one advertisement. Sometimes, Franklin distributed printed products for free. A complimentary pamphlet might entice a customer into his shop (where something else might catch the eye) and draw attention to his many projects and products. As well, the gazette did double duty—readers could buy it and also find in its pages other things to purchase.[24]

Franklin's chief commodity was knowledge. Quite early on, he imported and sold books, particularly if they were beyond his means to print (as was true of illustrated works) or if he was trying to gauge demand for something he might eventually print. One long 1734 *Pennsylvania Gazette* advertisement for imported books gave a good sense of what Franklin expected his customers to read. The list began with books on navigation and science: "Westindia Coasting Pilot. Newhouse's Navigation. Pattoun's Navigation. Key of Commerce. Lex Mercatoria. Euclid's Elements by William Whiston. Burnet's Theory of the Earth, 2 Vols." Histories and religious works followed. The advertisement concluded by noting that the printshop also stocked "Quadrants, Forestaffs, Nocturnals, Mariner's Compasses," further reminders of Philadelphia's burgeoning status as an Atlantic port city.[25]

Franklin circulated knowledge in other ways, including human form. In 1734, he advertised a buyer for an indentured servant who was "a Scholar, and can teach Children Reading, Writing and Arithmetick." He also used the paper to facilitate book loans in a network so extensive that he was always losing track of material. The same year he helped sell "a Scholar," he placed his own gazette advertisement, admitting that he had "Lent at different Times (and forgot to whom) the following [five] Books" that he now wished would be returned "to the Printer of this Paper." But Franklin had "in his Hands the 2d. Vol of Cowley's Works in Octavo, of which he does not know the Owner." Maybe all of these volumes made their way back to their rightful owners; if not, Franklin had, in his readiness to exchange ideas, gained one book at the expense of losing five.[26]

Above all, Franklin used his newspaper to circulate knowledge, including discoveries in the sciences. Indeed, the *Pennsylvania Gazette* is a very good measure of the popularization of natural science at midcentury. Franklin knew better than to fill his paper with learned discussions that the general public would skip or subscribers would resent paying for. So in his discussions of the natural world, he tended to favor a topic that never fails to grab a reader's attention: death.

The early editions of the *Pennsylvania Gazette* published what were then called "bills of mortality"—vital statistics, especially those for

Philadelphia. Most large cities published this information in order to notify the public of the growth or decline of the population or of any particularly dangerous conditions. In late 1730, the *Gazette* listed all Philadelphia burials for the past year: a total of 227, broken down by religion and race. Early the following year, an article pointed out to readers that from the number of deaths (assuming an average year), one could extrapolate Philadelphia's total population. It also proposed that the number could be compared to tallies in Boston, London, and some other European cities in order to get a comparative sense of the city's size.[27]

While considering death (and health), Franklin paid particular attention to smallpox. Unlike his brother, however, he heralded the efficacy of inoculation and urged its use. In May 1730, he published the description of inoculation from Chambers's *Cyclopedia*. That same month, Franklin reported that in cases of smallpox in Boston, of seventy-two people inoculated, only two had died, whereas one in four among the holdouts perished after contracting smallpox the ordinary way. In March of the following year, he reprinted an extract from the *Philosophical Transactions* of the Royal Society that described inoculation in Constantinople, and he rejoiced that "the Practice of Inoculation for the Small-Pox, begins to grow among us." In July, he was even happier that "the Small-pox has now quite left this City." Fragments though these may be, they are Franklin's first publications in natural history and his first printed discussions of matters debated by learned societies.[28]

He kept at it. Building on his coverage of smallpox, he next tackled the common cold (which may have interested him because of his struggle with pleurisy a few years earlier). In late 1732, the *Gazette* reported that "from all Parts of this Province, and even from Maryland, People complain of Colds." The reasons were debated: people either acquired their sneezes and sniffles from a sudden "hard Frost" or because of the disease's "contagious" nature, "after somewhat the same Manner as the Small-pox or Pestilence." Franklin conceded that learned men were divided on the subject, and he printed another extract from the *Philosophical Transactions* to prove the point. The piece, a 1694 description of colds, was a bit old, however.[29]

As Franklin expanded his coverage of the sciences, he tended to offer more up-to-date information. In 1737, for instance, the *Pennsylvania Gazette* gave an account of the recent appearance of the aurora borealis, with a text appended from astronomer Edmond Halley's description of it in the *Philosophical Transactions* for 1716.[30]

With its blend of news, editorials, advertisements, and natural knowledge, the *Pennsylvania Gazette* expanded and flourished. In short order, Franklin set up an independent business, dissolving his partnership with Meredith in mid-1730 and establishing himself as an important tradesman and property owner in Philadelphia. This improved situation allowed him, in late 1730, to take a wife, Deborah Read Rogers, and to set up a respectable household to which he could bring his illegitimate son William, who was born around the time of the marriage. The bastard child made the publicly acknowledged union crucial. Yet Franklin managed to keep his private life just that; we still do not know who William Franklin's mother was.[31]

Franklin's marriage reflected his principle of religious toleration. He may have been a deist, but Deborah Franklin belonged to the Church of England, and all the Franklin children would be raised in that faith. A *Pennsylvania Gazette* advertisement of 1737 notified readers that "a Common Prayer Book, bound in Red, gilt, and letter'd DF on each Corner" had disappeared from a pew in Christ Church. "The Person who took it, is desir'd to open it and read the *Eighth* Commandment" and put it back. Either Philadelphia was small enough or the Franklins were well known enough that readers knew immediately that "DF" was Mrs. Benjamin Franklin. Thus, Franklin economically advertised his wife's missing book, his household's general piety, and his services as advertiser.[32]

IN EARLY 1731, Franklin joined another club, the St. John's Lodge of Philadelphia. It was America's first Masonic lodge. His membership represented his initial attempt at a cosmopolitan status, one no longer linked to his provincial setting.

Freemasonry seems to have emerged in seventeenth-century Scotland, with a supposed ancestry in the ancient skill of stonemasonry. Like all trade guilds, stonemasons had long maintained rituals that conferred trade solidarity and protected secrets. As the guild structure declined at the end of the Middle Ages, its secrets and rituals reappeared in, of all places, social clubs for the elite and middle ranks. So-called Freemasons, or "Speculative Masons," people who could not have worked with stone to save their lives, relished exclusiveness and mystery in their clubs. The contrast between the working-class origins of Freemasonry and its attraction for propertied men meant that a Masonic lodge was a perfect place for Franklin.[33]

Their secrecy made Freemasons exciting and mysterious. Before learning Masonic mysteries, an initiate would have to swear never to "Write them, Print them, Mark them, Carve them or Engrave them" lest he then "have [his] Throat cut, [his] Tongue taken from the Roof of [his] Mouth, [his] Heart pluck'd from under [his] Left Breast," and so forth. Freemasons also referred to themselves, with a wink, as "the Craft" and claimed to possess knowledge descended from ancient Egyptian, Hebrew, or Greek traditions. While celebrating workers' culture, Freemasons rejected actual working people. In their ceremonies, speculative Masons employed silver trowels, silk gloves, and taffeta or lambskin aprons to mimic a working mason's iron tools, leather gloves, and apron.[34]

At the start of Franklin's Masonic affiliation, American lodges were exclusive and expensive. Philadelphia's lodge charged £5 for initiation, more than an ordinary worker earned in a month and probably a strain even for Franklin, however flushed with his new success. Gentlemen, merchants, and other men of property dominated the lodges. For example, sea captains and shipowners were Masons—but not ordinary sailors. But if real artisans, let alone workers, were not welcome in Freemasonry's ersatz guilds, Franklin was—as usual—the exception. He was made a Mason a mere year after the St. John's Lodge formed. More astonishing, he became grand master three years later, in 1734. The honor registered Franklin's material success. He resembled other Freemasons who practiced trades, such as printing, that required literacy and numeracy. Printers were also handy to Freemasons, as when Franklin printed material for his lodge.[35]

He was making brisk progress from workshop to drawing room. He still worked in his printshop and joined his fellow "leather aprons" at the Junto. But by joining the Masons, he had inched closer to gentility. He sometimes betrayed sympathy for workers, as when he said of Masons, "Their Grand Secret is, That they have no Secret at all." But Franklin placed increasing value on book learning as opposed to manual labor. In 1732, his lodge noted a plan to buy "the best Books of Architecture, suitable Mathematical Instruments, &c." in order to teach members "the excellent Science of Geometry and Architecture . . . so much recommended in our ancient Constitutions."[36]

Franklin would stumble, however, when a scandal exposed his indifference to Freemasonry's genteel creed. In 1737, some Philadelphians duped a young man into thinking they would initiate him into a lodge. They made him take a fake oath and, in a mock initiation ceremony, accidentally set him on fire. Franklin had asked for a copy of the oath, which he thought an excellent parody of Masonic ritual. When the burned youth died, Franklin was accused of complicity. He defended himself, and the scandal blew over. But his actions had revealed his amusement over Freemasonry's hallowed mysteries and had hinted at his leather apron background. Franklin had endured actual workers' callous treatment of initiates when his fellow printers in London had hazed him—that part of Freemasonry did make sense to him. He would, in future, be more careful about when and how he revealed his humble origins.[37]

This same trend—the growing focus on head rather than hands—was evident in the Junto. As its members prospered, the club generated a library. The original members had already been "clubbing" their "Books to a common Library." (Thus, Franklin found a way to re-create his experience in London, where he had discovered that wonderful trove of secondhand books.) But somehow, the system broke down, and the Junto members took away their books. So in 1731, Franklin proposed a "Public Subscription Library." Each of the roughly fifty subscribers paid a fee for admission as well as annual dues. "On this little Fund we began," Franklin remembered: "The Books were imported." The result was the Library Company of Philadelphia.[38]

We would not recognize this as a public library, yet its founders thought it one. Its subscribers did not need a particular status, occupation, or religion to join. Even nonsubscribers could borrow books if they left a sum proportioned to the volumes' value. A subscriber or borrower had to have some money but not as much as it would have taken to build a private library of comparable size. In 1741, Franklin praised his scheme because it meant "*Knowledge* is in this City render'd more cheap and easy to be come at."[39]

In the Library Company, Franklin had helped re-create the two learned institutions—Harvard College and the Royal Society—that he had failed to enter. He rejoiced that the Library Company "afforded me the means of Improvement by constant Study . . . and thus repair'd in some Degree the Loss of the Learned Education my Father once intended for me." And the Library Company was a small, provincial version of the Royal Society, a learned club with particular interest in the natural sciences. In 1738, for example, it acquired an air pump that allowed members to experiment with the creation and effects of a vacuum, as Robert Boyle had famously done. (The library also bought a full edition of Boyle's writings and two abridgments, part of a growing collection in the natural sciences.) The company began to sponsor lectures and demonstrations. In 1740, Isaac Greenwood, who had been first Hollis Professor of Mathematics at Harvard College (until he was sacked for drunkenness), offered lectures by subscription in which he used the library's air pump.[40]

The Library Company also invested in compendia. This genre, essentially the modern reference work, had emerged in the Renaissance. It came of age in the eighteenth century, culminating in the great French and British encyclopedias, versions of which we still consult today (increasingly, on-line). An early British example was Ephraim Chambers's *Cyclopedia; or, An Universal Dictionary of Arts and Sciences*, first published in 1728 and then in many subsequent editions. (This was the *Cyclopedia* Samuel Keimer had used in his *Universal Instructor*, less than a year after the compendium appeared, and that Franklin continued to reprint as well.) Chambers admonished those who jealously guarded secret knowledge or who claimed authorship for personal gain. He emphasized that "to offer a thing to the Publick, and yet pretend a Right reserved therein to one's self, if it be not absurd, yet it is sordid."[41]

Chambers's *Cyclopedia* was the warm-up act—two French projects, the *Description des arts et métiers* (1761–1788) and the *Encyclopédie* (1751–1777), were far more comprehensive. *Arts et métiers* surveyed trades, as England's Royal Society had once proposed to do before it turned its attention to learned gentlemen. Denis Diderot and Jean Le Rond d'Alembert originally conceived the *Encyclopédie* as a translation of Chambers's book. But they began to write and commission new articles, and the project grew and grew. Seventeen volumes of text appeared from 1751 to 1772, accompanied by eleven volumes of illustrations, the final one published in 1777. This enormous project represented the culmination of the long-term historical trends by which knowledge was published and used to criticize existing institutions and received wisdom. Diderot and d'Alembert courted arrest, for example, when they used their masterwork to launch critiques of the Catholic Church and of France's ruling orders.[42]

It was also significant that the *Encyclopédie* collapsed differences between learned and artisanal traditions. The authors believed that artisans, despite their low status and minimal education, knew how to do remarkable things and deserved respect and attention. Detailed engravings showed ordinary people at work; in the volume dedicated to the *marine*, or naval affairs, the workers construct ships, make sails, manipulate wind direction, navigate, and give signals at sea. These tasks were explained to the literate and—because illustrated—even to illiterate persons, such as children.

Encyclopedias made knowledge accessible, compact, and economical, which in turn made these volumes infinitely attractive to Franklin. He began to trade in and collect compendia. He bought "the best edition" of Chambers for himself in 1749 and would order two different editions of the *Description des arts et métiers* in 1763. Later, in 1769, the Library Company would ask Franklin to procure copies of all European learned societies' published transactions. He discovered that this would cost £300 sterling, far too much. He had already told them that the company should simply get a copy of the *Encyclopédie*, noting that it probably "contains Extracts of the most material Parts of all of them." The company agreed and directed him to purchase the latest edition.[43]

And so, Franklin's social progress continued. In the Junto, he had been a young worker who read; in the Library Company, he was a gentleman who read about workers, a man of letters, indeed. As they sat in the library and leafed through books, he and others from the Junto could catch glimpses of their earlier selves.

Franklin was edging his way into the "republic of letters." This was another kind of club, but an invisible one. A cosmopolitan and mostly elite network, its genteel or even aristocratic members agreed to consider each other equal citizens while snubbing ordinary, provincial people. This was the central paradox of knowledge as people in Franklin's era conceived of it: knowledge was sociable and collaborative, but not everyone could contribute to it. Franklin could not have hoped to barge into the real centers of learning, back in Europe. But by creating colonial versions of European learned societies, he could hope—not unrealistically—to become a corresponding member, someone who wrote actual letters to learned people abroad. To achieve that, he would need a bit more polish, a few more accomplishments, and greater wealth.[44]

IN LATE 1732, Franklin began to publish an almanac under a pseudonym, Richard Saunders—the indelible "author" of *Poor Richard's Almanac*. The *Pennsylvania Gazette* had advertised almanacs among the books Franklin had sold, so he knew there was a ready market. And he needed the extra income. He inaugurated his almanac shortly after the birth of his and Deborah's first child, Francis: a growing family needed growing income. Deborah may have encouraged the project, and Franklin may have immortalized her appeal to him. Consider that the first edition of *Poor Richard* introduced, alongside Richard Saunders, his voluble wife, Bridget. She tells her feckless, mathematical husband to "make some profitable Use" of his "Books and Rattling-Traps (as she calls my Instruments)" by producing an almanac. Was Franklin directly quoting Deborah or merely paraphrasing her? Did she appreciate or resent the joke? At the least, "Poor Richard" had increased her workload; Deborah was the one who folded and stitched together the pages of the almanacs.[45]

Poor Richard was, in many ways, conventional—Franklin had studied his potential audience shrewdly and knew they would recoil from blatant innovation. Unlike modern almanacs, which are the size of paperback books, colonial almanacs were pamphlet-sized. Highly salable and compact little wonders, they were printed on cheap paper and had no real binding. They were meant for daily use, and surviving examples are often blotched, scribbled in, or torn apart. The almanac was essentially a calendar. It devoted a page or two to each month; within each month's section, the almanac's author gave a compressed, day-by-day description of the main astronomical events (the position of moon and sun, information on the tides) in each month. This layout was exactly what Franklin used.[46]

Even the title of Franklin's product echoed a contemporary example, the *Poor Robin's Almanac* that his brother James published in Rhode Island. And the name "Richard Saunder" belonged to a real astrologer and almanac writer in seventeenth-century England. As in other almanacs, astrology was central to *Poor Richard*; the conventional man of signs illustrated the conventional wisdom that the hu-

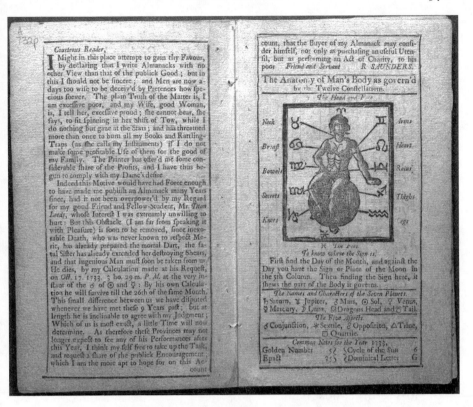

Poor Richard's man of signs. *Poor Richard* (1733).

man body, like all earthly matter, was governed by the motions of the planets. Franklin accepted the premise: the body's microcosm reflected the macrocosm of the universe.[47]

Franklin introduced *Poor Richard* into a crowded market. Pennsylvania already had five almanacs, and he suspected he would have to displace at least one. How could he win readers from the established competitors?

Wit helped. At the top of each month's section in the almanac, "Poor Richard" left a verse, something amusing or moralizing or both; the same followed for the daily listings. This proverbial material has made the almanac famous: "Eat to live, and not live to eat"; "He that lies down with Dogs, shall rise up with fleas"; "Fish and Visitors stink in 3 days"; "Don't throw stones at your neighbours, if your own windows are glass"; and—yes, Benjamin Franklin did really print it—"Early to bed and early to rise, makes a man healthy wealthy and wise."[48]

Few of these sayings were original to Franklin, but he notably tinkered with their wording to make them pithier. In some cases, he made sly references to his sources. For example, Poor Richard warned people to "make haste slowly"; this little adage had a pedigree. An early and important Venetian printer, Aldus Manutius, had adopted as his trademark a dolphin entwined with an anchor: *semp sestina tarde*, with the dolphin hastening and the anchor always slowing it. Thus, Franklin placed himself within the history of print while giving his neighbors some useful advice.[49]

He also differentiated his product from its competitiors by mocking astrology. In his first issue, Franklin mischievously undermined a rival, John Jerman, who published an almanac under the pseudonym Titan Leeds. Poor Richard used his astrological expertise to predict an awful event: the death of Titan Leeds. "He dies, by my Calculation made at his Request, on Oct. 17. 1733.3 ho.29m.*P.M.*," Saunders lamented. He allowed that Leeds calculated he would "survive till the 26th of the same Month." "This small difference between us," Saunders gossiped, "we have disputed whenever we have met these 9 Years past; but at length he is inclinable to agree with my Judgment." When the dreadful day arrived, Saunders mourned the loss of his colleague.[50]

Surely, Jerman would spot this obvious trip wire? But no, he proceeded to do a pratfall over it. He published a direct and therefore obtuse refutation of his alias's death and from then on steadily lost readers to Franklin. (William Bradford would take over publication of a local almanac under Titan Leeds's name, calling it *The Dead Man's Almanack*, which might have been a reference to either Leeds or Jerman.) Cleverly undermining yet another printer rival, Franklin also hinted that his readers should value his astronomical information for its practical application, not its astrological mysteries. They should read *Poor Richard* to figure out when to put a crop in or take a boat out, not to determine when Venus or Mars might improve their fortunes.[51]

Indeed, Franklin was among the few colonial almanac writers who did his own astronomical calculations; his early study of almanacs in London and of astronomy on board the *Berkshire* had paid off. *Poor Richard* became a how-to guide for backyard astronomers. In 1745, for example, Franklin instructed his readers how "to distinguish [the planets] from the fixed Stars." The latter maintained position in relation to each other and the horizon. The former were trickier but could be followed because, while they moved, each "had a particular and different Motion." They also looked different—Venus was brightest, Mars most red, and Saturn quite pale. Having told readers how to distinguish the main planets, Poor Richard next specified the moments of their rising. On January 6, for instance, shortly after acquiring the annual almanac, its readers could see Mars rise at "35 Minutes after 10 o'Clock at Night." Thus Franklin championed nature's regularity and its "glorious" and "beautiful" features—who would not want to be a backyard astronomer?[52]

Poor Richard proved successful, and Franklin grew more ambitious. In 1748, he renamed his expanded product *Poor Richard Improved.* The new version was twelve pages longer than its twenty-four-page predecessor. This expanded size gave greater room for Saunders's aphorisms but also for Franklin's publication of new developments in the sciences.[53]

He began not with details of natural science but with praise for its modern British practitioners. In his first and second issues of *Poor Richard Improved,* he restated the commonplace that two English pioneers, Robert Boyle and Isaac Newton, had defined modern natural science. In 1748, *Poor Richard* described Newton as "the prince of astronomers and philosophers." The next year, Boyle appeared in its pages as "one of the greatest philosophers the last age produced. He first brought the machine called an *Airpump,* into use; by which many of the surprizing properties of that wonderful element [air] were discovered and demonstrated."[54]

In these almanacs of 1748 and 1749, Franklin was careful to portray natural science's affinity with religion. He did so by using the argument from design, especially when he reprinted parts of English poet James Thomson's *The Seasons* (1726–1730). Three months after Newton's death, Thomson had produced a valedictory *Poem Sacred to the Memory of Isaac Newton* (1727) and had begun his longer opus, which described in verse nature's annual cycle, the four seasons. Franklin made a point of quoting Thomson's claim that Newton had "*Trac'd the boundless works of God, from laws sublimely simple,*" and then he cited the famous Alexander Pope epitaph. Thomson was useful again to describe "BOYLE, whose pious search / Amid the dark recesses of his works / The great CREATOR sought."[55]

Having introduced readers to the drama of discovery in the sciences, Franklin followed up with content. In 1751, he included a long description of the microscope, probably taken from a popular text by English author George Adams, *Micrographia Illustrata* (1746). (Franklin might have consulted this work at the house of a wealthy and learned Philadelphian, James Logan; the Library Company had owned a microscope since 1741.) He remarked on the "remarkably entertaining Objects" to be seen under "that admirable Instrument the MICROSCOPE." These objects included "the Globules of the Blood, which are computed to be almost a two thousandth Part of an Inch in Diameter," each with six even tinier subglobules. The instrument also revealed, within "various Fluids," teeming "Animalcules" that outnumbered all "the [human] Inhabitants of Europe, Asia, Africa, and America," a topic of interest to Franklin, who had earlier examined the tiny crab embryos that bred on gulfweed in the Atlantic.[56]

With his microscope, Poor Richard helped make one of the grandest claims about the new sciences: they made visible the invisible. Galileo Galilei's telescope and Antoni van Leeuwenhoek's microscope had let the human eye see distant or tiny parts of the universe. These devices relied on the paradoxical nature of glass: it was itself invisible, but when ground into lenses or made into instruments, it allowed the eye to see all the better. Glass devices had enabled the seminal experiments of the late seventeenth century. Through them, experimenters had seen the visible effects of invisible materials. No one had actually seen air, but, using an air pump with glass receiver, Boyle had made it an observable material. The device demonstrated that air had "spring," or pressure, a force that could be measured. And Newton had revealed the visible spectrum. He let sunlight through an aperture in a shutter and into a darkened room. There, he directed the beam of light through glass prisms, which refracted it. The light he saw was not unified but heterogeneous, with differently colored parts.[57]

Focused observation, use of instruments to assist the eye, and ingenious experimentation all revealed what might otherwise escape human sight. If Newton achieved fame because of his mathematically dense *Principia* (which Franklin never read), it was his carefully named *Opticks* (which Franklin did read) that put the human eye at the center of the sciences. As well, the invitingly speculative tone of the *Opticks*, which concluded with its chatty "Quaeries" soliciting new experiments, welcomed general readers. The Newton of the *Opticks* insisted, quite unlike the author of the far less accessible

Principia, that all disciplined observers could learn to see critically. And if their eyesight was naturally poor or had deteriorated with age, "their Sight is mended by Spectacles. For those Convex glasses supply the defect of plumpness in the Eye" that allowed an accurate refraction of light.[58]

It was a provincial education: Newton was on the high end, and popular texts on microscopy were on the low. Much is missing— Franklin seemed never to read Robert Hooke's important *Micrographia* (1665), for instance. Yet out of his scattered readings on nature and optical instruments, he managed to invent bifocals. Later in life, he would reveal that he had devised and begun wearing his trademark bifocals in the late 1730s or early 1740s, just as he was expanding his almanac. Eyeglasses of any sort were, at the time, classified alongside the specialized equipment of science, as they were in advertisements in colonial newspapers. Franklin could have bought an early, monofocal pair from Andrew Bradford, whose *American Weekly Mercury* sold a variety of imported instruments, among them "black Lead Pencils silver'd with Caps and Cases, Super-fine Spectacles with Steel Bows and Joints, either with Fish-skin Cases or without, with several other sorts [made] of Horn or Leather; also Reading and Burning Glasses, Pocket Compasses with Dials."[59]

The *Pennsylvania Gazette* also contained advertisements for spectacles, as well as other optical devices; Franklin instructed readers of his almanac how to use the devices. An elaborate chart from the 1753 *Poor Richard Improved* gave a schedule, down to the minute, for following that year's transit of Mercury over the sun. Readers could take the almanac out into their gardens and follow the planet's two-day progress for themselves. At one past five in the morning on May 6, 1753, "if you get up betimes, and put on your Spectacles, you will see Mercury rise in the Sun, and will appear like a small black Patch in a Lady's Face." Poor Richard might have been describing his author, famous for wearing spectacles (and for admiring ladies). And the description of the transit of Mercury assumed that at least some readers were active observers—they possessed accurate timepieces (and corrective eyewear), rose at the crack of dawn to practice astronomy, and wanted the very latest in learning.[60]

Franklin balanced his serious discussion of the sciences with entertaining puzzles. Predicting eclipses for 1734, he had punned that "since the Eclipses take up so little space, I have room to comply with the new Fashion, and propose a *Mathematical Question* to the *Sons of*

Art." The inaugural puzzle read: "*A certain rich Man had 100 Orchards, in each Orchard was 100 Appletrees, under each Appletree was 100 Hogsties, in each Hogstie was 100 Sows, and each Sow had 100 Pigs. Question,* How many Sow-Pigs were there among them?" Saunders warned, "*The Answer to this Question won't be accepted without the Solution.*" In other words, no lucky guesses were allowed—the multiplication mattered.[61]

The annual puzzles got more complicated, as with 1757's teaser. Imagine three ships, each occupied independently by Christians, Jews, or Muslims. Each vessel leaves the same place but travels a different route under its religiously distinct crew. All return to the original port, where "they shall differ so [much] with respect to real and apparent Time, that they all shall keep their Sabbath on one and the same Day of the Week, and yet each of them separately shall believe that he keeps his Sabbath on the Day of the Week his religion requires." What had happened? To circumnavigate the globe meant losing or gaining a day of the week, depending on the direction of travel. In the case of Poor Richard's three ships, some had gained or lost a critical day, creating a momentary Muslim-Christian-Jewish agreement over the Sabbath. Safe and dry at home, Philadelphia's readers could see, in their local almanac, just how capacious the world was.[62]

More than a diversion, the puzzle reflected Franklin's broader philosophy. Richard Saunders showed that the globe's rotation relative to the sun exemplified the wonder of the physical creation, a reminder that the cosmos—and its divine creator—constantly challenged human knowledge. Nature was a powerful reason to tolerate other faiths, all of them brought to unintended similarity by circumnavigation. This philosophy was a challenge to differences among religions but not to religion itself. The larger point, one that exemplified Franklin's deism and his religious toleration, was that the natural world inspired religious sentiment in everyone. Significantly, Franklin chose a maritime example to make his point. A ship was a conventional microcosm, a segment of the human world cast out on the waves of the great globe, bravely making its way against all storms, real and metaphorical.

By inserting a steadily increasing amount of material from the sciences into his newspaper and almanac, Franklin had established himself as Philadelphia's main disseminator of knowledge about the natural world. He even began to compare himself to famous men of science, such as Edmond Halley, the era's foremost astronomer, after whom the comet is named. Calculating an eclipse in 1756, Franklin would add that "Dr. Halley puts this Conjunction an Hour forwarder than by this calculation." He challenged Philadelphians, the amateur astronomers he had encouraged to look at things for themselves, to see who was right—London's learned man or, "Dear Reader, Thy obliged Friend, R. SAUNDERS."[63]

FRANKLIN was becoming quite careful in his choice of friends. At that time, the term *friend* could indicate not only a social equal but also a patron (or client, as Poor Richard had called himself in relation to his readers). Franklin had spent his twenties with his fellow tradesmen, but in the course of his thirties, he began to choose friends more strategically in order to consolidate his higher status.

He set his sights on John Bartram and James Logan, two Philadelphians who could not have been more different. Both men were interested in the sciences, but Bartram was adept at natural history, which described nature, whereas Logan excelled at the more prestigious branch of natural philosophy, which sought the causes of things within the material world. Their different ambitions reflected their social statuses—Logan was much wealthier and more influential than Bartram, a difference that was not lost on Franklin.

Bartram was the most gifted botanist in the continental colonies and a boon companion for Franklin. A Quaker and farmer, Bartram had come to the study of plants, the story goes, after pausing in his fields to admire a flower. Thus inspired, he read botany. Several methods of classifying plants and animals existed, but the taxonomy of Carolus Linnaeus (Carl von Linné), which sorted plants according to their organs of sexual reproduction, was beginning to win the day. Bartram not only described but also classified American plants. He sent samples and descriptions of them to European naturalists, who were always eager to learn of new world flora. His experimental garden outside Philadelphia would, by the second half of the eighteenth century, become a destination for travelers and cognoscenti as well as the training site for his son, William, also a famous botanist. European arbiters of knowledge marveled at the wisdom of a poor farmer. Linnaeus considered him the era's best "natural botanist"—a man with copious direct experience with plants but little ability to analyze them theoretically.[64]

At least as early as the 1740s (their actual introduction is obscure), Franklin and Bartram became extremely close friends, perhaps closer than Franklin and any of his fellow Junto founders. Each referred to the other as an "intimate," and Bartram (seven years older) seemed to be the only person outside Franklin's family to refer to him, in writing, as "Benjamin," as if addressing a younger brother. The friendship was also, in a small way, a business connection. In 1741, Franklin published Bartram's description of "*the true* INDIAN PHYSICK" in *Poor Richard*, and a year later, he printed in the *Pennsylvania Gazette* Bartram's call for subscribers to underwrite his work collecting specimens. That move was daring—it would be a real test of Franklin's ability to serve as a patron of the sciences in Pennsylvania. Bartram was also useful to Franklin for his array of friends. Through him, Franklin would establish another and far more formal relationship with James Logan.[65]

Almost thirty years older than Franklin, Logan had more money and influence than Benjamin and Bartram combined. Logan had retired from land speculation and the fur trade with wealth enough to enter politics and pursue learning. He was well established among the gentlemen who supported Philadelphia's proprietors, which won him their favor but also the ire of their opponents. Though he was crippled by a fall in 1728 and further incapacitated by a stroke in 1740, his mind remained unimpaired, and he steadily built an enormous library that focused particularly on classical learning and natural science. Logan seems to have been the first to import Newton's *Principia* to the colonies, and he had many other volumes that were rare in America, including a copy of George Adams's *Micrographia Illustrata* that Franklin might have consulted. Logan was also extremely well connected in and beyond Pennsylvania. When Sheik Shedid Allhazar of Beirut toured the British colonies, he arrived in Philadelphia in 1737 with a letter of introduction to Logan. (Franklin covered the sheik's visit in the *Pennsylvania Gazette*.)[66]

Logan wrote on an impressive range of subjects, including botany, optics, astronomy, mathematics, and numismatics. Unlike Bartram, who only collected and described plants, Logan offered analysis. In an important contribution to Linnaean botany, Logan described the sexual organs in maize that were necessary to pollenation. It was the first study that experimentally demonstrated the function of plant organs for sexual reproduction. The essay appeared in the *Philosophical Transactions* for 1736, as did Logan's pieces on why the sun and moon appeared larger at the horizon than at their zeniths and why lightning's angular appearance resulted from its refraction at different densities of air. If European men of science respected Bartram for his natural knowledge, they respected Logan for explaining how nature worked. It also did not hurt that he was a man of high social status. Confident of his position in the republic of letters, Logan corresponded with Linnaeus and with Sir Hans Sloane, to whom he sent a rare coin with Hebrew inscription—quite a contrast to Franklin's asbestos trinkets.[67]

Franklin was hardly Logan's social equal, but he became his intellectual peer as well as his client, something that would never have happened had Franklin not become both a property holder and a man of letters whom Logan could take seriously. Franklin was among the few to whom Logan showed manuscript works for criticism. Around 1737, in relation to Logan's analysis of virtue, Franklin offered that there was "some Incorrectness of Sentiment" in the discussion of "Temperance." He also printed Logan's work, as with his translation of Cicero's *Cato Major, or His Discourse of Old-Age* (1744). Franklin solicitously printed the book in large type so that elderly readers (beyond the help even of spectacles) "may not, in Reading, by the *Pain* small Letters give the Eyes, feel the *Pleasure* of the Mind in the least allayed." He claimed in his preface that Logan's was the "first Translation of a *Classic* in this *Western World*" (never mind that Spanish Americans had already done this). He expressed his hope that the Philadelphia publication was a "happy Omen, that Philadelphia shall become the Seat of the American Muses."[68]

By his thirties, after a decade in business in Philadelphia, Franklin was more than a printer. He had a reputation for learning and for particular expertise in astronomy and other sciences. He had undertaken plans to make Philadelphia an important site within the republic of letters. He had friends, especially James Logan, who valued his learning. He was about to become a man of public affairs. But Franklin was also about to learn that though he could study nature, he could not always control it.

In 1735, Franklin suffered a relapse of the pleurisy that had nearly killed him eight years earlier. This second bout was almost as bad. It lasted most of the spring, summer, and fall, climaxing when an abscess in the left lung ruptured and nearly suffocated Franklin with its discharge. When he published his major work of 1735, *Some*

Observations on the Proceedings against the Rev. Mr. Hemphill—an intervention in a local religious controversy—Franklin made an extraordinary personal aside. In the pamphlet's preface, he explained that "this *Answer* might have been published before the Printer was taken sick, whose Illness unexpectedly continuing six or seven Weeks has thus long retarded its Publication." (When he reprinted a popular medical tract, John Tennent's *Every Man His Own Doctor*, in 1736, he inserted a postscript from Tennent's *Essay on Pleurisy*.) Getting the paper out had been all that Franklin could do. Given his failing eyesight and persistently weak lungs, he must have wondered, as he turned thirty, whether he was falling apart.[69]

He recovered in time to receive another blow. In the autumn of 1736, his four-year-old son, Francis, died of smallpox. Franklin's sorrow increased when whispered rumors (none ever published) charged him with negligence: he, the great advocate of inoculation, had failed to inoculate his own child. In December, Franklin brought the matter into the open in the *Pennsylvania Gazette*. "I suppose the Report could only arise from its being my known Opinion, that Inoculation was a safe and beneficial Practice," he admitted. But the rumors were false. True, Franklin conceded, Francis had not been inoculated. But he had made the decision not to inoculate the boy because when smallpox loomed, his son had been suffering from a flux, or gastrointestinal disorder, and was too weak to be infected with anything else. If some of the later criticisms of Franklin's writings on matters of science were ad hominem, they would be nothing new and were perhaps never as painful as the first such instance over the death of his son.[70]

It was probably no consolation that Francis's death coincided with his father's political advance. In mid-October, Franklin was appointed clerk of the Pennsylvania House of Assembly, the colony's main representative body. This appointment was a logical progression from his earlier role as the assembly's official printer—he continued to enjoy the favor of those in power. (It was not until 1748, however, that Franklin would gain elective office, as a member of the Philadelphia Common Council.) The clerkship was an important job but not an onerous one. If we could have sneaked up behind Franklin and peered over his shoulder as he kept notes in the assembly, we could have seen him busily doing little arithmetic games known as magic squares. Each such square contained lines of numbers. Each line of numbers (horizontal, vertical, or diagonal) could be added up to the same number. Franklin would eventually move on to more complicated magic circles, in which concentric circles had numbers that could be totted up radially.[71]

The puzzles (see an example within the illustration on page 149), invented in the Renaissance, showed Franklin's fascination with numbers. They also revealed his (for the moment) arithmetic grasp of numbers. Mathematics can use numbers to explain phenomena—varying rates of physical motion are one example. Arithmetic simply expresses numerical values in relation to each other. It is a lesser skill, however nimbly executed in Franklin's magic squares and circles.

When he spared a moment to watch what was going on in the assembly, Franklin gained an education in politics. He did not yet have to involve himself in debate. He could instead watch others do so and learn from their triumphs and humiliations. Later observers would remark on his disinclination to speak in public—and his masterful backroom influence over those who did. Franklin learned these skills through his careful observation of Pennsylvania's assemblymen during his time as clerk.

In 1737, Franklin debuted in his most important public role—as colonial postmaster at Philadelphia. Taken for granted now, the circulation of mail was, for the colonies in the early eighteenth century, a confusing, erratic, and even violent affair. Throughout the previous century, colonists had lacked any regular mail service and had to pay or cajole travelers and merchant ships to carry their letters. A mail service within the colonies commenced in 1692; in 1702, packet boats began to cross the Atlantic during King William's War. This arrangement was very much an imperial effort, in which England threw its weight behind the small fleet in an effort to maintain contact with its colonial possessions. Even so, privateers captured ten of the nineteen total packets. Heavy government subsidies kept the mail arriving until around 1711, when, with the end of the War of the Spanish Succession, official and guarded packets seemed less important.[72]

Franklin began his postal career in 1737, when there was only the intercolonial system, no overseas post. A limited transatlantic service recommenced in 1745, as new wars pitted Britain against France and Spain and endangered British shipping. At first, Britain only risked its packets to communicate with the valuable West Indian colonies, but this service was expensive, and it was abandoned in

1749. The West Indian route reopened in 1755 along with a new one to New York. Franklin became deputy postmaster general for North America after 1755; he ordered the local post to and from New York, the continental center of the Atlantic service. It was a nerve-racking business. Postal service was as risky as commercial shipping and paid less. To address both problems, British officials encouraged Atlantic packets to take "prizes," enemy vessels whose seized cargo enriched the packet crews.[73]

Franklin's postal commission has never been found, so the reason for his selection is unknown. But colonial postal positions often fell to newspaper printers, who, after all, already circulated news. Franklin knew a postal position would complement his printing business by allowing him to send his own materials through the post. Years later, he presented his predecessor, Andrew Bradford, as unworthy of these privileges. Bradford published the *American Weekly Mercury,* and because he was postmaster, Franklin claimed, "it was imagined he had better Opportunities of obtaining News" and of broadcasting advertisements beyond the boundaries of the city. Franklin stated that he had to bribe postal riders to carry his newspaper outside Philadelphia, "Bradford being unkind enough to forbid it." He swore he would never serve his competitors so, and he regarded the mails as a public service that should be open to anyone—at least anyone who could pay for postage.[74]

Franklin's appointment to the postal service consolidated his influence over the circulation of information in Pennsylvania and the mid-Atlantic region generally. He took his new tasks seriously; in 1743, he would criticize the "disorderly" way in which people crowded onto ships to find their letters. He recommended that captains instead deliver all mail to the post office, where clerks could sort and distribute the letters and packages. More ambitiously, Franklin believed that Philadelphia, not New York, should be the center of the colonial postal system. In 1751, he claimed the city's importance, it "being the Center of the Continent Colonies, and having constant Communication with the West India Islands." Clearly, he no longer felt that after having left London, he was back on the ragged edge of the world. At least in his own mind, Philadelphia was now "the Center" of the Western Hemisphere.[75]

Franklin certainly put Philadelphia at the center of his printing network, which was moving steadily outward. Again, a growing family might have prompted his ambition—daughter Sarah, "Sally," was born in 1743. Franklin eventually formed partnerships with printers in several other colonial towns, including New York and Charleston. And he was always on the lookout for works he knew readers would buy. When the Reverend George Whitefield, a remarkable Church of England minister, took the colonies by storm with his revivalist preaching in the 1740s, Franklin eagerly printed his sermons.[76]

Whitefield even inspired in Franklin an interest in the transmission of sound. Franklin performed an experiment on the preacher's voice, gradually "retiring backwards" as Whitefield addressed a crowd from "the Top of the Court House Steps" in order to determine how far the sound carried. He estimated that Whitefield could project roughly 500 feet. "Imagining then a Semi-Circle, of which my Distance should be the Radius," he wrote, the minister could be heard by "more than Thirty-Thousand" auditors. Franklin's geometry was faulty (still), but his interest in the means by which ideas circulated within Philadelphia and beyond was no less keen for that.[77]

If Philadelphia were to become a center in the republic of letters, which Franklin wanted, it would need its own learned society and college. He helped create both. In 1743, he published a broadside in which he argued the need for a learned society. He contended that Philadelphia was already "the City nearest the Centre of the Continent-Colonies" and had an active library: it should therefore have a learned society that would establish contacts in the other colonies as well as Europe. His call went unheard for the moment, but it would eventually be one catalyst for the American Philosophical Society (APS). Franklin then proposed an academy for higher education in the fall of 1749. He printed *Proposals Relating to the Education of Youth in Pennsylvania* (1749) and cunningly distributed copies to "the principal Inhabitants gratis," meaning that he must have plied men such as Logan with the proposal. In this way, he solicited five-year subscriptions, promising £10 per year himself. His campaign raised £2,000, and the school was built; it opened in early 1751, a progenitor of the University of Pennsylvania.[78]

These steps were important ones. The Library Company had consumed knowledge, but a true learned society would produce it. The possibility was all the more likely if more of Pennsylvania's inhabitants gained a college education. Franklin was moving his town in the same direction as he moved himself. Once, he had circulated material on natural science; now, he itched to produce such knowledge on his own, hence his challenge to Edmond Halley.

It is not surprising, then, that when he proposed the academy, Franklin recommended that its curriculum include natural science. In his *Proposals Relating to the Education of Youth in Pennsylvania*, he insisted that "*Histories of Nature*" would be "delightful for Youth." Characteristically, he recommended materials that extolled the argument from design and listed several works famous for making this point. He believed all young men could study the sciences, whatever careers they later intended. Natural science would provide useful methods for understanding commodities (if they became merchants), physical materials (if artisans), or "Proofs of Divine Providence" (if ministers). Natural history combined with "Excursions" to the countryside would teach students practical information about health, diet, gardening, and agriculture. As a longtime arbiter of learning in Pennsylvania, Franklin had also become a genteel patron of learned establishments that would educate other men's children in the sciences. He had ascended to the level of the gentlemen he had once served.[79]

As significantly, Franklin made his first real friend in the republic of letters overseas. In 1743, London printer William Strahan was looking for a place to send a promising apprentice. One of Deborah Franklin's relatives, recently in London, told Franklin about Strahan's dilemma. Franklin quickly wrote Strahan to volunteer his Philadelphia printshop: "If the young Man will venture other hither . . . we can treat about the Affair." The young man, David Hall, ventured over, liked the arrangement, stayed on to master the business, and would eventually become Franklin's business partner. And Franklin gained in Strahan an important London contact, as he had surely expected.[80]

The Scot Strahan was extremely successful at the printer's craft. He eventually worked with David Hume, Adam Smith, Edward Gibbon, and William Blackstone; he published Samuel Johnson's *Dictionary*, among other great eighteenth-century works. Strahan purchased books for Franklin and for the Library Company, and the two men comfortably compared their opinions on authors, printers, texts, and presses. Strahan's value to Franklin only increased over time. He produced two London newspapers, the *Monthly Review* (begun in 1749) and the *London Chronicle* (in 1757), in which he would publish some of Franklin's political letters. Even as they rose in the world (Strahan became king's printer in 1770 and was a member of Parliament from 1774 to 1784), the two men would always remem-

ber their printshop origins. Promising a visit to Strahan in the
1750s, Franklin warned that "if a fat old Fellow should come to your
Printing House and request a little Smouting [part-time work], de-
pend upon it, 'tis Your affectionate Friend and humble Servant B
Franklin." Toward the end of his life, in 1784, Franklin recalled
Strahan's observation, as they sat together in the House of Commons, "that no two Journeymen Printers, within your Knowledge,
had met with such Success in the World as ourselves."[81]

Men of letters both, Strahan and Franklin did not share an interest in natural science. Franklin, having discovered an audience for
developments in the sciences, would delve into them himself; Strahan never bothered. Only one of them would become a household
name.

FRANKLIN had his first portrait painted around 1746. He was forty
and in his prime and ready to commemorate his successes. Robert
Feke, a mariner who became a self-taught artist, put Franklin on canvas. The image is, in some ways, disappointingly formulaic: here is a
gentleman from the provinces, dressed in respectable black with
good linen at neck and wrists, and finished off with a stiff and formal
wig. The background is even duller, composed of a brown wall and a
murky landscape with clouds, hills, and water. But Franklin probably
wanted his portrait to be conventional, the better to emphasize that
he had become indistinguishable from the bland burghers whose
ranks he had joined. The Boston chandler's son had become a club-
man, Freemason, printer and clerk to the Pennsylvania House of Assembly, civic improver, and man of letters. The portrait marks
Franklin's ascent into the ranks of the literate and propertied.

But one accomplishment still eluded him, even as he celebrated
his ascent to gentility. Note in the portrait his extended hand and
pointing finger. It is an empty gesture. It was meant to be—it indicated that the gentleman in question did not have to do anything,
least of all work, with his hands. But in later portraits, Franklin's
hands and especially a pointing finger would become significant as
indicators of nature and of natural properties. Paradoxically, it was
only when he had finally achieved status as a natural philosopher
that Franklin, the upstart gentleman, could afford to admit that he
worked with his hands.

A gentleman at last. Robert Feke, *Benjamin Franklin* (c. 1746).
HARVARD UNIVERSITY PORTRAIT COLLECTION.

Chapter 4

EXPERIMENTS AND OBSERVATIONS

C OURTEOUS READER," Franklin greeted anyone who opened his *Poor Richard* for 1747, one year after he sat for his portrait: "This is the 15th Time I have entertain'd thee with my annual Productions; I hope to thy Profit as well as mine." His words were a sly reference to his success. *Poor Richard* had turned Franklin many a profit. Its annual circulation had reached around 10,000, which indicated an audience extending beyond Pennsylvania and well into other mid-Atlantic colonies. His almanac and newspaper earned Franklin thousands of pounds each year. So he could afford to have Feke paint his portrait.[1]

Yet this success was not enough for him. Almanacs "have their daily Use indeed while the Year continues, but then become of no Value," Franklin observed, admitting the limits of his enterprise. *Poor Richard* and the *Pennsylvania Gazette* were ephemera, publications tied to the events of the time and destined to become outdated. The witty, moralizing phrases added a bit of life to the almanac because they survived in readers' memories "when both almanack and Almanack-maker have been long thrown by and forgotten." Indeed, it is striking that no collector or library today owns a full run of *Poor Richards*, which are, individually, quite rare. Franklin was right: his clients tended to use up his publications and throw them away.[2]

The Feke portrait of 1746 reflected Franklin's success as a printer; the *Poor Richard* for 1747 spoke to what Franklin had yet to achieve. He must have asked himself, Why not try something new, or to use a word rich with meanings, why not *experiment*? Indeed, by 1747, Franklin was experimenting in two fields—public affairs and natural philosophy. Each effort was a bold move for Franklin, but it was the philosophy that would ultimately earn him the most attention.

Franklin knew that the sciences posed the biggest questions of the age. And there was significant opportunity for a colonist to help answer them. When Newton had revised his *Principia* between 1709 and 1713, he explained that "the causes assigned to natural effects of the same kind must be, so far as possible, the same" everywhere. Examples included gravity, "the falling of stones in Europe or America." Were cause and effect always the same on both sides of the Atlantic? Perhaps experiments in America would answer the question, and perhaps Americans could do the experiments. Franklin seized the opportunity and moved definitively into natural philosophy. He vindicated the curiosity about nature that had in fact begun in his own body, head, hands, and all the rest. His investigation of nature, however, was never just about nature—it was always deeply connected to whatever Franklin wanted to explain about the human world as well.[3]

"WHEN about 16 Years of Age," he recalled, "I happen'd to meet with a Book, written by one Tryon, recommending a Vegetable Diet. I determined to go into it." Franklin was a vegetarian for at least a year, making his young body into an experiment in dietary extremes.[4]

The Tryon who converted Franklin to vegetarianism was a well-known English dietary crank. Thomas Tryon's *The Way to Health, Long Life and Happiness; or, A Discourse of Temperance* was first published in 1683. His related works ran through many editions and garnered some famous converts, including the playwright Aphra Behn. Tryon insisted that immoderate eating and drinking inhibited the circulations that maintained health. Water was the best drink, he said, because it "thins the Blood, causing it to circulate freely." Too much food and alcoholic drink "furs and stops the Passages, generates too much Blood, and thick dull Spirits, which makes the Body heavy and lumpish." The air necessary for vigor could not penetrate a richly fed body, nor could there be "the *free Circulation of the Blood*." The easiest way to maintain temperance and therefore health, Tryon argued, was to adopt "a Vegetable Diet."[5]

Justice as well as health motivated Tryon—he despised anything cruel or tyrannous. In the longest section of *The Way to Health*, "Of Flesh," he claimed that by slaughtering animals, humans took on a bestial quality that belied their assumption of moral superiority to the creatures they butchered. Why not just eat *"Human Flesh"*? Consuming meat was emblematic of the many sins Tryon listed in his diatribe: *"Hatred, Pride, Malice, Back-biting, Fighting, Killing, Violence* and *Oppression"* of *"Man* or *Beast."* No form of domination was just. *"Noble Birth and Blood"* did not justify legal privilege, let alone tyranny. All people were *"Couzens"* and of equal blood or *"Pedigree"*; all should therefore benefit from the "famous *Generosity* of the *red circling Juice."*[6]

The emphatic italics indicated that Tryon meant what he said. For example, he criticized enslavement of Africans when few other free, white people did so. Instead, most colonists and Europeans assumed that chattel slavery for Africans was part of an orderly system in which everyone's status was determined by birth.[7]

It took time for Tryon's larger moral program to surface in any of Franklin's thinking. But at sixteen, Franklin was convinced about the vegetable diet. (Questioned about her meat-abhorring son, Abiah Franklin sighed that he had read and perhaps aspired to be "a mad philosopher.") Franklin saw vegetarianism as a way to save money "for buying Books," to reserve time for study by lessening the hours spent at table, and to gain "that greater Clearness of Head and quicker Apprehension which usually attend Temperance in Eating and Drinking."[8]

But Franklin lapsed. When he ran away from Boston at seventeen and his ship was becalmed off Rhode Island, his fellow passengers caught cod and fried it up. "When this came hot out of the Frying Pan," Franklin remembered decades later, "it smelt admirably well." He was caught "between Principle and Inclination: till I recollected, that when the Fish were opened, I saw smaller Fish taken out of their Stomachs." That did it. "If you eat one another," he decided, "I don't see why we mayn't eat you." Franklin ate the cod, but his conscience pricked him a bit—he wryly reflected on how "convenient a thing it is to be a *reasonable Creature,*" as it gave one "a Reason for every thing one has a mind to do."[9]

Even after he had resumed eating meat and fish, Franklin remained convinced that the body functioned best with minimal sustenance. Add more fuel to the fire, as it were, and the heat would flare, wasting energy and causing discomfort and illness. As a printer in London, he breakfasted on a gruel familiar to the working poor—buttered bread softened in hot water, garnished with pepper and, in his case, with abstemious virtue. He also considered water superior to alcoholic beverages. Few shared the idea; most of his contemporaries believed liquor was an ideal dietary supplement that gave the body warmth and strength.[10]

Franklin annoyed his fellow printshop workers in London by shunning the beer they tippled throughout the day and by preaching temperance. "The Bodily Strength afforded by Beer," he told them, "could only be in proportion to the Grain . . . of which it was made"—and bread had more grain than beer. The gruel- and water-powered Franklin proved his strength by easily hefting heavy type up and down stairs in the printshop. The "great Guzzlers of Beer" marveled at "the Water-American" yet wasted their wages on drink: "Thus these poor Devils keep themselves always under."[11]

Franklin never thereafter lost an opportunity to extol temperance. In the early days of the Junto, he composed his famous list of thirteen virtues and put "Temperance" first. "Eat not to Dulness. / Drink not to Elevation," he admonished in his autobiography. Temperance was the key to all other virtues, "as it tends to procure that Coolness and Clearness of Head" necessary to resist "the Force of perpetual Temptations." Franklin claimed he maintained this virtue all his life, even though he notoriously let his youthful physique deteriorate into the mature "Dr. Fatsides," as he would later ruefully acknowledge himself to be.[12]

Fat though he grew, the adult Franklin's much-noted coolness and detachment may have been the result, at least in part, of his measured consumption of alcohol. His sobriety was striking in an age when people drank steadily—to consume calories, to keep warm, and to avoid tainted water. Tipsiness was so common that it went unnoticed, even in small children, pious clerics, and pregnant women. We might call these individuals drunk, but drunkenness at the time meant an inability even to stand.

Franklin's austere regimen was more than an eccentricity. Images of the body as a fleshy machine or furnace, to be stoked with care and minimal expense, showed that comprehension of the human body fit into larger conceptions of human society. Franklin agreed. It is obvious from the way he wrote about vegetarianism and sobriety that he considered them to be moral choices. "Thus these poor Devils keep themselves always under" was a somewhat uncharitable assessment of laboring men who spent their wages on drink. But for a wage earner who wanted to work for himself eventually, it paid to be vigilant about every penny, moment, or mouthful. Franklin was making a virtue out of his poverty. What a man ate was the best measure of his social status. The upper classes ate meat and fripperies and drank rich wines and liquors. Franklin was no gentleman, and he celebrated his inability to eat like one.[13]

He applied principles of moderation and balance to the whole body, not just its diet. He was deeply influenced by Sanctorius (Santorio Santorio), an Italian physician of the 1600s who studied metabolism or, as it was then called, "animal oeconomy." In 1612, Sanctorius was evidently the first person to describe the recently invented thermometer's use in medical analysis. He then performed an extraordinary autoexperiment in which he measured, perhaps for as long as a thirty-year period, the weights of the substances he ingested and those he excreted. Studying these data alongside measurements of his own weight, he discovered a gap: the food always weighed more than the excreta, even when he did not gain weight. (A lovely illustration from the period shows Sanctorius seated in his weighing machine in front of a dining table; as he tucks in, he will—briefly—sink in the balance.) In his *Ars Sanctorii Santorii de statica medicina* (1614), Sanctorius explained that the difference resulted from "invisible perspiration," the constant loss of matter through the pores and breath.[14]

Franklin read an English translation of Sanctorius, *Medicina Statica: Being the Aphorisms of Sanctorius* (1712), at some point before the 1740s and perhaps as early as the 1720s. It set off his lifelong fascination with perspiration and fluid equilibriums. He would later write that he believed the body capable, in theory, of maintaining a balance between fluids that entered and departed. (His views might have reflected old ideas about humoral balance as well as newer ones about fluid exchanges in the body.) When the runaway Franklin became feverish after tossing overnight in the surf off Long Island, he cured himself with "cold Water [drunk] plentifully," which caused him to "sweat plentifully."[15]

From these rather arcane works by Tryon and Sanctorius, Franklin moved to a famous one by William Harvey, *De motu cordis*, or the movement of the heart (1628). He would discuss Harvey directly in the 1740s, though his writings suggest he might have come across Harvey's work as early as the 1720s. In his remarkable studies, Harvey described a pattern, the movement of blood between heart and body, which he named circulation. (Previously, that term had usually described a solid body's motion, as a planet in the sky.) Harvey's was no ordinary circulating fluid. Blood was equated with life: no blood, no life—at least for humans and other animals. Blood also signified power: blood money, blood sacrifice, blood oath. And in the way it identified lineage and family ties, blood was the most important and legally recognized determinant of social standing. "Blood will out," people said, meaning a person could never escape his or her ancestry. Harvey's work may have demystified blood, but it impressed people precisely because each heartbeat now made them imagine the wonderful substance surging through their bodies.[16]

After Harvey, much medical work focused on problems of circulation. We may think that temperance in diet is beneficial because it restricts consumption of calories. But Tryon emphasized that temperance allowed better bodily circulation. Too much food and alcohol "furs and stops the Passages, generates too much Blood"—considerable hazards within a closed system. People still thought there were four humors within the body, but blood suddenly took pride of place; people still believed the body to be a bag of fluids, but now they paid more attention to organs, such as the heart, that were perceived to do something with these fluids.

Thanks to Harvey, circulation gained tremendous and lasting resonance within social thought. It was the first example of an idea within the modern sciences becoming a metaphor or even model for the human world. Thomas Hobbes, in *Leviathan* (1651), for example, wrote that money was to the commonwealth what "naturall Bloud" was to the human body; each, by "circulating, nourisheth" the state or body. The global expansion of European commerce, the growth of urban centers with complex social networks, and the government's increased regulation of trade and migration all elicited a barrage of publications on the circulation of goods, financial instruments, people, and ideas. Circulation as metaphor abounded. Even now, we talk about "pumping" money into the economy.[17]

Franklin and his contemporaries usually employed the concept of equilibrium to talk about circulation—hence Franklin's concern with a balance of fluids entering and leaving his body. This notion too had ancient ancestors, as with the idea that health resulted when the body's humors reached an optimal balance. Newton's work in physics, and particularly his universal law of gravitation, gave a modern emphasis to equilibrium: every action had an equal and opposite reaction. The field of statics examined the forces that created an equilibrium, a form of stasis. And like *circulation*, the term *equilibrium* became a catchword within the human sciences; balance among political agents could be compared to equilibriums within nature. The doctrine of checks and balances in the political system of the United States, for instance, reflected the eighteenth-century fascination with equilibriums.[18]

For better or worse, modern science had begun to influence theories of human society. Nature had always been a source of examples for human behavior. But now, its presumed *systems*, as established by natural philosophers, were models for human institutions. Almost as soon as the concepts of circulation and equilibrium emerged in natural science, they were appropriated into discussions of commerce and politics.[19]

And so, Franklin moved easily from physical equilibriums to moral equilibriums. His *Dissertation on Liberty and Necessity, Pleasure and Pain* (1725) had in its very title identified two opposing principles that characterized the human condition. And by the early 1770s, Franklin would develop what he called a "*Moral* or *Prudential Algebra*." This algebra was a system for making decisions. A worried decisionmaker had to list, in two columns, arguments for and against something. Once this was done, the person could then strike out the items that balanced each other and eventually see which column carried most weight.[20]

Again, Franklin's interest in balance was typical of his contemporaries' wider enthusiasm for the sciences as models for social inquiry. The crossover was most evident in the two fields of political arithmetic and political economy, both of which interested Franklin and both of which used numbers to establish some certainty about future events.

Political arithmetic studied human populations; political economy studied the commercial endeavors of those populations. At the end of the seventeenth century, Englishman William Petty had coined the term *political arithmetic* to describe the analysis of population dynamics. That field and political economy would then blossom over the course of the eighteenth century, eventually culminating in Adam Smith's famous *Wealth of Nations* (1776). Each field was considered political because it examined matters of state interest. A large population could be a significant political asset—the amount of wealth that a population generated definitely was. The size of a population and its ability to labor and spend its wages were fundamental measures of economic health. Political rulers now wanted—actually, demanded—numbers; printers who produced newspapers and almanacs began to print numerical assessments of public affairs, which indicated a popular audience for such matters as well.[21]

Political economists and arithmeticians admitted, however, that human behavior was not quite as predictable as the recurring patterns in the material world. But human bodies were themselves material. So political arithmeticians started with those bodies, the natural entities on which they built a science. To make their claims credible, however, these early theorists made a distinction between facts and probabilities.

The distinction existed in natural science as well. Different philosophers had different views as to whether facts outweighed probabilities or the reverse, but most agreed that the distinction was worth making. A fact was something that people could agree was certain or nearly so; a probability was something that people agreed was likely. Something probable was not a fact, yet it was not mere opinion. For example, a political arithmetician might state that data, such as the annual number of deaths in a city, were facts. But an estimate of how many people might die the next year was a probability. (A belief that God had struck down sinners while sparing the righteous was an opinion.) A probability was a kind of guess, a way to make a decision in the face of uncertainty. Any such decision was, in a way, a gamble.[22]

Indeed, Franklin's contemporaries referred to insurance, one aspect of political arithmetic, as a business that bet on lives. Someone who sold insurance, whether on a life or a piece of property, was gambling that he or she had correctly estimated the probability that payments for insurance would be greater than the cost of paying any claims. Conversely, whoever bought insurance was betting that the payment of premiums was worthwhile, given the estimated likelihood of personal disaster.[23]

Franklin had made his first foray into these questions of probability in 1722. That year, he used Silence Dogood to argue for *"An Office of Ensurance for Widows."* This proposal estimated death and survival rates based on the population dynamics for "Two thousand Women" and their husbands. The scheme would pay premiums tied to the amount each household had paid in and to the age of the widow's husband at his death. In support of this, the Widow Dogood rather learnedly cited "Sir William Petty in his *Political Arithmetick*."[24]

Petty came in handy again, seven years later, when Franklin recommended a paper currency for Pennsylvania. The colony had been trying to make do with an array of coins and currency from other places or with awkward forms of credit. But Franklin thought this was too limited and inconvenient a system to encourage economic growth. His *Modest Enquiry into the Nature and Necessity of a Paper-Currency* (1729) used Petty's *Treatise of Taxes and Contributions* (1662) to plead for a currency. Franklin's main argument was that "the Riches of a Country are to be valued by the Quantity of Labour its Inhabitants are able to purchase." A currency for Pennsylvania would, he argued, encourage the immigration of the *"Labouring and Handicrafts Men"* whose work was most valuable. The currency would also "occasion a much greater Vent and Demand for [British] Commodities here." Immigration, production, and consumption would all increase. It took a former workingman to define a rudimentary form of the labor theory of value.[25]

The pamphlet on this topic marked the first time that Franklin used circulation to explain something about human society. If financial transactions were easier, he said, "money which otherwise would have lain dead in [bankers'] Hands, is made to circulate again." It was paper bills that would in fact accelerate the movement of capital, commodities, and labor because they were "lighter in Carriage, concealed in less Room, and therefore safer in Travelling or Laying up." Members of the Pennsylvania Assembly were so taken with the idea that they hired Franklin to print the currency he advocated. It was "a very profitable Jobb," he congratulated himself.[26]

Thereafter, claims about population growth, economic value, and costs and benefits became hallmarks of Franklin's writings. This was true of one of his famous civic improvements, Philadelphia's Union Fire Company, which was essentially an insurance organization. Franklin had helped create it in 1736 for "the better preserving our Goods and Effects from Fire." Its members were bound in "Friendship" to maintain buckets and cloth bags, the former to douse fires and the latter to rescue portable goods. They promised to use this equipment to protect each other's property. Widows would inherit their husbands' status in the company. All this spread out the cost of fighting urban fires, a considerable hazard, much as insurance payments spread out the cost of reimbursement for other human tragedies.[27]

Political arithmetic and economy also made Franklin doubt the value of imported labor, especially slaves. Numbers were his proof. In 1731, he had analyzed the city's smallpox deaths in the *Pennsylvania Gazette*. Franklin reported that the total number of dead was "exactly 288, and no more." Sixty-four who died "were Negroes," meaning slaves. If slaves' average individual value was £30, the total loss was nearly £2,000. In his calculation, Franklin disapprovingly notified the public of the enormous expense that slaves represented. One year later, in 1732, the Junto asked if "the Importation of Servants [would] increase or advance the Wealth of our Country?"[28]

Clearly, Franklin and others in Philadelphia were concluding that their colony might become a destination so attractive that productive people would migrate there freely. By fostering the circulation of people to the colony, the circulation of paper currency would help to make the colony an economic success. Settled residents would then have no need to pay to import any workers, including slaves. All of this assumed, however, that a body was a body was a body—that humans were fairly interchangeable in their composition and therefore their capacity to work, to migrate, and to produce wealth.

Were they? Here, Franklin ran up against the crucial question that Thomas Tryon had raised: Were all humans alike? It had been traditional to think so. Christians were supposed to accept the scriptural admonition that humanity shared "one blood" and that each human had a soul equally subject to God. And in older theories of nature, the body was deemed a microcosm of the whole creation—each body had the same underlying composition. True, bodies seemed different, but only superficially. Different climates, it was thought, created differences in human bodies; Africans adapted to a burning sun and Europeans to cooler places. These characteristics did not weaken their underlying similarity because all were parts of God's Creation. As one seventeenth-century English commentator hoped, the "black Negro" and "olive-colored American" Indian would "with the whiter European become one sheepe-fold, under one great shepheard."[29]

But the newly precise ideas about bodies (about their hearts and blood, for instance) questioned whether humans had this cosmic connection with one another. Did the animal economy and the red circulating juice prove that all people were "cousins"? Or did some bodies digest food and pump blood differently?

Europeans tended to see differences, not similarities. The science of political arithmetic had turned humans into bodies to be studied, as if they were so many material objects, such as rocks or shrubs, that happened to have souls. Thus, William Petty speculated that human bodies were quite different. He compared Europeans and Africans, who differed not only in skin color but also "in the very outline of their faces and the Mould of their skulls." The same was true, Petty ominously asserted, of "the internall Qualities of their Minds." Another, anonymous seventeenth-century account, of the West Indies, assumed that Africans were "a people strong and able" to do heavy work in hot climates. As these emerging ideas of race were making clear, discussions about nature did not merely present facts. They made arguments—and sometimes troubling ones.[30]

Franklin never made up his mind about human difference. In *Poor Richard* for 1745, he declared, much as Tryon had done, that "All blood is alike ancient." That was his generous side. In other cases, Franklin concluded that different people might have different bodily characteristics. Why had smallpox devastated American Indians? Franklin cited the testimony of Charles-Marie de La Condamine, a French natural philosopher who had traveled to Peru and who became an advocate of inoculation—a contemporary dubbed him the "Don Quixote of inoculation." La Condamine wrote that he saw Indians in Peru swept away by smallpox. Indians in North America had suffered a similar fate. Climate could not explain this, for North American and South American Indians lived in quite different climates. So Franklin blamed their bodies, specifically, "the Closeness and Hardness of their Skins." Indians everywhere, he speculated, had less of the insensible perspiration Sanctorius had identified in European bodies. Inoculation was, he thought, all the more necessary for Indians.[31]

When Franklin discussed inoculation of whites, he presented data: so many people had been treated, and so many of them had died. He compared those figures to mortality rates among uninoculated people who got smallpox. His calculations implied the probability that it was safer to be inoculated than to wait to get smallpox the ordinary way. There was an element of uncertainty in Franklin's analysis, but it was as nothing compared to his hypothesis that Indians and whites had differently constructed skins. That was his opinion, merely.

FRANKLIN'S interest in the human body—its constitution, its health, its productivity—appeared to greatest effect in his *Account of the New Invented Pennsylvanian Fire-Places* . . . (1744). The pamphlet addressed a subject that he would consider throughout his life: heat. He seemed to have begun working on this topic in late 1739 and early 1740, in other words, in winter, the perfect time to worry about keeping warm.

Franklin's dread of pulmonary disorders might, in part, have spurred his interest in improving heating systems. He crammed his 1744 pamphlet on fireplaces with warnings that drafts in poorly heated rooms were deadly. It did people little good to huddle by a fire, he argued, if currents of cold air then buffeted them. "Many Colds are caught from this Cause only," Franklin lectured, "it being safer to sit in the open Street; for then the Pores do all close together, and the Air does not strike so sharply against any particular part." Franklin also cited an alarming Spanish proverb, "*If the Wind blows on you thro' a Hole, Make your Will, and take Care of your Soul.*" (He had first used this aphorism in *Poor Richard* for 1736, the year after his recent attack of pleurisy.) Over and over, he stressed the power of a "Crevice" or "Hole" to create "Colds . . . Fevers, Pleurisies, &c." He worried that women especially suffered from "Colds in the Heads," though interestingly, he did not assume an innate difference between men and women but instead suggested that the disparity occurred because women "sit much in the House" with its cold-producing drafts.[32]

Surely, houses and their occupants could be heated better. Franklin used the human body and its well-being—the "Comfort and Conveniency of our Lives"—as important measures of a successful heating system. He recognized that this was a new goal: "I suppose our Ancestors never thought of warming Rooms to sit in; all they purpos'd was to have a Place to make a Fire in."[33]

Franklin's "Pennsylvanian" fireplace was meant to warm a whole room, not just the space immediately around it. It could accomplish this because its interior, curving passage used convection. It would convey heat into the room and suck the smoke out. As it emitted heat, lighter air would rise "by the Mantle-piece to the Cieling and [spread] all over the Top of the Room," then sink as more warmed

PROFILE of the Chimney and FIRE-PLACE.

M The Mantle-piece or Breaſt of the Chimney.
C The Funnel.
B The falſe Back & Cloſing.
E True Back of the Chimney.
T Top of the Fire-place.
F The Front of it.
A The Place where the Fire is made.
D The Air-Box.
K The Hole in the Side-plate, thro' which the warm'd Air is diſcharg'd out of the Air-Box into the Room.
H The Hollow fill'd with freſh Air, entring at the Paſſage *I*, and aſcending into the Air-Box thro' the Air-hole in the Bottom-plate neaſ
G The Partition in the Hollow to keep the Air and Smoke apart.
P The Paſſage under the falſe Back and Part of the Hearth for the Smoke.
↑↑↑↑↑↑ The Courſe of the Smoke.

Profile of Franklin's fireplace. Benjamin Franklin,
Account of the New Invented Pennsylvanian Fire-Places (1744).
LIBRARY COMPANY OF PHILADELPHIA.

air flowed from the fireplace until "the whole Room [became] in a short time equally warmed." A cold draft within the fireplace pushed the smoke down the back of the chimney and through an "inverted siphon," allowing the heat to flow forward and then outward to the room. Franklin stressed the naturalism of his design by placing, on the front plate of his fireplace, a small sun with the caption "ALTER IDEM," meaning the fireplace was "another one," another sun.[34]

A properly heated room, like a properly maintained body, encouraged productivity, he asserted. In a room with an ordinary fireplace,

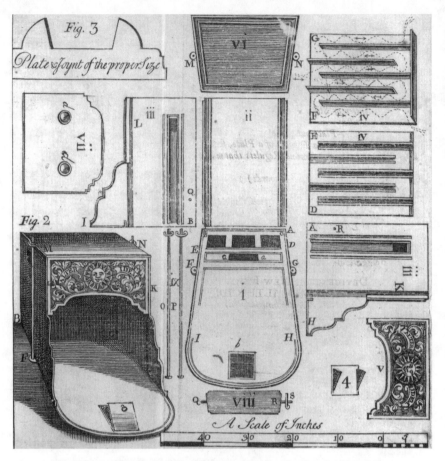

Franklin's fireplace—Guide to assembly. Benjamin Franklin,
Account of the New Invented Pennsylvanian Fire-Places (1744).
LIBRARY COMPANY OF PHILADELPHIA.

people had to crowd around the fire. By its dim, flickering light, they squinted at their reading or ran sewing needles into their fingers. But a room with Franklin's fireplace was fully heated. People could read or work in the light from windows. Unlike a closed stove, Franklin's design allowed people to see the "pleasant" sight of the fire and to have access to it so they could "boil the Tea-kettle, warm the Flat-Irons, heat [portable] Heaters, keep warm a Dish of Victuals by setting it on the Top, &c. &c. &c"—an infinity of domestic comforts.[35]

Franklin clearly knew the appeal of this domestic environment—a place of warmth, conviviality, and occupation. In this space, reading and housework might coexist, along with the male and female household members who did the reading and the work and enjoyed the comfort. Was this Franklin's own idea of domestic bliss? It is hard to tell. Consider that Poor Richard had offered, in the same almanac, two maxims on domestic and physical warmth. One was sentimental: "A house without woman and Firelight, is like a body without soul or sprite"; the other was misogynist: "Ne'er take a wife till thou hast a house (and a fire) to put her in."[36]

His vision of home and hearth was, above all, practical. Franklin used political economy and political arithmetic to promote his fireplaces, which consumed much less fuel than ordinary fires. "As the Country is more clear'd and settled" in America, he predicted, wood "will of course grow scarcer and dearer." Franklin's fireplaces used so much less fuel that America's wood could grow as fast as the expanding population could "consume it," which would prevent the development of an expensive internal market for wood or a ruinous traffic in coal brought "over the Atlantick." "We leave it to the *Political Arithmetician*," Franklin wrote, "to compute, how much Money will be sav'd to a Country, by its spending two thirds less of Fuel." There would also be concomitant savings in labor that could be shifted from cutting wood to cultivating land.[37]

How quintessentially Franklin the fireplace was. He had invented something! Moreover, the invention was practical: it made people more productive, and it was itself efficient—it embodied all the classic Franklin virtues. But this was a highly learned invention, whose description and directions for assembly and use came with footnotes, including footnotes in Latin. Those details were not strictly necessary. Why did Franklin bother to provide them?

In fact, the Pennsylvania fireplace was Franklin's first experiment, his first venture into natural philosophy. That philosophy explained the causes of things. With his fireplace, he was exploring the cause of motion in air—why did it move when heated?. To show that he had read and thought about this as a question within natural science, he cited in his pamphlet no fewer than six works of natural philosophy, several of which synopsized other sources; Franklin's phrasing in places betrayed a knowledge of still other texts in natural philosophy. If we look more closely at the pamphlet, we can determine what Franklin was reading and see what he was doing with all that reading.[38]

The first thing he did was define an experimental space, one he would use again and again: an enclosed room. This approach was a remarkably thrifty way of doing an experiment. Franklin could not afford the kind of specialized research spaces that gentleman philosophers commanded, but he owned a house, fireplaces, and his own heat-seeking body. Moreover, he could safely assume that his readers had access to rooms with fireplaces—and drafts—and thus could verify his findings if they wished.

He presupposed his experimental space to be full of air, a substance that would, when warm, rise and expand. Heating a room meant creating enough warm air to expand throughout it, repelling the cold drafts that plagued rooms where the warmth was too localized. (The problem could be detected, he advised, "by holding a Candle to a Keyhole.") An efficient fireplace would fill a room with heat because hot air expanded. Just the opposite happened when air cooled—it contracted. To verify this, anyone could make "very easy Experiments" with a bottle. Heat the bottle, Franklin instructed, and invert it in water and then watch water rise in the bottle as its air "cools and contracts."[39]

The "very easy Experiments" are a big clue that the pamphlet was more than a practical description of a fireplace. The bottle was a barometer, perhaps Franklin's nod to Robert Boyle and his air pump, which had established that air had a "spring" (meaning pressure). That pressure was an important reason to examine heat: temperature caused air to expand and contract, giving evidence of its material construction. Franklin was in fact accepting the prevailing learned opinion that matter was composed of an accumulation of particles that existed everywhere, even inside Philadelphia houses.[40]

Several figures in the early modern sciences had revived the ancient Greek idea that matter was composed of corpuscles or particles. They thought that these particles were (unlike our modern atoms) elemental, having no constituent parts. Where we see submolecular materials connecting and changing character, they thought corpuscles simply clumped or collided. The shape of the particles was, however, a matter of debate, with René Descartes and Isaac Newton offering the most important interpretations.

Descartes insisted that the configuration of the particles mattered. He observed that round objects, packed together, had spaces or channels between them. So if matter was composed of particles shaped like spheres, there must be other bits that fit the channels between them. He imagined another kind of particle shaped somewhat like a cube, one whose sides had round depressions into which spheres could fit. The spherical particles, he suggested, rotated within the channeled particles; together, they filled all available space but did so in a way that permitted them to move. Any motion could then be predicted according to this mechanical definition of matter. Things did not move in and of themselves; their physical configuration facilitated the motion.[41]

Cartesianism spread over the European continent and found advocates in England. But Newton, England's premier natural philosopher, found Descartes's theory too hypothetical. Yes, he believed, particles were the basis of matter. And yes, motion occurred. But there was no evidence that it happened because of the movement of spheres and squashed cubes, invisible to the naked eye. If the particles could not be seen, why not leave their precise shape unspecified?

In fact, Newton chose not to define the precise mechanism of particulate motion. His followers nevertheless inferred from what he had said about gravity that, just as a planet accelerated centripetally toward the sun, so there must be a mutual attraction between particles that generated distinct forms of matter. Motion, attraction, gravity—all three were evident in the macrocosm, and so, they very likely existed on a smaller scale. And Newton himself ventured to define, through experiment and mathematics, the size, shape, and force a particle exerted, making the particulate theory of matter into an exact science.[42]

It was a stalemate. Cartesians found Newtonianism disastrously unmechanical, inasmuch as its proponents spoke glibly about unseen forces such as gravity. In return, Newtonians found Cartesianism ridiculously unproven, unable to measure the forces among particles.

Warmed by his Pennsylvania fireplace, Franklin was a comfortable Newtonian. The chunks of wood he put on the fire, the hand that gingerly inserted the wood, the wife sitting opposite him—all were material, visible accumulations of invisible particles. The same was true of the smoke that went up the chimney and, even more invisibly, the hot air that came out of the fireplace. It took a powerful act of imagination to "see" everything as composed of particles, but that is what Franklin, following natural philosophy, was able to do.

When he pointed out that air got lighter, or "rarified," and bigger ("takes up more Space") as it grew warmer, he revealed his assumption that matter was particulate. When heated, the particles that formed air moved further apart, so the substance was less dense and lighter—this was a standard explanation. Franklin was indifferent to the question of the physical shape of these particles, which identified him as Newtonian, though it was not clear (and never was) that he consciously rejected Cartesianism.[43]

In his work on heat, Franklin, by accepting the idea of Newtonian particles, examined what other philosophers had termed the "imponderables." Imponderable substances had mass but not weight. Experimenters thought these "subtle fluids" would yield clues about matter's particulate construction. Newton had hypothesized the existence of an aether, a subtle and elastic substance that pervaded the universe; this proposition was an attempt to explain a cosmic force that caused gravity. But Newton was uneasy over his speculation, and discusssions of the aether were absent from subsequent editions of his work. But during the 1740s, when Franklin was working on his fireplace, information on Newton's aether was posthumously publicized, and theorists offered still other imponderable substances: heat, light, magnetism, electricity. All of these were material but not perfectly or directly visible, and they included substances we now divide among liquids, gases, and currents. Moreover, they were highly malleable, even entering other substances, as heat clearly did. Newton himself had ventured that electricity might be the central force of creation, running through the light he investigated in the *Opticks* and the attraction he posited in *Principia*.[44]

Franklin's frequent references to air becoming "rarified" by heat showed that he also was thinking in terms of fluid and elastic substances. Air was fluid (smoke flowed, for instance), and it was elastic (it expanded or compressed depending on its temperature). Yet some imponderables did not behave as conventional fluids. Franklin showed a knowledge of Newton's *Opticks* when he referred to the tendency of light and heat "to move in right Lines and with great Swiftness" and when he referred to "Rays of Heat" and "Rays of Light" that "shot" outward from a source, like a fire in a fireplace.[45]

Franklin's pamphlet drew on another and more obscure idea, that of an atmosphere. In the Renaissance, philosophers seemed to use the concept initially to explain a possible condition around the moon. Then they bestowed an atmosphere on the earth. By the sixteenth century, natural philosophers argued that the earth had not the concentric rings of air, water, and fire that the ancients had arranged around it but instead three layers of "air." The nearest was warmed by the earth, the next was cooler and had clouds, and the outermost was heated by fire and again cloudless. In 1686, Edmond Halley applied Boyle's "spring" of the air to the atmosphere, asserting that pressure varied with height and therefore with distance from the earth. The idea of an atmosphere thereafter became a way to distinguish one space from another, whether on the earth, over a town, or even around a human body. Each such space could sustain a field of unseen matter around its center.[46]

Franklin took the concept indoors. His ideal of indoor comfort reflected his beliefs that nature could generate and sustain atmospheres and that the body naturally preferred some over others. He cited Martin Clare's *The Motion of Fluids* to argue that a drafty room with a fire was less salubrious than one without. He pointed to Boyle's observation that Russians stayed perfectly healthy during their ferocious winters even though they went from their highly heated houses to the frigid outdoors; in each environment, they were at a stable temperature and so did not become ill from the stark contrast in temperatures. So too, Franklin contended, would a person maintain health even when going from a heated room to a cold bath or from a warm bed to a cold room. "The Reason is," he explained, "that in these Cases the Pores all close at once, the Cold is shut out, and the Heat within augmented." Repeated immersion in cold after warmth would, if anything, cause the blood to be "driven round with a brisker Circulation," aiding health the way that brisk circulation of currency aided an economy.[47]

In making these analogical leaps—from body to room, from fireplace to sun, from woodpile to forests, from heat to matter— Franklin joined an ongoing effort to use natural philosophy to improve everyday life. By the time he worked on his fireplaces, he knew the work of the foremost Newtonian experimenter, the Reverend Stephen Hales. Hales not only experimented with air and circulation but also used his findings to argue about health and public welfare, much as Franklin was doing.[48]

Hales described respiration and circulation within plants and animals in his *Vegetable Staticks* (1727) and *Haemastaticks* (1733). By attaching glass receivers to foliage or severed branches, Hales demonstrated that plants indeed emitted "air" as well as visible fluid. Placing mashed apple inside an air pump, he found that the air it respired weighed far more than the apple did. That discovery supported the Newtonian idea of an elastic, particulate matter, in this case compressed within the apple and then released when the fruit was smashed open. Animal circulation likewise revealed statical principles. For his hemostatic work, Hales would do an extraordinary series of bloody vivisections. In each, he tied down an animal, severed one of its arteries, and measured how high the blood would shoot in a glass tube and then ebb and finally stop.[49]

Drawing insights about health and circulation from these different experiments, Hales posited that the circulation of air benefited health and that the respiration of plants created a healthy atmosphere. He argued that better circulation of air on ships and in hospitals would keep people healthy; Franklin proposed the same for the circulation of heat at home. Both men used experimental results to make their cases.

Franklin had to proceed a bit more circuitously than Hales did. He had no reputation as an experimenter and could hardly assume his newspaper and almanac readers were eager to buy a philosophical pamphlet. So he disguised his experiment. He ingeniously packaged it as two products he could sell—the pamphlet and the metal parts of the Pennsylvania fireplace. The disguise was so effective that, after Franklin's death, people thought the pamphlet only proved that its author had invented a stove. He *had* done that, but he had also performed an experiment in the circulation of fluids, or elastic substances composed of particles.

The Pennsylvania fireplace was an ongoing experiment: Franklin would tinker with it for the rest of his life. In the late 1760s, he developed a hinged "sliding plate," or damper, with which to channel the smoke or close off the fireplace when it was not in use and simply made a room drafty. By 1771, he turned the whole thing into the freestanding vase stove, or "Franklin stove," the bulbous metal heater that survives to this day. Despite these improvements, Franklin never believed that he got things quite right. It is pleasant to envision him, even when older and grander, getting down on hands and knees to peer up his London landlady's chimney, banging out new metal fireplace fittings, advising Scottish aristocrats about their leaky chimneys, and drifting around drafty rooms, candle in hand, to locate currents of cold air. In the meantime, the pamphlet on Pennsylvania fireplaces, with its learned apparatus, was a kind of calling card for Franklin, a way to introduce himself as an experimental natural philosopher.

SEVEN YEARS separate Franklin's *Pennsylvanian Fire-Places* and the publication of his electrical experiments in 1751. Why was the ambitious Franklin so cautious? When it came to natural philosophy, he followed Poor Richard's advice: "Make haste slowly." We know that Franklin will dazzle the world. But there is no use wishing we could tell him to hurry up and go fly a kite. Franklin needed the gatekeepers in the republic of letters to pay attention to him, and they had no reason to do so. Had he continued to publish himself, as with his fireplace pamphlet or the tidbits on natural science in his newspaper and almanacs, few readers beyond the middle colonies would have noticed and he, like his brother James, would now be known to a handful of specialists on early America who study the mental world of colonial printer-publishers. The way to make a real mark in the world was to proceed slowly, build up a small stock of expertise, and then place ideas deferentially before the bigwigs.

Through a series of introductions (some fortuitous, others stage-managed), Franklin slowly inserted himself into an Atlantic network of correspondents interested in natural philosophy. For him, entry into this network was an intellectual goal—and a great deal more. He knew that all prominent colonists had friends and patrons in London, an absolute necessity for doing work in the sciences. Franklin had a friend in William Strahan, his fellow printer, but Strahan specialized in politics and political writers, not naturalists. Franklin needed to make friends who would connect him to natural philosophers in London.

Where should he begin? Franklin knew one other place where he was known, Boston, and his first thought was to promote himself there. It was not nostalgia that prompted him but rather the fact that the Bay Colony was layered with learning. Harvard College fostered scholars of all types, and, compared to Pennsylvania, the older and still somewhat richer colony of Massachusetts could support greater importation and production of books, scientific instruments, and experts. Having fled Boston ignominiously, Franklin wanted to return as a gentleman and scholar. He hoped his family and friends would help him. He told his parents about the Philadelphia botanist John Bartram, "an intimate Friend of mine," who would "be glad of a Correspondence with some Gentlemen of the same Taste" in Boston. A word to the right person could connect Franklin, via Bartram, to some Boston man of letters. But there is no sign that the elder Franklins managed to do this or that they even tried.[50]

So Franklin used family and business visits to Boston to do this work himself. During one sojourn in the spring of 1743, he attended Archibald Spencer's lectures on "Experimental Philosophy." As in Europe, such demonstrations used sensation—sparks, explosions, optical illusions—to present the sciences to the public. Spencer ran through the best-known discoveries, "the Circulation of the Blood," "Sir Isaac Newton's Theory of Light and Colours," and the fact "that Fire is Diffus'd through all Space," meaning brief exhibits of electricity. These were the first demonstrations of electricity Franklin had seen—"they equally surpriz'd and pleas'd me," he recalled. He also helped arrange for Spencer to give his lectures at the Library Company, a series he promoted both in the *Pennsylvania Gazette* and in the description of the lectures he printed in 1743.[51]

Having introduced his colleagues to Spencer, Franklin wanted them to return the favor. The two men he had been cultivating, John Bartram and James Logan, obliged him. They led him to two important contacts: Peter Collinson in London and Cadwallader Colden in New York. Further introductions to other men of science would follow. Indeed, Franklin's friends tended to know each other.

For Franklin, these colonial counterparts were also potential role models and sometimes cautionary tales. He studied his peers' strengths and weaknesses and learned a great deal. Above all, he could assess the trade-offs between doing natural history, which described things in nature (as Bartram did), or doing natural philosophy, which analyzed the universal causes of things in nature (as Logan and Colden did).

Peter Collinson, a Fellow of the Royal Society who had extensive political connections, was looking for a colonial protégé and slowly, via other Philadelphians, made his way to Franklin. Collinson was a cloth merchant from a Quaker family who had trained himself in botany. Through his trade, he corresponded with like-minded colonists, including Joseph Breintnall, a Philadelphia merchant and one of the Junto's founders. ("Very ingenious in many little Nicknackeries," Franklin remembered of Breintnall, demolishing a man who had been his elder and better for some time, "and of sensible Conversation"—a bit more generous.) At some point, Collinson asked Breintnall to introduce him to a botanically inclined Philadel-

phian. In short order, Bartram and Collinson became regular correspondents, and it was probably through the London merchant that
Bartram exchanged letters with Linnaeus.[52]

Collinson rummaged up no fewer than fifty-seven patrons who
underwrote Bartram's travels and gardening. (It was a sharp contrast to Franklin's failure to promote Bartram locally, in his newspaper and almanac.) But however indispensable Bartram became to
British men of science, they considered him a social inferior and let
him know it. Even Collinson considered his client completely inept
except when planted amid his plants; he gave Bartram (and his
wife) clothing as well as advice about how and when to wear it,
which was patronizing in both senses of the word. Bartram seemed
resigned: he was the naturalist's naturalist. His native genius with
plants never transferred to other realms, and he had no desire to
declare any universal principle about the vegetable world. Collinson
was therefore eager to find other Philadelphia protégés. He agreed
to act as agent for the Library Company (Breintnall was an original
subscriber) and to arrange some of its purchases of books and
equipment. Collinson would also make donations to the company.
In that way, by the 1740s, he began to focus his patronage on Benjamin Franklin.[53]

Franklin knew what to wear and when, and he aspired to be not
Collinson's client but rather his social and intellectual equal. To this
end, he needed to produce something more important than his
piece on fireplaces. This effort would require him to exchange ideas
and rough drafts with his peers in the colonies, lest he disgrace himself with an ill-considered essay sent to Collinson directly. Nearly all
of Franklin's thoughts on the natural world proceeded through a series of letters. He wrote initially to friends or select correspondents,
developed his ideas through continued correspondence, and culminated with refined letters he would then send on to experts. Such
was the case with the letters he eventually sent to Collinson to be
read (he hoped) before the Royal Society.[54]

Cadwallader Colden became the first link in the chain. Franklin
had probably known the New York resident, by reputation, for some
time. They both knew Logan and Bartram; Colden and Collinson
were correspondents, and Collinson had introduced Colden to Strahan. Yet Franklin and Colden ended up having an "accedental
Meeting on the Road" in Connecticut when Franklin was on his way
to or from Boston in 1742.[55]

Born to Scots-Irish parents, educated at the University of Edinburgh and in medicine in London, Colden had lived in Philadelphia but moved to New York in 1718, four years before Franklin arrived in Philadelphia—a near miss. When Colden failed to establish a medical practice in New York, just as he had failed in Philadelphia, he turned instead to politics as well as natural history and philosophy. He was among the original subscribers who underwrote the cost of Ephraim Chambers's *Cyclopedia*, a significant and ambitious undertaking for someone in the colonies. He had particular skill in botany, and Linnaeus praised him as "Summus Perfectus," or supremely perfect. Eventually, Colden turned over his botanical studies to his daughter, Jane, and by the early 1740s, he had moved into Newtonian mechanics, where the real action was.[56]

Franklin admired the ambition. Colden was addressing the question of universal causes—gravity making stones fall in Europe and America alike—that Newton had defined. Franklin professed to Colden that he could not "but be fond of engaging in a Correspondence so advantageous to me as yours must be." He used his 1743 plan for a learned society in Philadelphia to keep Colden, a potential corresponding member, interested in writing to him. Franklin pointed out that he and Colden were progenitors of the project, a short-lived ancestor of the American Philosophical Society. Colden had evidently advised Bartram to form the society; both Bartram and Logan passed the task to Franklin. "I tould Benjamin," Bartram wrote Colden, "that I believed he [Logan] would not incourage" the proposed society but that they should "Jog on without him." Logan did not, and they did, at least for a time. On a visit to New York in early 1744, Franklin left a letter for Colden, reporting that "the Society" had members (whom he listed) and held meetings; he promised future news of the meetings.[57]

This polite back-and-forth evinced enough trust for Franklin and Colden to begin a serious correspondence in 1744, when both were putting their thoughts on natural philosophy into print. Franklin did so with his pamphlet on fireplaces, which Colden read and then sent to Johann Friedrich Gronovius, a Dutch naturalist who had the pamphlet translated and printed in Leiden, the Netherlands. This edition was Franklin's first overseas publication.[58]

Colden meanwhile circulated drafts of some essays on "fluxions," a term (no longer used) that described the rate of change in a mathematical function. He claimed to have discovered the cause of gravitation, not through experiment or observation but by rational and mathematical analysis of some of the major texts in mechanics. Colden realized his work was speculative. "I have open'd to my self a large Prospect either into Nature or into Fairyland," he confessed to Franklin, and he wished to "lay it step by step before my Friends for their remarks." He sent Franklin part of his manuscript to share with Logan. Franklin was eager to tell Colden that he had passed the draft to Logan but was less keen to express Logan's disbelief ("he thought you had not fully hit the Matter"), and he was suspiciously slow to offer Colden his own thoughts.[59]

Colden was the anti-Franklin—he made haste hastily. Determined to make his mark, he published *An Explication of the First Causes of Action in Matter; and the Cause of Gravitation* in New York in 1745. His work explained the *cause* of gravitation, a problem on which even "Sir Isaac Newton [had] stopt short." Newton had proposed that aether filled the universe, exerting a force that caused gravitation; Colden said that it was the aether itself, its imponderable particles resisting matter, that created a special force on celestial bodies—it was gravity. On the strength of this claim, the book was translated and published all over Europe. Experts tore into it. Swiss mathematician Leonhard Euler wrote a critique, read at the Royal Society, that described Colden's explication as "so ill managed, that it is absolutely contrary to the first principles of Hydrostaticks." It was "an absurdity," he pronounced, for Colden to claim "that the Ether between Two of the Coelestial Bodies, has not the same Spring [resisting force] as that of the Rest" of matter. The Royal Society declined to read Colden's rebuttal.[60]

Yet Colden's boldness and reach obviously appealed to Franklin, who had offered to publish the book—no other colonist's work in natural philosophy had been so widely disseminated abroad. The mathematically challenged Franklin was unable to assess Colden's work, but he knew quite well that work in physics mattered more than any other attempt in the sciences. And he may have learned another lesson from Colden: do not publish your work in America but have it vetted and printed in Europe. He realized that the circulation of ideas in letters, which were essentially rough drafts, was very important.[61]

Colden and Franklin were on common—and safer—ground when they discussed the human body. In 1745, Colden sent Franklin the draft of another work, probably a version of his 1730s treatise entitled "The Animal Oeconomy." No strategic silence this time—Franklin sent back two letters that together formed a detailed response on the functioning of the body, starting with the question of invisible perspiration. "After I had read Sanctorius," he explained, "I imagin'd a constant Stream of the perspirable Matter issuing at *every* pore in the Skin." Yet the leaky body also managed to absorb fluids. How did the skin accomplish this two-way flow? Franklin and Colden agreed that the skin perspired and respired at the same time, through different "Ducts." This process had to be possible, Franklin insisted, even if the outward movement of fluids was better known and more powerful than any inward motion. If laid against the skin, for instance, a medicine's entry into the body "must go against Wind and Tide, (as one may say)."[62]

Their letters on this question revealed a crucial difference between Franklin and Colden: experiments. Whereas Colden reasoned his way through problems, Franklin liked demonstration.

At Archibald Spencer's Boston lectures, Franklin had just seen a glass mechanism that showed the circulation of the blood, and he may have bought the "Apparatus" around that time. With this as a possible model, Franklin built his own "little Machine" to show that fluids could, within the same system, move in opposite directions. He joined two pieces of hollow cane so they met at an apex, like a capital A. Water sent through the left-hand, ascending cane would rise and then descend through the right-hand cane. He then inserted two small glass tubes to stand above each cane, as if the A were now wearing horns. Water introduced through the cane on the left now spurted through the left-hand glass tube but not the right-hand one, even if some of the water traveled all the way through both sections of cane. As if they were two pores, one glass tube carried fluid outward, but the other resisted the flow and could (presumably) receive a different fluid if pressure in the system was low enough.[63]

Having corrected Sanctorius, Franklin also used his letters to Colden to comment on Harvey. He pointed out that Harvey's description of the heart's valves, which variously pumped blood inward and outward, indicated how a two-way circulation might exist in other parts of the body. Franklin then appended speculations on the cause of warmth in the blood. Friction could create heat—as anyone who rubs his or her cold hands together knows. Did it warm the blood? If so, where did the friction occur? Franklin concluded that the heart, moving as it pumped blood, had to "produce a Heat" that was then transferred to the blood, which circulated it through the body. This scenario was likelier than blood creating heat itself; fluids, though particulate, were too smooth to generate the necessary friction, which the heart's tissue could do.[64]

Franklin's "little Machine" (now lost) was inventive, but most of his arguments in his letters to Colden did little more than embellish Harvey and Sanctorius. He was more original when he posited analogies to the human body, moving outward to the macrocosm and reasoning about heat and fluid circulation as universal properties. Sun, heart, Pennsylvania fireplace—each one heated a fluid (air or blood) within a distinct atmosphere, whether around the earth, in the body, or through a room. In similar fashion, Franklin proposed that "Food in the Stomach" was equivalent to "Fuel in a Chimney"; they kept a body or a room warm. If the body was analogous to a room, an even larger atmosphere could resemble a set of rooms. Franklin would complain of London's dirty air in 1758, declaring, "The whole Town is one great smoaky House, and every Street a Chimney," thus making many sooty microcosms within the macrocosm of the metropolis.[65]

WAR called Franklin and Colden from their philosophical reveries in the late 1740s. The War of Jenkins's Ear (1739–1744) was merging into the War of the Austrian Succession (1744–1748), which the colonists called King George's War. Both conflicts involved land battles, but colonists probably worried at least as much about their naval maneuvers. Jenkins lost his ear to a Spanish coast guard vessel in 1739, provoking one war; New Englanders sent a private flotilla to seize French Louisbourg in the Atlantic Maritimes in 1745, escalating another. Men such as Colden and Franklin were still eager to discuss the natural world, but they now took up topics relevant to public affairs, including navigation, defense, and the value of the colonies within the empire.

Getting ships across the Atlantic was a paramount wartime concern, which may have been why, in a 1746 letter to Colden, Franklin considered "the much shorter Voyages made by Ships bound hence to England, than by those from England hither," which he had noticed on his own two Atlantic crossings. He thought the difference must be "in some Degree owing to the Diurnal Motion of the Earth" but also considered that ships' structure would affect the resistance of the water.[66]

Colden likewise attributed the phenomenon to multiple causes. The "more frequent westerly winds" across the Atlantic must play a part, he said; so too did the tides. Probably referring to the work of Edmond Halley, Colden observed that high tides could be mapped in regular patterns over the globe and their effects calculated, showing that a ship crossing westward in thirty days would have the tidal force "lessen'd 1/30 of the time as she approaches" America. Assuming that all ships could be constructed and loaded in the same way, an "equation" to calculate the rates of east and west passages at different times of year should be possible.[67]

But after this initial exchange on the topic, Franklin dropped it—for two decades. He may have done so because although the question had "entred" his "Mind," he was not sure if it ever had "any other's." This doubt had accompanied his first analysis of the North Atlantic in 1726, when he feared his perceptions might be his "opinion" alone. If he and Colden were the only two people who found the problem interesting, they might have no audience for their solution. And for the time being, there was no way to address the problem through experimentation and direct observation, both of which mattered to Franklin if not to Colden.[68]

Above all, the war-torn Atlantic world reminded Franklin that he was still on the edge of nowhere, as far as Europeans were concerned. In 1745, he assured his London book-buyer, William Strahan, that the colonial market for books remained steady—literate colonists fell over themselves to read whatever had been printed abroad. "Your authors know but little of the Fame they have on this Side the Ocean," Franklin explained; "we are a kind of Posterity in respect to them. We read their Works with perfect Impartiality, being at too great a Distance to be byassed by the Fashions, Parties and Prejudices that prevail among you." Only in far-off Philadelphia, Franklin implied, could one both read and appreciate European texts.[69]

But the distance—and difference—between the Eastern and Western Hemispheres was narrowing. As their populations grew, colonies were less dependent on Europe for immigrant labor and basic supplies. Instead, colonists imported more finished goods, including the piles of printed material that indicated their growing intellectual sophistication. Not that metropolitan authorities took note of this. The war made it apparent to Franklin that imperial officials would not even guarantee defense for the colonies, including Pennsylvania. In 1747, he published two essays that addressed, in remarkably different ways, the relationship between Britain and the American colonies.[70]

Plain Truth was Franklin's first overtly political statement. In it, he indicted the colony's leaders for abdicating their duty to defend Pennsylvania and recommended a voluntary military association to fill the void. Spanish privateers along the North American coast had raised fears of an attack on the mid-Atlantic colonies. Pennsylvania's elite (especially the Quakers) were nevertheless reluctant to invest in military defense. "Common Sense and Goodness" required greater vigilance, Franklin urged. Even if the war spared Philadelphia itself, privateering would hurt its trade, which was "in Danger of being ruin'd in another Year." To rely on the Royal Navy for defense was a foolish and short-term solution. If Pennsylvania paid for its own naval defense, the money given to its own shipwrights and sailors "remains in the Country, and circulates among us." Military investment was, therefore, an investment in both the economy and public safety: "Publick Money, raised *from All*, belongs *to All*."[71]

Franklin was not subtle. He signed his pamphlet as "A TRADESMAN of Philadelphia" and thereby made clear that he stood apart—socially and morally—from Pennsylvania's genteel elite. He also illustrated the piece with a cartoon that showed a man praying for divine assistance to get his cart out of the mud. A Latin tag to the cartoon ("Non Votis, &c.") roughly translates as "God helps those who help themselves."[72]

The pamphlet "had a sudden and surprizing Effect," much more than Franklin had expected and more than anything he had written before. If it was an experiment in promoting himself, it worked. When Franklin presented his scheme to "a Meeting of the Citizens," he "harangu'd them a little," read his essay, and then distributed copies of a plan for association. He garnered over 500 signatures on the spot, and that number doubled within a week. He also persuaded some powerful supporters, including Logan. By the fall of 1747, the colonial militia was formed. Franklin declined to serve as colonel of the Philadelphia regiment, but he had clearly become a figurehead in colonial politics. He won his first elected position the next year, 1748, when he became a member of the Philadelphia

Common Council. The military force he had helped create served two functions. It defended the colonies from external attack, and it deflected British critics who claimed the colonists were too weak to help themselves.[73]

Even as Franklin defended the colonies within the masculine world of politics and war, he adopted a female pseudonym to admit the colonies' backwardness. He wrote the "Speech of Miss Polly Baker" in 1746 and published it anonymously in a London newspaper the next year. In this piece, Miss Baker makes her speech from a Connecticut courtroom. Charged with fornication (the evidence was an illegitimate baby, her fifth), Baker protests that she had merely followed the "Command of Nature, and of Nature's God, *Encrease and Multiply*," her "steady Performance of which" was a benefit "in a new Country that really wants People." This inventive defense, among others, inspires the court to drop all charges against Baker and one of her judges "to marry her the next day."[74]

Prodigal daughter of Silence Dogood and errant cousin of Bridget Saunders, Baker shares her paper kinswomen's lively tone but transcends their bloodlessness. Baker exists because of her scandalous body, and she is suitably vivid in detailing its ability to work and to produce children. The smitten judge stands for us; we are meant to appraise Baker and then fall for her.

Through Baker, Franklin acknowledged his provinciality—he lived "in a new Country that really wants People." The colonies still depended on imports of all kinds, from finished goods to people, especially the young people who could work and reproduce. Baker argued that she did both, supporting her progeny without charity. (Poor Richard had already compared the two ways that the colonies acquired what they "wanted" when he declared in 1735 that "A Ship under sail and a big-bellied Woman, / Are the handsomest two things that can be seen common.") But the tide was turning. Franklin was, by the mid-1740s, beginning to see that natural reproduction would make the colonists powerful. With enough of the diligence that Baker exhibited, colonials would outnumber Britons. "God helps those who help themselves" indeed.[75]

In *Plain Truth* and the "Speech of Miss Polly Baker," Franklin was, for the first time, summoning nature to make a political argument. By the middle of the eighteenth century, languages of science and law had intriguing areas of overlap. Natural philosophers drew on the idea of law to argue for nature's uniformity and regularity; legal theorists called on the sciences to argue for law's inevitability. (The claims of political arithmetic, based on probability, were similar, if less certain.) Now, the concept of a *fact*—a hard, durable truth—became a political tool. People could not resist arguing that facts simply existed and spoke for themselves. The fruitful convergence of law and science was rhetorically seductive. Newton may have warned that even the idea of gravity (stones falling) needed to be tested; meanwhile, many a second-rate lawyer and would-be politician insisted that facts, truth, nature, and law all confirmed whatever point he was trying to make.[76]

Franklin had stuck to probability when he examined political arithmetic, but actual politics made him bolder. The two words in the title of his call to arms, *plain* and *truth*, made a rhetorical bid for the self-evident nature of his argument. Meanwhile, Baker, like her anonymous creator, leans hard on the argument from design. Note that she does not cite scripture; she credits nature, not the book of Genesis, even though her words "Encrease and Multiply" come from the King James Bible. Indeed, nature matters more than its Creator, if the order in which Baker/Franklin listed them is any indication. It was a rather scandalous package, had anyone bothered to catalog its contents.

———————————

FRANKLIN had produced *Plain Truth* and "Polly Baker" almost as asides—natural philosophy was, finally, demanding every moment of his time as the war wound down in 1747. His experiments consumed him. "I have, during some months past, had little leisure for any thing else," he confessed. Franklin had fallen under electricity's spell.[77]

He was not alone. His contemporaries were fascinated by electricity, even though no one knew quite what it was. People had long known about static electricity, associating it with substances (amber, glass, kittens) that, with a little friction, generated a weak charge. In the seventeenth century, philosophers had remarked on electricity's resemblance to magnetism and had begun to explain it in similar terms, as an elastic fluid or imponderable. In this way, investigators made electricity into a substance they could visualize, as if it were an oddly fine, dry, and crackling form of water. But how could they explain it? Answering the question might define electricity and, even better, shed light on the universal construction of matter. Was electricity akin to Newton's aether, the subtle fluid that pervaded the universe and helped explain physical things? Or might electrical matter show new things about all of matter, challenging natural philosophers to redefine their theories?[78]

By the 1740s, electrical investigations had become a kind of craze. Demonstrators' equipment and vocabulary had grown fairly complicated. To experiment with electricity, natural philosophers (and popular demonstrators such as Archibald Spencer) produced it by revolving a large and smooth piece of rounded glass against their hands or a padded surface. An experimenter could then put the electrostatic charge through something—sometimes a metal rod, sometimes a light person (a child, for instance) suspended in silk cords. By 1739, an Englishman had coined the terms *conductor* and *insulator* to indicate which substances did or did not carry a charge.[79]

An illustration within an electric treatise of 1748 showed some of these experiments. At the bottom right-hand corner, an assistant rotates a wheel connected to a glass globe, which spins against an experimenter's hand. The consequent electrostatic charge travels through a metal rod, or conductor. A man standing on an insulating platform grasps the end of the conductor and conveys the charge into his upraised sword, with which he ignites spirits of alcohol that a woman, who is grounded, holds in a spoon. Above them, two children are demonstrating electricity's effects on chaff. The boy, insulated on a disk of pitch or wax, holds the end of the conductor. He proffers a plate with the chaff in his other hand. The girl, who is grounded, holds another plate above, and the chaff is mysteriously suspended in midair.

The invention of the Leyden jar in 1746 made electrical experiments even more exciting—and dangerous. This jar was usually a glass container coated with metal plate or foil and filled with water or small pieces of metal shot. (The jar, or sometimes bottle, showed investigators' conviction that electricity was a fluid.) The apparatus dramatically condensed an electrical charge. With the Leyden jar, "electricians" could see what a stronger electrical force did to the array of materials they had already been testing.[80]

Electrical demonstrators reexamined many of the questions about fluids and particles that Franklin had already considered. It was particularly puzzling that electricity exhibited both attraction and repulsion, the two concepts Newton had used to explain gravity.

Electrical amusements. William Watson, *Expériences et observations . . .
[sur] l'électricité* (1748). HARVARD COLLEGE LIBRARY.

Before he died in 1727, Newton had made many and not always matching statements about electricity. Some of those statements asserted that electricity showed how attraction and repulsion could occur in the same substance, but others were not convinced. Some investigators concluded that there were, in fact, two electrical fluids: electrical attraction and repulsion lay in separate, if related, substances. And Newton's posthumous critics used electricity to attack his theories. French Cartesians, above all the Abbé Jean-Antoine Nollet (soon to be Franklin's nemesis), insisted that explanations of electricity should stick to mechanical causes, not unseen forces. Nollet proposed that there was only one electrical substance but that it had two streams, outgoing ("effluent") and incoming ("affluent"), depending on the material that generated them.[81]

All of this serious electrical work coexisted with extremely popular feats of autoexperimentation and audience participation. One trick, the Venus Electrificata, ran a light charge over a lady, who could then "repulse" any gentleman bold enough to "salute" her with a kiss. Demonstrations of Leyden jars knocked children backward, stunned trusting assistants, killed small animals, and sent charges through astonishing numbers of hand-holding people. In 1746, Nollet reported that he made 200 monks jump and yelp. No wonder Franklin had been entranced when he saw Spencer reveal the electrical fire in Boston. No wonder he jumped at the chance to play with fire himself.[82]

But this kind of experiment was more complicated than anything Franklin had done with his Pennsylvania fireplace. For the new experiments, he would need collaborators, special equipment, an experimental space, and patronage. It was extremely fortunate that he had already managed to guarantee his access to all four.

Fairy godmothers give glass slippers; Peter Collinson, the English patron of the Library Company, gave his American godchildren a glass "electric tube." Collinson was, of course, in the habit of sending books and equipment to the library. The glass cylinder he now sent would, when rotated against hands or padding, generate static electricity. The tube arrived early in 1747 and was probably intended for general use. But it was Franklin who, in March, wrote the note thanking Collinson for his "kind present" and "directions for using it." This is the first extant letter between the two men, initiating a correspondence in which Franklin documented his electrical experiments—and made himself Collinson's most important American client. Soon after, in July, Thomas Penn, the proprietor of the colony, sent an apparatus, probably one in which the tube could be mounted and rotated. "I never was before engaged in any study," Franklin reported, "that so totally engrossed my attention and my time."[83]

It was quite an operation: collaborative, sociable, and located in the heart of public life. Franklin named his fellow experimenters, about whom we know quite a bit, but was unhelpfully vague on the place of the experiments, which, as it turns out, has since been demolished. Franklin's three collaborators were Thomas Hopkinson, Philip Syng, and Ebenezer Kinnersley. Hopkinson was a lawyer, Syng a silversmith (and Junto founder), and Kinnersley a Baptist minister and itinerant electrical demonstrator. Together, the four "electricians" embodied head and hands professions, the sciences, and religion.[84]

The Library Company still lacked its own building. Only later would its members use rooms at Philadelphia's Carpenter's Hall and, still later, build the group's current house. In the meantime, the company convened in the west wing of the State House (where the assembly met), on its second floor. The house's two wing buildings were pulled down in the early nineteenth century; early twentieth-century reproductions now sit where they once did. The second floor of the west wing measured about fifty by twenty-two feet and was divided into two rooms. The best estimate of the size of the room where electricity snapped in the 1740s is that it was perhaps twenty by ten feet. The room would have accommodated a table to hold the electrostatic equipment, half a dozen or so active people who could comfortably move about the table, and spectators who could stand or sit along the walls. Thus, in the colony's center of government, Philadelphians could perform and witness experimental philosophy in action.[85]

In the very first experiments, the ones Franklin described in his first substantial letter to Collinson, he and Hopkinson made their first distinctive observation of "the wonderful Effect of Points [pointed bodies] both in *drawing* off and *throwing* off the Electrical Fire." The Library Company men discovered this effect when they placed a piece of iron shot, three or four inches in size, "on the Mouth of a clean dry Glass Bottle." Then, attaching a silk thread to the ceiling, they suspended a marble-sized "Cork Ball" to rest on the side of the shot. They electrified the shot and saw the cork jerk back four or five inches, "more or less according to the Quantity of Electricity."[86]

Then someone extended "a long, slender, sharp Bodkin," or metal pin, within six or eight inches of the piece of shot: "The Repellency is instantly destroy'd, and the Cork flies to" the shot. (In the dark, the bodkin glowed as it approached.) A "blunt Body" had to be placed "within an Inch, and draw a Spark to produce the same Effect." Moreover, a metal conductor had no effect unless it was attached to some other substance, such as wood, that was a non-conductor.[87]

The Philadelphians discovered other ways to break the charge around an electrified object. They breathed on the air around the shot, sifted sand over it, waved woodsmoke toward it, plunged it in darkness, and lighted it with a candle—all of these did seem to weaken the charge. But sunlight thrown off a mirror had no effect. And smoke from rosin did not affect the repulsion "but [was] attracted by both the Shot and the Cork-ball, forming proportionable Atmospheres round them," as in diagrams of the planets "in Burnets or Whiston's Theory of the Earth."[88]

The point of the experiments was to visualize electricity, the invisible fluid—fleeting even when it flashed in the dark. The experimenters sought their quarry by exposing it to different conditions, seeing its reactions, and then assigning it traits. The American experimenters had to verify experiments done in Europe (the directions Collinson had sent with the electric tube had described previous experiments and their terminology, *electrify* and *electrise*). And they needed to show that electricity had universal properties; stones had to fall in America as they did in Europe. The Philadelphia experiments were important in confirming that electricity exhibited repulsion, the size and strength of which could be manipulated (as when a bodkin approached an electrified object). They also revealed which materials were conductors or nonconductors of electricity.

But Franklin's group had also revealed two new properties of electricity: the significance of pointed objects and the importance of nonconductors. Each finding established greater experimental precision. Yes, metal conducted electricity, but a metal point probed the subtle fluid more subtly: the smaller the conductor, the greater its effect on electricity. And the probe performed best when it was itself grounded, placed within a nonconducting substance. Earlier experiments had established that metal conducted electricity and wood did not; the Library Company experimenters helped show that the shape and interaction of these materials were relevant, too.

Franklin next tackled the biggest question of all: What kind of matter was the electrical fluid? To answer this, he modified an experiment described in the text Collinson had sent. In that trial, the experimenters had stood a man on a nonconducting layer of pitch and then electrified him; anyone who tried to lay a finger on him felt a painful charge. The experiment established that electricity could be artificially concentrated in something as ordinary as a human body. But that did not reveal what it was or where it came from. Did the machine generate it? Or did it already lurk within the air, floor, walls, or experimenters?

Franklin and his associates did the experiment again. They stood their electrified man on a slab of wax and got the same results. But then they put two men on two wax slabs. One man put his hands against the rotating electric tube, and the other took the "fire" from the machine's conductor. Surprise! They carried different charges.

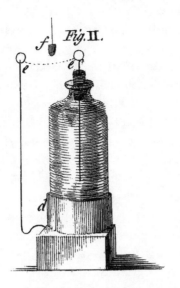

Franklin's Leyden jar experiment. Benjamin Franklin,
New Experiments and Observations on Electricity (1754).
HOUGHTON LIBRARY, HARVARD UNIVERSITY.

Each of the two was electrified—a third person felt a painful shock
on trying to touch either—but they could also shock each other.[89]

From this experiment, Franklin argued that electrical matter was
present everywhere yet in two different quantities, negative and positive. The man who rubbed the electric tube was "electrised . . . *negatively*" because he had given his "fire" to the tube; conversely, the
man who received the charge from the conductor was "electrised
positively"—he had an excess. Two humans had divided the fluid and
then brought it back together, with a snap, when they touched. Positive and negative charges were also revealed when these two people
approached a third person insulated on wax, who had the usual
(meaning equally mixed) distribution of charge—more snaps.[90]

Franklin illustrated these principles in a demonstration with a
Leyden jar. He placed a jar on a nonconducting base, ran a wire up
from its outside bottom, charged the water inside, and then ran a
second wire from inside and through its stopper. He let a suspended
bit of cork play between the two wires and their different charges,
carrying the positive charge from top to bottom until the "Equilibrium" was restored and the cork rested.[91]

From this experiment, Franklin argued that electricity's two states could exist anywhere and were necessary to create an equilibrium, meaning the usual form of electricity itself. "If the Persons standing on Wax touch one another during the exciting of the Tube, neither of them will appear to be electrised" because both were: "The Equality is never destroyed, the Fire only circulating" from tube to human. In electricity itself, the "*plus* and *minus* [were] combined and ballanced"; if separated, the charges returned to "Equilibrium" or "the original Equality." Here is where the concept of fluid circulation helped Franklin visualize electricity, as something that did not change or vanish but simply moved in streams. As well, he stressed that an "Atmosphere" existed around an electrified body and governed its reactions to other bodies that might disrupt this equilibrium. His earlier experiments with heat (which also circulated, formed equilibria, and generated atmospheres) had clearly prepared him to see electricity in these particular ways.[92]

Above all, Franklin thought his experiments helped establish knowledge about all matter. Those pointed bodkins confirmed that the electric fluid (and other matter) was composed of particles. The points, because of their narrowed ends, drew electricity "Particle by Particle," whereas a blunt instrument had the opposite effect. The electric fluid was a perfect example of an imponderable, that is, a weightless, elastic substance. Yet it was distinctive because it had particles that were mutually repellent, hence its positive and negative qualities. And electricity was opposed to solid, or "ponderable," matter. Each attracted the other—"common Matter is a Kind of a Spunge to the Electrical Fluid." The latter's material was "extreamly subtile" and therefore able, like heat, to "permeate common Matter." A doubter could be convinced by receiving, in the common matter of his or her flesh, "a shock from an electrified Glass Jar."[93]

The glass of that jar itself hinted at matter's construction. A rotating glass tube could generate an electrostatic charge, but a residual charge would remain in the glass. Franklin demonstrated this by charging a Leyden jar and then pouring its water into another glass vessel. Which was now electrified? Not the one with the water but the original, emptied of the visible fluid but not the invisible fluid of electricity. It was not, after all, the water that contained the electricity. Franklin pondered the implications. "If that due Quantity of Electrical Fire so obstinately retained by Glass, could be separated from it, [perhaps] it would no longer be Glass," he speculated. If, somehow, electricity could be poured out of all other matter, material reality might alter. There was no way to do that experiment, but it was quite an idea! Lacking a divine ability to drain electrical matter from the universe, Franklin simply observed that a battery need not be shaped like a jar or bottle. In a rare moment of agreement with Nollet, Franklin stated that electricity was a fluid that could exist within planes, as with sheets of glass and metal sandwiched together.[94]

From bits of cork, metal, and glass, using their own breath and hands, Franklin and the other Library Company experimenters made some astonishingly assured claims about the nature of matter. Newton had hypothesized that electricity was a great force running through the cosmos, perhaps even unifying the other forces he examined, light and gravity. Franklin had defined protocols for investigating these possibilities—he had made electrical experimentation into a science. The sciences still revealed the wonderful nature of Creation, but the wonders apparently could be controlled and measured. And Franklin had proposed an elegant way to understand electricity—as one fluid with two qualities, negative and positive, that were beautifully balanced in nature. The theory needed neither multiple fluids nor the Cartesian hypothesis of differently configured particles in order to explain electricity's effects on other forms of matter.

Yet again, Franklin had discovered an equilibrium. Money, heat, electricity—all circulated, and all returned to a state of balance. A flow of analogical reasoning had brought Franklin to his definitions of positive and negative charges. Because his theory passed from his era to ours—it survived him—we now think of electrical circuits and of positive and negative charges as natural, as simply the way electricity occurs. But these explanations of electricity were highly contingent. Circulation and equilibrium had not always existed as concepts within natural philosophy. Yet they emerged in time for Franklin to use them to describe electricity. Moreover, he had already tested those concepts in his economic writings and his work with heating systems.

If electricity had been more thoroughly investigated earlier or if its accepted definitions had come later, maybe we would now be thinking that other concepts were "natural" explanations of it—the four humors, perhaps, or capital accumulation. Franklin's contribution was brilliant because it immediately made sense to his contemporaries, who were likewise weaned on Harvey, Petty, Sanctorius, and Newton—not because he invented concepts specifically for electricity.

As well as brilliant, the Philadelphia experiments were highly sociable. The tests needed a cast of characters: thinkers to design and modify the experiments, standers to perch on wax, rotaters to turn the glass tube, and observers to point out what the nervous and excited experimenters might be missing. And everything depended on a transatlantic economy—note the variety of imported commodities, the electric tube especially but also the silk, cork, mirror, and glass bottle. (To lessen the experimenters' dependence on imports, Franklin encouraged a local glassmaker, Caspar Wistar, to make more electric tubes.) Unlike in electrical experimentation in Europe, men dominated the Philadelphia experiments. An occasional Venus Electrificata did, however, help show that the Philadelphians could "encrease the Force of the electrical Kiss vastly."[95]

There was no shortage of electrical standers or kissers. People came "continually in crouds" to see the experiments, which spilled over into Franklin's house. His letters to Collinson used plural pronouns—"us" and "we"—to describe his efforts. Thus, it is impossible for us to know exactly who did what. (Did Franklin stand on a slab of wax? Did his collaborators shock him and laugh?) But the anonymous plural pronouns assured Collinson (and others) that many people saw and believed the American demonstrations. Even when he performed some experiments "alone," Franklin made a point of "repeating them to my Friends and Acquaintance," all of whom appeared in Franklin's communications to Collinson: "We fire Spirits with the Wire of the Phial. We light Candles just blown out, by drawing a Spark. . . . We represent Lightning. . . . We electrise a Person. . . . We encrease the Force." Even in his first letter to Collinson, Franklin had remarked that the electric tube had "put several of us on making electrical experiments, in which we have observed some particular phaenomena that we look upon to be new."[96]

Through his experiments, he cleverly transformed his provinciality into a philosophical asset. True, he lived on the far edge of the British empire, but that meant he was able to give "an Account of American Electricity." Just as stones fell in Europe and America alike, so "it is now discovered and demonstrated, both here and in

Europe, that the Electrical Fire is a real Element, or Species of Matter, not *created* by the Friction [of the generator], but *collected* only."[97]

Franklin knew he was doing something unprecedented. Midway through the seminal electrical experiments of 1747 and 1748, he retired from his printing business. He now had considerable assets, including his house and printshop. A private business would still make him money, but he no longer needed it. And the business took up time, made him seem more like a worker than a philosopher, and raised the question of whether he might force into print philosophical ideas that no one else would publish. So on January 1, 1748, Franklin and David Hall, who had progressed from being Franklin's journeyman to his foreman, signed "Articles of Agreement." The document made them partners, each receiving a share of the printing business's income, but Hall would thenceforth be the active partner. (The friendship between the two men was clear in the statement that "the said Benjamin and David" entered a new business connection.) Not until he set up a press in France in 1779 would Franklin again have a printshop of his own.[98]

Yet having given up working with his hands, Franklin showcased their value in his experiments. His hands and fingers became electrical equipment. Because of the stigma of manual labor, the hand was still a complicated body part. Even quite rarified manual tasks were considered rather low. (One splendid snob dismissed musical talents in this way: "Those Embellishments are more *noble* and *rich* that lie in the Brain, than those that sink into the Feet, or *perch* on the Finger's End.") Amateur status in the sciences distinguished gentlemen from those who generated income by use of their hands.[99]

Hands were nevertheless acquiring dignity within the sciences. Experimenters grew accustomed to manipulating things. They even regarded their hands (and bodies) as sensitive indicators of whatever phenomena interested them. In doing so, they knew that their actions made them resemble artisans and manual laborers, who were referred to as "hands." (In his first substantial letter to Collinson, Franklin had punned that "many Hands" on both sides of the Atlantic were busy with electrical experiments.) Like Freemasons, experimenters emulated skilled laborers without eliding any social boundaries between workers and men of science. For a former "leather apron" to do this took some nerve—and newfound confidence—both of which Franklin, now retired from his printshop, had in abundance.[100]

In one of his longest letters on electricity, he referred many times to the necessity of actually touching various mechanisms in order to detect an electrical current or to redirect it. Electricity could be drawn out of a "Bottle" (Leyden jar) "by touching the Wire" protruding from its top. Another electrical device would emit a charge at a distance up to two inches, "a pretty hard Stroke, so as to make one's Knuckle ache." Franklin loaned the rest of his body to science when he filled a glass vial with a "Purgative" (laxative or emetic), charged it up, then "took repeated Shocks from it" to see if the purgative effect would pass electrically into his body. It did not. Franklin had to content himself with feeling electrical currents wash through his body and with surviving an electrical "Blow" that briefly knocked him out while he was trying to electrocute a turkey—Thomas Tryon's revenge?[101]

THROUGHOUT HIS LIFE, Franklin began his experiments indoors and then took them outside, to the greater natural world. This was the case for his two first experiments, both of which began in a room and then moved out into the larger atmosphere; thus with heat, so with electricity.

He pursued the electric fluid outdoors. In an early 1749 letter to John Mitchell, on "a new Hypothesis for explaining the several Phaenomena of Thunder Gusts," Franklin explored the atmospheric behaviors of electricity, air, and water, both fresh and salt. He analyzed these forms of matter as particulate and as differently disposed to electricity. Electricity "loves Water" and so was attracted to it; air was itself electric, so it was less attractive. But when water was electrified, it rose into the air in the form of clouds. Not all clouds were equally charged, however, and Franklin thought those arising from saltwater tended to be more so than freshwater clouds.[102]

If these clouds encountered something less electrified, such as a mountain range, the obstacle would draw down the water as rain and the electricity as lightning and thunder. Franklin used as an example the storms along the eastern Andes, which intercepted "all the Clouds brought against them from the Atlantic Ocean, by the Trade Winds." (He had probably learned about the Andes from La Condamine, who had written about smallpox among Indians in Peru.) Like mountains, clouds formed from freshwater would draw electricity, again with thunder and lightning. "If the foregoing Hypothesis be a true one," he wrote, "there ought to be but little Thunder and Lightning far at Sea."[103]

Note, within this brief explanation, Franklin's accumulated interests: particles, electricity, an atmosphere, circulation of air, Atlantic storms. There was as yet no clear explanation of the behavior of electricity up in the earth's atmosphere—whoever could provide one would make a signal contribution to philosophy by revealing that electrical matter did seem to pervade all of creation. Franklin would be the one to make this contribution in experiments that represented the culmination of his reading and investigation into physical circulation.

On the same day he wrote to Mitchell, Franklin wrote Collinson that the Philadelphia electricians had celebrated their labors with a picnic on the Schuylkill River. The frolic marked a seasonal end to electrical investigations, with "hot Weather" making indoor experimentation "not so agreable." The party arrived on the riverbank with plenty of provisions—and equipment. Using electricity, they killed and roasted a turkey and then ate it while enjoying wine in "Electrified Bumpers" that tickled the lips of the quaffer, "if the Party be close shaved, and does not breathe on the Liquor." For many people, all this would have been fun enough. But those irrepressible pranksters could not resist running some electricity through the river in order to ignite, with a dramatic flash, some spirits of alcohol on the opposite bank.[104]

It was a lovely flourish, that trans-Schuylkill flash. It summed up so many of Franklin's interests in physical circulation. And it symbolized the letter that recorded it, an over-the-water salute to Collinson, distant patron of the experiments that had taught Franklin's circle how to send fire through water. The picnic also embodied the Philadelphians' claim to universal knowledge: they brought their indoor activities out into the larger world. Indeed, given that he wrote to Mitchell about the "Phaenomena of Thunder Gusts" on the same April day that he wrote Collinson about the picnic, we can imagine Franklin looking to the skies during the frolic. The weather and the electricity were linked in his mind, just as he and other Philadelphians braced themselves for the muggy season of thunder and lightning.

Chapter 5

THE FRANKLIN PARADOX

TWO MONTHS LATER, it was too hot to picnic. On June 18, 1749, the temperature in Philadelphia reached "100 in the shade." Some mad dogs and English settlers may have gone out in the noonday sun, but Franklin stayed home. "I sat in my chamber without exercise, only reading or writing," he later wrote a friend, recalling that he stripped down to "a shirt, and a pair of long linen drawers." He was still too warm. "The windows [were] all open, and a brisk wind blowing through the house, the sweat ran off the backs of my hands, and my shirt was often so wet, as to induce me to call for dry ones to put on."[1]

Franklin's recollection of the sweltering summer of 1749, which he related almost nine years later, registered physical discomfort and an almost unbearable tension between action and inaction. As he sat sweating in his underwear, he was waiting for something to happen.

It finally did: the two letters he had written to Mitchell and Collinson on April 29, 1749, would that autumn be the first of his two read at the Royal Society of London. At forty-three, Franklin had his long-awaited metropolitan audience. Then the letters, along with most of the others he had written to Collinson, were published, first in London and then in France. Celebrity of every kind followed. In the period between 1749 and 1757 (when he reentered London as a recognized "genius"), Franklin achieved fame as a natural philosopher. He joined the international republic of letters— and immediately became its most important British colonial member. Through his prowess in natural philosophy, he came to exemplify universal knowledge. And the fact that a colonist of obscure birth could ascend to this status lent credibility to the idea that nearly anyone could comprehend the new science.

As he was proclaimed a philosopher and genius, Franklin plunged into politics. "I shall never *ask*, never *refuse*, nor ever *resign* an Office," he promised, a good way to ensure he would be busy, too busy for the experimental science that had made his political authority possible. It was the Franklin paradox: his fame made him unable to continue working in the area that had made him famous. Instead, many of Franklin's subsequent interests in the sciences— cartography, hydrography (the science of bodies of water, an ancestor of oceanography), and political arithmetic—did double duty in the political realm. At the time, politics meant empire, and all of Franklin's new interests in science had imperial implications. They helped to determine which places the British would rule and which people would benefit from that rule. These were no small questions as North America headed into the cataclysmic Seven Years' War, the most important geopolitical event of Franklin's lifetime.[2]

———————

HAVING his letters read at the Royal Society gave Franklin his first notable publicity, yet his initial statement on electricity and meteorology had appeared slightly earlier, in a surprising (and still overlooked) place—Lewis Evans's 1749 *Map of Pensilvania, New-Jersey, New-York, and the Three Delaware Counties*. Why a map—and why this map?

Cartography was yet another of the eighteenth century's momentous contributions to modern science. We now unfold maps confident that they accurately represent physical places. But it was only during Franklin's lifetime that maps were so defined, as direct representations of what the eye supposedly sees when it scans the earth. So powerful was this new vision that mapping became a metaphor for a thorough survey of anything. Ephraim Chambers had called his *Cyclopedia* "a map of knowledge"; Diderot and d'Alembert claimed their *Encyclopédie* was "a kind of world map." And actual maps were now the product of surveys that measured space on the earth and then transcribed it on paper. Surveyors used triangulation to determine positions among three visible objects, then another three, and so on, in order to generate a topographical field in which the distances among places were proportionate to their placement on the land itself. Sometimes, the surveys addressed more abstract questions; the field of geodesy, for instance, determined the size and shape of the earth.[3]

Pennsylvania as center of empire. Lewis Evans, *Map of Pensilvania,*
New-Jersey, New-York, and the Three Delaware Counties (1749).
HARVARD MAP COLLECTION.

The idea of measuring the world emerged in an age of wild imperial competition. Maps attempted to provide order amid the chaos.
Cartography was the offspring of a complicated marriage of science
and politics. People proclaimed the sciences to be universal, above

nation and party, but they then embedded them within political concerns—and quarreled over the way to do so. A single map or other representation of nature could easily do all three things, that is, make a universal claim, score a partisan point, and deplore someone else's partisan point.

The globe was a contested place; maps recorded the contests and were also weapons used in them. Europeans could not even agree on a prime meridian, a zero point from which a cartographer could calculate longitude, or east-west positions. (Latitude was easier—since antiquity, the equator had been the zero point.) Until the nineteenth century, when Europeans accepted a prime meridian at Greenwich, England, that point could be—and was—placed anywhere. In the meantime, European powers were essentially mapping their quarrels with each other, as when they put the prime meridian through their capitals. Even as they did so, they agreed that their surveys could claim non-European land for their empires, appropriating or erasing non-European views of territory as well as the territory itself.[4]

The globe we would recognize, one of fixed units of measurement and clearly demarcated zones, was nevertheless coming into view. Cartographers began to use the words *continent* and *ocean* to describe discrete masses of land and water; they linked the terms to proper names, such as Asia or Atlantic. They mapped the globe's physical traits (as with magnetic or barometric variation) in order to visualize patterns within nature. And they took a new interest in precise, fixed national boundaries, at a time when wars over these borders shed enough blood to stain all eighteenth-century maps crimson.[5]

These were grand imperial goals, but colonists had their own and distinctive view of what maps should accomplish. They identified themselves in a middle position between high imperial strategy and practical local needs—and they definitely inscribed those needs on their maps. By the 1740s, Franklin and other Pennsylvanians worried that their colony's original borders, which William Penn had carefully negotiated with the Delaware Indians, were too restrictive. The colonists wanted to expand outward, which was bound to bring them into conflict with Native Americans and with French settlers farther west. Since 1689, conflict between France and Britain had been escalating—war was an almost routine occurrence in the colonies, as Franklin had acknowledged at least since he had published *Plain Truth.*

Franklin also knew very well that maps played a significant role in the politics of empire. In 1746, he ordered, for the Pennsylvania Assembly, two sets of Henry Popple's *A Map of the British Empire in America with the French and Spanish Settlements Adjacent Thereto* (1733). He also wanted "some other large Map of the whole World" of equal size to Popple's, "they being to be hung, one on each side the Door in the Assembly Room" so the assemblymen could see the whole world, see Pennsylvania's place in it, and see its borders with its French and Spanish competitors.[6]

Lewis Evans, a Welsh-born draftsman and surveyor, shrewdly judged this a good moment to produce a regional map locally. Evans had gone to Franklin's shop in 1736 to buy a copy of Edward Cocker's *Arithmetick* (the same book Franklin had studied as an adolescent), and somehow, he became a clerk in the shop. Gradually, the two men became collaborators and friends; Deborah Franklin was godmother to Evans's daughter, Amelia. Evans had executed one of the diagrams for Franklin's 1744 pamphlet on the Pennsylvania fireplace and copied all of Franklin's reports on electricity to make a 155-page manuscript for James Bowdoin of Massachusetts, who was fast becoming one of Franklin's most important American correspondents by the end of the 1740s. Franklin also sold Evans books on mathematics and surveying, which helped him prepare for his survey of the middle colonies.[7]

To make his survey, Evans joined a 1743 expedition that also included John Bartram and Conrad Weiser, the colony's main contact with Indians. Bartram quietly botanized; Weiser negotiated with Algonquian- and Iroquoian-speaking natives. Evans had the shadiest task: measuring Indian land without telling its owners what he was doing. He would use his survey to claim for Pennsylvania land that was disputed among colonial officials, Indian traders, and the Indians themselves. (This encroachment was particularly unfair to the Delaware, who had recently been cheated out of a vast expanse of territory in the so-called Walking Purchase. The Delaware had agreed to cede land but only to the extent that a man could walk in a day; the Pennsylvanians arranged men to cover ground in relay to guarantee that the "man" and the "walk" would yield the greatest amount of territory.) Native Americans knew all too well that colonists had designs on their land, so how Weiser explained Evans's surveying instruments to them is anyone's guess.[8]

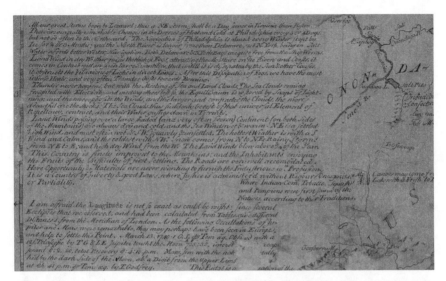

Putting electricity on the map. Close-up of Evans's map (top left corner).
HARVARD MAP COLLECTION.

It took six years for Evans to map the results of his survey, during which Franklin advised him about its preparation. David Hall, who ran Franklin's printshop after 1748, probably produced the map, using an engraving by Lawrence Hebert. The final product presented the three colonies of the mid-Atlantic, plus part of Delaware; it also indicated waterways and mountains as, respectively, conduits and barriers for anyone pushing westward. Above all, the map implied a potential British control over territory extending hundreds of miles inland. Evans used both British and colonial measures to stake his claims. He provided two readings of longitude: on the very bottom of the map, he indicated longitude as drawn from London (in defiance of French territorial claims), and on the top, he indicated it as drawn from the State House in Philadelphia. Franklin's hope that Philadelphia might become the center of the American colonies was now rendered on paper.[9]

Evans then added to his map a philosophical flourish, courtesy of Franklin. The left-hand side of the map offered a compressed version of Franklin's explanation of Atlantic storms, which he had sketched at the end of his electrical experiments. The text noted the prevailing northeast direction of the storms, asserted the presence of electricity in the "Sea Clouds" that collided with "Land Clouds" to create lightning and thunder (thus restoring the "Equilibrium"), and depicted the general directions of winds along the Atlantic coast. Franklin's first statement on electricity was also his first venture into cartography—early evidence that he thought about science and empire together. Yet if Franklin had wanted to begin contributing to printed works that would survive longer than almanacs, maps were an odd choice. The Evans map was not produced in very large quantities, and it was made to be used. In consequence, surviving copies are now rare and not in the best condition.[10]

Even before the Evans map, Franklin had been thinking about Atlantic storms for some time. He had intended to explain them to Jared Eliot, a Connecticut clergyman and physician, another in Franklin's expanding network of correspondents. In a letter of 1747, Franklin told Eliot that storms along the Atlantic coast moved southwest to northeast (up the coast of North America) even though the prevailing winds blew northeast to southwest, "i.e. the Air is in violent Motion in Virginia before it moves in Connecticut" even as the wind itself seemed to move in the opposite direction. There were exceptions, he noted, but the pattern was frequent, and the worst storms were always leeward rather than windward. Franklin promised to give Eliot "Reasons for this Opinion" in his next letter but then became too entranced by electricity to do so.[11]

Eliot waited almost two years before he learned Franklin's "Reasons." In 1750, Franklin finally related how he had wanted to observe a lunar eclipse several years earlier. He was foiled by a sudden storm that, blowing northeastward, drew clouds over the moon. He was then surprised to learn that the eclipse had been visible in Boston—why, if the storm came from the northeast, had it not obscured skies in Boston earlier than in Philadelphia? By questioning travelers and correspondents, he found that this was "a constant Fact, that N East Storms begin to Leeward; and are often more violent there than farther to Windward." The reason, he believed, lay far to the south, in the Gulf of Mexico and the Florida straits. There, air was "heated by the Sun," and being thus "rarified," it drifted northward, where it met the "chill'd and condens'd" air over the British colonies. The collision sent the warm air still higher even as the cool draft sank, with each current tending in the opposite direction, warm to the north and cold to the south. This created a whirling corkscrew, with cooler eddies that curled under, slinking northeast to southwest.[12]

These descriptions of Atlantic storms betray their intellectual ancestry. Both Franklin's 1726 observation of drifting gulfweed and his experiments with heat had primed him to see storms as products of thermal variation and circulation. Franklin's letter to Eliot even compared windflow along North America's coast to the way in which "a Fire in my Chimney" created an upper outflow of heat that eventually met a cooler, lower "Current of Air constantly flowing from the Door to the Chimney." Like a Pennsylvania fireplace, North America channeled currents of air. The Appalachian range, running from northeast to southwest and parallel to the coast, helped propel winds alongside the "Continent." Again, Franklin had generated universal principles from local observations.[13]

Perhaps Atlantic storms might reveal more general properties of nature, particularly when they produced electricity. How did storm clouds become electrified? When they were, did they tend to carry a positive or a negative charge? If clouds could carry a charge, Franklin reasoned, electricity must exist in the atmosphere. Lightning, which certainly looked like a spiky electrical discharge, was just that.

Friction explained everything. In the early 1750s, Franklin explained to several correspondents that atmospheric electricity made sense if one assumed, as he did, that matter was made of particles. The sea clouds that seemed to generate electricity were, for example, constituted of water and salt; the particles of each coexisted without transforming one another. "The separate Particles of Water" were like "hard Spherules, capable of touching the Salt only in Points" where their outside curves touched. (See his "Fig. VI" on the plate of illustrations that accompanied his *Experiments and Observations.*) The friction they created had to produce atmospheric electricity, Franklin theorized, much as the friction between a revolving glass "Globe" and a "Cushion" produced static electricity. Saltwater thus had "constituent Particles of Salt and Water (as in a Sea of Globes and Cushions)." Franklin realized that this finding meant "there must be Interstices" within any form of matter, "yet the Mass incompressible." In 1753, he would portray air, which conducted electricity, as doing so through its "Particles," which "in hard Gales of Wind," friskily rubbed themselves against things like trees and houses "as [if] so many minute electric Globes, rubbing against non-electric Cushions."[14]

So Franklin had a hypothesis. What he needed next was an experiment to demonstrate that electricity did occur in the atmosphere,

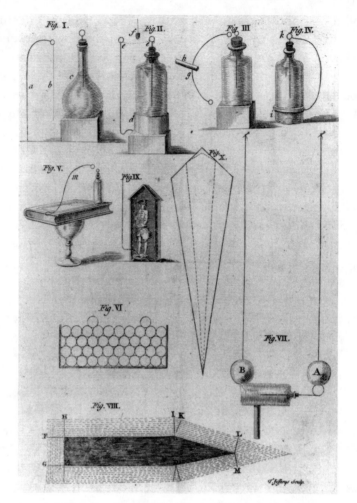

Electrical points, made in Philadelphia. Benjamin Franklin,
New Experiments and Observations on Electricity (1754).
HOUGHTON LIBRARY, HARVARD UNIVERSITY.

most dramatically as lightning. He would propose elevating a
pointed metal rod into the clouds to conduct atmospheric electricity downward, where its properties could be verified.

In July 1750, Franklin suggested an experiment "on the Top of
some high Tower or Steeple." There, an investigator would stand on
an insulated floor within a "Sentry Box" (see Franklin's "Fig. IX"
above) that supported an ascending metal rod with a point. The
pointed rod would, like an experimental bodkin ("Fig. VIII"), draw
electricity down in a particulate stream, making the sentry equally
(but not fatally) "electrified" with the atmosphere.[15]

Collinson had this protocol read to the Royal Society—further evidence that Franklin's work mattered in the metropolis. Then, Edward Cave published all of Franklin's electrical letters in April 1751 as *Experiments and Observations on Electricity, Made at Philadelphia in America, by Mr. Benjamin Franklin* . . . , edited and introduced by London physician John Fothergill, Fellow of the Royal Society (FRS), who seems to have done so at Collinson's request. After this edition appeared in London, it was translated into French and published in Paris in 1752. These printed instructions invited (or perhaps dared) interested men of science to try Franklin's experiments, including the sentry box test.[16]

Who would risk it? Several Frenchmen, as it turned out, were willing to do so. Franklin had the good fortune to be caught up, perhaps unwittingly, in a distant battle between French Cartesians and Newtonians. The Cartesians blocked acceptance of Newtonianism in France. They ridiculed universal gravitation and championed instead their master's assertion that vortices in elementary bits of matter explained everything. A few, including Pierre Louis Moreau de Maupertuis, defended Newton, arguing that gravitation must create a shortening of the earth's axis, resulting in the earth's fattening at the equator and flattening at the poles. Two geodesic expeditions, one to Peru in 1735 and the other to Lapland in 1736, set out to measure the earth. Charles-Marie de La Condamine went on the expedition to Peru that measured several degrees of the meridian near the equator, and Maupertuis led the venture that did the same in Arctic Lapland. Their measurements confirmed a shortening of the earth's axis.[17]

But the Cartesians fumed and refused to yield ground, insisting on their superior attention to mechanical causes—such as those underpinning the Abbé Nollet's theories of electricity—as opposed to vague Newtonian forces. The stalemate continued. The Newtonian Georges Leclerc (later Comte de Buffon) and the Cartesian Antoine Ferchault de Réaumur, who was Nollet's patron, had been sandbagging each other for years. Then, in 1751, Buffon read Franklin's essays and discovered something wonderful: a mere colonial, in far-off Philadelphia, had devised a convincing theory of electricity that supported Newton's claims. (Note the timing. War between France and Britain had ended in 1748—it was, politically, an uncontroversial moment for a Frenchman to sing the praises of a Pennsylvanian.) Buffon made sure an ally, Jean François Dalibard, translated Franklin's book. Then, in 1752, Buffon and Dalibard showed Franklin's indoor experiments to the king. This was a direct rebuke of Nollet, who was the king's official experimenter.[18]

In May 1752, Dalibard instructed an assistant to perform "the Philadelphia experiment" at Marly, outside Paris. The attempt worked: a pointed metal rod conducted atmospheric electricity down to the earth. A later experiment by a still-unidentified man named "Delor" in Paris confirmed the finding. Nollet sputtered and pointed out problems with Franklin's theory, including the odd concept of electrical atmospheres. What were these? What did they explain, anyway? Regardless, Dalibard and Delor published their results immediately, and Franklin was now famous in a place (and a way) he had never expected to be. Translated, the two French reports appeared in two London newspapers. June's *Gentleman's Magazine* featured a letter from a convert in Paris, who confessed how "we ridiculed Mr *Franklin's* project for emptying clouds of their thunder" and "could scarce conceive him to be any other than an imaginary Being." In August, the *London Magazine* version of the reports appeared in the *Pennsylvania Gazette*, Franklin's former paper. After a celebrated tour of Europe, the Philadelphia experiment had come home.[19]

What did Franklin think of the Descartes-Newton debate, the one that had made him a success? He didn't give a fart. He said so in 1780, when living in France. When he read some philosophical questions the Royal Academy of Brussels had just proposed, offering medals for the best replies, Franklin hooted at what he perceived as the preciousness of the mathematical question. It reminded him of the kind of sterile academic debate that had consumed the French Cartesians and Newtonians for almost half a century. So Franklin wrote a bagatelle, a slight and amusing essay, purporting to address "the Royal Academy of * * * * *" on the problem of human flatulence. "What Comfort can the Vortices of Descartes give to a Man who has Whirlwinds in his Bowels! The Knowledge of Newton's mutual *Attraction* of the Particles of Matter, can it afford Ease to him who is rack'd by their mutual *Repulsion,* and the cruel Distensions it occasions?"[20]

For decades, Franklin kept his indifference to the theories of his French detractors to himself, but then, he finally let it out. This gaseous essay is Franklin's only mention of Descartes, ever. Was he Newtonian? Yes. Was he anti-Cartesian? No, not really. Then, was he pro-Franklin? Ah, that was the whole point, the reason never to acknowledge criticism, starting with Nollet's.

Remember again Poor Richard's advice: make haste slowly. Franklin cared only for his own success, not the theories, objections, or resentments of others. He did seem to know something about the Cartesian-Newtonian debate. He followed the geodesic expeditions that, by measuring the flattening of the earth, indicated the force of gravity. He requested the account of Maupertuis's expedition from James Logan in 1748, and when he commented on Indians' susceptibility to smallpox in 1750, he cited La Condamine. He had followed the triumphs of these Newtonians just as he himself was making an impact in France.[21]

But he knew better than to claim a place in the debate. As he had learned as clerk in the Pennsylvania Assembly, passionate and prolonged argument on one side of a question could make enemies. The republic of letters expected its citizens to be sociable and to use wit and persuasion, not angry denunciation or guile. (This expectation was sometimes honored in the breach, as Buffon and Nollet had made very clear.) So Franklin carefully crafted his statements on nature, then let them fare for themselves, whatever detractors might say. He started to compose a letter to Nollet in 1754 but never sent it—hence his belated (and coded) comment on the Newton-Descartes debate in 1780, the closest he ever came to a response to Nollet.[22]

Yet given how much he wanted to promote himself, it must have been frustrating for him to contemplate, in 1752, that he could not even execute his own experiment, sticking a pointed probe into the clouds. Philadelphia, vexingly, lacked any site high enough for Franklin to do the demonstration, even when the city crackled with thunderstorms—the *Pennsylvania Gazette* for 1752 snapped with references to lightning and thunder.[23]

So Franklin thought of another method, his kite experiment. In two elegant paragraphs, he told readers of the *Pennsylvania Gazette* in the fall of 1752 how to build, from wood, cotton, silk, and metal, an electrical apparatus. "Make a small Cross of two light Strips of Cedar," he advised, and then knot to the frame a silk handkerchief and attach a wire point. This kite would conduct electricity down a cotton string terminating in a silk ribbon tied to a metal object, the famous key. The experimenter was to watch for a promising set of rumbling clouds and then send up the kite. The critical moment had arrived when the kite-string's fibers would "stand out every [which] Way"—it was electrified. The experimenter should then calmly allow the rain to wet the kite and string but *not* the ribbon and key, so that when the ribbon was lashed to the kite-string, "the Electric Fire" would "stream out plentifully from the Key on the Approach of your Knuckle."[24]

If this protocol seems sketchy, maybe that is because Franklin had forgotten to mention one very important element: an assistant (and witness). Twenty years after the *Pennsylvania Gazette* description of his kite had appeared, Franklin would assure electrical experimenter Joseph Priestley that he had flown one shortly after Dalibard's assistant had done the sentry box version but before news of this got back to him. When he made this claim, Franklin finally remembered to note that his son, William, had "assisted him in raising the kite."[25]

So we have to think of the experiment as a two-person operation, involving William (or "Wet") Franklin (WF) and Benjamin or ("Bone-dry") Franklin (BF). WF went out with the kite, set it aloft, watched for the prickling of fibers on its string, and then got everything thoroughly wet. Consequently, WF got soaked but could have contemplated his father's cheerful assertion that "a wet Rat can not be kill'd" by electricity "when a dry Rat may." Meanwhile, BF, the dry rat, stood inside some kind of shelter, keeping the ribbon and key dry. After WF sloshed inside, tugging the kite behind, BF attached the ribbon and key and presented a knuckle. Keep in mind that, in addition to an assistant, Franklin had something else he did not bother to explain: an almanac maker's keen awareness of the local weather. Trade knowledge mattered. How else could anyone decide whether clouds promised a thunderstorm that would stay at the right distance and height?[26]

Quickly, imitators of the two forms of the Philadelphia experiment generated multiple verifications that electricity existed in the atmosphere. As far as Franklin was concerned, this was indirect evidence that, if friction created static electricity, the same might be true of its atmospheric form. Again, he was addressing questions about the general nature of matter and the presence of electricity throughout the material creation. Here, however, his belief that indoor laboratory results could explain outdoor natural forces was beginning to strain the evidence.

From his indoor experiments, Franklin argued that, if pointed conductors drew electricity better than blunt ones, then they could drain electricity from clouds. This topic addressed a real problem—when lightning struck, it could cause terrifying and fatal damage. Franklin recommended the erection of pointed lightning rods atop buildings and ships. He first described these rods in *Poor Richard* for 1753. There, Richard Saunders dismissed any religious doubts that humanity should defy natural disaster. Indeed, he hinted at a divine revelation of lightning rods. "It has pleased God in his Goodness to Mankind," he preached, "at length to discover to them the Means of securing their Habitations and other Buildings from Mischief by Thunder and Lightning."[27]

Instructions followed. Alongside each building, an iron rod should be planted "three or four Feet in the moist Ground" and "six to eight Feet above the highest Part of the Building." That was a lot of costly metal, but Saunders added that the readily available lengths of iron that builders cut into nails were perfectly acceptable. Each should be topped by "a Foot of Brass Wire, the Size of a common Knitting-needle, sharpened to a fine Point." The same principle would protect a ship if a shorter rod was secured to its topmast and then an attached wire was run down into the water, which grounded it.[28]

Whenever atmospheric electricity ominously rumbled, pointed metal rods would discharge it. Individual houses or ships would be protected, and multiple rods in towns and cities provided collective benefit; together, they might prevent electricity in the atmosphere from building up in the first place. Franklin's insistence that lightning could be managed by ordinary building materials, familiar to anyone who paid the least attention to everyday items ("the Size of a common Knitting-needle"), showed his hope that his invention could serve anyone.

Franklin had demonstrated that atmospheric electricity existed and had recommended a way to limit its threat to life and property. But he found it harder to answer his other philosophical question: Did clouds carry a positive or negative charge? The answer would shed light on the formation of electricity and its interaction with other forms of matter. Was a positive or negative charge associated with the genesis of electricity? Franklin thought clouds were "*most commonly* in a negative State." But the electricity drawn from actual clouds was inconclusive. So he went back to indoor experiments. He had read of a way to generate vapors for experiments. He placed a brass plate on an electrified metal stand, heated the plate, and then sprinkled it with water. Franklin expected that the resulting steam would also be electrified. It never was, so he never satisfied himself as to whether clouds, when first generated, tended to be more frequently positive or negative in charge.[29]

Again, the underlying problem was the assumption that experiments indoors were analogous to nature outside. Franklin had, for instance, used the concept of an atmosphere, usually applied to the larger natural world, to explain electrical phenomena indoors. But these electrical "atmospheres" were, as the Abbé Nollet had pointed out, rather puzzling. In his first letter on his first electrical experiment, Franklin had asserted that an invisible force had to surround a charged body, as rosin smoke had revealed when it settled around a charged piece of iron shot.

Nonsense, declared Londoner John Canton, a self-taught experimenter and schoolmaster who greatly resembled Franklin (and would later meet him). Canton was the first to successfully repeat Franklin's experiments in England, and drawing electricity from the clouds, he discovered independently that clouds might be charged positively or negatively. But he disbelieved Franklin's idea of atmospheres and designed an experiment to disprove it.[30]

Canton hung a cylinder from insulated cords and suspended cork balls from it. He moved a charged glass rod toward the apparatus to see if it would break the atmosphere. Instead, the balls retreated gradually from its approach, ebbing and flowing, not breaking out of an atmosphere. He published the results in the 1753 *Philosophical Transactions*. Instead of being defensive or hurt, Franklin was so convinced by the evidence that he embraced Canton's criticism—and began a correspondence with him—and gamely improved the experiment by using silk tassels that spread at the approach of the glass rod and contracted when it was withdrawn. Franklin also eased the term "atmosphere" out of his descriptions of electricity. If his long study of heat and atmospheres had encouraged him to portray electrical force in an unconvincing way, he nonetheless knew when to relinquish the idea.[31]

Franklin was most fascinated by those parts of the earth's atmosphere he could never reach, even with the world's longest kite-string. The electrical experiments prompted him to speculate further on the composition of the earth's atmosphere, especially how the atmosphere might occur in distinct layers of air. A "lower Region of Air" was cooler than an "upper" one—the macrocosm's inversion of a cozy room heated by a Pennsylvania fireplace. The thermal variation created a dynamic field. In a 1749 letter to John Mitchell, Franklin had noted that the varying motions of clouds at different heights showed there were "different Currents of Air." Warmer air would rise in the tropics, and the denser and cooler air of northern areas would keep pushing it up until it arrived in polar regions, where it had to descend so "that the Circulation may be carried on." Considering the formation of rain and hail in 1753, Franklin ventured that there was, high in the atmosphere, a frigid zone where moisture froze.[32]

From this chilly level, Franklin pressed on to consider a higher, hotter layer above. He was puzzled that although he had demonstrated that atmospheric electricity existed, air itself did not easily conduct electricity. Something else must help do so—perhaps the aerial "Atmosphere" was only one of several layers above the earth. "Who knows then, but there may be, as the Antients thought, a Region of this Fire, above our Atmosphere, prevented by our Air and its own too great Distance for Attraction, from joining our Earth?" And "perhaps the Aurorae Boreales are Currents of this Fluid in its own Region above our Atmosphere." Fire and electricity might be revealingly similar fluids. Unable to design an experiment to verify any of this, Franklin merely concluded that "there is no End to Conjectures."[33]

He speculated similarly about magnetism, admitting that this "Fluid" puzzled him. He suspected "that Magnetism fills all Space," indicating north and south throughout the known universe and making it possible for any "Being capable of Passing from one Heavenly Body to another" to use a compass as "a Mariner on our Ocean," a lovely interstellar image.[34]

And still his conjectures about fluids did not end. Franklin considered the nature of light, starting with Newton's assertion that it resulted from moving corpuscles. Franklin was "not satisfy'd" with this doctrine, comically confessing himself "much in the *Dark* about *Light*." He explained to Colden in 1752 that he believed "Universal Space" was filled "with a subtle elastic Fluid, which when at rest is not visible, but whose Vibrations affect that fine Sense the Eye, as those of Air do the grosser Organs of the Ear." With this idea, Franklin accepted Newton's concept of the aether as a material that filled space. But he also emphasized aether's extremely subtle nature—was it even material, really? With these speculations, Franklin rounded out his repertoire. He had now made claims on areas of natural philosophy in which he had done no experiments and had attempted a unified theory of the subtle substances whose forces pervaded the cosmos.[35]

IT IS EASY to trace the spread of Franklin's fame—it followed his *Experiments and Observations on Electricity* (1751). Initially brief, the essays went through five English editions from 1751 to 1774. Each included the primary electrical writings but then gathered more and more of Franklin's letters and essays. (Increasingly, they would address nonmeteorological and nonelectrical topics.)[36]

Franklin used these successive editions to craft his image as a philosopher. It would have made sense for Franklin to open the *Experiments and Observations* with his initial letter of 1747 to Collinson, thanking his patron for the electric "Tube" and breathlessly relating his first use of it. Instead, he wrote a stiff note to Collinson in 1750, thanking him and Penn for the tube and apparatus. It was almost as if someone had told Franklin he had to write the letter and he reluctantly did—a bit late in the course of the experiments and a mere year before he published his findings. And then he buried the letter within the other essays. Indeed, Franklin's slowness to thank patrons matched his determination to ignore critics—why shift focus away from himself? Moreover, the electrical experiments themselves, done collaboratively, were published under his name alone. Carefully, relentlessly, he had worked his way to center stage. He intended to stay there.[37]

Translations of Franklin's writings introduced him all around Europe. After the initial French edition of 1752, an enlarged one appeared four years later. Subsequent editions in Italian, German, and Latin would follow, for a total of eleven in Europe before the American Revolution. The Philadelphia experiment thus spread from Spain to Russia. (The latter country saw the only electrical fatality, when an ungrounded Georg Wilhelm Richmann unwisely approached a charged Leyden jar during a St. Petersburg experiment.) The proliferation of Franklin's works in Europe sharply contrasted with the situation in his native land: the first American edition of the *Experiments and Observations* appeared in the nineteenth century, and the first scholarly edition was not issued until 1941.[38]

Franklin may have been American, but his initial fame as a natural philosopher was not—it depended entirely on European approbation. He was absolutely right to look to Europe for validation. Anglo-America could not yet support the elaborate culture of learning necessary for natural philosophy. No American printer thought that an edition of Franklin's essays would sell; any colonist who bought the *Experiments and Observations* was probably used to ordering such things from London. And London had been essential to Franklin's philosophical success. The metropolis had given him a patron (Collinson), equipment (the electric tube), and published validation (the 1751 edition of his essays). That he was a colonial client clearly irked Franklin, hence his muffled thanks to Collinson and Penn in early versions of the story of his success. But colonial client Franklin was, and only by his meticulous cultivation of friends and patrons in the republic of letters had he been able to claim a place in that cosmopolitan realm.

Not that Franklin's native land neglected him entirely. In 1752, he received honorary master's degrees from Harvard and Yale Colleges. Alas, his Boston parents could never swell with pride that their youngest son was, after all, a college man; his father had died in 1745 and his mother in 1752—just before her son's triumphs made news on both sides of the ocean.

The sweetest plum for Franklin was the Copley Medal of London's Royal Society. This was the society's highest distinction, one previously given only to its British fellows. But "Benjamin Franklin Esquire of Philadelphia in America" received it in 1753, "on Account of his Curious Experiments and Observations on Electricity." The society's president, George, Earl of Macclesfield, emphasized that the award had no precedent. Though Franklin was neither "a Fellow of this Society nor an Inhabitant of this Island," he was "a Subject of the Crown of Great Britain." Moreover, all "learned men and Philosophers of all Nations" were "Fellow members of one and the same illustrious Republic, and look upon it to be beneath Persons of their character to betray a fond partiality for this or that particular district." In a way, the Royal Society needed Franklin as much as he needed it. By giving the Copley Medal to Franklin, a commoner and colonist, the society made its point that the sciences established universal truths apparent to everyone across the globe.[39]

Franklin had probably not anticipated receiving the Copley Medal. His surprise might be roughly equivalent to that of a modern scientist who, trying for years to land an article or two in a major journal, suddenly finds she has succeeded—and has also somehow won the Nobel Prize. For Franklin, it was dizzying. He must have practiced and practiced drafts of the thank-you note he sent to the Royal Society; it is powerfully succinct (no telltale gushing) and one of the loveliest examples of the Franklin hand. The note is the bookend to the letter he had sent to Peter Collinson seven years earlier, acknowledging the glass electric globe. And it is the antithesis of the supplication he had sent almost thirty years earlier to Sir Hans Sloane, offering a view of his asbestos curiosities. It was a wonderful vindication of Franklin's faith that the republic of letters would recognize talent of whatever nation and rank. In his case, it had—spectacularly.[40]

In no time at all, admirers attached the terms *philosopher* and *genius* to Franklin. The first word did not even need the modifier *natural* before it: the sciences were the apex of learning, philosophy for the modern age. Poets, clergymen, naturalists, and complete nobodies all agreed. When Franklin received his honorary degree from Yale, clergyman and Yale professor Ezra Stiles wrote a Latin oration calling his subject "Philosophorum Princeps" (first among philosophers). James Turner, who had done engraving work for Franklin and for Lewis Evans, went further, extolling Franklin as "the eminent philosopher," indeed "the admiration of the world!"[41]

Above all, his admirers claimed that Franklin, as natural philosopher, commanded nature itself, making him equivalent to deities and giving him a place in the pantheon. In a 1753 poem published in the next year's *Gentleman's Magazine*, Charles Woodmason insisted that Franklin could:

> Dictate science with imperial nod,
> And save[,] not ruin[,] by an *iron rod.*
> If for thy birth, when latest times draw nigh,
> As now for Homer's, rival cities vie.

Richard Brooke maintained in 1755 that Franklin's feat, identifying lightning with electricity, was "a Discovery far more Philosophical and beneficial than those for which many of the Antients were Deifyed!" An anonymous poem, circa 1756, claimed that heaven would welcome Franklin's "Genius"; there, "Bacon [and] Newton will our F—lin greet. / And place him in his Electrisic seat," a somewhat

Gentlemen,   Philad. May 29. 1754.

The very great Honour you have done me, in adjudging me your Medal for 1753 demands my grateful Acknowledgements, which I beg you would accept as the only Return at present in my Power.

I know not whether any of your learned Body have attain'd the ancient boasted Art of *multiplying Gold;* but you have certainly found the Art of making it infinitely *more valuable.*

You may easily bestow your Favours on Persons of more Merit; but on none who can have a higher Sense of the Honour, or a more perfect Respect for your Society and Esteem of its excellent Institution, than

Gentlemen,

Your most obliged
& most obed. Servant

B Franklin

Presid. & Council of
the Royal Society.

A short letter of thanks. Benjamin Franklin to the President and Fellows of the Royal Society (1754). THE ROYAL SOCIETY.

alarming prospect. Even Franklin's electrical collaborators, who did not exactly share the glory, praised him immoderately. Ebenezer Kinnersley expected that the "Posterity of Mankind" would "make the Name of FRANKLIN like that of NEWTON, *immortal.*"[42]

The praise of Franklin's immortal wisdom did not let up. In 1766, Stiles (still eager to flatter Franklin) claimed that just as "Confucius and his Posterity have been honored in China for Twenty Ages—the Electrical Philosopher, the American Inventor of the pointed Rods will live for Ages to come." John Walsh even implied Franklin's divinity when he repeatedly capitalized the pronouns addressing him: "He, who predicted and shewed that electricity wings the formidable bolt . . . : He, who analysed the electrified Phial . . . ; He, who by Reason became an electrician." No one had ever rhapsodized about Franklin as a printer, civic booster, or clerk to the Pennsylvania Assembly. Science made it happen.[43]

People went a bit crazy, it must be said. In Germany especially, the idea that Franklin had supernatural power became a commonplace. In 1756, Immanuel Kant proclaimed Franklin the Prometheus of the modern age (*Prometheus der neuern Zeiten*) because he had, like the mythological figure, defied the gods in order to draw "fire" (electricity) from the heavens. A German acolyte sent Franklin some verses (styled as a dialogue between Earth and Moon) celebrating how the great American had protected "Mankind" from lightning; what was needed next, the Earth tells the Moon, was "still one Francklin more, to secure us [from] the Power of Death." He was no longer quite human, our colonial chandler's son.[44]

Again, it is worth noting the new meaning of *genius.* It had once meant a quality or trait a person *had;* by the middle of the eighteenth century, it had also come to mean what a certain kind of person *was.* That kind of person did not possess mere talent—a genius was born, not made. Franklin's rapid rise—he sprang from the dust of the Newton-Descartes squabble in France—greatly reinforced the idea. We can trace the transformation of genius from modifier to noun over the rest of Franklin's life. For example, Woodmason's 1753 poem wished for Franklin "those honours that are virtue's meed, / Whate'er to genius wisdom has decreed!" and in 1761, Kinnersley described his compatriot's "superiour and more penetrating Genius." But Penuel Bowen in 1771 called Franklin "the distinguish'd genius of America," not only *a* genius but *the* genius.[45]

Now, Franklin had to decide what to do with his fame. His reputation made him indispensable not only within the republic of letters but also in the political realm. For the rest of his life, he would have to balance the demands of philosophy and politics. Elevated by his experimental achievements, he could never again pursue natural philosophy on a full-time basis, as he had done during his two-year, headlong pursuit of electricity.

Franklin was aware of the problem and looked to other philosophical careers as cautionary tales. In 1749, *Poor Richard* had quoted James Thomson's *Seasons* yet again, this time on Francis Bacon, "The great deliverer he! who from the gloom / Of cloister'd monks, and jargon-teaching schools, / Led forth the true Philosophy." But Bacon was "hapless in his choice" of politics; "Unfit to stand the civil storm of state. . . . Him for the studious shade / Kind nature form'd." A year later, Franklin offered the opposite choice—politics not philosophy—to Cadwallader Colden, who was smarting anew from reviews of his book. "Let not your Love of Philosophical Amusements have more than its due Weight with you," Franklin warned. "Had Newton been Pilot but of a single common Ship, the finest of his Discoveries would scarce have excus'd, or atton'd for his abandoning the Helm one Hour in Time of Danger; how much less if she had carried the Fate of the Commonwealth." Colden, in short, was no Newton, the philosopher he had attempted to correct. Thus, Franklin dismissed his friend's aspirations in the sciences: "Forgive this Freedom," he begged Colden, which he, North America's ranking philosopher, offered "with the sincerest Esteem and Affection."[46]

Franklin was determined to do better, to combine philosophy and public affairs. If he did so, he would outstrip even Newton, whose contributions to public life had been limited. Demands on Franklin's political energies were growing. He had been elected a member of the Philadelphia Common Council in 1748, was elected president of the trustees of the Academy of Philadelphia (which he had helped create) a year later, and became a member of the Pennsylvania Assembly and a Philadelphia alderman in 1751. Many men would have decided that they had no more time for natural philosophy—but not Franklin. He was determined to keep his hand in.

But how could he? Franklin conserved his energy: he worked on problems for which he already had background. He would ever after follow developments in electricity and meteorology, for instance, but he did not—could not—keep up with everything. He ignored most discussion of earthquakes, as just one example, even though they were thought to be connected to atmospheric electricity (as he had briefly speculated) or even caused by lightning rods. Others pleaded for Franklin's further thoughts on electricity and earthquakes; he declined to elaborate. It is most remarkable that he never even mentioned the devastating Lisbon earthquake of 1755, which obsessed most learned figures in the Atlantic world—it had in fact inspired Kant's declaration that Franklin was the modern Prometheus, someone who could comprehend and master nature's terrible forces. But 1755 was just a few years too late; by then, Franklin lacked time to start research on earthquakes.[47]

He coped, as well, by integrating his ongoing research on electricity into his household routine. In that way, he could keep an eye on his investigations, whatever else was happening. Having earlier used his home as an experimental space for heating systems, Franklin now rigged the place up as a big piece of electrical equipment. In September 1752, he erected a lightning rod "to draw the Lightning down into my house." Suspended on wire running down from the lightning rod, two bells gave "Notice when the Rod should be electrified. A Contrivance obvious to every Electrician." The bells were sometimes so loud "as to be heard all over the House." Franklin gave "orders in my Family that if the Bells rang when I was [away] from home, they should catch some of the Lightning for me in electrical Vials, and they did so."[48]

It would be interesting to know who "they" were, exactly. In 1752 and 1753, when Franklin was trying to fill his electrical vials, his household included his wife, Deborah; young daughter Sarah; older son William; and two slaves, Peter and Jemima. It is unlikely that Deborah Franklin tried to "catch" any lightning—she complained about having bells announce the presence of electricity in her house. William was the obvious suspect, but surely Franklin wanted a backup as well. He could have enlisted his daughter or simply ordered his slaves to respond to the sound of the bell, as servants did anyway. Any of these options would have made Franklin's ongoing investigations typical of an age when laboratories existed in households, workshops, rectories, and naval vessels—whatever location was convenient to the experimenter.[49]

But the presence of Peter and Jemima is telling. The slaves remind us that this experimental space existed in the British colonies at midcentury, the heyday of imperial expansion and of a drive to control extra-European territories and peoples.

———————

As FRANKLIN ENJOYED his new consequence in the 1750s, Britain's first empire entered its most significant period of growth. Everyone in North America was, for different reasons, obsessed by territorial expansion. Conflicts among different nations, Indian and European, took center stage. But there were also signs of tension between Britain and its colonies. In all this, the sciences played a part. It would be too simple to state that natural science was the handmaiden to empire. But whether as metaphor of power over the globe or as source of actual power, the sciences certainly served British imperial ambitions. And the empire provided men of science new scope for their investigations.

Consider James Alexander's plan, in the early 1750s, to use British North America to measure the speed of electricity. Earlier tests had been inconclusive. In one English trial, reported in the Royal Society's 1748 *Philosophical Transactions*, two men held between them a wire, four miles long but twisted back and forth so many times that they could stand side by side. They connected one end of the wire to a Leyden jar but did not detect any interval between the charge's initiation and transmission.[50]

A greater distance was perhaps necessary: where was there a better place to find it than on the vast North American continent? Alexander proposed to Franklin that (after an initial test spanning the Delaware and Schuylkill Rivers) thousands of miles of wire be run along yet more waterways, even down to the Ohio River, thence to the "Missisippi, to the Bay of Mexico, round Florida, and round the South Cape of Virginia; which, I think would give some observable time, and discover exactly the velocity." Franklin gently responded that the experiment, "though well imagined, and very ingenious," would merely confirm "the extream facility with which the electric fluid moves in metal."[51]

But was it such a mad idea? Franklin and his merry Philadelphia electricians had, after all, conducted electricity through the Schuylkill River when they picnicked on its banks in 1749. Franklin had told Collinson that they had done this, and Collinson had told the Royal Society—Alexander probably read the letter in question, which was why he consulted Franklin. Wiring a great expanse of North America was not even the remarkable part of his plan. More astonishing was Alexander's assumption that the continent must somehow lack creatures of any kind to snag or snip his wire. That was, indeed, the usual fantasy. British subjects, including Franklin, were convinced that North America was a vast, underpopulated space in which they could carry out some unprecedented scheme or another.

Indeed, Franklin was preparing to scheme his way into the most important political role of his career. The postal service was reinstating the Atlantic packets that connected the continental colonies to England. In early 1751, Franklin learned that the deputy postmaster for North America, Virginian Elliott Benger, was dying. Franklin wanted the job, a promotion from his local postmastership, and knew he needed friends in London to help. So even before Benger ceased to draw breath, Franklin asked Peter Collinson for assistance: "The Place is in the Disposal of the Postmasters General of Britain, with some of whom or their Friends you may possibly have Acquaintance." Franklin somewhat disingenuously professed himself "quite a Stranger to the Manner of Managing these Applications" but provided Collinson with a copy of the previous occupant's commission so his patron would know the job requirements to the letter.[52]

The position was reputed to be worth £150 a year, income Franklin could use now that he was retired, but he claimed a higher motive. The Post Office would support his "Proposal for Promoting Useful Knowledge." Location mattered, too. "I need not tell you," Franklin nevertheless told Collinson, "that Philadelphia being the Center of the Continent Colonies, and having constant Communication with the West India Islands, is by much a fitter Place for the Situation of a General Post Office than Virginia." Franklin won the campaign. In 1753, he and William Hunter of Williamsburg, Virginia, were appointed, the Post Office having decided that the volume of mail warranted two men on the job. Franklin the Copley Medalist thus gained his first significant political appointment. Prowess in natural philosophy led to patronage in the republic of letters—and in the carrying of letters. Already, science had brought Franklin successes he might otherwise never have achieved.[53]

In hindsight, he would conflate his blooming political career and his new status as a philosopher. In his *Autobiography*, he wrote that Pennsylvania's new governor, William Denny, had delivered the

Copley Medal to him in 1756. Denny bore the award along with "very polite Expressions of his Esteem for me" and took Franklin aside to confide that "his Friends in England" had advised him "to cultivate a Friendship with me, as one who was capable of giving him the best Advice." Franklin misremembered. He had received the medal two years earlier, when the (sadly forgettable) Reverend William Smith took it to him. But the false memory revealed the truth: Franklin's fortunes rose generally as his philosophical reputation shot heavenward.[54]

So confident was Franklin that he began to criticize British imperial policy, using political arithmetic to defend colonists' interests. He thus built on his earlier analysis of colonial populations—and his fascination with numerical addition and multiplication—but renounced his earlier statements that the colonies might need migrants. (That notion had underpinned his plea for a Pennsylvania currency, and it had influenced Polly Baker's spirited defense of her duty to increase and multiply.) In *Poor Richard Improved* for 1750, Franklin claimed for the first time that the colonies were growing too fast to need immigrants. English political arithmeticians had estimated that the continental colonies doubled their population every thirty years but assumed that migration accounted for much of the growth. Franklin accepted the estimate but doubted its cause: "I believe People increase faster by Generation in these Colonies, where all can have full Employ, and there is Room and Business for Millions yet unborn," in contrast to "old settled Countries" that offered no such opportunities.[55]

Franklin next used this argument to question British colonial policies. Since the previous century, British officials had been sending convicted felons to the colonies, where they served out their sentences in the employ of whoever purchased their labor. (The assumption was that the rough-and-ready colonies needed any kind of labor and guaranteed conditions that would both punish and reform criminals.) Then came the British Iron Act of 1750, which prohibited most new iron and steel production in the colonies in order to secure markets for British metal manufactures. Together, these policies made clear that Britons valued the colonies as a marketplace for their exports but also considered them a dumping ground for people they did not want.

Franklin, who had worked so hard to prove himself worthy of metropolitan regard, was offended. In a biting 1751 "letter" to the

Pennsylvania Gazette, he complained of the policy on convicted felons. British ministers argued that the convicts would assist the "WELL PEOPLING of the Colonies," but Franklin wondered whether the migrants were such a prize. He suggested a swap: British convicts for American rattlesnakes, which could happily slither in English gardens, "particularly" those belonging to "the *Prime Ministers, the Lords of Trade,* and *Members of Parliament*" who had advocated the traffic in felons. Those "*Rattle-Snakes* seem the most *suitable Returns* for the *Human Serpents* sent us by our *Mother* Country."[56]

That same year and possibly in response to the Iron Act, Franklin began a longer analysis, "Observations Concerning the Increase of Mankind." He circulated it in manuscript while his fame was building and only published it in 1755 as an appendix to another man's pamphlet. His pamphlet rejected estimates of population based on "Bills of Mortality." He had earlier accepted this as a model, derived from William Petty's groundbreaking analysis, for examining his colony. This method would not "suit new Countries, as America," where ample land gave ample "means of subsistence." "Plants or Animals" would increase until they crowded each other out—unlikely in the colonies. Franklin calculated an even faster rate of population growth: colonists doubled every twenty years, exclusive of immigration, which must soon tip the population balance of the British empire to the western Atlantic. It would then be absurd for the small metropole to make colonial commercial policies unilaterally—"Britain should not too much restrain Manufactures in her Colonies. A wise and good Mother will not do it."[57]

This was a shattering conceptual shift and possibly the most aggressive claim that Franklin could have made against Great Britain. Britons had long feared that the small population of their island nation would diminish their efforts to establish colonies, and they worried about overextending their power. Franklin preyed on that fear and nimbly reversed the transatlantic balance of power. Size and productivity of population should, he declared, determine political authority.[58]

Tempting though it may be to see a revolutionary message smoldering within this tract, Franklin intended his criticisms to strengthen the empire, not declare independence from it. In fact, he argued, the more numerous colonists became, the greater their economic contribution to the British state: they produced valuable commodities for sale and then used the profits to buy British manufactures. As they increased, so did their production and consumption—"a glorious Market wholly in the Power of Britain." Rather than regulate colonial economies, as in the Iron Act, British officials should consider the natural increase of colonial population "an Accession of Power to the British Empire by Sea as well as Land! What Increase of Trade and Navigation! What Numbers of Ships and Seamen!" Franklin's imagery summoned a vivid image of the British Atlantic empire at full tide, producing wealth, consuming goods, and dominating the sea.[59]

More than any other of his investigations into the natural world, Franklin's political arithmetic politicized an argument about nature. He was, in fact, consciously comparing human and animal populations. In 1751, the same year he drafted his "Observations," Franklin had published in *Poor Richard* his essay on microscopy, in which he referred to the teeming unseen animalcules that vastly outnumbered humans. Microscopes also allowed people to examine the polyp, an aquatic creature whose self-regeneration raised interesting questions about the nature of life. Franklin's "Observations" duly compared a colonizing nation to "a Polypus." "Take away a Limb" from the home country and "its Place is soon supplied" while the severed limb grew into another polyp. Thus, he wrote, "you may of one make ten Nations, equally populous and powerful."[60]

But this analogy between animal and human populations brought Franklin back to the vexing question of human difference and particularly the racist categories he had used in his earlier writings on mortality. In his "Observations," the increase of white colonists mattered most to him. They married earlier and oftener, compared to Europeans, and produced twice as many children per marriage. So their overall numbers "must at least be doubled every 20 Years." His assumption was, of course, that America's land lay open to colonists, whether Indians lived on the land or not. And slaves introduced a complicated variable into the equation. The excruciating conditions under which they worked prevented their natural increase (here, Franklin focused on the sugar islands), "so that a continual Supply is needed from Africa." The more slaves, the less natural increase and the greater the dependence on expensive, imported labor.[61]

Franklin probably did not care about the sugar islands—he simply wanted to be sure that the continental colonies did not end up resembling them. For that reason, he wished to see the slave trade to the continent slowed, if not ended. Europeans, he said, "make the principal Body of White People on the Face of the Earth. I could wish their Numbers were increased." In America, "we have so fair an Opportunity, by excluding all Blacks and Tawneys," meaning Africans and Indians, and "increasing" those with complexions of "the lovely White and Red" mixed together.[62]

Nor were all white and red complexions welcome. In his essay, Franklin gave ill-considered vent to his dislike of Pennsylvania's German-speaking population. "Why should the Palatine Boors be suffered to swarm into our Settlements," crowding out English "Language and Manners"? He used a watery metaphor to tell Collinson he hoped that "the Stream" of Germans might be "turned to the other Colonies you mention," ones too new to be choosy about their settlers. Pennsylvania's Germans unsurprisingly resented Franklin's prejudice—and they could vote. His political opponents would find it easy, in future, to turn his statements against him. Franklin would later repent and omit the offending material, as well as the assessments of black and tawny complexions, from reprintings of his treatise during the 1760s.[63]

And Franklin was far from consistent in his opinions. Recall Poor Richard's claim that all blood was ancient and that inherited statuses were not natural facts. In the same year Franklin composed the openly racist "Observations Concerning the Increase of Mankind," Poor Richard published another jibe at hereditary entitlements. He considered it "an amusing Speculation to look back, and compute what Numbers of Men and Women among the Ancients, clubb'd their Endeavours to the Production of a single Modern." Over the course of twenty-one generations, a person's ancestors would run, "supposing no Intermarriages among Relations," to the number of 1,048,576. If a "Nobleman" traced his genealogy back to "the Norman Conquest," he would discover that over a million people had sired him. Indeed, the more ancient an ancestry, the less likely its nobility. The "Purity of Blood" was "a mere joke," and all the world's people were of one "Blood."[64]

Humanity's red circulating juice even connected the hated Germans to Pennsylvania's British settlers, including Franklin. Despite his objections to German migrants, he explained in a private letter of 1753 that he did not think them physically distinct from the British peoples. After all, following the myth of Germanic settlement of ancient Britain, "the English are the Offspring of Germans," and both peoples lived in a "Climate" that was "much of the same Temperature." Therefore, Franklin confessed, "I can see nothing in Nature that should create this Difference, I am apt to suspect it must arise from [human] Institution." English-language schooling and familiarity with English customs would make Germans British. In the same letter, Franklin allowed the same possibility for Indians, who if "brought up among us" were virtually European in their beliefs and manners. Whether the same was true for Africans was something Franklin did not, at that point, explore.[65]

Whatever his inconsistencies, he continued to think of his work in the human sciences as similar to his investigation of the natural world. Thus, to his brother John, he complained that he had never heard back about "my Electrical Papers nor of that on the Peopling of Countries, nor that on Meteorology, which have passed thro' your Hands." To Collinson, Franklin sent drafts of three pamphlets dating from the 1750s: "The Increase of Mankind / The Properties and Phaenomena of the Air and / The present State of the Germans in America." The bundle of ideas made clear, however, Franklin's different conceptions of the natural and human realms: air circulated freely, but the humans who lived around the Atlantic should not.[66]

FROM POLITICAL ARITHMETIC, Franklin turned to hydrography, especially to questions about the extent, configuration, and characteristics of the Atlantic. He was already familiar with maritime cartography. In the sixteenth century, the Dutch had created detailed and highly coveted sea charts. Many were packaged in "quarter waggoners," maritime atlases named after the Dutch publisher Lucas Wagenaer. These images proliferated in the early eighteenth century as practical guides to navigation but also as political—meaning imperial—statements that designated European overseas holdings. In 1745, with an eye to this demand, Franklin had advertised for sale the fourth book of the canonical *English Pilot* (first published in London in 1737), an atlas that described "the West India Navigation, from Hudson's-Bay to the River Amazones."[67]

He was venturing into literally uncharted waters. Despite all the advances in mapping land, open ocean cartography barely existed. Instead, charts mostly surveyed known sea routes and indicated coastline—meaning what navigators were trying not to run into. Most of the open ocean was known only to the sailors who managed to stay afloat in it.[68]

Edmond Halley had pushed further. Franklin had followed much of Halley's work, so he probably knew of his pioneering attempt, from 1698 to 1701, to chart the entire Atlantic. Halley wrote on many nautical subjects, including tides and the trade winds, explaining the latter according to thermal trends, which may have influenced Franklin's analysis of Atlantic storms. Halley had also been the first English person to command a naval vessel for work in the sciences. Three times, he commanded the *Paramore* to determine the lines of magnetic variation in the North and South Atlantic—an unprecedented mapping of physical pattern over the earth, of immense value to the British navy and merchant marine. The premier London maritime cartographic firm, Mount and Page, published Halley's chart in 1701. It circulated widely as a model of how to investigate a vast and turbulent part of nature. Yet Halley had charted an ocean whose very boundaries remained unknown.[69]

Around the time he was forming his "Observations on the Increase of Mankind," Franklin explored those boundaries by investing in an attempt to find the Northwest Passage. We now scoff at this fantasy, the geographic equivalent of the philosopher's stone. But many reasonable people had, since the sixteenth century, sought a passage through the northern part of North America. Such a waterway would unite the Atlantic and Pacific, giving whatever European power controlled it unprecedented access to two oceanic systems. For the time being, only the Spanish could claim this advantage because their empire straddled the isthmus of Panama and held strategic islands in the Philippines and West Indies.

The French and British, in contrast, had their greatest holdings in North America and none in the Pacific. As their empires expanded and vied in the eighteenth century, the French and British sought a Northwest Passage that would, by heading north, circumvent the Spanish empire. This passage was especially important for the British because they lacked access to the Mississippi and St. Lawrence Rivers, great advantages to the French and Spanish.

In 1745, Parliament promised £20,000 to anyone who could sail from Hudson's Bay to the "South Sea," or Pacific Ocean. Franklin was motivated. He studied accounts of voyages into Hudson Bay. Both Christopher Middleton and Henry Ellis had sailed there between 1741 and 1742 and between 1746 and 1747, respectively. Franklin dismissed their doubts that a further passage flowed out of the bay and concluded that ships might "sail easily" through an "expected Passage." Then, in 1752, Franklin joined venturers from Philadelphia, Maryland, New York, and Boston. Together, they bought a vessel, the optimistically named *Argo*, and sent it to Hudson Bay. The men sought geographic knowledge (and the prize) but also wanted to expand trade and fishing in the northern waters that Britain and France disputed. The *Argo* set out in March 1753, then turned back when ice blocked it as winter set in. A second attempt in 1754 was even less successful. The ship returned to Philadelphia with only some Inuit artifacts for the Library Company.[70]

His investment in the *Argo* revived Franklin's fascination with the sea and sailors. The *Argo*'s captain, Charles Swaine, had left his manuscript notes and charts with Franklin before he left on the second attempt. Franklin retained the two journals from the journeys, the relevant "Charts," and "a Number of Letters and Papers" about the northern venture. All the documents were subsequently lost. But his interest in them showed that he was turning the nautical interests of his boyhood into ones suited to a mature natural philosopher.[71]

Franklin also took another look at Atlantic storms, especially the winds within them. In a 1751 letter to Collinson, he remarked on "the more equal temper of sea-water, and the air over it" compared with their counterparts on land. Franklin suggested that the winds "agitated" large bodies of water, which thereby "continually change[d] surfaces," blending cold and warm waters and creating a general moderation in temperature. To explain why wind blew westward from Africa to America, Franklin declared that the rotating earth was itself moving "West to East, and slipping under the air," which created an apparent wind. And he concluded in 1753 that it was "a Mistake, that the Trade Winds blow only in the Afternoon." Instead, they blew almost all the time, making the ocean a constant field of forces. He believed that system could, like magnetic variation, be charted, though perhaps not easily reduced to any single force, such as the rotation of the globe.[72]

Franklin next considered something that wind caused, waterspouts. These whirlwinds over water were highly dangerous to wooden sailing vessels. He concluded that a spout formed when opposing currents of warm and cold air collided. The warm air rose and the cold sank, and together, they created a visible vortex. The consequent force sucked upward the surface water around it. Franklin maintained that spouts ascended rather than descended, violently raising water rather than smashing down into it. Others, including Colden, argued that the spouts descended. Franklin insisted on the logic of warm air ascending—"The Rising will begin precisely in that Column that happens to be the lightest or most rarified; and the warm Air will flow horizontally from all Points to this Column, where the several Currents meeting and joining to rise, a Whirl is naturally formed." It would have been a tall order to Franklin or anyone else to plunge into a waterspout and look up into it in order to see its internal shape. Franklin instead visualized the dynamic by comparing it to the descending motion of a fluid draining out of a tub with a central hole in its base.[73]

How did he know anything about waterspouts? It was not clear Franklin had ever seen one. Since he had returned from London in 1726, he had had no excuse to go to sea. (While in Annapolis on postal business in 1755, however, he spotted a whirlwind and remembered that mariners believed waterspouts could be dissipated by firing cannon through them. He tried to "break" the whirlwind by "striking my whip frequently through it, but without any effect.") But he had a great treasure trove of information in his maritime family, the Bostonians and Nantucketers he had grown up with.[74]

He had been quizzing New England mariners for some time. Pehr Kalm, a Swedish naturalist who visited North America from 1748 to 1751, reported that Franklin had, perhaps in boyhood, "heard from sea captains in Boston, who had sailed to the most northern parts of this hemisphere." (These tales might have nudged Franklin toward the *Argo* venture.) And Franklin praised his maritime informants. During his work on meteorology in the 1740s and 1750s, for example, he credited "an old Sea Captain" with testimony that there was little thunder and lightning on the high seas and "an intelligent Whaleman of Nantucket" for information about whirlwinds' occurring to the leeward.[75]

Between 1754 and 1755, Franklin dived into written works about hydrography and nautical science. Characteristically, he blended learned and unlearned sources, as when, in 1754, he ordered for the Library Company the volumes of "the Philosophical Transactions" that it lacked as well as a copy of "Dampier's Voyages." Each source—the *Philosophical Transactions* and the Dampier work—is worth consideration.[76]

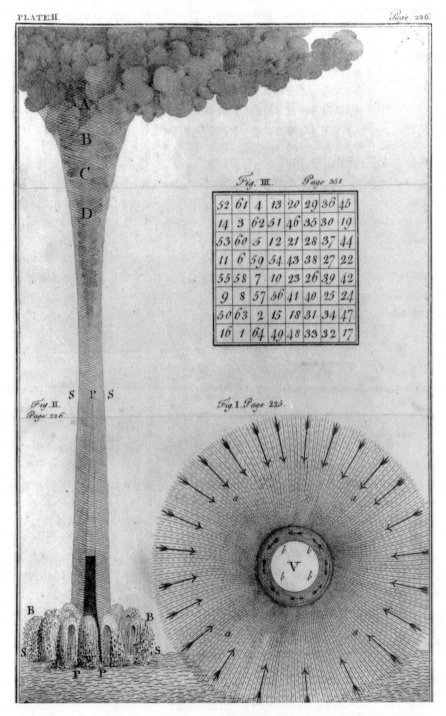

Waterspout. Benjamin Franklin, *Experiments and Observations on Electricity* (1769). HOUGHTON LIBRARY, HARVARD UNIVERSITY.

The Royal Society volume of 1753, for instance, included an account of a historic episode in hydrography. In a 1751 letter, Captain Henry Ellis described to the Reverend Stephen Hales the experiments he had done off the coast of West Africa. On the *Earl of Halifax*, Ellis had tested "ventilators" that Hales had designed to improve the circulation of shipboard air. This work was part of Hales's effort to use experiments with fluid circulation to benefit humanity (as Franklin did with his Pennsylvanian fireplace). The ship's ventilators worked: of the 130 people on board the *Earl of Halifax*, Ellis reported, all were "very healthy." He then went on to recount his experiment with another Hales invention, a "bucket sea-gage." This device was an ordinary wooden bucket sealed at top and bottom. Each end was fitted with a unidirectional valve activated by water velocity; the valves opened as the bucket descended and closed when it was drawn up. Weighted and lowered on a line marked at regular intervals, the bucket could take discrete samples of seawater from specific depths.[77]

Ellis then analyzed the samples. He used a Fahrenheit thermometer to measure the water temperatures at various depths, ranging from 360 to 5,346 feet—over a mile deep. At the ship's tropical location, the air temperature was 84 degrees, but the temperature of the water dropped, "in proportion to the depths," to 53 degrees. It stayed at this temperature, even in samples from lower depths. Ellis also discovered that the water from the lowest depths weighed more and hence was "the saltest water."[78]

It was astonishing. Since the 1660s, natural philosophers had been trying to craft instruments to observe the sea at depths where humans dared not venture. But it was Ellis who, using the Hales sea gauge, recorded the first subsurface temperature measurements in the open ocean. Hales's inventive instrumentation—very cheap, something a cooper could knock together on board a ship—made it possible to investigate the globe's hidden reaches. The sea gauge is the electric kite's watery cousin. Imagine a kite on a mile-long string—it could easily sample the upper atmosphere that fascinated Franklin. Ellis did the same under water. He admitted that he could think of no immediate use for his discovery, other than that it "supplied our cold bath, and cooled our wines or water at pleasure; which is vastly agreeable to us in this burning climate."[79]

The cold baths and wine were chilling in every sense. Ellis commanded a slave ship, and many of the people on the *Earl of Halifax* were African captives bound for the British West Indies. When he rejoiced that Hales's ventilators made the passengers healthy, his comparison was to slavers with appalling mortality rates. He was pleased that running the ventilator was "good exercise for our slaves, and a means of preserving our cargo and lives." In this case, the lives were the cargo. Slave ships were sites for science and for empire.[80]

What might Franklin have made of this? In the spring of 1754, he reported that he "perused the 47th Vol. of the Transactions." It is not impossible that he turned first to the piece on him, one of the accounts of his electrical experiments. That letter ended on page 211, where Ellis's letter then began. Franklin might have been flattered by his proximity to Hales, whose work on circulation he admired. He had read other Hales publications in the *Philosophical Transactions* (as in the preceding volume, number 46), knew Ellis from his attempts to find the Northwest Passage, and took an interest in shipboard health. Franklin lamented that many migrants (Germans, felons, and others) arrived in Philadelphia with "gaol fever," the name for contagions associated with poverty and crowding. In 1755, he urged the Pennsylvania Assembly to outlaw the overcrowding that would "poison the Air those unhappy Passengers breathe on Shipboard, and spread it wherever they land, to infect the Country which receives them."[81]

We know Franklin made a mental note of Hales's sea gauge—he would use one at sea in 1785. But he could only get so much hydrographic material out of the *Philosophical Transactions*. Franklin was wise to turn to other sources, such as "Dampier's Voyages," that focused on maritime phenomena exclusively.

William Dampier, privateer, adventurer, and hydrographer, was one of the best-known mariners of Franklin's day. He had done what Franklin had not, gone to sea as a boy. Dampier circumnavigated the globe twice and became a privateer who harassed enemy vessels on behalf of the Royal Navy. He is best remembered now as the captain who deposited Alexander Selkirk on Juan Fernández Island, giving Daniel Defoe an idea for a book called *Robinson Crusoe*.[82]

But Dampier was also a maritime expert. In 1699, he published an influential *Discourse of Winds, Breezes, Storms, Tides, and Currents*, the book Franklin ordered in 1754. Like Halley, Dampier had tried to determine what regular patterns, if any, played over the world's oceans. He postulated that some ocean winds and currents were stable (they "never shift at all") and that even those that changed did so in regular patterns. He explained that Atlantic currents followed the trade winds, beginning off the coast of Africa and continuing over to the Americas. Yet these wind-driven currents paled in comparison to the one that emerged from "the Gulph of *Florida* which is the most remarkable Gulph in the World for its Currents."[83]

So the reading material Franklin selected in 1754 gave him two models for hydrographic work. On the one hand, gentleman Henry Ellis flourished his instruments and data; on the other, tarpaulin Dampier recounted his long experience at sea. Despite their different methods, these investigations sometimes yielded complementary results. Gentleman Edmond Halley included "Dampier's Passage" on his chart of magnetic variation; Dampier returned the favor, using Halley's thermal explanation of trade winds in his *Discourse.* But the land-bound Franklin would have to lean toward Dampier's descriptive mode and to use sailors' own descriptions to do so.[84]

Franklin started to question mariners more pointedly in 1753. Indeed, he made time to do so. In his letter on waterspouts, later read before the Royal Society, he explained that he had postponed writing due to "Business partly, and partly a Desire of producing further Information by Inquiry among my Seafaring Acquaintance." The seafarers confirmed that waterspouts, like whirlwinds, pulled things up into the air—boats at sea and animals on land. Franklin then credited his "intelligent Whaleman of Nantucket" as well as "some Accounts of Seamen" for this information. He also cited some printed sources. These latter included works by Dampier and Cotton Mather, who had published an essay on whirlwinds in the *Philosophical Transactions.* The intelligent mariners, who filled in Franklin's knowledge while he was wrapped up in "Business," were anonymous sources, certainly not the equals of the published experts.[85]

Franklin's father would have been pleased: his son now thought sailors were his inferiors. At the time he sought information on waterspouts, Franklin began to act as patron to individual seafarers. He was personally responsible for admitting Francis Buckley, "a poor Sailor . . . in a very bad Condition with sore Legs," to the Pennsylvania Hospital in 1753; Franklin stood "Security" for all charges for Buckley's treatment and maintenance. He would send a gift in 1761 to Charles Hargrave (or Hargrove), who was at the Royal Hospital for Seamen in Greenwich, England. Hargrave had rendered frequent service to Franklin, as when he carried to Philadelphia David Hall, Franklin's business partner and relation by marriage.[86]

Franklin was ambivalent, as befitted a former artisan who had become a philosopher. He concluded his letter on waterspouts by announcing that he had "not with some of our learned Moderns disguis'd my Nonsense in Greek, cloth'd it in Algebra, or adorn'd it with Fluxions." He must have realized that this sentence might offend gentlemen who donned all three disguises, so he omitted it when he published the letter. Without this phrase, Franklin's praise of ordinary and "intelligent" seafarers gave credit to the unlearned without digging too sharply at the learned. Indeed, sailors seemed to value his opinion. William Falconer, a scribbling mariner, cited "Dr. Franklin" as an expert on waterspouts in his *Universal Dictionary of the Marine* (1769); Falconer had also versified on waterspouts in his sea poem "The Shipwreck" (1762).[87]

But Franklin also began to criticize mariners' trade knowledge. He was dissatisfied with captains' accounts of waterspouts and wanted them to give "more accurate Observations of those Phaenomena, and produce more particular Accounts, tending to a thorough Explanation."[88]

Inclusive and collaborative when he had done his electrical experiments, Franklin had acquired a hectoring tone and patronizing attitude. He sidled yet further from his plebian origins. He was now confident in his status as *gentle*man of letters. Franklin would get another boost when the war that everyone had been expecting finally blew up.

OVER the protests of its Quaker leaders, Pennsylvania threw itself into the French and Indian War (1754–1763), the American phase of the Seven Years' War. In 1753, Virginia sent a young George Washington, with a small militia unit, to persuade the French to withdraw from the Ohio Valley. The French easily repelled the Virginia band and the larger British threat behind it. That small incident then exploded outward through the colonies, over the Atlantic, and eventually into Africa and South Asia, exacting an unprecedented toll on places, populations, and governmental budgets.

Many readers of Franklin's *Autobiography* wonder why Franklin spent so much time describing his military activities during the

French and Indian War, right down to the amounts of provisions he ordered for the troops. He was thorough because the conflict changed everything. Until the end of his life, he lived with the war's consequences. The great struggle would divide and redivide the world and would incite the initial colonial protests against Great Britain that would culminate in the American War of Independence.

The Seven Years' War pitted Great Britain against France and Spain, the main rivals for North America. It also threatened British colonists' delicate relations with Indians. By the 1750s, the most powerful Indian group was the Iroquois Six Nations. The Iroquois had a much-qualified alliance with the British colonies, represented as a Covenant Chain that bound the two peoples together. "Keep bright the chain" was the ritual exhortation of Anglo-Iroquois diplomacy.[89]

Franklin wanted a stronger as well as a brighter chain, which gave him reason to soften, temporarily, his attitudes toward Indians. In 1754, he attended a congress of colonial and Iroquois delegates at Albany, New York. "In our Way thither," Franklin remembered, "I projected and drew up a Plan for the Union of all the Colonies." This Albany Plan offered a permanent intercolonial council, drawing representatives from each colony as well as from the Iroquois, and a royally appointed governor over all. Colonists worried that this body would give too much power to the Crown; imperial administrators feared it gave colonists the upper hand. The plan was an interesting harbinger of Franklin's role in planning pancolonial organizations and the first sign that he took Indians seriously as political actors, not just "Tawney" people who needed to be cleared out of North America. But it was never adopted.[90]

Franklin, approaching his fiftieth year, still had vigor enough for the front lines. In 1755, he commanded the troops in Northampton County, located between Philadelphia and the New York-Pennsylvania border. There, he directed construction of three forts over the mountain range that was the hoped-for barrier to Franco-Indian invasion. He had few good things to say about the nearby enemy Indians, yet he admired the "Art in their Contrivance" at keeping warm with fires hidden in depressions in the ground, invisible to spies on the British side.[91]

In 1756, Franklin was elected colonel of Philadelphia's militia regiment, and his military title went to his head. ("The People happen to love me," he confided to Collinson; "perhaps that's my Fault.") His political opponents sniped that his troops' parading was an "infinite distraction" in the city. Franklin's men felt differently. After their first muster, they marched him home and saluted him with "some Rounds fired before my Door, which shook down and broke several Glasses of my Electrical Apparatus." Too much love, perhaps.[92]

The republic of letters continued to adore Franklin, too. Of the more technical praise, appreciated by cognoscenti, he confessed to Jared Eliot that he felt quite like a girl with "a pair of new Silk Garters." The specialized compliments, like silky undergarments, were acquisitions appreciated only by those in the know but were no less pleasing for that. (Franklin roguishly offered to "take the Freedom to show them" to Eliot.) In late 1755, he became a corresponding member of London's Society (later Royal Society) of Arts, which gave premiums for new devices and useful discoveries. He received another honorary master's degree, this from the College of William and Mary, which confirmed the spread of his fame up and down the colonial seaboard.[93]

Then, in April 1756, Franklin was elected a Fellow of the Royal Society. He at last joined the club whose members he had long admired: Newton, Sloane, Hales, Collinson. He surely enjoyed Collinson's indiscreet testimony that "there was not one negative Ball," or vote, against him, "an Instance of Unanimity" that the society's president said "*he never before saw.*"[94]

Shortly thereafter, in 1760, Franklin joined another London organization, Dr. Bray's Associates. The Reverend Dr. Thomas Bray, who died in 1730, had founded the Society for the Propagation of Christian Knowledge in 1699 and had also established libraries in England and Wales. His associates, a small philanthropic group, sponsored the education and evangelization of African slaves. Franklin knew by reputation several of the associates, including a leading member, the ubiquitous Stephen Hales. The associates, as individuals and as a group, also sought to better slaves' lives. Hales's desire to ventilate slave ships was a classic example of their meliorism. The associates shared an unusually humanitarian concern for non-European peoples, while leaving the slave trade itself unchallenged.[95]

Franklin's sympathy with the associates made sense, given his ambivalence toward slavery. He owned household slaves yet regarded slaves as a poor way to stock his colony with labor. He questioned whether they were naturally the equals of Euro-Americans. Now, he also worried that slaves were a liability in time of war. In a plan for settling any new western land won from the French, Franklin warned that "loose English people," Germans, and slaves were likely to desert to the French. (So, too, would aggrieved Indians.) Slavery was not only economically irrational, in his view, but a weakness within the empire.[96]

Franklin gained a direct voice within that empire when, in 1757, the Pennsylvania Assembly chose him as its agent and sent him to London. Many of the British colonies were hiring agents to lobby for their interests. Franklin's task was quite specific—and delicate. The Pennsylvania Assembly was locked in battle with the colony's proprietors, Thomas and Richard Penn, heirs of Quaker founder William Penn. The Penns refused to let their colonial properties be taxed. Franklin was to persuade them and other British officials that taxing the proprietors would generate significant revenue for the colony, benefiting it and the empire.

That Franklin got this job reflected the colonists' confidence that he was a Pennsylvanian famous enough to shine in the metropole. His appointment resulted in a five-year stay, during which Franklin—busy on behalf of his colony—nevertheless found time to settle himself into the learned societies to which he had just been elected.

He faced doing so alone, for Deborah Franklin was determined never to cross the Atlantic. Her caution was typical—it was her husband's eagerness to play sailor that was unusual. Deborah and Benjamin were both unusual, however, in their agreeing to disagree. Wives were supposed to obey their husbands; husbands expected to command all members of their households. But Deborah and Benjamin Franklin had negotiated a different sort of marriage. They addressed each other in letters as "dear Child" to signify a familial equality. In his letters, Franklin frequently persuaded or advised his wife, but he never commanded her outright. So when she decided not to embark, that was that. William Strahan, Franklin's London bookseller, refused to believe it. "Instead of being afraid of the sea, we ought to have a particular regard for it," Strahan pleaded with Deborah, "as it is so far from being a bar to the communication and intercourse of different and far distant countries, that it facilitates their correspondence." As Franklin had predicted, his wife was unmoved: "There is no inducement strong enough," he pronounced.[97]

Franklin's reentry to London was otherwise a personal triumph and he brought the entourage to prove it. He embarked with his son, William, and each took a slave, Peter and King. Thus, Franklin, at fifty-one, took his place in London as a somebody—as the electrical genius, the winner of the Copley Medal, and the famous American philosopher. His son and heir visited the capital as a gentleman who would read law at London's Inns of Court; the slaves indicated social and financial consequence, an unapologetic display of colonial wealth by someone who both held slaves and criticized slaveholding.[98]

Even his passage to London was memorable. This was Franklin's fastest Atlantic crossing ever. His ship, the postal packet *General Wall*, was protected partway by a large military convoy bound for Nova Scotia, where it would besiege French Louisbourg. The convoy lingered over two months in New York (the Franklins and other passengers ate up their "Sea Stores" and had to buy more) before Lord Loudon, commander in chief of the British forces in North America, gave it permission to sail. The *General Wall* was the only packet that dared complete the voyage—the other two postal vessels turned back. Franklin recalled how the packet's captain, Walter Lutwidge, had "boasted much before we sail'd, of the Swiftness of his Ship" but "she proved the dullest of 96 Sail, to his no small Mortification."[99]

Franklin then witnessed some superb seamanship. Lutwidge measured the *General Wall*'s speed against a straggling vessel "almost as dull as ours" and then experimented with the way his ship was loaded. He ordered all hands and passengers to stand as a group and then moved them about to test weight distribution. The experiment reduced roughly forty people (officers, crew, landsmen) to the direct authority of the captain—and to the status of mere ballast. Franklin was, briefly, equal to his slave. Discovering that the water supply, loaded too far forward, retarded the ship, Lutwidge had the casks "remov'd farther aft; on which the Ship recover'd her Character, and prov'd the best Sailer in the Fleet." Lutwidge bragged that it reached speeds of thirteen knots per hour. Another officer scoffed but lost a bet to Lutwidge when the log-line (a device that determined rate of travel) proved the astonishing speed. Cracking on, the *General Wall* reached Falmouth in just over three weeks, making Franklin's passage a record postal crossing.[100]

Franklin used his time at sea to get some writing done. He composed a preface for *Poor Richard Improved*, his expanded almanac. He called his essay the "Speech of Father Abraham," the musings of a village elder who had a remarkable familiarity with the many aphorisms of Richard Saunders. In a rapid-fire synopsis of Poor

Richard, Father Abraham told poor young men how to get ahead—
"The Way to Wealth," as the essay became known. As with Franklin's
Experiments and Observations, the "Way to Wealth" would enter multiple editions in multiple languages, making him not just a philosopher but a charmingly provincial one. In a way, it was a farewell
speech for Franklin. He bid good-bye to his early career as a colonial printer. Retired from that business, he could live as a London
gentleman, the antithesis of Father Abraham.

When he arrived in England in July 1758, Franklin took up
rented rooms with Margaret Stevenson, a widow whose house was
on Craven Street, just off Charing Cross. This was a happy choice.
Mrs. Stevenson (and her daughter, Mary, nicknamed Polly) offered
Franklin an upper-middle-class address yet not one so grand as to
make Franklin seem pretentious (or bankrupt him). The two
Stevenson women gave the two Franklin men a surrogate and respectable family. The location itself was well chosen. Charing Cross
was not far from Holborn, where William would read law, and lay at
the intersection of Whitehall, which ran southwest toward the governmental centers of London, and the Strand, a cultural prome-
nade that included several important clubs and societies.[101]

Within two weeks of his arrival at Craven Street, Franklin presented himself and the Pennsylvania Assembly's complaints to the
Penns; within three weeks, he attended his first meeting of the Society of Arts. He thus marked out the political and cultural paths he
would continue to tread for the rest of his London career. Then, he
collapsed.

For two months, Franklin was too ill to do anything. He later admitted, in a letter to his wife, that he had at first refused to believe
that what he thought "a violent cold and something of a fever" was
very serious. "I ventured out twice, to do a little business and forward the service I am engaged in," which made him worse. His doctor "grew very angry," having cautioned him against exertion, and
took the extraordinary step, Franklin recalled, of forbidding him
the use of pen and ink. Franklin must have thought back to the
pleurisies that had nearly killed him decades earlier and feared that
his violent cold might turn in that direction. No wonder the doctor
lost his temper. Franklin conceded to his wife that the current malady was no ordinary one but was, in fact, his "seasoning," the contemporary term for a traveler's often miserable and sometimes fatal
adaptation to a new physical environment.[102]

In the hot Philadelphia summer of 1749, Franklin had waited for fame while stripped to his shirt and drawers; in 1757, he arrived in London famous—but there he was, back in his underwear, confined to bed while brilliant London bayed outside. That vast Atlantic Ocean still exacted a toll on those who dared cross it. What if Franklin had died then, at the height of his philosophical celebrity but long before playing his role in the American Revolution? How would he now be remembered?

Chapter 6

DISTANCE

F RANKLIN carefully tended his flame, even as it threatened to go
out. He not only survived but also used his enforced leisure to
burnish his image and make an important contact. Lying in bed, he
had his portrait painted and befriended the doctor who kept him
confined. The portrait was a miniature on ivory by an obscure artist,
one C. Dixon. In it, Franklin the invalid wears the comfortable
clothing of a philosophical gentleman at home—a turban (instead
of a scratchy wig) and a banyan, or dressing gown. Franklin sent the
miniature to Deborah to forward to his sister, Jane Mecom, as an intimate memento of his ascent to gentility (or a possible memento
mori). Franklin's new friend was John Fothergill, FRS, a physician to
several important Britons and the editor of the first edition of
Franklin's *Experiments and Observations*. Fothergill became, like Peter
Collinson, a useful ally in several spheres of activity—and in eight
weeks, he got Franklin back on his feet.[1]

Once recovered, Franklin threw himself back into the London
whirl. On November 14, 1757, he resumed his meetings with the
Penns. Ten days later, he attended his first meeting of the Royal Society and was formally admitted as a fellow. The following month,
Franklin made his first appearance before the Board of Trade, an
important arbiter for colonial affairs. It was as if he had never been
ill. William Franklin, marveling over his father's steady devotion to
the sciences, said, "It is surprizing how you could find Time to attend to T[hings?] of that Nature a[mid all?] your Hurry of public
Business."[2]

It was indeed "surprizing." Franklin faithfully executed his mission in London to wring money out of Pennsylvania's proprietors.
As he did so, he waged a much bigger war: to enlarge the scope of
the British empire and his place within it. He succeeded on both
counts. The Seven Years' War, the conflagration that had started in
one small part of North America, burned its way across much of the

rest of the globe and brought unprecedented expansion and change to the British empire. It also brought Franklin new power and influence.

Yet his and the empire's successes raised new problems. Distance was the real dilemma. Although its global reach gave the British empire might and grandeur, it was now much harder to regulate and to communicate across the empire's vast distances. As people employed natural sciences in their quest to master the globe's expanse, those sciences became more politically valuable than ever. And as Franklin extended his influence—through travel, correspondence, and force of character—his status as a philosopher became an essential passport in multiple realms.

———

As EVER, the sciences served Franklin's broader ambitions. In London, he had many opportunities to make himself known more widely and for a wider range of accomplishments. He began to build up a circle of acquaintance that eventually encompassed a range of Britons and other Europeans. They were a more heterogeneous group than he had known in Philadelphia—more affluent and sometimes aristocratic; some were interested in arts rather than sciences, and some were women, his first female intellectual peers.

Franklin clearly enjoyed being a member in good standing—and high repute—of the republic of letters. While he lived in London, he attended the Royal Society's meetings and, more unusually, served on its committees. He was elected a member of its council in 1760. He followed suit for the Royal Society of Arts, where he kept track of new inventions and, in 1761, served on a committee.[3]

Franklin also executed new experiments and entertained new theories. Soon after his recovery, he reconsidered his ideas about heat. (Maybe the recent illness had reminded him of his fear of drafts.) He moved away from his earlier theory that bodily heat was produced mechanically, as by friction, and considered that it might instead result from a process of fermentation akin to digestion. He continued to regard heat as a fluid. He visualized heat (a quality) in terms of quantity, something that might be measured as it flowed one way or another, creating warmth or coldness in its wake.[4]

Above all, Franklin began to think of substances as "conductors" of heat—he seems to have been the first to apply that electrical term to thermal phenomena. In 1758, he worked with John Hadley, professor of chemistry at Cambridge, to examine evaporation and cooling. He and Hadley confirmed that evaporation, either of alcohol or ether, would drive down the mercury in a thermometer, whatever the ambient temperature. "From this experiment," Franklin blithely concluded, "one may see the possibility of freezing a man to death on a warm summer's day" were the poor soul placed in a breezy passageway and repeatedly doused with ether. The result made Franklin suspect that some materials were "better fitted by Nature to be Conductors" of heat than others.[5]

As proof, he recalled the hot Philadelphia day of 1749 when he had streamed with perspiration and called for dry shirts. That, he now realized, was a mistake. The evaporation of sweat kept cool "the atmosphere round, and next to our bodies"; moisture conducted the heat away. Franklin remarked that, unlike his animate body, "inanimate bodies immers'd in the same air" became as hot as the surrounding temperature. His desk, chair, and "a dry shirt out of the drawer . . . all felt exceeding warm." Metal felt warmer than wood and hence had to be a better conductor of heat.[6]

Franklin was presenting these thoughts in letters of 1757 and 1758 to John Lining, a South Carolina physician and a fellow Sanctorius disciple. (Lining replicated Sanctorius's metabolic autoexperimentation, correlating the readings of his body with those of Charleston's balmy climate.) To Lining, Franklin described evaporation in colonial terms, especially in the context of productive work. He considered that evaporation might be "why our reapers in Pensylvania," working "in the clear hot sunshine," found themselves cooled by their sweat, as long as they could "supply matter for keeping up that sweat, by drinking frequently of a thin evaporable liquor, [such as] water mixed with rum."[7]

Franklin next compared the bodies of his colony's free white workers with those of the enslaved "negroes" in the West Indies, where sugar and rum originated. These workers, Franklin believed, had "a quicker evaporation of the perspirable matter from their skin and lungs, which, by cooling them more, enables them to bear the sun's heat better than whites." He added that this was "the alledg'd necessity of having negroes rather than whites" to work the Caribbean's sugar fields. The use of the word *alleged* hinted that Franklin did not entirely believe in slavery's necessity. (He did not admit that it was probably his own slave, Peter, who had fetched him dry shirts to replace the sweat-soaked ones.) Finally, Franklin turned back to questions about circulation in the natural world and wondered whether evaporation did not tend to cool the earth, offsetting the sun's heat.[8]

Franklin's writings on meteorology, from about the same time, likewise blended the local with the universal. Atmospheric electricity had universal properties. But it occurred more in some places than others, and Americans, blessed (or cursed?) with frequent thunderstorms, were natural electricians. In London, where thunderstorms were rare, experimenters had found it difficult to "extract the electricity from the atmosphere" in order to verify "Mr. Franklin's hypothesis." North Americans, in contrast, had greater appreciation for the dangers of lightning—and for the benefits of lightning rods and chains. Political arithmetic proved it. In England, Franklin estimated, "those who calculate chances may perhaps find that not one death (or the destruction of one house) in a hundred thousand happens from that cause." The implication was that Americans did not enjoy the same odds.[9]

As he pursued questions in the sciences, Franklin was unable to keep up with everything, even with the work of his disciples. From the 1750s onward, Franklinists abounded throughout Europe. Franz Ulrich Theodor Aepinus was the most important. Aepinus admired Franklin's theory of electrical matter, but he made one key modification to it. Franklin had said that glass would resist an electrical force because it already contained electricity. In a 1759 treatise, Aepinus argued that this resistance was essentially true of most nonelectrical matter. In fact, all matter had to be composed of mutually repulsive particles, as Franklin had posited of electricity. Aepinus used this idea to explain magnetism. Together, magnetism and electricity revealed that different forms of matter could attract and repel each other. This must be how matter constituted itself, with particles repelled from or attracted to each other, depending on what other particles were around them.[10]

In 1759 or shortly thereafter, Franklin learned of Aepinus's work. He briefly commented on some of it, seemed to agree with its major points, but did not further develop his own theories in response. His fame had, paradoxically, made him central to philosophical discussions on which he had little time to comment.[11]

It was clear, however, that Franklin's reputation preceded him— so he proceeded to introduce himself to men of science around

Britain. London may have been the nation's center, but Franklin knew that the provinces were his logical home away from home. (Scottish and English provincials, like Philadelphians, were also eager to assert their places in the republic of letters.) And so, in 1758, during the hot months when fashionable Londoners fled the city, both Benjamin and William visited Franklin and Read ancestral sites. Birmingham had many Read relations, a large number of them with the delightfully specific surnames Cash, Salt, and Wheat. (The Norths and Whites were the family's abstract characters.) Amid the cheerful breakfasts and dinners with his wife's kin, Franklin realized that his distant daughter, Sarah, had inherited the "blue Birmingham eyes" he saw all around him.[12]

Birmingham also swarmed with learned artisans who admired Franklin or whom he admired; quite often, they happily admired each other. Franklin was already Matthew Boulton's role model. Boulton, a metalworker with scientific interests, including the nature of heat, would eventually collaborate with Isaac Watt to develop a working steam engine. He was overjoyed to meet Franklin, "the best Philosopher of America," a mutual friend proclaimed.[13]

Franklin had another felicitous meeting, with John Baskerville, a "japanner" (black-enameler) and fellow printer whose name still designates a distinctive typeface (a version of which you are now reading). Through Fothergill, Franklin had subscribed to Baskerville's 1757 edition of Virgil, signing up for six copies. Franklin later told Baskerville how he had "mischievously" tricked a critic who complained, as did many, that Baskerville type was "a Means of blinding all the Readers in the Nation." Franklin had handed the man a page and led him to believe it was the offending font; it was actually the Caslon typeface the man claimed to prefer but now obliviously reviled. Baskerville promptly printed the endorsement—who better to advertise a new typeface than Philadelphia's famous man of letters?[14]

Franklin departed Birmingham but remained a presence nonetheless. In 1775, his new friends would organize themselves into the Lunar Society. This club, very like the Library Company, eventually included luminaries such as Erasmus Darwin (evolutionist grandfather of the evolutionist), Josiah Wedgwood (the potter), Joseph Priestley, and James Watt, along with Boulton. Franklin found his closest Birmingham friend in Priestley, a dissenting minister and experimental natural philosopher. Franklin would help him prepare his *History and Present State of Electricity,* first published in 1767, and would follow Priestley's subsequent chemical experiments. When Franklin wrote to any of these Lunar Men, it was as one provincial genius to another and often as one self-improved workingman to another. By working, reading, tinkering, and printing, they had all, on opposite sides of the Atlantic, helped build the republic of letters and extend an enlightened society throughout the English-speaking world.[15]

Scotland presented the world with yet more provincial geniuses who befriended Franklin: David Hume; Henry Home, Lord Kames; Adam Smith. From Scotland, Franklin received his first honorary doctorate, bestowed by St. Andrews in early 1759. Meet "Dr. Franklin," as he would thereafter be known. Receiving the honor was an excuse to visit Scotland, and so the Franklins summered there in 1759. Dr. Franklin adored "North Britain," where he experienced "the *densest* Happiness I have met with in any Part of my Life." Even more than the Lunar Men, the Scots celebrated Franklin's marvelously mixed qualities: genteel artisan, philosophical provincial, famous everyman. In rapid succession, the cities of Edinburgh, Glasgow, and St. Andrews admitted Franklin as a burgess, a person legally entitled to enter and roam at will. Edinburgh welcomed him as a guild brother whose character had "reach'd them, Across the Atlantick Ocean." William Strahan, the Scot who had cleverly befriended Franklin before he was the famous Dr. Franklin, triumphantly swept him around Edinburgh.[16]

It is striking that Franklin's Scottish friends were more aristocratic than his English ones. The circle included the Duke of Argyll and Sir Alexander Dick as well as Lord Kames. Being American and a philosopher doubly endeared Franklin to the learned Scots, who, like colonists, lived rather self-consciously within the English-controlled British empire. Indeed, the Scottish aristocrats delighted in Franklin's hands-on quality. They solicited his advice on fireplaces and heating, which says something about the social warmth (and physical chill) in Scotland. Mentioning another man's "Paper on *Fire*" in a 1761 letter to Kames, Franklin described himself as one who had long "been dealing in *Smoke.*" In 1769, Kames remembered the joke and gave the punch line: "I apply to you for a remedy as to an universal Smoke Doctor." Franklin explained why Kames's heating vent leaked smoke, advised how to solve the problem, and stated that the whole thing was "merely the Effect of a Law of Nature."[17]

Franklin would continue the custom of traveling every summer, and each time he expanded his network of correspondents. In 1760, he went to Wales and several northeastern destinations in England. The following year, he went abroad to Flanders and Holland, returning just in time to see George III's coronation procession. It must have disappointed Franklin that, because of the Seven Years' War, he could not meet the Frenchmen who had vindicated his Philadelphia experiment. (Correspondence among philosophers separated by war was permitted—the republic of letters was neutral territory—but actual contact was dicier.)[18]

When in London himself, Franklin reinforced his mixed character—provincial philosopher, artisanal gentleman—in two important ways: he was painted as a natural philosopher, and he invented his glass armonica.

Earlier portraits tended, like the first one by Robert Feke, to emphasize Franklin's gentlemanly status. Benjamin Wilson's bust-length work of 1759 best captured Franklin at midlife. Wilson was a Fellow of the Royal Society (where he probably met Franklin) and a noted chemical and electrical experimenter as well as an artist. Wilson painted Franklin from life and did a pendant of Deborah from a now-lost colonial image; his Franklin has a lively expression but is otherwise indistinguishable from hundreds of other images of provincial gentlemen. Some subsequent portraits, from 1759 onward, resembled Feke's and Wilson's in their emphasis on Franklin's gentility: wigs and fine clothing emphasize his passivity—he just sits there, the idle creature.[19]

After Wilson, however, most portraits also portrayed Franklin as a natural philosopher. And Franklin's hands emerged as active indicators of knowledge. In James McArdell's 1761 mezzotint based on Wilson, Franklin holds a book of his electrical experiments and points to lightning striking a distant town. The warning is softened by two patches of light: the heavenly beams above the storm and, gleaming benignly behind Franklin, the glass globe for generating electricity; experimental philosophy resembled providential power.[20]

The next important image of Franklin, which Mason Chamberlain executed in 1762, also celebrated the sciences. This private image circulated in Edward Fisher's cheaper mezzotints. Fisher's Franklin had no pointing finger—the moral is clear enough without it. An electrical storm crackles outside and smashes several buildings. At his desk, Franklin pauses to listen to the bells behind him,

Franklin with his book and electrostatic globe.
James MacArdell after Benjamin Wilson (1761).
FRANKLIN COLLECTION, YALE UNIVERSITY LIBRARY.

their vibration signaling the atmospheric electricity conducted by
the lightning rod atop the house. (On the right-hand bell, Franklin
self-deprecatingly hung tiny cork balls, a nod to John Canton's experiment disproving his theory of electric atmospheres.) These depictions would become standard Franklin images, the busy man of
science who used his hands.[21]

Franklin's glass armonica, like his portraits, emphasized the human hand but in a way designed to stress its gentility. A year or two

Franklin with his electric bells. Edward Fisher after Mason Chamberlain
(c. 1762). FRANKLIN COLLECTION, YALE UNIVERSITY LIBRARY.

after 1759, an associate in the Royal Society had demonstrated that
by fixing glasses to a table and filling them with different amounts
of water, one could create music by sliding wetted fingers around
their rims. Franklin had long been interested in music and played
several instruments. Looking at the awkward arrangement of upright glasses, he imagined a "more convenient" device "all within
reach of hand to a person sitting before the instrument," and by
1761, he had built it. He reported that his armonica was a set of
glass half-globes mounted sideways, in descending size, along a spin-

Franklin's glass armonica. *Oeuvres de M. Franklin* (1773).
HOUGHTON LIBRARY, HARVARD UNIVERSITY.

dle and set into a water-filled trough. To revolve the glasses, a player pressed a pedal. His or her "fingers should first be a little soaked in water," Franklin noted, "and quite free from all greasiness," the better to elicit an uncanny ringing. William Stukeley, who "visited Dr. Franklyn, the electric genius" in May 1761, remarked on his "glass bells, that warble like the sound of an organ," a rather fragile, watery, and ethereal organ.[22]

Soon, the "celebrated *Glassy-Chord* invented by Mr. Franklin, of Philadelphia," enjoyed a slight craze, carrying Franklin's name abroad yet again. The device was extremely difficult (and expensive) to make, tricky to transport, and amazingly hard to play well, so it is all the more surprising that it gained a following. Wolfgang Amadeus Mozart, no less, played and composed for the device. To honor friend Giambattista Beccaria's "musical language," Italian, Franklin dubbed his instrument "the Armonica."[23]

The glass armonica has puzzled those who think of Franklin as a no-nonsense American, a practical inventor. Whence these warblings, which delighted hoity-toity European audiences? Put the armonica alongside the machine for generating static electricity, however, and the family resemblance is clear: both devices have revolving pieces of round glass, both require the human hand to generate or verify their sensible emissions, and both have emissions that can be varied or sustained, depending on manual effort. The hand was the connection. Keyboard instruments, such as harpsichords—the nearest things to armonicas—did not allow a player to vary sound according to finger pressure. Pianofortes were an exception, but they were still rarities in Britain in the 1760s. Independently, Franklin had invented an instrument that used the hand to elicit modulated sounds. He loved the "incomparably sweet" tones of his armonica and that "they may be swelled and softened at pleasure by stronger or weaker pressures of the finger," the whole point of the device.[24]

Stroking an armonica, a finger created a sound that stimulated a sentiment, a sweet or heavenly mental state. Some of Franklin's contemporaries insisted that the sentiments connected mind and body in the deepest way possible. Franklin concurred. When he played any instrument, touch and sound affected him. After a friend gave him a small harp, he declared, "I shall never touch the sweet Strings of the British Harp without remembering my British Friends." Instructing armonica players how to manipulate the instrument, he noted both the player's manual sensation and the listener's aural and mental "Pleasure." Franklin may have been an American inventor, but this invention revealed his desire for a sophisticated, cosmopolitan reputation.[25]

Franklin's intellectual interaction with women during his time in England was another strong sign that he was becoming more European than American. He had always asserted that women would benefit from the same education as men, but his active circles of friends, from the Junto through the Library Company, had been en-

tirely male. That situation changed once he encountered more
women, in Britain, who did have education comparable to men.
The first truly accomplished armonicist, for instance, was Franklin's
protégée Marianne Davies. She performed publicly to great acclaim
from London to Vienna and gave Marie-Antoinette lessons on the
instrument.[26]

Franklin's new interest in female learning was apparent in his
witty correspondence with his landlady's daughter, Mary "Polly"
Stevenson. While Franklin traveled, they had exchanged letters—
Franklin missed his blue-eyed daughter and Stevenson's father was
dead, so they comforted each other a little. Then, Stevenson decided to make Franklin her teacher as well. She had studied her
mother's lodger well and, in 1760, dropped into a letter two questions about fluid dynamics: Why did water become "warm by pumping"? And how was it that the moon (as "you told me in your last
obliging Conversation") affected tidal flow in rivers?[27]

Franklin obliged Stevenson, again, with a detailed account embel-
lished with a sketched cross section of an estuary. He concluded by
asking, "After writing 6 Folio Pages of Philosophy to a young Girl
[Stevenson was twenty], is it necessary to finish such a Letter with a
Compliment? Is not such a Letter of itself a Compliment?" "Such a
Letter is indeed the highest Compliment," Stevenson agreed. It
lessens the charm of their dialogue only slightly that Franklin and
Stevenson were performing stock characters: the gentleman and
(younger) lady who improved each other in philosophical conversation. Several examples of popular guides to science took this form
and "complimented" women by considering them the intellectual
equals of men, even though they were still barred from universities
and learned societies.[28]

Yet the discussion was to be respectable, avoiding scandal (in this
context, a philosopher was *not* to use his hands) or scandalous topics,
such as a materialism bordering on atheism. "I would not have
trusted myself in the Hands of a Philosopher who regards only Second Causes," Stevenson confided to Franklin, referring to his faith in
the Prime Mover. Her phrasing betrayed her awareness that others
might not think their conversation innocent, let alone edifying.[29]

But on they went, the young woman from London and the older
man from Philadelphia, discussing all manner of natural phenomena, including, of course, electricity. Stevenson read Franklin's *Experiments and Observations*; he proposed experiments for "my dear

little Philosopher." By tying a rope to an upper window and, from the garden below, shaking it into undulations, she could observe the formation of waves. By placing light and dark patches of cloth over snow, she could see the dark sink faster as it absorbed heat and melted the snow beneath. The Junto's members had earlier devised this experiment to demonstrate a point from Newton's *Opticks*— Franklin now included a woman in the club.[30]

Franklin taught Stevenson the usefulness of philosophy. Should she ever find herself short of freshwater while at sea, he advised, she and her fellow passengers could wet their clothes with saltwater or, better still, "make Bathing-Tubs of their empty Water Casks" and sit in seawater for an hour or two each day. The specialized pores in their skin would absorb the water and filter out the salt (impossible if they drank the water). He thus shared with Stevenson the point he had proposed to Cadwallader Colden about the two-way flow of perspiration.[31]

Franklin paid Stevenson the greatest compliment by inserting her into his web of learned correspondents, which grew bigger and more tangled with each passing year. When he sent her a "Paper" with his "Sentiments" on the evaporation of water in 1761, his accompanying instructions indicated how the republic of letters crossed boundaries of nation and sex: "It is Mr. Collinson's Copy, who took it from one I sent thro' his Hands to a Correspondent in France some Years since; I have, as he desired me, corrected the Mistakes he made in transcribing, and must return it to him; but if you think it worth while, you may take a Copy of it." Everyone worked this way. Writing from Harvard, John Winthrop IV asked Franklin to circulate his thoughts on light. Franklin did so, adding the note, "This Letter to be return'd to B.F. after Drs [Richard] Price and [Joseph] Priestly have perus'd it." Franklin's access to the postal system subsidized such circulation. In 1762, he told Sir Alexander Dick that he could provide, "free of Charge for Postage in America," any specimens or seeds for a professor of botany at the University of Edinburgh.[32]

———

THE SCOPE of British botany in America was about to be considerably enlarged. The British and French were hammering out a treaty to end the Seven Years' War. There had been no American hostilities since 1757, just after Franklin crossed the Atlantic. But the conflict had continued elsewhere—it was the first truly global (or world) war, involving military action in Europe, Asia, Africa, and both South and North America. So much territory was involved that as Britain and France (and their allies) met to negotiate in Paris, it was clear that the presumed victor, Britain, could expect incredible gains.[33]

The prospect scared Britain's rulers. Could they really control so much of the globe? Franklin would not soothe their fears. He reminded anyone who would listen that British America, where the population constantly increased, was destined to become the center of the empire.

It was now obvious that Spain's empire, once the mightiest in the modern world, had waned; Britain and France were vying to become the new dominant power in the Americas. Denouncing French aspirations in 1761, Franklin cited Tommaso Campanella's alarmist *De monarchia hispanica discursus* (Discourse on the Spanish Monarchy), written in 1601 and first published in German in 1620. That work decried Spain's dangerous ascent to hemispheric power. "The matter contain'd is so *apropos* to our present situation," Franklin declared, "only changing *Spain* for *France*." Then he supposedly quoted passages from Campanella that he had, in fact, wickedly invented—they cannot be found in the original. All was fair, Franklin evidently believed, in the struggle to get more American territory for British settlers.[34]

British ministers feared, however, that if the colonies expanded, they would also become more autonomous. Even when Britain conquered New France (later Canada) and even though they held the upper hand in the peace negotiations, British officials were reluctant to add Canada to British America. So much new territory, covering such a distance, would be difficult to administer and protect and would worsen the physical disparity between the colonies and the home country. The alternative, to add easily managed Guadeloupe to Britain's lucrative sugar islands, was a serious consideration.[35]

Franklin wanted Canada, which, he believed, would add glory to both the continental and the Atlantic dimensions of the empire. During the war, he had written a pamphlet to plan two western colonies that would stretch from the Ohio River to the Great Lakes. (Such schemes were legion during and after the war.) Citing his "Observations on the Increase of Mankind, &c.," Franklin complained of the expanding colonial population "being confined to the country between the sea and the mountains." He stressed that the "inland navigation or water-carriage by the lakes and great rivers" gave the region "natural advantages" for its settlers, connecting them back to older settlements, to the sea, and from there to the home country. In 1760, he emphasized to Lord Kames that the conquest of Canada would allow "all the Country from St. Laurence to [the] Missisipi" to fill with British settlers and "the Atlantic Sea" with British ships.[36]

Once he got wind of British dithering over Canada, Franklin banged out yet another pamphlet, *The Interest of Great Britain Considered, with Regard to Her Colonies, and the Acquisitions of Canada and Guadaloupe* (1760). In this "Canada Pamphlet," he stressed that the increase and spread of the colonial population would not make the empire too unwieldy but instead would strengthen it. More settlers meant more British imports and stronger economic and social ties between colonies and metropole. Distance was not a disadvantage, in his opinion. "No body foretels the dissolution of the Russian monarchy from its extent," Franklin pointed out, "yet I will venture to say, the eastern parts of it are already much more inaccessible from Petersburgh, than the country on the Mississipi is from London."[37]

Rather than duck the issue, Franklin confronted the British fear of a growing colonial population. Demographic increase would indeed alter the tie between colonies and capital but in a positive way. "When we first began to colonize in America," Franklin observed, "it was necessary to send people, and to send seed-corn; but it is not now necessary that we should furnish, [even] for a new colony, either one or the other." Instead, the colonies imported manufactures, a measure of their societies' increased complexity as well as their connection back to the home country. If British ministers truly feared these developments, Franklin proposed a Swiftian solution: "Let an act of parliament, [then] be made, enjoining the colony midwives to stifle in the birth every third or fourth child," a modest proposal that compared British legislators to scriptural tyrants such as Herod.[38]

Franklin's political arithmetic—long gestating in his almanac and newspaper—underpinned his first significant critique of the British empire. In case anyone missed the point, he appended his "Observations on the Increase of Mankind" to his "Canada Pamphlet." If Franklin's fascination with the Atlantic Ocean reflected an older colonial mind-set, his consideration of continental matters hinted that a later generation of Americans would worry over their "manifest destiny."

Yet Franklin loyally championed the British empire's destiny. He was patriotically gleeful over the possibility that Britons might command the New World, thereby stepping into Spanish shoes, richly buckled with American silver. For this reason—and as his comments on colonists' trade with Britain were indicating—he welcomed any new water route in and around North America, whether the Northwest Passage, the Mississippi River, or the newest problem in hydrography, the Gulf Stream.

The Gulf Stream itself was not new, but public discussion of it was. Indians had probably known parts of the current, and the Norse might have learned about it when they crossed the North Atlantic in the early Middle Ages. And any number of people could have observed the strange debris that the Atlantic scattered, which included pieces of tropical wood that washed ashore in North America and North American native watercraft that drifted over to Ireland. The Spanish gave the first written accounts of transatlantic currents, starting in 1492 with Christopher Columbus. Thereafter, European sailors grew familiar with the currents, though they never put all this knowledge on paper.[39]

The Gulf Stream's southern flow, up past Florida, had been essential to the initial Spanish settlement of the Americas. Spanish mariners used the current to shoot eastward across the Atlantic. The very name Gulf Stream reflected political rather than natural realities. Euro-American observers by and large thought that the current issued out of the Gulf of Mexico, then flowed upward past the coast of North America. The current's name, after its presumed source, acknowledged the old center of power in the Atlantic: Spanish America. Spain's holdings in South America, its long-standing presence in Mexico and the Caribbean, and its command over the Pacific in places such as the Philippines were continuing reminders of its hemispheric and oceanic dominance. It is little wonder, then, that observers of the Atlantic convinced themselves a mighty current thrust out of the Gulf of Mexico toward the Caribbean, then snaked its way alongside North America—they were visualizing Spanish sea power.[40]

In the momentous chess game of European colonization of the Americas, the current represented a command over the Atlantic Ocean that was, in the mid-eighteenth century, suddenly available to new players. Britons understood quite well, at the end of the Seven Years' War, that they needed to understand and exploit the northern part of the Atlantic.

Information about the Gulf Stream began to flood British publications. Robert Bishop's *Instructions and Observations Relative to the Navigation of the Windward and Gulph Passages* (1761) was a good example. Bishop explained that the windward passage guided mariners from Africa to the Americas; the gulf passage, around the Caribbean, was trickier. He recommended routes that used the "current of the *Gulph*" to swing west and north but also ones that avoided the current in order to maneuver around Florida. In that way, they could reach the Mississippi River. It was still in Spanish hands but, if transferred to the British, would give westward settlers access to the Atlantic. The Mississippi River, the Gulf Stream, the Northwest Passage—all were coveted routes that added value to territory in North America. The prospect that Britain might command all three was breathtaking.[41]

Indeed, Franklin wrote the words *Gulph Stream* for the first time, in 1762, while discussing the Northwest Passage. He told John Pringle (a Scottish friend) of the promising northwest "exploration" of one Bartholomew de Fonte, "now Prince of Chili." The explorer's grand-sounding but obscure title should have warned Franklin: the voyage never took place, and there was no such person as the prince of Chili. The hoax was so clever that even Silence Dogood was fooled. Franklin's credulous discussion of de Fonte made two connected points: the Gulf Stream prophesied Britain's eventual supremacy in the North Atlantic, and it indicated the larger pattern of circulation in that ocean. Put another way, British empire was a natural fact.[42]

Franklin dismissed Spanish protests that de Fonte's voyage was imaginary. The Spaniards, he asserted, were simply "jealous" of "the maritime Power of their Neighbours, and apprehensive for their extensive Settlements on the Coasts of the South Sea" or Pacific. As peace negotiations ground on, Franklin anticipated that an ability to navigate the Gulf Stream, the Mississippi, and a possible Northwest Passage would add value to whatever American territory that Britain might receive and that rapidly increasing Americans might settle.[43]

Before the Seven Years' War, Franklin had interpreted the Gulf Stream as a local phenomenon. But now, he viewed it within the context of the greater Atlantic, particularly the ocean's wind vectors. So powerful were these air currents that they created distinct hemispheric climates; the North American side had much harder winters than the warmer European side. While cooling the western Atlantic, the winds sent its waters clockwise. "The Trade Wind blowing over the Atlantic Ocean constantly from the East, between the Tropics," Franklin explained, "carries a Current to the American Coast, and raises the Water there above its natural Level." Once elevated, the water poured through "the Gulf of Mexico, and all along the North American Coast to and beyond the Banks of Newfoundland in a strong Current called by Seamen *the Gulph Stream.*" From Newfoundland, the northwesterly winds "mov'd [the currents] away from the North American Coast towards the coasts of Spain and Africa, whence they get again into the Power of the Trade Winds, and continue the Circulation."[44]

Using the Gulf Stream, Franklin traced both circulation and equilibrium. By rising and then returning to their natural level, the waters of the North Atlantic traveled in a circle. That circle may have always been there in the middle of the ocean, but it only became a topic of public discussion at the end of the Seven Years' War, when European nations were redividing the globe's land and water. Was it a natural fact? The Gulf Stream had to wait for the right political context. For Franklin, wind and waves were both natural forces and vehicles of British empire.

IN 1762, Franklin sailed back to America, crossing the Atlantic he had just been studying. His official business in London was done. He and the Penns had fought out a compromise that had the one advantage of displeasing everyone equally. Thomas Penn had labeled Franklin a "malicious V[illain]." For his part, Franklin conceived a "more cordial and thorough Contempt for [Penn] than I ever before felt for any Man living." The Penns snubbed Franklin and ordered him to meet with their lawyer; he and the lawyer quickly learned to detest each other as well.[45]

But the proprietors had underestimated Franklin. To a correspondent who worried that Fothergill and Collinson would "introduce [Franklin] to the Men of most influence at Court," Thomas Penn had sneered, "Franklin's popularity is nothing here . . . there are very few of any consequence that have heard of his Electrical Experiments." He was wrong. Ultimately, Franklin won the day—in August 1760, the Privy Council ruled mostly in favor of the Pennsylvania Assembly and against the Penns, who had to pay some taxes, if not the amount the assembly wanted. Franklin conceded a truce but itched to get the Penns out of Pennsylvania entirely.[46]

A return home would allow him to gather more support for his bid to establish his colony as a royal one. It would also remove him from a sticky family situation. William Franklin was poised to marry an heiress, Elizabeth Downes, and to accept a royal commission as governor of New Jersey. Whether Franklin disapproved of the social climbing or merely felt slighted by his son's increasing independence, we will never know. But he planned to depart before the wedding and the ceremony of royal appointment. This also meant he would travel separately from his son and daughter-in-law. Perhaps this was wise. It allowed Franklin to cool his temper so he could bless the young couple rather than pick a quarrel with them.

Franklin's departure was a blow to his distinguished British friends and a reminder of the distance between Britain and the colonies. William Strahan wrote that "there is something in his leaving us even more cruel than a Separation by Death; it is like an *untimely Death*." (Franklin agreed, writing Lord Kames that his departure from "the old World to the new" made him "feel like those who are leaving this World for the next.") David Hume, made of sterner stuff, put it best. "America has sent us many good things," he declared, such as the "Gold, Silver, Sugar, Tobacco, Indigo, &c.," that had inspired European colonization. "But you," he assured Franklin, "are the first Philosopher" from America, "the first Great Man of Letters for whom we are beholden to her." Given that Europeans would "never send back an ounce of" American gold, why should they relinquish American "Wisdom?"[47]

If he was sad when he left London, Franklin had cheered up by the time he reached Madeira, where the passengers refreshed themselves with the island's fruit and fabled wine. He described how the ships in his convoy then ran "Southward till we got into the Trade Winds, and then with them Westward till we drew near the Coast of America." Perhaps because of the warm southern route and the fresh fruit, Franklin arrived home in uncharacteristically good health. It was his first experience with the westward movement of the Atlantic winds on which he had commented. (In 1726, he had traveled back to Philadelphia, much more slowly, through northern waters.) He had defined a circle of air and water that swept clockwise around the North Atlantic—now, he had traversed both halves of the circle.[48]

Back in Philadelphia, Franklin busied himself with building a house and being reelected to the assembly. Big news then arrived from Paris: peace. In the 1763 Treaty of Paris, Britain indeed swapped Guadeloupe for Canada. The French retained some fishing rights off Newfoundland but otherwise withdrew from the former New France. The British finally had access to the Mississippi and St. Lawrence Rivers, the two big continental conduits. France even ceded greater access to India to Britons. The British—and British Americans—were delirious about their nation's unsurpassed strength over continents and oceans. Franklin rejoiced that Britons would "retain our Superiourity at Sea" and give the colonists "all the Country" on "this Side [of] the Missisipi." It was only the start. In future, Franklin told his son, any British military force "might easily be poured down the Missisippi upon the lower country [Louisiana], and into the Bay of Mexico, to be used against Cuba, or Mexico itself."[49]

The expansion of British territories in the Caribbean, North America, and South Asia convinced the free inhabitants of the English-speaking world that they belonged to the most powerful empire seen since the Rome of Caesar Augustus—George III was a new Caesar; the age itself was Augustan. It was a dangerous analogy. The Roman empire had declined and then fell. Could Britain do better? Or would maladministration and barbarian invasion doom its empire as well?

Colonial administration was adjusted to meet new demands. Postal service needed reform, which was where Franklin came in. Deliveries to the West Indies and New York had staggered on through the war, though enemy action took out fourteen packets. After a brief respite during the peace negotiations, a permanent British Atlantic postal service began in 1763 and has lasted ever since, through all the wars that have lashed the ocean. This system required not only boats and captains but also colonial postmasters to organize the collection and distribution of the mail and keep track of expenses. Franklin and his counterparts in Virginia (first William Hunter and then John Foxcroft) studied their half of the coastline and decided that they needed to determine new rates, based more precisely on mileage traveled. They published the new rates on a broadside circa 1763. Franklin had discovered one way to conquer distance: make every mile of it pay.[50]

But the rate-related distances were unclear because they had never been measured, despite the frenzy of mapping that had begun even before the war. Franklin and Foxcroft thus set out to do their own postal surveys. From April through November 1763, Franklin made trips to Virginia, New Jersey, New York, and New England, spending almost six of his twenty-four months in America away from home. He measured some of the distances himself, a grueling task for a man of fifty-seven. While riding in New England, he suffered two bad falls, dislocating a shoulder in the second tumble. Perhaps at this point, a bigger empire seemed less appealing.[51]

Bigger for whom? It was not enough that the Seven Years' War had expanded the British empire—it had also raised unprecedented questions about the rights of colonized persons. Britons on either side of the Atlantic discovered a new solicitude for the non-European peoples who lived within the empire, most of whom wished they did not. The French had been able to count on more Indian military support than the British, which highlighted Britain's comparatively poor diplomatic relations with native peoples. Ottawa leader Pontiac made the point clear when he began an Indian rebellion in 1763, once he and other Indians heard that their lands now belonged to Britain. British ministers took note. In a proclamation of 1763, they drew a line down the western edge of the colonial settlements. This border would separate and, it was hoped, prevent conflict between the settlers and the Indians, who thoroughly distrusted each other and threatened the peace.

Slavery troubled British consciences even more than Indian policy. Criticism of the slave trade gained ground, and for the first time, there was public debate over the possible rights of black (and Indian) people. Might they not be subjects of Great Britain, with at least some of the obligations and rights that this legal status would entail? Was it just to exploit African Americans in ways unlawful for people of European descent? Or did their inherited physical and mental characteristics reflect a natural inferiority?[52]

Franklin was beginning to think not. He had been elected to Dr. Bray's Associates in 1760, while living in London. He agreed to inspect the "Negro School" in Philadelphia on his return. In assenting to this, he had perhaps capitulated to Deborah Franklin. She had expressed concern over slaves before her husband did and, as an Anglican, believed in the Anglican evangelism of the associates. In December 1763, Franklin visited the Philadelphia school, and its pupils astonished him. They gave him "a higher Opinion of the natural Capacities of the black Race, than I had ever before entertained. Their Apprehension seems as quick, their Memory as strong, and their Docility in every Respect equal to that of white Children." Franklin could no longer account for his earlier "Prejudices," which had been considerable.[53]

He made no attack on slavery itself, and he continued to own slaves, but Franklin had come to see that people of African ancestry possessed sufficient intelligence to claim a place in civil society. He had earlier conceded that Germans and Indians differed from British settlers only in custom and language; now, he thought the same of people of African descent. This mattered to Franklin—only by thinking of Africans as people who might acquire knowledge could he consider them equal to free people of European descent. He continued to work with Dr. Bray's Associates to educate freed blacks. In 1767, he and two other associates would be delegated to invest £1,000 in Philadelphia real estate in order to generate income "for the Support of Negro Schools in America."[54]

In the 1760s as well, Franklin expressed a new sympathy for Native Americans and questioned his earlier belief that their skin marked their inferiority to whites. The paranoia and racism of Pennsylvania's western colonists prompted his change of mind. In December 1763, around the time Franklin visited the "Negro School," a group of armed settlers, the "Paxton Boys," attacked some Indians in Lancaster County, killing and scalping six. Two weeks later, the Paxtonites tracked down and slaughtered the fourteen Indians who had survived the earlier attack and fled to the town workhouse in Lancaster. Between this and Pontiac's uprising, it looked as if British officials had been right to worry about their ability to keep order over so many new people—and the expanse of new territory—at such a distance.

The murder of the Indians shocked Franklin. He almost immediately produced a pamphlet to denounce it. He decried how "the only Crime of these poor Wretches seems to have been, that they had a reddish brown Skin, and black Hair." To a British agent in charge of Indian affairs, Franklin stressed that new western settlements would "be of great National Advantage with respect to Trade" only if done "with the Approbation of the Indians." Recent attacks on the Indians had proved that "our Frontier People are yet greater Barbarians than the Indians." More significantly, Franklin—who, in his "Observations on the Increase of Mankind" had wished to see America "scoured" of its indigenous population—began to defend Indians' territorial claims.[55]

This move was not entirely selfless. If Indians had land rights, they could legally transfer them to colonists, which would undermine Britain's claims to govern these transactions. It was a bit disloyal of Franklin to flout British law, though it was very common for colonists to do so in this regard.

Taken together, Franklin's ideas of blacks and Indians nonetheless represented an important readjustment. He had once coldly eyed them as things to be analyzed, as with the pores in Indians' skin or the rates of smallpox deaths among African Americans. Now, he considered them as sociable beings similar to people of European descent. They were crafters of custom, respecters of property rights, students of written language. His prejudices moved from physical to cultural criteria, as when he agreed that freed blacks needed to be educated and Christianized. It was a limited advance but, in that era, an advance nonetheless. Still, it was not clear whether Franklin had repented his earlier opinion that Indians were a doomed population. Did he think that because their populations would inevitably decline, there was no need to mistreat them in the meantime? Or did he think they would be a lasting presence in the land—hence the need to treat them with more justice than the Paxton Boys handed out?

The Paxtonites may have claimed another casualty: Franklin's political reputation in Pennsylvania. The Paxton Boys marched on Philadelphia in early 1764 to attack Indians (and pro-Indian policy); Franklin drummed up a volunteer defense force. At the governor's request, he led a delegation that persuaded the Paxtonites to disperse—a narrow escape. But then, in his pamphlet *Cool Thoughts on the Present Situation of Public Affairs,* Franklin argued that the Paxton riots demonstrated the proprietors' incompetence; the Crown should take over. The colony's present government, he wrote, "has scarce authority enough to keep the common Peace. Mobs assemble and kill (we scarce dare say *murder*) Numbers of innocent People in cold Blood." Meanwhile, even the colonists, "People of [the] *three Countries*" of Britain, Ireland, and Germany, suffered under the

Penns' misrule. At least some Pennsylvanians agreed—Franklin was elected speaker of the assembly in May.[56]

The debate over making Pennsylvania a crown colony was extremely divisive, however, and Franklin was reckless in putting himself at its center. His 1764 campaign for reelection to the assembly was a grim affair. His detractors painted him as a hypocrite—he had benefited from the attentions of the proprietarial party before he turned on them. They also mocked him as a philosopher. One critic offered an epitaph: "He was the first *Philosopher* / Who, contrary to any known System, discovered / How to maltreat his / PATRONS." Franklin lost in Philadelphia by a mere nineteen votes, his first defeat after thirteen consecutive elections. One wit concluded that he "died like a philosopher." He never served in the assembly again. He summarized the Paxtonite affair and its fallout in the outline for his autobiography: "Sent out to the Insurgents—Turn them back. Little Thanks. Disputes revived."[57]

FRANKLIN RETURNED to London with almost unseemly haste. He lost his assembly seat on October 1 but was reelected as the assembly's agent on October 25. He may have lost authority within the colony, but he was still prized for the famous face he presented in London. He embarked on the *King of Prussia* on November 9, leaving his family to finish the new house.

Coming so late in the season, the voyage ran into "terrible Weather." Friends had prayed that Franklin would get "thirty Days fair Wind"; the thirty days expired—the wind then whipped up. A borrowed woolen gown kept Franklin warm. It also helped, he wrote Deborah, that "every body on board" treated him well, particularly the captain: "No Father could be tenderer to a Child, than Capt. [James] Robinson has been to me." Franklin arrived in Portsmouth on December 9. He drew up to Craven Street the next day, and the maid showed him in. Returning home herself, Mrs. Stevenson "was a good deal surpriz'd to find me in her Parlour," Franklin chuckled to Polly. Of course, an Atlantic crossing meant illness; he dutifully suffered "a most violent Cold" for nearly a dozen days in mid-December.[58]

Franklin settled back into his metropolitan roles as a famous man of letters (he was reelected to the Royal Society's council in 1765,

1766, and 1772), a man of influence (he helped Collinson engineer the title of Royal Botanist for John Bartram in 1765), and a high-ranking postal official. He was more determined than ever to wrest Pennsylvania away from the Penns and put it under Crown rule. His antiproprietorial campaign made him a champion of colonial interests. Other colonies procured his services, so that Franklin began representing the Georgia colony (in 1768) and the New Jersey and Massachusetts assemblies (in 1769 and 1770, respectively). He took these appointments seriously. His records indicate payments to the "doorkeeper of ye Board of Trade"—tipping the servants kept the door open.[59]

Franklin was also watching out for his own interests, and during this time, he became a land speculator. His retirement from the printing business meant he could not expect any significant increase in income from his printshop, and his salaries as colonial agent were small; being a philosopher paid nothing. He needed other income. All that new territory in North America led to many settlement schemes, if not outright land grabs. Franklin followed debates in the Board of Trade over western territory, where colonists and British traders jockeyed for access to the fur trade, and he invested in several land companies. His earlier contribution to cartography proved useful; in 1766, he showed a potential investor the boundaries of a projected land company by giving him "one of [Lewis] Evans's maps" on which he had "marked with a wash of red ink the whole country included" in the scheme.[60]

Like many others, Franklin looked north and west for new land. He tried to help "the Nantucket Whalers, who are mostly my Relations," to get land on St. John's Island. There, they would be less cooped up and would gain access to "excellent" whaling and fishing. For himself, Franklin petitioned and in 1767 received a grant of 20,000 acres in Nova Scotia, a nice scrap snipped from the immense tapestry of French cession. Though he was ordered to settle one inhabitant per 200 acres within ten years, he never did. The grant eventually lapsed.[61]

Franklin took more seriously a collective venture, the Grand Ohio Company, also called the Walpole Company, organized in 1769. This company sought the lands west of Virginia and south of the Ohio River—territory that Indians had ceded in 1768, following the collapse of Pontiac's and other uprisings. The company's royal petition for nearly two and a half million acres described the "said

Tract of Land" as "vacant and unsettled by any of your Majestys Subjects." (Even after the United States spurned Britain, Franklin retained his Walpole Company shares, hoping they would enrich his heirs.)[62]

With borders in a constant state of flux, the sciences of surveying and cartography were more important than ever. In 1764, British America was divided into northern and southern districts, each endowed with specialized administrators. A Surveyor General presided over each section, Samuel Holland in the north and William Gerard De Brahm (for East Florida) and George Gauld (for West Florida) in the south (the south was informally divided into two sections). Colonists worried that new surveys might slice into their holdings. At great expense, the astronomers and geodetic surveyors Charles Mason and Jeremiah Dixon labored from 1763 until 1768 to determine the line between Pennsylvania and Maryland that still bears their names. The mission was both scientific and imperial. Mason and Dixon measured a degree of longitude and a degree of latitude during their survey and determined the magnitude of gravity at the forks of the Brandywine Creek in Pennsylvania, comparing it to a reading done at the Royal Observatory in Greenwich.[63]

Franklin, the colonial man of letters, was a consultant on this project. Acting as colonial postmaster and as a Fellow of the Royal Society, he advised the society how to contact Mason and Dixon, who together made a distant—and moving—target during their survey. The monthly packet had already sailed by the time the society made its inquiry, so Franklin offered another way to get the materials to the surveyors, via his remarkable network of friends and ships' captains.[64]

As important, he followed developments in marine cartography. There were few seaborne counterparts to North America's official surveyors. Until 1795, Britain lacked a governmental hydrographic office (which France had), so it usually encouraged such work indirectly, by permitting private firms to publish charts. Little was censored—an unprecedented amount of maritime information was publicly available, especially in Portsmouth and London. The London market flourished on Tower Hill, a lively nautical nest where "Press Gangs" snatched men for His Majesty's ships (one in ten British men had been impressed into wartime naval service) while customers perused charts. Anyone with enough money—women, landsmen, even foreigners—could buy a British chart of the Atlantic.

Franklin was one such customer, purchasing several new maps and charts during his third London residence.[65]

By the 1760s, three agencies dominated British marine cartography, and Franklin patronized them all. The oldest, Mount and Page, was a grand old firm that, under a variety of names, spanned four centuries. By the early eighteenth century, it was the sole publisher of the canonical *English Pilot*, a classic sea atlas. Mount and Page produced several editions by Samuel Sturmy and John Seller, which Franklin had conquered in his youth, and it had published Edmond Halley's charts of magnetic variation. The second firm, Sayer and Bennett, was newer, dating from 1720, and specialized in charts rather than atlases or books. It scored a coup in 1775 when it obtained the rights to Captain James Cook's surveys of the Canadian coastline, then carried on to publish Cook's cartographic surveys of the Pacific. Last, there was Thomas Jefferys, a newcomer who published two important maritime atlases, *The American Neptune* and *The Atlantic Pilot*. The former gorgeously represented the coastline; the latter was more innovatively hydrographic in that it indicated the routes of voyages of exploration.[66]

Hydrographic and navigational discoveries were of sufficient interest to appear in cheaper media, such as newspapers, including Franklin's old paper. In early 1765, the *Pennsylvania Gazette* recounted the ordeal of a ship that, sailing to Philadelphia from Connecticut, "got into the Gulph Stream, and was carried so far to the Eastward, that the first Land she made was Newfoundland." The current was not so well known that it was avoidable, yet it was familiar enough that the gazette felt no need to explain what the "Gulph Stream" was—by the 1760s, colonists knew.[67]

This was the moment, above all, to solve the problem of longitude, the empire's greatest problem of distance. Franklin had arrived back in London in time to get a front-row seat on the final race for the prize, from 1763 to 1773. Parliament had yet to pay anyone the money it had promised in 1714, when Franklin was a child on the far side of the Atlantic Ocean.

Two solutions were possible. A navigator could either compare a celestial body's position at sea against that at a fixed point on land (represented by an accurate timepiece) or determine position based on the locations of the celestial bodies that had predictable patterns.

Franklin knew the men, John Harrison and Nevil Maskelyne, who championed each solution. Harrison, an artisan, made the first working chronometer, a timepiece whose elaborate gimbaling enabled it to keep time despite a ship's jarring motion; Maskelyne, astronomer royal, produced the *Nautical Almanac* and the *Tables Requisite* with which navigators could determine longitude by lunar distances. Franklin served on the Royal Society's council when, in 1761, it advised the Board of Longitude on the equipment to accompany Harrison's celebrated chronometer during its test voyage to Jamaica. (Franklin sent Harrison's 1767 essay on his marine "Watch" to a friend in Philadelphia.) But chronometers were prohibitively expensive, unlike star charts, which was why Maskelyne's solution remained competitive. In an uneasy compromise, Parliament awarded some of the prize money to Harrison but did not proclaim him the contest's winner.[68]

Born an artisan (like Harrison) and formerly an almanac maker and currently a Fellow of the Royal Society (like Maskelyne), Franklin was uniquely suited to be cordial to both men, who hated each other. Despite this antipathy, each had helped to make the oceans safer.

FOR EVERY chronometer that crossed the Atlantic, there were thousands of letters. Quieter and less flamboyant than the quest for longitude, the further development of the postal system was nevertheless the most effective way to bridge distances. For that reason, reforms of the post were central to the empire and to Franklin's imperial career.

The reforms were ongoing. In 1764, Franklin met with the secretary of the Post Office, Anthony Todd, probably to discuss the changes Franklin and Foxcroft had recommended in September. Their main point, that postage should be based on distance, was accepted. The two American officials published a table of rates based on travel outward from New York, where the Atlantic post arrived. More ships were laid on between North America and Britain, and service within the continent became more frequent, partly by "making the Mails travel by Night as well as by Day, which has never heretofore been done in America." Franklin and Foxcroft requested "Maps delineated and adapted to the Post Roads of America" to keep postal riders moving even in gloom of night. After the Postal Act of 1765, the northern postal district gathered up the new Canadian territories and the southern one added East Florida.[69]

With the expansion of the British Post Office, communication across the Atlantic became both regular and regulated. It still took from one to three months, depending on the route and sailing conditions, but service became more predictable and more frequent, which was a tremendous boon. No longer would colonists suspect that they received news, books, and letters only haphazardly; no longer would merchants and ministers fear that colonists were unaware of official news and policy.[70]

Imagine a postal customer—say, Franklin himself—using this system. Look at all the paper he used. Paper, that marvelous substance, represented him to distant friends, and it let him glimpse those friends from a distance.

At a stationers', Franklin could buy writing paper and, if he did not make them himself, quills and ink. He might also purchase an epistolary novel for himself or, for a young friend, a how-to guide on writing letters—both were best-selling genres. He could consult a newspaper, which published the schedule for packet boats. After that would come writing, folding, sealing, and addressing the letter. He could take it to the local post office (usually a shop licensed to handle mail) or wait until a postboy blew a horn or rang a bell in the street and then hurry the letter out to him. If he felt very grand or pitied his correspondent's poverty, he sent the letter "post paid." This was rare—mostly, he paid postage on whatever arrived. Thus, the sociable souls of the eighteenth century honored their relations with each other: they paid for each other's letters. (In this regard, we live in a similar era, as anyone who has printed out a long e-mail attachment knows.)[71]

Thousands of eighteenth-century letters show signs of having been written according to postal schedules, not the writer's inclinations. Even postal officials were caught unawares. To apologize for the brevity of one letter to Deborah, Franklin scribbled at its bottom, "I write this in hopes of [it] reaching the Packet" in time. Shortly after Polly Stevenson married William Hewson, Franklin began a chatty letter to her that ended abruptly when he heard "the Post-man's Bell, so can only add my affectionate Respects to Mr. Hewson, and best Wishes of perpetual Happiness for you both." But a regular post was a marvel—proof positive that human sociability defied distance. Writing to Polly Stevenson, as she then was, Franklin called down "Blessings on his Soul that first invented Writing, without which I should, at this Distance, be as effectually cut off from my Friends in England, as the Dead are from the Living."[72]

The administrators and packet captains of the postal system were themselves a sociable group. Franklin became friends with Anthony Todd, and both men invested in the Ohio Company. London-based postal officials, including Franklin, regularly dined on venison that the postmasters general provided. And Franklin, long a collector of maritime clients, became patron to several packet boat captains, especially Nathaniel Falconer. He gave business advice to Falconer; Falconer in turn carried news of Franklin's Philadelphia family (including his yet-unseen grandchildren) and transported books from London for the Library Company. Falconer had a standing invitation to spend Christmas with Franklin at Craven Street.[73]

Other useful captains were kinfolk. Nantucketers were always to be found swarming around Franklin. Among these, Timothy Folger had pride of place. Franklin's sister, Jane Mecom, used "capt. Foulger" to send letters to Craven Street; Jonathan Williams Sr., Franklin's nephew, employed Folger to communicate with Franklin. The family also relied on another Nantucket relation, Seth Paddock, as well as Captain Isaac All, Franklin's nephew by marriage, to keep in touch with each other. As Franklin summarized in a note to Deborah in 1765, he "receiv'd kind Letters per [Captain James] Friend and per the Packet"—both private and public services solved, for the moment, some of the dilemmas of distance.[74]

Franklin also used transatlantic correspondence to participate in the republic of letters. Sea captains and kinfolk sent him an astonishing range of American specimens and commodities. In return, Franklin packed scientific equipment off to America. From Jamaica, for example, Falconer sent a turtle (probably to eat) and two exotic birds (as pets or specimens). Taking advantage of London's unparalleled workshops for scientific instruments, Franklin purchased several items for Harvard College, including "an equal Altitude Instrument" possibly intended for Harvard's observation of the 1769 transit of Venus. He sent a reflecting telescope, microscope, and thermometer to Humphry Marshall, and a perspective glass to a friend in France.[75]

Franklin next figured out how to make himself visible throughout the Atlantic world: he circulated his likeness on paper. He broadcast Edward Fisher's mezzotints of himself to friends, family, and patrons—anyone with space on a wall. These inexpensive images showed him at his desk, electrical wires and bells dangling behind him. William and Benjamin Franklin bought one hundred copies of the 1763 print. William evidently sold many of them. His father took a dozen to roll up, slide into tin cases, and send to Boston, "it being the only way in which I am now likely ever to visit my Friends there." In the autumn of 1768, his old friend John Bartram remarked that "thy pretty exact picture" (probably the mezzotint) was "a dayly fresh membrance of intimate frindship" between himself and his "dear Benjamin." The Bache family, into which Franklin's daughter Sarah had married, owned another copy, which they evidently moved between dining room and parlor so that "Franklin" could stay with the assembled company. The mezzotint showed Franklin's grandson, Benjamin Franklin Bache, what his famous grandfather looked like. Little Benny was reported to kiss the icon.[76]

Above all, Franklin trafficked in groceries—"Goodeys," he drooled. He harvested an amazing range of treats from members of his North Atlantic family. Deborah Franklin forwarded Indian nocake (maize roasted and then ground) from Nantucket. Nantucketer Seth Paddock sent "Salted Cod fish Cured" from Timothy Folger. Other shipments included salt beef and pork, the dried tongues and air bladders of codfish (a delicacy, when reconstituted), dried venison, Deborah Franklin's hams, ordinary ground maize, cranberries, buckwheat, and American apples, which Franklin particularly relished. These foods comforted the homesick Franklin but, in the quantities he received, it is hard to believe that he—even in his stout middle age—ate everything himself. More likely, he proffered American treats to his hosts and his guests. He thus distinguished his hospitality from Mrs. Stevenson's and gave Deborah Franklin a virtual presence in the house on Craven Street.[77]

LETTERS, feasts of venison, favors to friends, American goodies— postal work was pleasant. The same could not be said of the commercial traffic across the British Atlantic. Franklin found himself at the center of a political storm when Parliament passed the 1765 Stamp Act, which imposed a tax on a range of paper items that were to bear the stamp. The revenue was desperately needed—Britain had run up an unprecedented debt during the Seven Years' War, and officials were taxing everything they could think of. But the Stamp Tax affected all the paper items that the letter-posting, newspaper-reading, novel-buying colonists had come to regard as part of everyday life and that served as an important link between the colonists and the metropole. This tax was the first in a series that stirred up the colonial protests that would culminate in the American Revolution.

Colonists argued that because they were not represented in Parliament, that body had no right to tax them on goods they had to import from the home country. British officials smoothly assured the colonists that they were "virtually" represented—members of Parliament for whom they had never voted nevertheless took their interests to heart. Indeed, many Britons lived in districts that had no member of Parliament at all. But qualified colonists (white men who owned property) were accustomed to electing representatives to their local houses of assembly. Without their own members of Parliament, they did not consider themselves "actually" represented. And the distance between them and their putative representatives in Parliament made it seem unlikely that those men knew much, if anything, about them.[78]

Franklin adopted a position of compromise, midway between British and colonial extremes. He would maintain his balance until 1775. He remained convinced that the source of the colonies' power lay in their rapidly increasing populations. Even if untaxed, their commerce with Britain would eventually yield prodigious amounts of revenue—that was what he wanted Britain's ministers to accept. But he thought that, in the meantime, colonists should comply with the Stamp Act. He planned for the implementation of the act while recommending its repeal—a compromise that was out of step with American opinion. Colonists were rioting, burning tax officials in effigy, and blocking the distribution of stamp materials. Some British officials advocated force to administer the stamps; Franklin and others deplored this approach.

Under the pseudonym Homespun, Franklin trumpeted colonial consumer power: a general boycott on imported British goods would demonstrate colonists' real value. Did Americans really need tea at breakfast? They could instead start the day with good solid food, especially "Indian corn," one of the most "agreeable and wholesome grains in the world." Did they need imported cloth?

They could shear rather than eat their lambs—"the sweet little creatures are all alive to this day, with the prettiest fleeces on their backs imaginable." (These were sweet and pretty phrases from a lapsed vegetarian.) A boycott of nearly "two millions of people," in "a country of 1500 miles extent," would easily destroy British merchants and manufacturers.[79]

In London, cool heads urged consultation with the Americans. And who would be better to consult than America's only true philosopher, Benjamin Franklin? He was summoned for an interview in the House of Commons in 1766. No orator, Franklin found that the question-and-answer format suited his gift for dialogue. He claimed, yet again, that the empire's center of power—meaning the majority of its producing and consuming subjects—was shifting to the western side of the Atlantic. He stressed that American consumption of British manufactures grew not only because the population was expanding but also because Americans had increasing wealth. Untaxed, their buying power would be all the greater. Do not alienate us, Franklin was warning the members of Parliament. He lectured them that colonists used to have "particular regard" for Britons and "a fondness for [British] fashions."[80]

Yet Americans' increasing buying power, Franklin's trump card, was a tricky one to play. It was hard to deny that colonists already paid for imperial services and could afford to pay more. Cross-examined about the Post Office, Franklin insisted that postage was not a tax but "a quantum meruit [as much as is deserved] for a service done." One member sharply asked why colonists increased so rapidly. Franklin admitted that people could marry earlier in the colonies because so much land was available—land was the key to their fecundity and wealth. But he denied that this meant colonists could pay more taxes than land-starved Britons. Rather, he pointedly said, ordinary people in America were "better paid for their labour" than the oppressed workers of Britain.[81]

To make his point, Franklin distinguished between "duties" on commerce and "internal taxes." Commercial duties had to be paid when an item was landed; an internal tax was paid once the good circulated in America. Americans accepted the former, he claimed, but not the latter, as with the Stamp Act. He emphatically stated that Americans would never accept parliamentary taxation: "No power, how great soever, can force men to change their opinions." *Opinion*—the term defined matters that could not be defined by facts, sensory experience, or even reason. His use of the term in this context made clear that Franklin did not necessarily believe that Americans were right but also that Britons were unwise to use force against them. But his proposed compromise, a distinction between external versus internal taxes, was a distinction without a difference. Americans would accept neither. That Franklin claimed the difference showed, again, how he was out of step with American opinion at home.[82]

Members of Parliament, however, bought his story and repealed the Stamp Act. The architect of the repeal, William Pitt, later Lord Chatham, became a hero to Americans. His image—often in toga and always with implied halo—proliferated throughout the colonies. Franklin presented a bust of him to Harvard College. He also enjoyed a bit of the afterglow. "Caress'd by Ministry," he bragged of himself. Fothergill may at this time have presented Franklin with a silver milk jug engraved, "Keep bright the chain," appropriating the imagery of Anglo-Iroquois diplomacy to represent Anglo-American relations.[83]

The repeal of the Stamp Act was fortunate for Franklin. Although his interview in Parliament had won him British plaudits, he was nevertheless making enemies in several camps. His criticism of the Pennsylvania proprietors unsurprisingly annoyed those in the proprietary party, as well as the Penns' powerful friends in Britain. At the same time, many colonists suspected him of a kind of virtual representation of them once they learned he had planned to implement the Stamp Act. The distance over the Atlantic muffled the criticism, as did loud rejoicing over the Stamp Act's repeal.

What did Franklin do with his reprieve? He shaped, yet again, his image as a philosopher. A Scottish friend, Robert Alexander, commissioned a portrait of him by David Martin. Completed in 1766, the painting presented Franklin as a man of science. In it, he wears a short wig in the style known as "physical," favored by physicans and men of science. He sits and reads, one hand holding a book, the other his chin. The head-on-hand position was the classic pose of contemplation, but here, it is accessorized by that pointing index finger. The finger was not part of the classical convention but evidently was recognized as Franklinian. A huge bust of Newton looms, but Newton's intellectual heir is the more brightly lit of the two figures. Franklin's eyes are lowered over his reading material, his trademark spectacles perched on his nose. The Society of Artists exhibited the

Franklin with a bust of Newton. Benjamin Martin (1767).
PENNSYLVANIA ACADEMY OF THE FINE ARTS.

picture in spring 1767; Horace Walpole noted in his copy of the ex-
hibit catalog that it was "a great likeness." Franklin himself liked it
so much that he requested a copy from Martin, the only change being to his chair, which was ornate in the original but simple in
Franklin's version.[84]

Franklin also used the reprieve to enjoy two summer visits to the
European continent, much of which had been off-limits during the
recent war. In 1766, he and his Scottish physician friend, John
Pringle, traveled through the German-speaking territories. Both

were elected to the Royal Society of Science at Göttingen in July. The following summer, the two men went to France. Franklin finally met his electrical champion, Dalibard, as well as many other French men of science. He also began to make contacts in the French political world. He was presented to Louis XV and met several so-called physiocrats. Physiocracy was a French field of political economy. Physiocrats eagerly read Franklin's work on political arithmetic, and they mistakenly assumed him to be, as they were, opposed to all taxes. He was not, but his odd distinction, when grilled by Parliament, between internal and external taxes had misled many. And it was to that problem he had to return, once the pleasant summer rambles were over.[85]

Franklin's views on taxes and commerce were never quite clear. He hoped that "in time perhaps Mankind may be wise enough to let Trade take its own Course, find its own Channels, and regulate its own Proportions." This was yet another of those images that was supposed to convince readers that nature proved the truth of some point that was actually debatable. Colonists did not believe it. Many of them instead found their own solution in smuggling. Franklin denounced them in the *London Chronicle* in late 1767, pointing out that commercial duties contributed to the "publick treasure" and common good of the empire. Smugglers were "pickpockets." Among the offices thus shortchanged was the Post Office, which had recently restricted public officials' franking privileges; this decreased the potential for corruption but made it more important to safeguard lawful forms of revenue. Franklin seemed to sympathize with British officials; Americans had reason to suspect him of going native, what with his long residence in London.[86]

The fact that Franklin lived in London also raised questions about his ability to oversee, at a remove, postal affairs in America. In May 1768, the Commissioners of Customs in Boston complained to the Lords Commissioners of the Treasury about the "want of a proper establishment of the posts in this Country," particularly the slowness of mail service. One problem they claimed was inefficient service along the American coastline. This was a criticism of Franklin's supposedly reformed service and may have generated gossip about him. Only a month later, Anthony Todd related to a correspondent that Lord Sandwich had hinted that Franklin "ought, after some year's absence, to return thither [to America] to his duty."[87]

How could Franklin prove himself dutiful, even in absentia? The commissioners' second complaint proved useful. They pointed to the peculiar fact that travel from London to Boston was much quicker than that from Falmouth to New York, even though these were roughly similar distances. It provided Franklin with the perfect opportunity to say something about the Gulf Stream. He made his first public statement about the current in an October 1768 letter to Todd. "The long passages made by some Ships bound from England to New York," he claimed, resulted from their sailing in the middle of the "*Gulph Stream*"—hence the post's different arrival times in North America, depending on which route a ship had taken across the North Atlantic.[88]

This simple observation about nature allowed Franklin to make three complicated points about empire: the Gulf Stream was useful to the empire (particularly the postal system); Americans had superior knowledge of it; and he himself, in London, had access to this knowledge. To make his case, he named his source, "Captain Folger a very intelligent Mariner of the Island of Nantuckett," and appeared to be quoting a conversation he had had with him. Folger knew the Nantucket whalers, who in turn knew "that the Whales are found generally near the Edges of the *Gulph Stream,* a strong Current so called which comes out of the Gulph of Florida, passing Northeasterly along the Coast of America, and the[n] turning off most Easterly running at the rate of 4, 3 1/2, 3 and 2 1/2 Miles an Hour."[89]

By paraphrasing his cousin to Todd, Franklin gave him the authority to define natural facts. *Folger* had claimed that whalers had to "Cruise along the Edges of the Stream in quest of Whales," becoming "better acquainted with the Course, Breadth, Strength and extent of the same" than did "Navigators" who "only cross it in their Voyages to and from America." Those navigators made the mistake of sailing west in the eastward path of the Gulf Stream, which slowed them considerably. They did so for good reason, however, in order to stay clear of "Cape Sable Shoals, Georges Banks or Nantucket Shoals," putting them smack in the middle of the current. They avoided grounding or wrecking their ships at the cost of a slower crossing—probably a reasonable trade-off.[90]

But Franklin thought that navigators could steer a path between the shoals and the current. He reported to Todd that he had asked Folger to mark "on a Chart, the Dimentions Course and Swiftness of the Stream from it's first coming out of the Gulph, where it is narrowest and strongest; till it turns away to go to the Southward of the Western Islands, where it is Broader and weaker." He had also solicited from Folger "Written directions" about avoiding both the stream and the dreaded banks and shoals. Folger marked the chart in red, and Franklin sent it to the Post Office to engrave and distribute to packet boat captains. The Post Office dutifully printed the chart, complete with Folger's instructions. The teamwork between a philosopher and a mariner was crucial; the philosopher's generosity in giving the mariner coauthorship unusual.[91]

It seems incredible that British captains were entirely ignorant of the Gulf Stream. Yet maritime knowledge was sometimes highly segmented. From 1765 to 1770, the Post Office neither requested nor required packet captains to gather information about navigation or give advice about charts. And the journals of one very able seaman, James Cook (later the famed Captain Cook of Pacific exploration), bear out Franklin's claim. Cook surveyed Newfoundland from 1764 to 1765, under the guidance of Surveyor General Samuel Holland, who mapped the area in order to regulate the French crews that continued to fish there. Cook's charts were published individually by both Mount and Page and Thomas Jefferys, then gathered into Sayer and Bennett's *The Newfoundland Pilot* (1769). Cook indeed kept an eye out for currents and discovered them both to east and west. But after he "Try'd the Current but found none" on May 26, 1765, he stopped looking, despite pestering local fisherman about "the hidden dangers" of the tricky Newfoundland coast.[92]

Cook may have been just a few years too early for the locals to be forthcoming with him. In 1768, when Folger told Franklin about the Gulf Stream's significance to whalers, it was no longer a commercially advantageous trade secret. In the seventeenth century, American whalers had begun their hunts just offshore. By the 1730s, they had abandoned offshore whaling for deep-sea whaling, and around the 1750s, they headed to the Gulf Stream. But after 1760, whalers were moving into Arctic waters, and around 1768, they went south toward the Caribbean, Africa, and Gulf of Mexico. By publicizing the Gulf Stream, Folger had the satisfaction of knowing his name was circulating among high-ranking British officials without any nagging guilt over ruining another man's trade. Secretary of the Post Office Todd now knew Folger as a maritime expert; Franklin's letter was copied at least twice in 1769 (the copyist mistakenly gave that year for its composition) and made the rounds in the Treasury.[93]

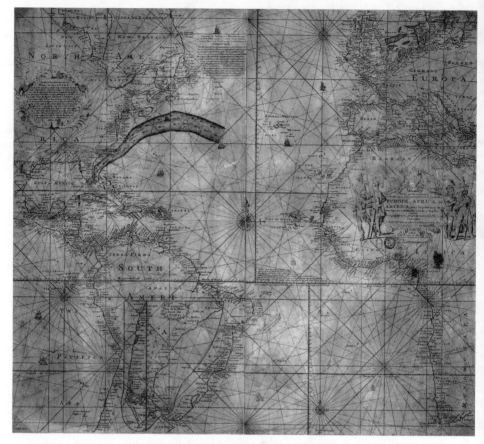

The first chart of the Gulf Stream. Mount and Page (1768).
LIBRARY OF CONGRESS.

So, here it is, the first known chart of the Gulf Stream, done
(Franklin later recollected) in 1768. Mount and Page was, by late
1767, the Post Office's contract stationer and produced the chart.
The firm often reprinted from its own stock, so it thriftily reused an
older map of the whole Atlantic Ocean from its new sea atlas, *Atlas
maritimus novus* (1702). The result is an odd chart, so big it nearly
drowns the small feature Folger and Franklin added to it. Folger's
instructions are similarly marginal, even smaller than Franklin's description of Atlantic storms inserted into Lewis Evans's map of the
mid-Atlantic colonies. Spanning the major landmasses of the Western and Eastern Hemispheres, the chart had to be printed in four
panels, joined at the readings for 16 degrees north and 32.5 degrees west. There was plenty of room to depict the full sweep of the

Timothy Folger's sailing instructions.
Close-up of Mount and Page chart.
LIBRARY OF CONGRESS.

Gulf Stream, which Franklin had both described and seen, but the current stops far short of the "Azores or Western Isles," where Folger had indicated the Gulf Stream dipped south. It was an especially odd image for a natural philosopher who thought of circulation in terms of equilibriums. Someone truly interested in balance should have worried about where all the Gulf Stream's water went.[94]

In fact, Franklin, Folger, and the Post Office had little interest in presenting the entire circle of water around the North Atlantic. No map merely represents what lies in nature. This, the first chart of the Gulf Stream, made a statement about British overseas power. The Gulf Stream was an imperial ornament, one that measured out Britain's hemispheric power and connected an enlarged British America to Britain. Laid over a chart that included all the nations bordering the Atlantic, the current swept the viewer's eye along the new boundaries of British power, from Florida to Nova Scotia. Look at the chart again: imagine the Gulf Stream as an eyebrow arched over an invisible British-American smirk.[95]

A REMARKABLE CONTRIBUTION to hydrography and maritime cartography, which were only beginning to map the open ocean, the Franklin-Folger chart of the Gulf Stream also holds an important place in the prehistory of the American Revolution. The chart, like many of Franklin's pamphlets on British policy in the late 1760s, represented at once a promise that Americans would help create a powerful British empire and a threat to withdraw from this project. Colonists, Franklin emphasized, could help conquer the vastly expanded territory of the empire—if treated well by British rulers.

The growing atmosphere of colonial suspicion and defensiveness out of which the map emerged helps explain Franklin's reliance on Captain Timothy Folger. By invoking Folger's name, he alluded to a greater community of American knowledge. Franklin conveyed collective wisdom to the Post Office in order to "be of general Service." British ingratitude for such service would damage the empire. "Subjects will be dutiful and obedient," Franklin had promised in his "Canada Pamphlet," only "when the government is mild and just, [and] while important civil and religious rights are secure." "The waves do not rise," he darkly predicted, "but when the winds blow."[96]

Chapter 7

WRECKED

The Waves never rise but when the Winds blow: Franklin used this metaphor again in 1768, to readers of the *London Chronicle*, and again to question British policies toward the colonies. Even as he called on nature to make his point, it was not clear whether he blamed the winds (British ministers) for all the trouble. Perhaps the problems in the empire were not as inevitable as the motion of wind over water. Franklin did not, at that stage, despair of Britain, and he happily remained in London. He criticized British colonial policies in order to get them repealed or adjusted, not to make any great change in the political order.[1]

Franklin's moderate politics and his loyalty to the ruling elite were evident in his response to the 1768 Wilkes controversy and to sailors' role in it. Indeed, his distaste for John Wilkes set him apart from many colonists—and Britons—who thought that the government's treatment of Wilkes revealed its disdain for the rights of ordinary subjects.

Wilkes was a radical English writer who had been gleefully antagonizing Britain's rulers with essays in his periodical *The North Briton*. But in 1768, after he attacked the king himself in the forty-fifth issue of the paper, Wilkes was tried and found guilty of seditious libel. He fled to France where, in absentia, he was elected to a parliamentary seat for Middlesex County. He returned in triumph, but his election was nullified on the grounds of his sedition. Many Britons were outraged that the popular will could be ignored and a writer silenced.[2]

Suddenly, American complaints about British tyranny seemed less far-fetched. Cartoons immortalized Wilkes, whose hunched back and leering squint made him immediately recognizable. Riots broke out. Referring to the issue of the paper that carried the attack, Londoners chalked up "No. 45" everywhere, all over buildings and coaches. "Light up for Wilkes," crowds would shout outside a house, breaking its windows if the inhabitants did not light candles to show their support. A number of colonial assemblies and groups officially protested on Wilkes's behalf; some of their actions commemorated the number forty-five, as in drinking forty-five stupefying toasts to the "Member from Middlesex."

Even sailors, most of whom lacked enough property to vote, demonstrated their support of Wilkes. Rioting was clearly a popular pastime for the British—but especially so for sailors, who had plenty to protest. The state was consolidating its authority over them, as the waves of impressment during the Seven Years' War had shown. Even landspeople grew uneasy over how press gangs seized maritime laborers. Some began to compare the situation to slavery; both African captives and impressed sailors were snatched from their homes to labor involuntarily. Across the Atlantic, colonists thought they were protected from impressment, but naval captains assumed otherwise. The difference in opinion had erupted back in 1747 in Boston. When officials tried to impress colonial men, they incited a three-day riot. Thereafter and certainly through the Seven Years' War, sailors' protests continued in the colonies, and they spread to the metropolis. When sailors refused to work, they would "strike" the sails, inventing a term that other workingpeople eventually used for their own work stoppages. London-based sailors did this in solidarity with Wilkes.[3]

Franklin was horrified. As the 1768 riots swept around London, he denounced Wilkes as "an outlaw and exile, of bad personal character, not worth a farthing." The "drunken mad mobs" had cost the city an estimated £50,000 in physical damage, not to mention "the expence of candles." The capital was "a daily Scene of lawless Riot and Confusion." Mobs were "knocking all down that will not roar for Wilkes and Liberty." Just as bad were the "Sailors unrigging all the outward-bound Ships . . . Watermen destroying private Boats and threatning Bridges."[4]

This was a surprising attitude for a former workingman, let alone a colonist whose own maritime kin might easily have been impressed. (Growing older, Franklin grew yet more like his father. In 1773, he would tell his sister, Jane Mecom, that one of their step-nephews was "fit, I should think for a better Business than the Sea.") But the maritime strikes and acts of sabotage were, for Franklin, beyond the pale, much like the colonial smuggling he constantly condemned. He had his own doubts about British law and politics. But he was a law-and-order man who had no patience with Wilkes's insistence that the British government was rotten to the core, to say nothing of Wilkes's taunting of George III. Franklin's stance was a contrast to his earlier defense, in the 1730s, of John Peter Zenger against similar charges of seditious libel.[5]

Franklin's position represented compromise, the kind of compromise he wanted on colonial policy, and it made him look compromised on either side. He knew it. At the end of 1768, he confessed that his "impartiality" made him suspected "in England of being too much an American, and in America of being too much an Englishman." He would keep deploying metaphors based on nature (waves rising with the wind) in order to argue for the plain truth of his positions. But his authority as a philosopher was increasingly difficult to wield in the political realm. This remained Franklin's dilemma until 1775. That year marked the most frustrating moment of his life, when his status as a natural philosopher failed to give him any political leverage whatsoever. His sudden undoing in 1775 had a radicalizing effect on him and forced him to leave London, the empire's center of learning, where he had clearly preferred to be. In his case, "the winds" blasted him clear out of the British empire— just when he had hoped the empire's increasing glory might redound to him.[6]

GLORY had indeed been his. In November 1768, Franklin was elected president of the American Philosophical Society. The honor crowned him, in absentia, as supreme among American philosophers. Two infant and rival Philadelphia societies, the American Society (formed by Quakers and assemblymen) and the Philosophical Society (with the proprietary faction), had long played tug-of-war over Franklin as their founding member. In 1768, the two groups merged into the American Philosophical Society, held at Philadelphia, for Promoting Useful Knowledge, which has retained this amalgamated, eighteenth-century name to the present day. The first APS presidential election pitted the two earlier societies' presidents, Franklin and James Hamilton, against each other. Franklin's election lost the society any hope of patronage from the proprietors.[7]

The APS election was fitting reward for Franklin's long efforts, starting with the Junto, to found a learned society in Philadelphia.

He would be reelected annually until his death in 1790. The APS president was no mere ornament; the letter notifying Franklin of his election stated that the other officers "hope for your Patronage and assistance." Franklin was expected to woo foreign members, the great and the good who, flattered at the Philadelphia society's attentions, would promote it to learned societies in their home countries. Franklin accepted the charge. He would disseminate the first volume of the society's *Transactions* (1771) to British learned societies and individuals.[8]

Franklin was also revisiting several questions about physical circulation. On his 1766 tour of Europe, he encountered some interesting "Glasses from Germany." These were pulse glasses, tubes filled with alcohol or ether and then sealed with a slight vacuum, that registered small gradations of heat by generating bubbles. Franklin had more sensitive versions made in London in 1768. He did not specify with whom he worked, but clearly, he was continuing to collaborate with artisans, as when he had encouraged Caspar Wistar's production of glass electric tubes in Pennsylvania.[9]

With these improved pulse glasses, Franklin could detect differently heated currents of air. "I bored a very small hole through the wainscot in the seat of my window," he explained of what was, in fact, Mrs. Stevenson's window. He placed the top of a pulse glass against the draft of cold winter air. The heat from the room was enough to generate bubbles from the bottom of the glass, despite its chilled top. All of Franklin's "philosophical" visitors marveled at the sensitivity of the device. He himself could not decide whether the bubbles resulted from some heat-activated "subtil invisible vapor" within the fluid or whether they were heat—"fire"—itself.[10]

Either way, the pulse glass rekindled Franklin's interest in using the atmosphere of a heated room to experiment with circulation. Shortly thereafter, he developed and mounted a damper in the fireplace he had installed at Craven Street a decade earlier. And by 1771, he perfected a vase-shaped metal stove that, like a Pennsylvania fireplace, consumed smoke rather than leaking it into a room. He used the device for three winters in London and then took it home to use in Philadelphia.[11]

Franklin also addressed new questions about fluids and circulation. He considered the formation of waves in the sea and raindrops in the sky. He wrote up new observations on electricity, perhaps reinvigorated by his ongoing correspondences with Joseph Priestley and John Canton. Franklin and Canton rhapsodized over news of a "beautiful" American experiment. In this investigation, Ebenezer Kinnersley, one of Franklin's old electrical collaborators, used an electric charge to melt a fine wire, thus proving that electricity made "a hot and not a cold Fusion"—it was fire, all right. Then Franklin served on a Royal Society committee that investigated Canton's claim that water and other liquids were compressible and that the compressibility depended on ambient temperature and barometric pressure. Franklin had earlier assumed that liquids were not compressible. But the committee verified the findings and voted Canton the 1764 Copley Medal, his second.[12]

In 1768, Franklin consolidated his own reputation as a philosopher by publishing an expanded edition of his writings. A fourth edition of his *Experiments and Observations on Electricity* appeared in December of that year. (It was not advertised for sale until the following month, so it bears a 1769 publication date.) This edition differed from its predecessors substantially, not least of all in size. It had tripled in length, growing from 154 pages in the third edition to 496 in the fourth. And the bulk of the volume was new, though it hardly exhausted what Franklin still had in manuscript form. Many of the new portions were in fact old letters that he had been meaning to revise before publishing them either in the *Philosophical Transactions* or in his own volume of essays. But "finding that he is not like to have sufficient leisure, he has at length been induced, imperfect as they are, to permit their publication."[13]

In some cases, these letters had been waiting for Franklin's attentions since the 1750s—no wonder his friends pleaded for their publication. (Franklin's reticence may be why his letter on the Gulf Stream to Anthony Todd appeared neither in the 1769 edition of his writings nor in the succeeding one five years later.) Readers of the fourth edition of the *Experiments and Observations* enjoyed the freshness and spontaneity of Franklin's unrevised essays; it all added to his seeming effortlessness. "There are not very many philosophical writers . . . who can suffer so little," the *Monthly Review* concluded, "by appearing in an undress before the public."[14]

The description of an undressed Franklin—lounging at home, wigless, turbaned, in banyan—was apt. Despite the fourth edition's learnedly stout size, it had a warmer and more personal tone than the earlier versions, which had showcased letters on physical science written to fellow philosophers. The 1769 *Experiments and*

Observations added letters meant for a popular audience and therefore a larger one. For example, the fourth edition contained eight of his letters to Mary Stevenson, which made public Franklin's inclusion of women in the republic of letters.

He also included his classic essay on swimming in the fourth edition. Sometime before 1769, Franklin had written to a friend who assumed he was too old to learn to swim yet had new employment on the water, which he dreaded. Franklin reassured him that the skill would keep him safe, "to say nothing of the enjoyment in so delightful and wholesome an exercise." His friend had a river at the bottom of his garden in London, "a most convenient place" to gradually master his fear. Like all swimming instructors, Franklin told his pupil to start with floating. The trick was to think of water as an element that naturally suspends the body, rather than one that might oppress and invade it. If the novice kept calm, Franklin assured his pupil, he could feel this. Franklin pointed out that freshwater had greater specific gravity than the trunk of the human body and saltwater had greater specific gravity than all of it. "You will be no swimmer," Franklin cautioned, "till you can place some confidence in the power of the water to support you."[15]

This definitive edition of the *Experiments and Observations* showed Franklin at his most confident. By including his "Observations on the Increase of Mankind," he noted his critical engagement with imperial affairs, but he went no further. And he finally published his first letter to Collinson, in which he acknowledged the gift of a glass electric tube that had started it all. Maybe he felt that he could finally admit he had had that assistance. His place within the Atlantic republic of letters was assured, as the other essays showed. They included Franklin's correspondence with grand figures, including Lord Kames, and foreign worthies, such as Dalibard, who had done the sentry box experiment.[16]

And Franklin was likewise completely at home among London's learned circles. He attended Royal Society meetings and lectures and became a frequent guest at dinners of the Royal Society Club, an offshoot (more Junto than Library Company) where conviviality made the learned conversation go down sweetly. He also joined the Club of Honest Whigs, which met at a coffeehouse every two weeks. Formed by the water-compressing John Canton, this club mixed dissenting clergymen, men of science, and men of letters. The "Whig" in the club's name indicated that its members favored some of the reformist politics of the day. (The opposing Tories favored tradition, meaning an established church and social hierarchy, both embodied in king and Parliament.) But the Club of Honest Whigs could hardly be termed daringly radical—it suited Franklin very well.[17]

Abroad, his reputation continued to spread. In 1772, the Académie Royale des Sciences, the French equivalent of London's Royal Society, elected Franklin an *associé étranger* (foreign member). He was one of only eight honorees, Franklin bragged to his son, and only because one of the previous eight had died. His French contacts now included Jean-Baptiste Le Roy, whose science was undistinguished but service to the Académie prodigious; Franklin followed the work of Le Roy's brother, Pierre, who had developed a chronometer that was successfully tested at sea from 1771 to 1772.[18]

Franklin also met Jacques Barbeu-Dubourg, who would become his main French translator. Barbeu-Dubourg had trained for the priesthood but had instead become a physician. He also took an interest in legal reform, and he and Franklin would discuss both nature and politics. Though the two men had evidently been corresponding for some time, the first surviving letter between them is dated 1768. In it, Barbeu-Dubourg mentioned his bold criticism of France's legal order, *Code de l'humanité* . . . , published in part in 1768. In 1773, Polly Stevenson Hewson (with Franklin's advice) translated the essay, and Barbeu-Dubourg published it in full in London, beyond the reach of French censors.[19]

Two other European friends were more substantial figures in the sciences. Franklin corresponded about electricity with the natural philosopher Giambattista Beccaria (for whose musical language Franklin had named his glass armonica). And he discussed an astonishing range of topics with Dutch physician and experimenter Jan Ingenhousz. Ingenhousz had developed some improved methods of inoculation that won him the patronage of the imperial family in Austria. Whenever the court in Vienna would allow it, Ingenhousz lived in England. He joined the Club of Honest Whigs and became such a frequent visitor at Craven Street that he corresponded with the Stevensons, as well as their lodger. Legendarily genial, Ingenhousz got along with everyone and helped connect Franklin to everyone as well.[20]

These people and connections conveniently intermingled. When Le Roy became a foreign member of the Royal Society, Franklin greeted him as his "dear double Confrere," referring to their shared memberships in the Royal Society and Académie Royale. Congratulating Lord Kames on his election as president of the Philosophical Society of Edinburgh, Franklin artlessly segued into a discussion of his own accomplishments. "I think I formerly took Notice to you . . . that I thought there had been some Similarity in our Fortunes, and the Circumstances of our Lives." Franklin offered a "fresh Instance": his and Kames's simultaneous elections as presidents of their provincial learned societies. He then mentioned the impending delivery of "a little Box," just big enough for "a few of the late Edition of my Books for my Friends in Scotland," including one for Kames and one for the society he now headed. Le Roy tidily summarized Franklin's multiple roles in the republic of letters when he addressed a missive to the "Deputy Post Master of North / America, Fellow of the Royal / Society."[21]

HE WAS FETED as a philosopher throughout Britain and Europe, but Franklin's shining reputation mostly depended on things he had already done. His continued revisions to his collected essays indicated that he wanted to do more. Franklin's correspondence made clear that he managed to read about and keep up with an astonishing range of issues. But he had limited time to conduct new experiments and to revise the essays he had not managed to get into the 1769 edition of his writings.

He was too busy with political affairs. Franklin now tended multiple colonies' interests. To London's newspapers, particularly William Strahan's *London Chronicle*, he sent a steady stream of essays that took shots at British policies. Again, all this was done within the bounds of loyal criticism of public affairs (Strahan would not have published anything that ventured further), but it was time-consuming. Meanwhile, Franklin watched younger men conquer new areas in science, ones he could only admire.

This was especially the case with the emerging field of chemistry. Chemical experimentation was to the second half of the eighteenth century what electrical experimentation had been to its first: fascinating, revolutionary, and widely reported. Sober experiments jostled with dramatic public demonstrations featuring flashes, crashes, and small animals dying horribly. For the sciences, these experiments mattered because they described elements other than the ancient quartet of air, earth, fire, and water.

Air now came in parts. In 1766, Henry Cavendish had isolated "inflammable air" (hydrogen), and Joseph Priestley did the same with "dephlogisticated air" (oxygen) in 1774. Anything that burned or altered when heated was believed to contain *phlogiston,* an inflammable substance. Priestley believed that by burning ash derived from mercury, he had produced a version of air separated from phlogiston. In 1775, a mouse confined to a glass vessel with this new air survived longer than a mouse shut up with ordinary air. Priestley also managed to impregnate water with air, inventing soda water, which he and other people soon could not stop drinking. Franklin had collaborated with Priestley in electrical investigation, but when it came to chemical experiments, he could only marvel—and drink the fizzy water.[22]

A dawning sense that several chapters of his life were over may have motivated Franklin, at the age of sixty-five, to record the events of that life. He had long used portraits to craft his image; now he used his pen. In 1771, during his second summer visit to the home of Jonathan Shipley, the Bishop of St. Asaph, Franklin wrote the first of four sections of what would be his posthumous (and incomplete) autobiography. He claimed to be writing a private account, describing it later as "several little family Anecdotes of no Importance to others" and composing the first section as a letter to his son. The writing of this autobiography was an odd and unconvincing retreat into private life by a man who remained a highly public figure.[23]

But Franklin might have felt himself in an odd position. He was still highly visible but not only for his philosophical work. His political reputation now announced him to the world. And even in areas where he had done stunningly new work, as with his Gulf Stream chart, he was already losing ground to competitors. First and foremost among them was William Gerard De Brahm, whose work on the Gulf Stream would eclipse Franklin's efforts for 200 years.[24]

De Brahm belonged to the lesser German-speaking nobility and had trained as a military engineer. He had emigrated to Georgia in 1751 and became surveyor to the colonial governments of South Carolina and Georgia. In 1764, he was appointed Surveyor General for the Southern District of North America. Shortly thereafter, in 1767, De Brahm served, with Franklin, on a royal commission to determine the New York–New Jersey boundary. (The commission never convened, so its members knew each other by name only.) De Brahm also became surveyor general of lands for newly acquired British East Florida. There, he learned of the Gulf Stream and began studying it.

But he ran afoul of the colony's governor, James Grant, who complained to the Earl of Hillsborough, Secretary of State for colonial affairs, that De Brahm spent money faster than he produced work. Hillsborough summoned De Brahm to London to explain himself.[25]

In London, De Brahm published his preliminary "Observations on the American Coast" in the *Gentleman's Magazine*. During his recent passage, he recounted, he had "traced" a great current from Florida "along the Atlantic coast to the Newfoundland bank." Knowledge of this Gulf Stream would "not only guide [vessels] clear of all shoals projected from the Capes on the coast of North America, but also accelerate their voyage [away from America] in a near incredible measure." At a stroke, De Brahm proved that he had indeed been working on behalf of the expanding empire, in much the same way Franklin had done with the Gulf Stream. But De Brahm, unlike Franklin, published his efforts in a newspaper read both in Britain and all over the colonies.[26]

The following year, De Brahm published *The Atlantic Pilot* (1772), a portable guide that coaxed navigators through the tricky currents of the Florida straits. The book included a "Hydrographical Map of the Atlantic Ocean" that traced De Brahm's passage from Florida to the English Channel, with the Gulf Stream accompanying him most of the way. In his canny dedication to Hillsborough, De Brahm expressed concern for "the safer conduct of ships in their navigation from the Gulf of Mexico along Cuba and the Martieres, through the New Bahama Channel, to the northern part of his Majesty's dominions upon the continent of North America, and from thence to Europe."[27]

De Brahm's assessments of the Gulf Stream were bolder than Franklin's in three respects. First, the engineer described the current's place in a full circle around the North Atlantic. He narrated its course out of Cape Florida, through the New Bahama channel, and then north and northeast along North America; it then joined the currents coming from the Gulf of St. Lawrence, Baffin Bay, and Hudson Strait, which forced it southeast toward the Azores and thence to Africa. The trade winds along Africa then sent it back, "after its rotation in the ocean, to the gulf of Mexico." This statement was either a rational deduction (as it had been for Franklin in the 1750s) or something De Brahm heard from sailors. It was not the result of direct observation—only when he returned to Florida in 1775 did De Brahm finally see that the current crossed westward from Africa to America, "as I always supposed."[28]

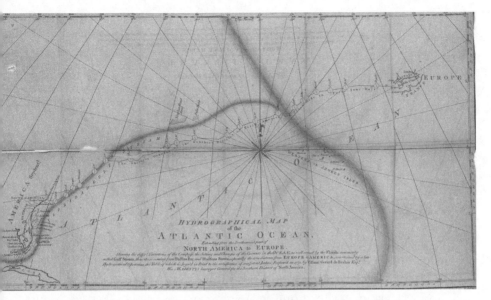

The Gulf Stream, another view. William Gerard De Brahm, *The Atlantic Pilot* (1772). JOHN CARTER BROWN LIBRARY AT BROWN UNIVERSITY.

Second, De Brahm elaborated the Gulf Stream's geomorphic significance—it had the power to wear away the edges of continents. He hypothesized that Florida's reefs and keys were parts of two ancient peninsulas that the Florida Current had long since gnawed off, and he provided a chart that ingeniously reconstructed this land, "Ancient Tegesta, now Promontory of East Florida." Indeed, the current continued to erode land. Mariners had to be wary: a stream of water that beat peninsulas to tatters could leave "many vessels wrecked."[29]

Finally, De Brahm presented the Gulf Stream as a variable current rather than the fixed one Franklin had described. De Brahm argued that wind, lunar cycles, and seasonal meteorologic conditions all affected the Gulf Stream. His manuscript map of East Florida, from which he prepared his published charts, noted that the places where the current altered course would themselves shift over the different seasons. The published "Hydrographical Map of the Atlantic Ocean" noted these variable conditions. The parallel lines that indicated the current on this chart hinted that the current's width and path were only approximate—navigators had to look up from the chart and peek at the actual ocean. De Brahm also identified an interior, southwest "eddy" between the Gulf Stream and Florida; navigators could stay in the stream proper or in the countercurrent hugging the shore, depending on which way they headed.[30]

With the publication of *The Atlantic Pilot*, De Brahm made himself the recognized expert on the Gulf Stream. It was he, not Franklin, who put the name "Gulf Stream" on the map. Franklin's 1768 letter to Anthony Todd, in which he had described the Gulf Stream, had circulated much less widely. The printed Franklin and Folger chart, produced in small numbers, had an only slightly larger audience. And then, for reasons that are not clear, it vanished from the public record. So much did De Brahm eclipse Franklin that by the early twentieth century, he was assumed to have charted the Gulf Stream first. Not until 1978, when a determined oceanographer turned up a copy of the Franklin and Folger chart in Paris, was Franklin's priority recognized.[31]

It is impossible that Franklin did not notice what De Brahm had done. (Though De Brahm might not have known of Franklin's work.) De Brahm advertised his findings in the *Gentleman's Magazine*, and at least two other London newspapers reviewed his *Atlantic Pilot*. Franklin, an old newspaper man, seems to have read most of the main London papers. Without someone to tidy them, he confessed, "they lie about in every Room, in every Window, and on every Chair, just where the Doctor lays them when he has read them." Hillsborough and probably others in the colonial office kept track of Franklin's correspondence with Todd and of De Brahm's work in Florida. Finally, both Franklin and De Brahm lived in London between 1771 and early 1775 and encountered many of the same people. De Brahm's foremost patron was George Legge, Lord Dartmouth, British politician and Fellow of the Royal Society. Dartmouth and Franklin shared a doctor, the ubiquitous John Fothergill, and they corresponded at several points on colonial policies.[32]

But despite their overlapping lives, the two rival hydrographers differed crucially over questions of social rank. Franklin, the American arriviste and champion of colonial rights, had pointedly observed that simple, hardworking Americans best knew the northern stretch of the Gulf Stream, and he credited one source, Timothy Folger, by name. De Brahm gave no one credit, though it was clear he had talked to ordinary sailors in America. The current in question was, he explained, "commonly called [the] Gulf stream." He differentiated this colloquial name from the Florida Current known to cartographers.[33]

De Brahm made his loyalties clear when he wrote the dedication of his *Atlantic Pilot*: "To the Right Hon. the Earl of Hillsborough."

Franklin despised the sycophancy. "My Character," he summarized himself: "Costs me nothing to be civil to inferiors, a good deal to be submissive to superiors &c. &c." He also loathed Hillsborough. Franklin felt that English aristocrats, including Hillsborough, had not always respected him, despite his philosophical status. In 1768, he had sought a ministerial appointment under the earl, which would have been a real coup, placing him at the center of colonial administration. But Hillsborough chose another man. Thereafter, when Franklin pilloried British ministers in his pamphlets, Hillsborough had good reason to take offense. "Our new Haman, the S[ecretar]y" of colonial affairs, Franklin mocked him. The abuse was a risk. He published such pieces under pseudonyms ("Daylight," "Twilight," "Homespun," "N.M.C.N.P.C.H.," and so on), but people suspected him as the author.[34]

De Brahm took no such risk. His dedication to Hillsborough extolled the earl as "ever attentive to the welfare of his Majesty's American subjects," and he craved his "Lordship's protection and patronage." (He would go even further, eventually insisting that the current he studied should be called the George Stream, after the king.) It is hard to imagine Franklin ever begging anyone's patronage for his work in science—he wrote that one of Hillsborough's faults was that he was "fond of every one that can stoop to flatter him." Franklin's attitude was a bit stiff-necked, if not narcissistic. Patronage made the sciences possible, as he knew very well from Collinson's attentions to him. Several friends, including Fothergill and Ingenhousz, relied on aristocratic or royal patrons.[35]

Patronage had its costs. In 1772, Franklin watched Joseph Priestley agonize whether to accept William Petty the Earl of Shelburne's offer to serve as his paid librarian. It was a good job, but the patronage would compromise Priestley's independence. He turned to Franklin for advice. "Wishing sincerely that you may determine for the best," Franklin recommended to Priestley his *"Prudential Algebra."* He should list pros and cons against each other and then see which column was longest. Maybe it helped—Priestley accepted the offer, though he would later leave Lord Shelburne's employ. Franklin refused to weigh in on the question itself. Perhaps he feared he would offend his friend by admitting that he would never accept such support, a daily reminder of dependent status.[36]

De Brahm's and Franklin's preferences were deep-seated. De Brahm was, after all, a nobleman himself and could play the patron-

and-client game without a sense that he might be groveling. Franklin knew how to be extremely polite to the political leaders with whom he worked as a colonial agent, but unless they had worked on questions of philosophy, he expected the gentlemen and lords to respect his standing in the republic of letters. In that realm, the colonial commoner and self-made philosopher could not have flattered an aristocratic patron without feeling the man's boot on his neck. Indeed, it is telling that Franklin, unlike most other authors in the British Atlantic, never dedicated any of his philosophical works to anyone. He sought no more patrons. His belated publication of his thank-you note to Peter Collinson was the closest he came. Eager to minimize his reliance on anyone, let alone a social superior, he may have sacrificed opportunities to become more firmly embedded in Britain's social hierarchy.

Thus, by the early 1770s, Franklin was accomplished and influential but a bit touchy about his philosophical reputation and somewhat slippery politically. Endlessly conciliatory, he was critical of Britain yet clearly relished his place in its centers of learning. Could he really have it both ways? As debate over British colonial policy mounted, so, too, did speculation about Franklin's intentions.

Consider a 1770 engraving. "Political Electricity" traces an electrical chain that carries an evil current. The charged chain starts with Lord Bute, former prime minister and George III's much-hated pet adviser (who was mocked for his interests in science). Making many connections along the way, the chain terminates at a gun aimed at a supporter of John Wilkes. Thus, Lord Bute, "in ye Character of Doctor Franklin," uses electricity to pervert royal authority, ultimately murdering a loyal, if protesting, British subject. Or is the point that extreme authority is needed to maintain order? Anything was possible in this topsy-turvy Atlantic world. London appears under the label "Boston," fulfilling Franklin's prophecy that the center of the empire must move westward. Yet the ships sit idle, as had indeed happened during the controversies over Wilkes and over the taxes on colonial imports. Meanwhile, Franklin flies a kite in France.[37]

Necessarily anonymous and deliberately ambiguous, this remarkable cartoon restated, visually, every possible problem that was besetting the empire: political corruption, violence, conspiracy, waste of wealth and resources, and abuse of ordinary subjects.

Whoever concocted the engraving was keeping up with electrical discoveries. One year earlier, Joseph Priestley had reported, in his second edition of *The History and Present State of Electricity* (1769),

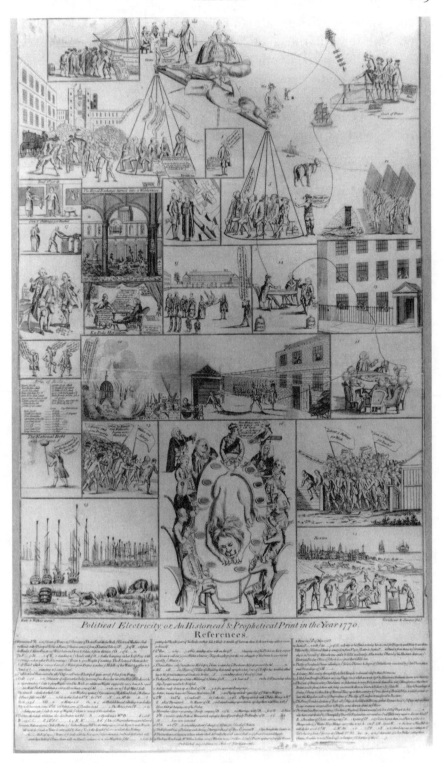

"Political Electricity" (1770). AMERICAN ANTIQUARIAN SOCIETY.

some experiments with a metal chain that he had performed in 1766. Priestley laid the chain atop a sheet of paper and then electrified it. He discovered that it left a telltale stain along the paper (and reported the finding to Franklin). The cartoon marked on paper a stain of another sort, one over the British nation and empire.[38]

In all this, Franklin's "Character" was suitably ambivalent, his reward, yet again, for appearing to play all sides. It was probably known that he was an anti-Wilkesite. And he was known to admire Bute, whose picture adorned his house in Philadelphia. (John Adams claimed that Bute was trying to use Franklin to advance his philosophical standing while Franklin hoped to benefit from Bute's political patronage.) But was Franklin truly as evil as the king's hated adviser? Even if not, was this any time to be flying a kite? It is remarkable that Franklin is represented as so powerful, roughly equivalent to a British prime minister. Equally, it is remarkable that his electrical power, the force so much associated with him, could be lethal. He commanded nature's power, but in the service of what? [39]

Franklin left few indications as to what he really thought. But he did leave us one amazing clue. At some point before the middle of 1773, he arranged on a piece of paper two columns under the headings "Stay" and "Go." He was thinking about getting out of London. The agonized note is a rare example of Franklin's prudential algebra. (Perhaps he used it frequently and then burned the results but forgot to this time.) The first column had nine reasons for staying in London; the second had six for going home. Franklin put his philosophical ambitions first. Four of the nine reasons for staying indicated his wish to travel in Europe and work on his philosophical writings, including a fifth edition of his works. Only one of the reasons for returning to Philadelphia might have had an intellectual foundation. "Repose," Franklin wrote, as if a weary traveler with a vague memory of a clean bed, somewhere. To have repose would mean being free from public affairs and having free time to think clearly again about philosophy.[40]

These were his choices. For Dr. Franklin, there was the heady republic of letters based in London, a city that used up so much of his time and money that he could barely answer family letters or pay his landlady but gave him access to all the learned heads of Europe. Or for Poor Richard, there was a quiet, thrifty, provincial life in America. Stay or go?

Dr. Franklin stayed, of course.

HIS DECISION to stay in London meant that he remained at the
heart of an expanding empire, which daily offered up new opportunities in the sciences and just about everything else.

The British incursion into India was probably the most gripping
development—tigers and nabobs easily chased electrical Americans
and rioting Wilkesites out of the headlines. England had held trading interests in South Asia since the early seventeenth century, when
the East India Company was formed, but Britain remained a minor
player in comparison to Portugal and France. The situation changed
after the Seven Years' War, when Britain won important concessions
from France and its South Asian allies and gained a meaningful
foothold on the subcontinent.

India was a long way from British America, but it had important
implications for American colonists, as Franklin knew. The British
East India Company was the trading monopoly that had had access
to India since the early seventeenth century. Its officials did not lose
a second, after the war, in expanding company interests—and offering more revenue to the state, more commodities to consumers,
and more work to sailors. It was as these opportunities were expanding that Franklin recalled his half brother Josiah's return from the
fabled Indies. Now, the younger generation of his family hankered
to go east. Jonathan Williams Jr., Franklin's grandnephew, intended
to go "to East India as a Writer in the Company's Service"; Franklin
applauded the idea because "he cannot fail bringing home a Fortune." Williams instead returned to Boston but solicited East India
Company ships and goods for his trade in America. He asked his
London-based granduncle to "recommend their Business" there.[41]

Through merchants such as the Williamses, many new goods
from Asia made their way to Britain and America, permanently
changing the texture of everyday life. Cotton became a standard
fabric for ladies' dresses; tea, the standard drink that the awakening
ladies sleepily sipped before they donned the dresses; and china,
the standard container for the tea. "Mark how Luxury will enter
Families," Franklin warned. His household had long breakfasted on
"Bread and Milk, (no Tea)" served in earthenware and pewter until
one morning his wife presented him with "a China Bowl with a
Spoon of Silver." It was all done "without my Knowledge," Franklin

claimed; Deborah justified it as a matter of keeping up with the neighbors, which was probably how the eastern "luxuries" did infiltrate the colonies.[42]

Other "Indian" imports included Asian specimens that naturalists solicited and then passed on to others. These joined the stream of seeds, dried plants, preserved animals—and live ones—that were crossing the Atlantic at the same time. Britons transported Asian plants to the tropical and subtropical American colonies in order to generate new crops. In 1771, for example, Franklin distributed "a few seeds from India" to Georgia, for which he was acting as colonial agent. Calcutta to London to Savannah—a seemingly small gesture brought seeds across two oceans and halfway around the world.[43]

It only remained for the British to command the Pacific, and their empire would span the globe. Unfortunately, others had the same idea. From 1763 and through the Napoleonic Wars that would rage into the next century, Europe was possessed by a "South Seas" craze. Although Europeans had traversed parts of the Pacific since the 1520s and although the Spanish had claimed the Philippines since 1521, the greatest part of the ocean remained known only to its native populations. (It was not even clear whether it was a single ocean or whether it held mere islands or another whole continent.) The French South Pacific voyage from 1766 to 1769 set off a race for the Pacific. Louis Antoine de Bougainville's account of the venture spread rapidly. It helped produce an important stereotype of the peoples of the South Seas as "noble savages," loving creatures who transcended the violent ambitions that plagued Europeans. Recall Franklin's new regard for Indians, after the Seven Years' War; the concept of noble Pacific savages also exemplified this changed attitute toward non-European peoples.[44]

Britons wanted the Pacific people and places for themselves, but first, they had to elbow the French out of the way. The French commandeered New Zealand and some smaller islands, but the British planned to beat them to the rumored continent, *terra australis* (southern land), in the South Pacific. From 1769 to 1771, James Cook, commanding the *Endeavour*, made the first of three voyages into the Pacific, with orders to navigate as much of that ocean as possible and, in particular, to chart the coast of what came to be known as Australia. It turned out not to be connected to Antarctica, so it was not quite the long-rumored continent of the South Seas.

But all the other news from Cook's ventures was so astonishing that the disappointment was fleeting.[45]

It was the British state's most ambitious undertaking to date, an unprecedented merger of naval power and the sciences. Joseph Banks, the naturalist who later became president of the Royal Society, and Daniel Solander, a protégé of Linnaeus, both sailed with Cook, as did a train of other naturalists and sketch artists. The *Endeavour* returned with natural history specimens, charts of the ocean, maps of the coastlines, and a vast quantity of narrative material to encourage further British advance into the Pacific. Cook's second voyage, from 1772 to 1774, was even more spectacular. He hauled back still more scientific material as well as a Tahitian man, Omai, who was sent around London's dinner-party circuit and painted by Joshua Reynolds. One naturalist, from the second voyage, rejoiced that "what Cook has added to the mass of our knowledge is such that it will strike deep roots and will long have the most decisive influence on the activity of men."[46]

Well into his sixties, unable to cross the Atlantic without endangering his health, Franklin could not even hope to join Cook's expeditions. But he advised the ventures to a remarkable degree. The admiralty was interested in testing whether Joseph Priestley's method of making soda water might also sweeten saltwater at sea; Franklin advised Priestley how to persuade Banks and Solander to do the experiment, and Cook took samples of the soda with him. (Cook also experimented with using citrus juice for scurvy.) Franklin must have been especially gratified that the *Endeavour* proved the efficacy of a chain conductor as a means of protecting ships against lightning. Cook's ship emerged unscathed from a storm at Batavia, while an unprotected Dutch ship was "almost demolished by the Lightning."[47]

Franklin also knew that Cook's first expedition would help answer a big question: how far away was the sun? The 1769 transit of Venus across the sun and the expanded dimensions of the British empire gave Britons a unique opportunity to determine the distance. If an observer could measure the time it took an object to pass over the face of the sun and then compare the interval with those measured elsewhere on the earth, the distance between the earth and sun could be calculated. Edmond Halley had predicted Venus's two transits, in 1761 and 1769, noting that the planet's slow movement would allow such calculation, whereas faster objects, such as comets, would not.[48]

The second transit was not observable in Europe. Only Britain's greatly expanded empire could hold a suitable mirror up to the vast heavens. There were now many global outposts for science, from the middle of the Pacific Ocean to the middle of Philadelphia.

Poor Richard had worked hard to transform his provincial readers into backyard astronomers, and just in time for the 1769 transit, he succeeded. Colonists had failed to observe the 1761 transit. (Franklin's friend John Winthrop IV, Hollis Professor at Harvard and Fellow of the Royal Society, had arranged the only significant attempt.) Now they outdid themselves. In the northern colonies especially, observers with every level of skill and every kind of instrument rallied. In Philadelphia, for example, Mary Norris offered her telescope to the official observers. Franklin himself sent telescope lenses to Harvard, though the Pennsylvania observers nabbed them when it was clear they would not get to Massachusetts in time. On the day of the event, people poured outside and silently waited— with, we hope, the right protective eyewear—for the crucial minutes of transit. Philadelphians gathered in the square outside the State House, where Franklin had done his electrical experiments. The excitement was overwhelming—at a critical moment, Philadelphia astronomer David Rittenhouse fainted. And the event left its mark: Providence, Rhode Island, still has a Transit Street.[49]

Philosophy united colonists and Britons. The result, a statement of the distance between the earth and sun, is not now accepted as definitive, but the attempt to measure it was astonishing, especially because it organized so many people in so many places to do the same thing at the same time. In the end, twenty-two reports on the transit made their way into colonial newspapers and other publications and then crossed the Atlantic. Franklin could report that the official American measurements arrived at the Royal Society before those "made in the South Sea." The first volume of the American Philosophical Society's *Transactions* (1771) would be devoted to the transit. It proved colonial aptitude in the sciences and publicized the society's president, Franklin, as the acme of American learning.[50]

But the colonial interest in philosophy was superficial and fractured—it reminded Franklin that London seemed a far better place for him. He was annoyed that the APS's proprietary faction had sent their observations to Thomas Penn rather than to him, as president. In contrast to the undisciplined American society, Franklin scolded, "the Royal Society is of all Parties, but Party is entirely out of the

Question in all our Proceedings." Initially hopeful that Pennsylvania might build an observatory (the transit observers had worked from a mere platform), Franklin then heard otherwise from doubters: "I begin to fear the Expence will be thought too heavy for us," he regretted. The American colonists did not intend to invest much in learning, in sharp contrast to Cook's state-sponsored activities in the Pacific.[51]

Franklin himself could not hear enough about the Pacific. In 1768, just after Bougainville's return, he sent to a British acquaintance "a Piece of the Bark Cloth with which the new-discover'd People dress themselves." Franklin had known Banks before Cook's first Pacific voyage and met Solander during the Pacific craze. In August 1771, he dined with Sir John Pringle and the newly returned Banks and Solander, hearing them describe "the People of Otahitee" (or Tahiti) as "civilized in a great degree." He was interested that those people had "a considerable Knowledge of the Stars, sail by them, and make Voyages of three Months westward among the Islands." Franklin also heard flattering things about the New Zealand Maori and derogatory ones about the people of New Holland, or Australia. Knowing that Franklin was among the lucky few who knew Banks and Solander, a friend pumped him for "a few of the Particulars you have heard of the Voyage of the Endeavour."[52]

So taken was Franklin with the Pacific that he endorsed a scheme to bring the "Arts and Conveniencies of Life" to the New Zealanders in exchange for any of its plants that Britain might profitably grow. A 1771 prospectus solicited investors for a three-year expedition costing £15,000, and Franklin wrote its introduction. He, the constant thorn in the side of the British colonial office, argued that colonization could be a benign force. Only by being colonized and brought into trade with other peoples had ancient Britain gained "vast advantages," he contended, including a cornucopia of flora, fauna, and arts, all of them introduced by outsiders. The nation should return the favor. "Britain is now the first Maritime Power in the world," he observed, blessed with innumerable ships and "bold, skilful, and hardy" seamen. Moreover, the British knew the use both of compass and celestial navigation.[53]

"Does not Providence, by these distinguishing Favours, seem to call on us," Franklin demanded, "to do something ourselves for the common Interests of Humanity?" Other oceangoing "voyages have been undertaken with views of profit or of plunder, or to gratify resentment." Rather than cheat or enslave a people, this venture would "do them good."[54]

Keep in mind the year when Franklin wrote these phrases. In 1771, any pleas to avoid profit and plunder echoed colonial protests against taxes on Atlantic commerce. References to providence and to the common good were sure signs of an argument in need of rhetoric. Yet, more positively, Franklin's interest in New Zealand represented the new trend to make empire into a benign or even benevolent force. The Pacific Ocean's very name invited a pacific empire. It was a place acquired peacefully, in contrast to the territories gained in the recent and ruinously expensive war for empire. Above all, Franklin was conceiving of Britons and (white) British Americans as partners in empire, the Christian and enlightened people who together would improve the world.

It was the optimal moment for an abolition movement to gain ground. Concern over the injustice of slavery, which had started with people such as Thomas Tryon, the ranting vegetarian, were beginning to find moral and political purchase. Few advocated freeing slaves, but they spoke and wrote angrily about the slave trade itself, which created new slaves. Moreover, they expressed sympathy with the plight of slaves in a way that hinted at disapproval of slaveholding, as well. These ideas entered public debate—they appeared in newspapers and even at the doors of Whitehall and Parliament. This was the advent of the monumental antislavery campaign that would, after the American Revolution, end the British slave trade and then move on to dismantle slavery in the West Indies.[55]

Though Franklin still supported Dr. Bray's Associates and deplored the slave trade, he did not immediately accept any criticism of slaveholding. He perceived within it an implicit critique of the American colonists who held slaves. In January 1770, he wrote a defensive dialogue between an "Englishman" and an "American," published in Strahan's *Public Advertiser*. The dialogue's Englishman argues that white colonists have little right to talk of liberty if they keep slaves. The American objects that Britons have no right to point a finger when their own poor suffer more than domestic slaves do in America. Most British coal was dug by "Wretches," argues the American, who are "absolute Slaves by your Law, and their Children after them." (This was true: colliers inherited their miserable lot.) Nor could subjects in the home country frown on colonial forms of subjection; national security depended on conscripted soldiers and impressed sailors. The latter were "well described" as slaves, states the American. (Clearly, Franklin was getting over his 1768 revulsion at London's striking sailors—or was willing to pretend to be in order to make his point.)[56]

But Franklin's doubts about slavery were mounting. Just as he had needed Deborah Franklin to chide him into supporting Dr. Bray's Associates, so he now had another better angel, Anthony Benezet, to lead him beyond his defensive reaction to the antislavery movement. Benezet was a French-born Quaker who had moved from London to Philadelphia and pressured Friends there to disavow slave trading; he recruited Franklin and Fothergill as London-based allies. Franklin also received antislavery writings from Benjamin Rush in Philadelphia and "commenc'd an Acquaintance with Mr. Granville Sharpe," or Sharp, the abolition movement's foremost leader.[57]

These were nudges, but then a legal case gave Franklin a shove. James Somerset, a slave, had been taken to England by his owner, Bostonian Charles Stewart. Somerset ran away while in England but was later recaptured, and Stewart intended to take him back to America. Somerset's bid for freedom came before the Court of King's Bench, which ruled in 1772 that it was illegal to remove slaves forcibly from England. The decision shocked many colonists, especially West Indians, because it stigmatized their way of life. Franklin broke rank with many well-off Americans by declaring the decision inadequate. He rallied his old ally against slavery—political arithmetic. He cited Benezet's estimate that there were already 850,000 "Negroes" in the British colonies and that 100,000 more were shipped there each year. Franklin questioned whether the Somerset case, which affected only a tiny number of slaves in England, was any great threat to the trade in fellow humans—the numbers were against it. "Can sweetening our tea, &c. with sugar, be a circumstance of such absolute necessity" that the "pestilential detestable traffic in the bodies and souls of men" should continue?[58]

Now, Franklin conceded that colonists who defended their liberties while holding other humans in bondage were indeed hypocrites. His change of mind was particularly apparent in 1773, the year following the Somerset decision. That year, Franklin pointedly visited Phillis Wheatley, the enslaved poet, in London. He offered "any Services I could do her," a clear invitation to take advantage of the Somerset decision and remain, as a free woman, in London. (Wheatley's master, lurking in a nearby room, was outraged.)

Despite the continued presence of slaves in his own family, Franklin wrote Benezet that the colonies must "get clear of a Practice that disgraces them" without "producing any equivalent Benefit."[59]

He even concluded, rather remarkably, that all Atlantic migration should be free. He had long been arguing that the colonies needed no migrants. He finally got his way in 1773, when British ministers proposed restrictions on emigration to the unruly colonies. Franklin immediately switched his position, invoking nature to do so. "It is the natural Right of Men to quit when[ever] they please the Society or State, and the Country in which they were born," he now insisted. In a letter he sent to the *Public Advertiser* that year, he argued that the laws of nature proved this "Liberty":

> The Waters of the Ocean may move in Currents from one Quarter of the Globe to another, as they happen in some places to be accumulated and in others diminished; but no Law beyond the Law of Gravity, is necessary to prevent their Abandoning any Coast entirely. Thus the different Degrees of Happiness of different Countries and Situations find or rather make their Level by the flowing of People from one to another, and where that Level is once found, the Removals cease.

Ocean currents obeyed natural laws—why not British ministers? If Franklin thought that invoking Isaac ("Law of Gravity") Newton might lend authority to his argument, he miscalculated. The *Public Advertiser* declined to publish his letter.[60]

———————

JUST as Franklin's stock was faltering in London, it rose in Paris. (The 1770 political cartoon showing him flying a kite in France had been oddly accurate, on this point at least.) If the fourth edition of the *Experiments and Observations* had expanded Franklin's English-speaking audience, Jacques Barbeu-Dubourg's two-volume translation of his works, *Oeuvres de M. Franklin* (1773), strengthened his philosophical reputation on the Continent and hinted at a political radicalism Franklin himself had never publicly avowed. Three years later, this political character would come in handy in ways neither Barbeu-Dubourg nor Franklin could have anticipated.

The previous French edition of Franklin's work was nearly twenty years old. Unless they read English, French natural philosophers had access to a mere fraction of his recent work. When Franklin made his second visit to France in 1769, just after the expanded English edition of his works had appeared, it was obvious that something needed to be done. Barbeu-Dubourg translated the 1769 English edition and added pieces from other sources (including Franklin's letters to him). He also begged Franklin for some new tidbits to make the French product distinctive. Franklin dutifully expanded his treatment of swimming, to Barbeu-Dubourg's delight—not even the landmark *Encyclopédie* had discussed swimming.[61]

Barbeu-Dubourg also introduced a new Franklin to the world. His "M. Franklin" may seem uncannily familiar—he is the mythic American we know quite well. In Britain, Franklin was a dignified figure of learning, moderate in religion and politics, completely at home in London, and fundamentally loyal to Great Britain. Barbeu-Dubourg's Franklin, in contrast, was a wilderness autodidact, a Quakerish bundle of radical virtues, and an American at odds with British government. Franklin had worked with Barbeu-Dubourg on the edition. He presumably had his own reasons for wanting his French audience to see him as a radical figure who favored eccentric bodily therapies, the education of women, and the destruction of British tyranny. Maybe it provided a kind of release from his willed serenity and moderate politics in London.

Barbeu-Dubourg's Franklin was a fleshed-out philosopher, not a brain without a body. If the English-speaking Franklin appeared in "undress," his French counterpart was stark naked. He swam more, and he took an "air bath" that was most effective when entirely nude, the better to facilitate a healthy flow in and out of the pores in the skin. (This topic had been the subject of earlier letters to Barbeu-Dubourg, first evidence of Franklin's nudism.) Barbeu-Dubourg found none of this scandalous. Of the Franklin-Stevenson correspondence, for instance, he was "persuaded that many fathers of families would wish such a Mentor for their daughters."[62]

Barbeu-Dubourg lionized Franklin, body and soul, as an exemplar of the "peoples of America." In the paragraph directly following the one on naked air baths, Barbeu-Dubourg addressed the "dissentions" between London and the colonies. His Franklin defended colonial rights against the British court, something Franklin himself did not do in the London editions of his works. Barbeu-Dubourg also mentioned his earlier translations of Franklin, including his hero's 1766 interview before Parliament and his 1768 essay in the *London Chronicle*, the one that represented British ministers as winds that lashed colonial waves.[63]

By turning Franklin's philosophical sagacity against Britain, Barbeu-Dubourg rendered him more appealing to a French audience. The French philosophes were discovering in America a boundless source of examples for their social theories. But this was tricky. How could they praise their former antagonists in several colonial wars? Barbeu-Dubourg needed his French readers to overlook the awkward fact of Franklin's active military career in the Seven Years' War and his considerable prejudice against the French—in his Canada pamphlet, Franklin had described New France as populated by "barbarous tribes of savages" who were "strongly attach'd" to France "by the art and indefatigable industry of [Catholic] priests."[64]

The Quakers had stood aside from the recent warmongering, which may be why Barbeu-Dubourg did his best to transform Franklin into a Philadelphia Quaker, friendly to all, including the French. (There is no mention of Boston in Barbeu-Dubourg's introduction, and London is only hinted at.) Philadelphia had sprung up, Barbeu-Dubourg explained, "in the midst of America's savages" (*au milieu des Sauvages de l'Amérique*) and Franklin had been raised among "les Trembleurs (ou Quakers)," the pious pacifists who had been persecuted in England. It is not clear whether the editor knew the truth about his subject. But Franklin surely remembered his past, though he never corrected Barbeu-Dubourg's version. (Maybe he closed his eyes, held his breath, and thought hard of his mother's Quaker relations on Nantucket.)[65]

Barbeu-Dubourg's portrait of Franklin as a cheerful, simple, life- and liberty-loving American was enhanced by the inclusion of the "Speech of Father Abraham," the almost comically concise compendium of Poor Richard's years of advice. Barbeu-Dubourg described it as a kind of "bonhomie," economic sermons (*leçons oeconomiques*) suited admirably to the spirit of Franklin's native land.[66]

But above all, Franklin was a genius. Barbeu-Dubourg sandwiched Franklin's less philosophical essays and letters among the pieces "de physique générale," but it was those general essays on physics that gave readers the best sense of "la fécondité de son génie," his fecund genius. Franklin had been labeled a philosopher and genius in English; now, in French, he was a philosophe endowed with génie.[67]

HIS FAME across the channel would prove useful in future, but for the moment, Franklin was more concerned about his authority in the British Atlantic world. He still expected that British officials and American colonists could reach some compromise, one in which Britain would gain cooperation and some revenue from the colonies without reducing Americans to second-class citizens. He may have been unduly optimistic because he worked for the Post Office, the one imperial service that clearly worked and pleased just about everyone.

It certainly worked for him. The avalanche of American groceries continued to arrive at Craven Street. In one 1773 instance of excessive affection, different members of Franklin's family sent him six barrels of American apples within a month. He could, day after blissful day, crunch into the fresh apples he loved. He could also snack on the "Applepye" he had praised, in the character of "Dr. Fatsides" ("the *great* Person"), in the "Cravenstreet Gazette," which he wrote in 1770 to amuse the Stevensons. But six barrels was quite a load. If a contemporary barrel held about 365 apples and a pie generously used five apples, Mrs. Stevenson could have baked her lodger 438 pies. Even allowing for spoilage and snacking, that's a lot of "applepye."[68]

Franklin kept adding items to his list of American imports. He had long ago learned, in his father's chandlery, to appreciate a good candle. Now, he disdained English candles and wanted only spermaceti ones from New England. He requested them, usually from his relatives and often as part of the regular exchange with them. Was this untaxed traffic legal? In a private letter, Franklin jokingly reported to Timothy Folger that Mrs. Stevenson was "vex'd to hear that the Box of Spermaceti Candles" Folger had tried to send her from Nantucket had been "seiz'd." Stevenson, Franklin warned Folger, promised that "if ever she sees you again, she will put you in a way of making Reprisals. You know she is a Smuggler upon Principle; and she does not consider how averse you are to every thing of the kind." Franklin was soon assuring Folger, unrepentently, "I have since received a Box of Spermaceti Candles from you that are excellent."[69]

Other imports were legal, if unusual. Franklin asked his wife to send young American apple trees or their cuttings for a British friend; the fresh apples or pieces of pie might have been advertisements for American pippins. Deborah Franklin also sent pet squirrels for her husband to bestow on friends' children, including the daughters of Jonathan Shipley, the Bishop of St. Asaph, who delighted over "Mungo" (killed by a dog and eulogized by Franklin) and "Beebee" (who lived to a good age for a squirrel). More than apples or even apple trees, the hapless squirrels showed Franklin's authority over and trust in his network of ship's captains, who, agreeing to transport the animals, accepted the delicate task of keeping them fed, watered, and out of the hands of ravenous, rodent-roasting midshipmen.[70]

These small, happy trades existed, however, within an otherwise quite troubled Atlantic economy. In 1767, the Townshend Duties had laid taxes on a variety of British manufactures imported into the colonies. Colonists responded with some well-organized boycotts. Franklin wrote pamphlets supporting them, deploying political arithmetic to defend continental colonists' value to the empire. They were like geese that laid golden eggs: they generated revenue by voluntarily consuming British goods but might be killed by obtuse ministers of finance. Carried away with this idea, Franklin overstated the potential impact of Americans' nonimportation of British goods. He predicted that "suspending our trade with the WEST INDIES will ruin every plantation there."[71]

The less the colonies were regulated, Franklin maintained, the greater their wealth and ultimate contribution to the empire. The continental population was growing, America was expanding as a market for consumption, and colonists were increasingly able to navigate the continent and Atlantic themselves. When British ministers were anxious about the burgeoning colonial fishing trades, Franklin, writing as "N. N.," advised them to regard colonial fishing, "coasting trade," and commerce with the West Indies and Europe as activities that—independent of metropolitan regulation—would increase "the numbers of English seamen" and augment "our naval power."[72]

Again, the colonists won. The Townshend Duties were removed in 1770, except for the tax on tea. Throughout the debate over the duties, Franklin mixed his messages. Americans could contribute to imperial might, he promised, but they would resist any attempt at close regulation.

Hydrography proved it. Warning Britain to anticipate a "populous and mighty" British America, one that could "shake off any Shackles that may be impos'd on her," Franklin included among North America's assets its "great navigable Rivers and Lakes." When he read a 1770 pamphlet that described how the spread of colonial population would increase the costs of trade and transportation, he jabbed angry marginalia into his copy. North America was "full of Rivers and Lakes: which this Writer seems not to know." In notes on agriculture and manufacturing that he made circa 1771, Franklin again stressed the power of internal navigation, though with tempered optimism. A mutually beneficial relationship among farmers and manufacturers was obvious but only if farms were "near the Sea or navigable Rivers . . . those distant will find it difficult."[73]

Where American nature failed, canals might help. Canal building—like chemistry, soda water, India, and the Pacific Ocean—was a craze in the late eighteenth century. Franklin duly researched its possible use for landlocked colonists. In 1766, he had overheard a Dutch boatman say that slow progress in a canal resulted from a low level of water. Franklin thought this might result from displaced water; the shallower the water, the more of it had to pass along the sides of the boat rather than underneath it, which would slow the boat. He "did not recollect to have met with any mention of this matter in our philosophical books," so as he made his way around London, he chatted to Thames watermen. They confirmed that shallow water meant delay. In a wooden trough, Franklin conveyed a miniature boat by silk thread and pulley to perform eight timed experiments in 1768, each test at three different depths of water; the deepest water allowed the swiftest passage. He concluded that even if deeper canals cost more to build, they were cheaper to operate— horses could more easily drag boats in deep water.[74]

Franklin began keeping track of colonial canal projects, particularly in the mid-Atlantic region. In 1769, for example, he read of a possible canal between the Chesapeake and Delaware Bays; from 1770 to 1772, he learned about plans to connect the Susquehanna and Schuylkill rivers. He researched the optimal construction of canal boats by consulting a Dutch authority; he solicited help from a British cartographer and surveyor. Thus, science assisted empire yet again, but the question remained: Could Britons and British Americans unite in efforts to improve the colonies?[75]

BY THAT TIME, the years 1771 to 1774, Franklin's political involvement alternated between explosive confrontations and tranquil

achievements. Remarkably, the pattern was also true of the philosophical topics he chose to address at the same time.

A political bomb landed early in 1771, when Lord Hillsborough
took his revenge on Franklin, his pamphleteering opponent. Franklin had just been appointed agent for the Massachusetts Assembly.
He called on Hillsborough, who, still Secretary of State for the American colonies, had to approve the appointment. The interview went
badly. His lordship refused to acknowledge any appointment that
did not carry the consent of the governor. This had indeed been the
usual practice, though it had lapsed. Hillsborough's insistence on it
looked like a way to deny that colonists could choose their representative to the metropole (and a way to humiliate Franklin). Franklin
was taken aback, Hillsborough was adamant, and both men lost their
heads, Franklin worst of all, since he crossed a line by insulting his
opponent. "It is," he declared, "of no great importance whether the
appointment is acknowledged or not." Thus dismissing Hillsborough—and the authority he held—Franklin stormed out.[76]

It was only a momentary victory for Hillsborough, who was replaced by Lord Dartmouth in the summer of 1772. Franklin thought
Dartmouth might broker a compromise over colonial affairs and
left for his annual summer tour in a good mood. He had journeyed
to Ireland, Scotland, and the north of England in the summer of
1771; he returned to the northwest part of England in 1772. It was
very nearly a trip to the future, a form of time travel. In several of
these places, Britain was quickly advancing into the industrial era
and the age of steam. Franklin toured two different coal mines (one
gradually sloped "80 Fathoms under the Surface of the Sea") and
several factories, two of them ironworks. He liked what he saw, even
though what he was seeing was the production of the troublesome,
taxable manufactures over which colonists and British ministers
were squabbling.[77]

He remained torn over his place in the British Atlantic. Returning
to London in August 1772, Franklin confessed to his son that "a violent longing for home sometimes seizes me." His situation in London was, however, very "agreeable." There, he enjoyed "a general
respect paid me by the learned," the primary reason for his happiness. He also had many friends; "my company [is] so much desired
that I seldom dine at home in winter, and could spend the whole
summer in the country homes of inviting friends if I chose it." (That
October, Franklin fled to the home of Sir Francis Dashwood, Lord

Le Despencer, Postmaster General, while Mrs. Stevenson moved to another house on Craven Street.) Above all, Franklin confided, the new ministry promised less trouble over colonial affairs, and "the K[ing] too has lately been heard to speak of me with great regard."[78]

The royal attention was a first and entirely welcome to Franklin. Among all British monarchs, George III is still the one who received the best education in science. His (working) collection of scientific instruments—including electrical devices—was vast. He was in a position to appreciate Franklin's expertise.[79]

But his service to the Crown led Franklin into an explosive scientific debate. Between 1763 and 1768, the royal powder magazine had been moved—very carefully—from Greenwich to Purfleet. Then, in 1769, lightning had struck the powder magazine in Brescia, Italy, killing more than a thousand people and destroying the town. In response to the disaster, Parliament passed two acts in 1771 and 1772 regulating private stores of gunpowder. In 1772, the Board of Ordnance also took a hard look at its powder-houses. Benjamin Wilson, who had painted Franklin's portrait in 1759 (the men were both fellows of the Royal Society and remained on good terms) initially proposed to protect Purfleet with blunt-ended lightning rods. The board then consulted Franklin. He inspected the arsenal and recommended pointed conductors instead. The head of the Ordnance Board ordered the Franklin plan "executed as above proposed." But someone worried over the difference between Wilson's and Franklin's plans, and the work stopped. The Board of Ordnance asked the Royal Society to adjudicate, which they did with a committee that included Wilson and Franklin.[80]

It is worth noting a political difference. Wilson identified with his aristocratic patrons and had no record, as Franklin did, of complaining about the British government. In contrast, Franklin's loyalties lay with the middling sort and with the Whigs, indeed, the Club of Honest Whigs; his steady if moderate criticism of British authorities had become the hallmark of his political career. There was no politically inflected difference in the two men's theories of electricity. And the two behaved themselves for the most part, never stooping to insults, as Franklin had done with Hillsborough. But their political antipathy would certainly add verbal sparks to their exchange over lightning rods. It also belied Franklin's assertion, when members of the APS had misbehaved, that the Fellows of the Royal Society never took partisan positions against each other.[81]

In August 1772, the Royal Society committee inspected the magazine yet again and then met four times. Neither Wilson nor Franklin budged, but the doctor carried the day, probably because he, unlike Wilson, offered experimental evidence, which convinced the committee members. They advised the Board of Ordnance to attach two lightning rods to each building within the Purfleet magazine. Each was grounded by a lead pipe buried in the ground and then fastened to an iron rod—with "a sharp point" terminating in copper. Outvoted, Wilson asked Franklin to reconsider his position. "I will *never* give it up," Franklin replied. (The former friends never reconciled.) Wilson filed a minority report, which accompanied the advice to use pointed conductors to the Council of the Royal Society and then to the Board of Ordnance.[82]

After this thunderous affair, Franklin calmed himself by investigating how oil had a calming effect on water. As usual, this was a problem he had been considering, on and off, for more than a decade. He had first noted the phenomenon on shipboard in 1762 when, needing some light, he rigged up an "Italian" lamp, a glass tumbler "slung in wire" and containing water topped with a layer of oil and a wick. Franklin hung the lamp from his cabin's ceiling and watched it sway. He related to John Pringle in December 1762 that, even as "the water under the oil was in great commotion, rising and falling in irregular waves," the oil followed an unexpectedly different pattern: "The surface of the oil was perfectly tranquil, and duly preserved its position and distance with regard to the brim of the glass." "We are all agog," Pringle responded, "about this new property of fluids." The 1769 edition of *Experiments and Observations* included the letter on the new property.[83]

What was the new property? Franklin marshaled his trademark blend of sources: books, artisanal knowledge, and direct observation. He remembered reading, in his youth, Pliny's description of the smoothing effects of oil and "wondered to find no mention of them in our Books of Experimental Philosophy." Where the philosophers failed, mariners excelled. Franklin had received reports of oil's calming effect on water from "an old Sea Captain" as well as a witness in Newport, where spilled whale oil kept the harbor's water smooth as glass.[84]

But sea folk were not always helpful. Franklin recalled his transatlantic voyage in 1757. He had observed the smoothness in the wake of two ships in the fleet bound for Louisbourg and queried Captain

Walter Lutwidge, who had just used him as ballast in his experiments relading the ship. Ludwidge responded impatiently: "'The Cooks, says he, have I suppose, been just emptying their greasy Water thro' the Scuppers, which has greased the Sides of those Ships a little.'" Franklin had felt humiliated: "This Answer he gave me with an Air of some little Contempt, as to a Person ignorant of what every Body else knew."[85]

His own demonstrations were more satisfying. He started with the rather placid pond on Clapham Common, London. On the windward side, just where the air began to make the water shudder, Franklin poured oil and saw it instantly erase the ripples. From this observation, he drew yet more proof of matter's particulate nature; when they touched water, a "mutual Repulsion" among the particles of oil sent them skidding over its surface, ready to rebuff the breeze in a way water could not do. He explained that "the Wind blowing over Water thus covered with a Film of Oil, cannot easily catch upon it so as to raise the first Wrinkles" that led to waves. Franklin was entranced by his discovery and commemorated it with a clever invention. He transformed the top of his walking stick into a receptacle for oil, handy whenever he and the right kind of breeze arrived together at a body of water.[86]

He decided that oil should be effective on large bodies of water as well. He knew from Captain Cook that violent surf could prevent boats from reaching shore. But perhaps a ship could sail back and forth off the "Lee Shore, continually pouring Oil into the Sea" until it subsided. There was only one way to find out. On a "blustring unpleasant Day" in October 1773, he tested his theory near Portsmouth, accompanied by Banks and Solander, Cook's naturalists— three men in a boat. In a near storm, they made several "Trips of about half a Mile each, pouring Oil continually out of a large Stone Bottle." The test was inconclusive (not enough oil, perhaps), though Franklin congratulated his companions for their "Patience and Activity that could only be inspired by a Zeal for the Improvement of Knowledge." Then, he wrote up his findings in a long, much-delayed letter to William Brownrigg, who would present it to the Royal Society.[87]

But in December 1773, soon after Franklin had poured oil over the water near Portsmouth, irate Bostonians poured tea over Boston harbor. The exotic goods flowing out of India had become a problem. The recent Tea Act, the one surviving part of the Townshend

Duties, had lowered the cost of East India Company tea. This step, it was hoped, would guarantee sales for the troubled company. Only the restive North Americans could see the lowering of prices as reason for revolt. Cheaper tea be damned—the colonists hated the Tea Act's monopoly, which undercut colonial profits from smuggled Dutch tea. Massachusetts residents had for some time been leading the most truculent protests against any and all British commercial policies. Now, they made tea with muddy, salty water. They had destroyed private property, and British officials lost patience with them.

Things seemed to be at an impasse, but Franklin was determined, still, to reach a compromise. He worked on a peace commission, whose members included Fothergill, to broker a repeal of certain taxes in exchange for colonists' cooperation with commercial regulation. In March 1773, he repeated his claims about the value of the colonies—their growing populations, their ability to consume, produce, and transport valuable goods—to make sense of the Boston affair. Cooperation between colonists and British officials was a necessity, he said, and British force was ill advised. "A Coast, 1500 Miles in Length," he warned, "could not in all Parts be guarded, even by the whole Navy of England." Franklin even offered to pay for the destroyed tea, which would have cost him a ruinous £9,000. The gesture made clear that, however unruffled he appeared on the surface, he boiled within and was desperate for resolution.[88]

Franklin finally saw why colonists might feel driven to unlawful defiance. He himself began to fear persecution. He worried that his enemies might manipulate the postal system to block the colonists' access to information and even feared that officials would divert his letters to British ministers and put copies about to prove him treasonous. In 1772, he and William Franklin had wondered whether their private letters were being opened. (William even suspected Anthony Todd of snooping, though his father defended the man.)[89]

And then, Franklin suffered the worst humiliation of his life. It was his own fault—he had himself interfered with the circulation of the mail. Londoner Thomas Whately had, years earlier, received several letters from Massachusetts friends, including Thomas Hutchinson and Andrew Oliver. (Hutchinson was chief justice and lieutenant governor; Oliver was secretary.) The two men wrote how they wished to use more forceful action against the intransigent Bostonians, perhaps by removing government from popular control.

Someone (still unidentified) sent the letters to Franklin, and he forwarded them to Thomas Cushing, speaker of the Massachusetts Assembly. They considered the letters to be evidence of a British plan to destroy colonial autonomy. Franklin advised Cushing, probably ingenuously, against printing the letters, but they were published in Boston in 1773. The publication angered both those who feared what the correspondence said and those who deplored that a private correspondence had become public. On Christmas Day in 1773, Franklin identified himself as the source of the miscirculated letters in order to prevent suspicion from falling on others.[90]

Franklin's confession came only nine days after the Boston Tea Party—bad timing. Even British moderates were turning against colonists. Were none of them dutiful? That a deputy postmaster for North America would read and circulate private letters was a serious matter. Called to account for his actions, Franklin prepared carefully for a hearing in late January 1774, where he would face questioning in the "Cockpit," where the Privy Council held public meetings.

Circulation, one of the great themes of his life, had turned toxic. As the crisis surrounding the circulation of the mail drew to a climax, Franklin was obsessed with the common cold and how it circulated. In one 1773 letter, he fretted about both colds and the Hutchinson letters, running from one topic to the next in a revealing train of thought.[91]

To a series of correspondents, Franklin wrote letters in which he rejected most of the conventional wisdom on colds. He insisted that they had "no Relation to *Wet* or *Cold*," the proverbial causes that encouraged people to stay indoors, sweltering in wraps or bedclothes. Even doctors recommended these tactics, but Franklin thought they prevented a healthy flow of air and moisture through the body. "No one ever catches the Disorder we call a Cold, from cold Air"; sailors were healthy despite their damp surroundings. Conversely, going out into fresh air caused vigor, as did exercise proportioned to diet. Franklin assumed that the body perspired even if it was cold, which did not entirely close the pores and cause illness. He argued that a different kind of circulation explained colds—people circulated them. "People often catch Cold from one another when shut up together in small close Rooms, Coaches, &c. and when sitting near and conversing so as to breathe in each others Transpiration."[92]

Franklin thus revisited several of his earlier concerns about circulation, including the metabolic cycles of the human body, the movement of air in enclosed atmospheres, perspiration and respiration, and the effects of hot and cold. His interest in the circulation of air was partly rekindled by Joseph Priestley's chemical work. As Priestley investigated air, he explored its contribution to life, the question Boyle and Hales had investigated earlier. Tormenting yet more small animals, Priestley watched a lone mouse in a bell jar die in tortured gasps as it depleted its air supply. But he gave one lucky mouse a mint plant for company, and it lived. When Priestley related that plants could thus "repurify" foul air, Franklin marveled that "the vegetable creation should restore the air which is spoiled by the animal part of it." He hoped the discovery would "give some check to the rage of destroying trees that grow near houses." Instead of being unhealthy, trees might impart health.[93]

But Franklin's long manuscript notes on the common cold, circa 1773, drew no clear conclusion. He did define a cold as "a Siziness [viscosity] and thickness of the Blood, whereby the smaller Vessels are obstructed, and the Perspirable Matter retained." That matter then "offends [the body] both by its Quantity and Quality." It is not surprising that Franklin thought impeded circulation caused ill health. But what caused or prevented this thickness and slowness of the blood?[94]

Franklin guessed himself into circles. Warm rooms were healthy unless they overheated a body; fresh air helped except when it did not. Colds resulted from exposure to cold air "without Exercise," yet exercising in a "close Room" could increase the chances of a cold because the exertion might "fill the Air with putrid Particles." Nor was going outside any safer, as colds resulted from "cooling suddenly in the Air after Exercise." Other culprits might include wet newspapers, putrid fish, damp books, failing to relieve the bladder frequently, intemperance in eating and drinking, and exposure to rotten glue. Franklin looked everywhere for clues: the high mortality in the Black Hole of Calcutta, the rate at which Pennsylvania reapers drank water, and the fact that American Indians slept with their feet to the fire (retaining health), and that "Hottentots" greased themselves (courting illness).[95]

These principles—gathered from Franklin's long inquiry into circulation and from the expanding geography of the British empire—defy synopsis, let alone analysis. They exist almost as diary entries. In one, Franklin first read Tryon on temperance; in another, he saw Indian spies keeping warm on American frontiers; and then, he pondered questions about labor and perspiration in Pennsylvania's wheat fields. Franklin may have given the best summary of the issue when he concluded, with Poor Richard's epigrammatic, if mocking, common sense, that "People often don't get Cold where they think they do, but do where they think they do not." He had asked a question about nature he could not answer. Given his history of near-fatal colds and pleurisies, he surely would have welcomed an answer. Having thus undermined his confidence in himself, mind and body, Franklin entered the Cockpit for the hearing on the Hutchinson affair.[96]

It was a denunciation. If Franklin had hoped to reprise his brilliant performance in the question-and-answer interview in Parliament eight years earlier, he had deceived himself. In fact, he had little opportunity to defend his conduct at all—it was, he said later, like a "bull baiting." Before a packed audience, Solicitor General Alexander Wedderburn lambasted him at length, leaving no opportunity for rebuttal or counterattack. Wearing his best suit, Franklin, who had just turned sixty-eight, managed to remain standing with an impassive expression for the hour that it took Wedderburn to wreck his reputation as a servant of the British empire.

Devastatingly, the solicitor general attacked each of the accomplishments that had elevated Franklin to the status of philosopher and genius. Poor Richard's astronomy took a hit when Wedderburn sneered that "the rank in which Dr. Franklin appears, is not even that of a Province Agent: he moves in a very inferior orbit." Twice, Wedderburn mocked the master electrician with his own terminology by calling him the "prime conductor" in the affair. (As Franklin left, he grasped hands with fellow electrician Priestley, who knew the nerve Wedderburn had struck.) Worst of all was a vicious pun—Franklin's nefarious work in the postal service had so compromised him, Wedderburn claimed, that "he will henceforth esteem it a libel to be called *a man of letters.*"[97]

Franklin's status as a member of British officialdom was destroyed. Two days later, Anthony Todd dismissed him from the Post Office. It was a humiliating end to twenty years of service and no thanks for his having helped make American postal delivery turn a profit rather than suffer continual losses. Postal service had been Franklin's first imperial role, his first significant political function. It had become second nature to him; at least once after his termination, he automatically dropped an unfranked letter into the post, forgetting he had lost his franking privileges.[98]

Friends rallied and tried to console him. Some Philadelphians used electricity to burn effigies of Hutchinson and Wedderburn. But Franklin had entered a state of controlled rage against the British government. He never emerged from it. In a "Letter from London" printed in the *Boston Gazette* in April 1774, Franklin dismissed the service that had dismissed him, warning that "the post officers will in a little time become as formidable as the Commissioners of the Customs and their numerous levee." The former postmaster was no longer conciliatory: "*Behold Americans where matters are driving!*"[99]

———————

MAYBE it comforted Franklin that, over at the Royal Society, it was as if nothing had happened. In June 1774, five months after the Cockpit hearing, William Brownrigg presented the society with Franklin's experiments on pouring oil over turbulent water. During a peaceful moment in the British empire, Franklin had introduced himself to the Royal Society of London with a bang—with a paper on thunder and lightning. Now, as the empire collapsed, he would take his leave of London with a farewell paper on how to calm troubled waters.

Franklin's demonstration of oil on water, like his electrical experiments, was dramatic and easily done and hence widely imitated. In early 1775, Thomas Percival reported that the experiment was successfully repeated in Manchester; in Birmingham, Matthew Boulton "astonished our rural philosophers exceedingly by calming the waves a la Franklin." The quick popularization of Franklin's new experiment—and its association with him—meant that the world now had two dramatic images of Benjamin Franklin: he was the modern Prometheus who drew fire from the skies in the "Philadelphia experiment," and he was a wise old man who could calm the raging seas "a la Franklin."[100]

But even Franklin could not calm the political storm rising over the British Atlantic. So far had Anglo-American relations deteriorated that, beginning in 1774, everyone assumed letters and packages carried on British packets were being opened. In a showily sentimental letter to his sister Jane (meant to reproach anyone else who read it), Franklin complained that "the Letters between us, tho' very innocent ones, are intercepted. They might restore me yours at least, after reading them." Even the republic of letters suffered. When John Winthrop wrote Franklin to acknowledge a letter and new volume of the Royal Society's *Philosophical Transactions*, he related that the once-sealed package was now "only tied up loosely . . . without any seal."[101]

Until February 1775, Franklin continued to work and hope for some kind of resolution to the colonial crisis. He achieved nothing, and as February ended, he decided to go home. Both the decision and its timing were sad. By prolonging a pointless fight in London, Franklin guaranteed that he would never again see his wife. Deborah Franklin, smitten by a series of strokes, had died in December 1774.

Shipwrecked: in the eighteenth century, the word described a man who had lost everything—livelihood, reputation, prospects, hope. There were moments in 1774 and 1775 when Franklin must have felt himself to be wrecked, though he still had some hope—and rage—to sustain him. As he wrote his son from the ship that carried him back to America in March 1775, the "wrong politicks" had prevented Americans and Britons from "extending our Western Empire [by] adding Province to Province as far as the South Sea." So much for the pacific—and Pacific—promises of the British Empire. "The Waves never rise but when the Winds blow." Did Franklin feel any satisfaction, however grim, that his political and philosophical sentiments had converged?[102]

Chapter 8

THE SCIENCE
OF WAR

FRANKLIN had waited until the fifty-ninth minute of the eleventh hour to leave London. On March 22, 1775, he embarked from Portsmouth on one of the packets that still, barely, connected the colonies to Britain. The six-week passage gave him ample time to write a bitter journal of the failed peace negotiations in London. And he worried, yet again, about "Voyages from & to America why not of equal Length," as he titled a note he wrote "at Sea" on April 5.[1]

In the political essay, Franklin addressed a problem with a solution he could now define: separation from Britain by any means necessary. There would be no more compromises. In his essay on science, in contrast, he addressed a problem that continued to puzzle him. The Gulf Stream caused different lengths of passage across the Atlantic, but what on earth caused the stream? Such was his indefatigable curiosity about nature that even at that moment, still reeling from a grave political defeat, Franklin attacked a major philosophic topic, one emblematic of the dangerous distance between Britain and America.

He still suspected that the earth's rotation was involved; a ship sailing east must gain speed as the world turned, perhaps "two miles in a minute faster." When a ship went the other way, "just the contrary must happen." But perhaps the current had other causes, and Franklin now examined a new factor, thermal variation in seawater, that revived his old interests in temperature and circulation. He joined a clutch of naturalists, including those on Cook's second Pacific voyage, who were starting to collect sea-surface temperature readings.[2]

How do you take the ocean's temperature? In the eighteenth century, if you were nearly seventy years old, you could do it handily with the help of a Fahrenheit thermometer and a spry young person. Franklin's assistant was his teenaged grandchild, William Temple Franklin. Temple was William Franklin's son, born in London (out of wedlock) but now going to America to join his father, who was serving as governor of New Jersey. While he and his grandfather were at sea, it was probably Temple who hauled up buckets of seawater or lowered the thermometer in a protective device. We have the final assessment of their data, published as part of Franklin's 1786 "Maritime Observations," which may be only a subset of the readings he and Temple had collected a decade earlier. These data recorded the sea's surface temperature on thirteen days in April and May. Franklin also took the air's temperature, and for the final six days of readings (April 28 through May 3), he made measurements of air and water several times a day. The data allowed Franklin to see how the temperature of the ocean varied according to the time of day and atmospheric temperature. The records included, for each reading, prevailing wind direction, the ship's course, position at latitude and longitude, and narrative remarks.[3]

The latter were mostly notes on the color of the ocean's water and whether it contained any "gulph weed," the two visible clues Franklin had noticed in 1726. He remarked on two places where the temperature of the water rose, gulfweed appeared, and phosphorescence vanished. One note referred to an older thermal interest, a "Thunder-gust"; another followed Timothy Folger's advice for locating the great current: "saw a whale." Franklin seemed to be compiling all he had learned and was continuing to learn about the Gulf Stream.[4]

Then Franklin dropped the matter—again. As never before, public affairs—meaning the birth of the United States—robbed him of time to address the sciences. It was the Franklin paradox in its starkest form.

We could look at this situation in two different ways. In one way, the American Revolution destroyed Franklin's scientific career; the event made it impossible for him to maintain even the low level of activity he had managed in London while the crisis was brewing. But in another way, the Revolution guaranteed his immortal fame. The event made clear that Franklin had surpassed all other modern philosophers. He had gained glory in natural science, as figures such as Newton had also done. But then he guided a new nation through war and into international recognition, tasks even Newton had never had to face.

Franklin was surely not oblivious to the trade-off. In essence, he made a silent pact with his new nation: he laid his reputation as a philosopher on the altar of the Revolution. He guaranteed his apotheosis as a genius but sacrificed any time to do further work in the sciences.

Moreover, Franklin brokered his fame to win European allies. This was yet another of his astonishing balancing acts. The republic of letters was supposed to stand above nation, but Franklin used his status as man of letters to help found a nation. During the war that created the United States, he embodied the complex relations between science and politics—sometimes studiously separated, sometimes opportunistically conflated.

———————

DISEMBARKING in Philadelphia on May 5, Franklin learned of the battles of Lexington and Concord. The next day, he was selected as a Pennsylvania delegate to the Second Continental Congress, whose members debated whether to break with Britain. Knowing his time for science would soon vanish, Franklin quickly wrote Joseph Priestley on May 16 that "in coming over I made a valuable philosophical discovery, which I shall communicate to you, when I can get a little time." Priestley waited. Later in May, Franklin began another letter, possibly to him, on the question the Boston Board of Customs had sent "to the Lords of the Treasury," five or six years earlier, about different lengths of voyages across the Atlantic. He ran through the available explanations, adding that he "could not but think the Fact misunderstood or misrepresented," a sign that his work on thermal variation might have followed. But the letter stopped there and was never posted. He had other things to think about.[5]

Franklin had always wanted Philadelphia to be at the center of things—now, he got his wish. The city was the heart of the "United Colonies," the seat of the Continental Congress, which met in Pennsylvania's State House. (There, Massachusetts delegate John Adams saw Henry Popple's map of British America, which Franklin had ordered in 1746—Adams reported that it was the largest map he had ever seen.) Franklin joined congressional committees meant to establish independent power for the United Colonies. The Committee of Secret Correspondence sought diplomatic and military aid; the parallel Secret Committee sought materiel to use against Britain.[6]

Then, in late July of 1775, Congress founded a post office, and fittingly, Franklin was appointed its first postmaster general. His old friend and now political critic William Strahan was alarmed. Strahan recognized that, by creating an American postal authority, Congress was declaring colonial independence and that Franklin, by becoming postmaster, was declaring his as well. "I see with Concern that you have accepted of the Place of Postmaster from the Congress," Strahan wrote, "a Step of itself which sufficiently indicates your Opinion, that *a Separation will take Place.*" Strahan noted that he communicated his suspicion via "the last regular Packett that is to sail from hence for some time at least." He thus retracted an earlier promise to write Franklin by every packet and withdrew his friendship. Franklin had already written him a note signed, with clever fury, "You are now my Enemy, and I am, Yours, B FRANKLIN." But he could not bring himself to send it.[7]

As the first British empire fell apart, so did its postal system, ominously severing thousands of human connections between Britain and America. On August 23, 1775, the king declared the colonies to be in open rebellion. One month later, on September 28, the British General Post Office announced in the London newspapers that mail to the thirteen rebellious colonies would leave one last time on October 4. Many scribbling Britons, including Strahan, posted their letters on that day. Thereafter, North American packet boats ran only to and from Halifax. A final round of mail for Britain left the United Colonies the following spring, which was how Franklin sent a package of letters to Anthony Todd. Assuring Todd of his friendship despite the "Breach" between their homelands, he did not expect him to frank the enclosed letters but to forward them and charge the cost to Franklin.[8]

When the imperial postal system collapsed, paper could no longer easily span distance. Thus began a long period during which Franklin had to use circuitous means to communicate with friends in England. One transatlantic packet of letters, from Mary Stevenson Hewson, took over a decade to reach Franklin. When Franklin's letters stopped, Hewson plaintively wrote him that "the Atlantic is now the *great gulph,* indeed; for there seems no possibility of passing over it to each other."[9]

Franklin still hoped that good sense might avert a costly war—a little political economy revealed the folly of British invasion. In a letter "to a Friend in London" dated October 1775, he offered their mutual friend, Richard Price, "some data to work upon." These morbid numbers consisted of the revenue the British ministry had already spent on the war, the "mile" of ground they had gained at Lexington and Concord minus the half mile they subsequently lost at Bunker Hill, the British casualties, the American casualties, and then the 60,000 to 70,000 children who had been born in the United Colonies since fighting had broken out in New England. Given these data, Franklin concluded, it would take roughly forever "for England to conquer America." Americans could breed faster than they could be killed—a doggedly cheerful scenario.[10]

But the American invasion of Canada between 1775 and 1776 severely tested this political arithmetic. The rebels had decided, somewhat ambitiously, not only to defend themselves but also to strike back at the British. So American forces assaulted Quebec. They did so in December, hardly the ideal month in which to invade the frigid territory to the north. The Americans lost their commander, and as myth has it, a small band of survivors left bloody footprints in the snow as they retreated.

Congress then appealed to Franco-Canadians, who had endured British rule since the Treaty of Paris and were presumably eager to overthrow their conquerors. But there was no reason for Franco-Canadians to trust the predominantly Protestant colonies in British America, with their rich anti-Catholic history. So Congress carefully selected four emissaries to Montreal. Members of that body ransacked Maryland, Britain's only originally Catholic colony, and came up with Jesuit-educated Charles Carroll of Carrollton and Catholic Father John Carroll. The other two men were Anglican Marylander Samuel Chase and deist Benjamin Franklin.

Franklin was the first delegate listed on Congress's official letter and the only man introduced at length: "Member of the Royal Academy of Sciences at Paris FRS &c. &c." The other delegates had no "et ceteras" after their names. Franklin, the man of science, was above faith and nation—that was why his membership in the Académie des Sciences mattered. (The "FRS" hastily disclosed Franklin's affiliation with British learning.)[11]

Northward the four men went in March 1776, but the francophone Canadians swiftly rebuffed them. The delegation trailed back to Philadelphia in May, and leaders of the Canadian campaign conceded defeat the next month. But the venture foreshadowed Franklin's role in wooing the French. Jacques Barbeu-Dubourg's creation of a peacefully Quakerish Franklin in the French *Oeuvres* already had interesting possibilities. Even at that early stage, members of the nascent Congress recognized that Franklin's international reputation could serve the national interest.

For the same reasons, the somewhat crazed idea of Franklin's Promethean power reappeared. William Goforth conjured up the image in a 1776 letter to Franklin. Goforth was a New York artisan and radical leader, already a veteran in the war. He begged Franklin for an unearthly assistance against British Canada: "I understood you are a great man that you Can Turn the Common Course of nature that you have power with the Gods and Can Rob the Clouds of their Tremendious Thunder." Franklin needed merely to "Collect the Heavey Thunders of the United Colonies" to "Shake the Quebec walls or on the other hand inform us how to Extract the Electric fire" to do so. Obviously, Goforth knew the power of flattery.[12]

But it almost did not matter that the idea of Franklin as a Merlin or Prospero was overstated—as patriotic guff went, it was pretty powerful. The *New-Jersey Gazette*, for instance, would crow that Franklin would, at any moment, put together "an *electrical machine*" that could "disunite kingdoms, join islands to continents." He could also concoct "a certain chymical preparation" to "smooth the waves of the sea in one part of the globe, and raise tempests and whirlwinds in another."[13]

Clearly, the American Revolutionaries thought they might need supernatural aid. And indeed, they were facing Europe's most powerful empire, flushed with victory from the Seven Years' War and equipped with the world's best navy, meaning the best means to invade and retake the rebellious colonies. It made perfect sense that the Americans were scared—scared enough to want to believe they had a sorcerer on their side.

Franklin, man of letters, rallied a weapon more effective than thunder: Tom Paine. Paine was an English workingman—a corset maker—possessed of a ready wit, an interest in natural philosophy, and radical political sentiments. When Franklin had first met him in London sometime in the 1760s, he recognized a kindred spirit, even if the two men's politics did not match, exactly. When Paine emigrated to America in 1774, he arrived with Franklin's letter of introduction to Richard Bache, Franklin's son-in-law, who got him printer's work in Philadelphia. Like Franklin before him, Paine honed his writing skills while setting type for other authors' works.

Political essays became his forte, and in 1776, Paine crafted a short, sharp treatise, *Common Sense*, probably the most important piece of propaganda ever published in what was about to become the United States.[14]

Common Sense's tone, indeed its very title, asserted that truth was perfectly apparent, perhaps as obvious as material reality itself. On these grounds, Paine mocked the still prevalent arguments for reconciliation with Great Britain, urged a final break, and championed a republican form of government, meaning one without a king.

Franklin critiqued a draft of *Common Sense*, which, published anonymously in January 1776, was so persuasive that people suspected Franklin wrote it. (Mistakes are rarely compliments, but this misattribution complimented both Paine and Franklin.) Many parts of *Common Sense* articulated Franklin's own emerging sentiments, including a plea for a navy, "that nice point in national policy, in which commerce and protection are united." Nature had been "liberal" to America: the world's great powers had either coastline or inland materials for shipbuilding, but America had both. It already produced "tar, timber, iron, and cordage" and had enough "able and social sailors" to instruct "active landmen in the common work of a ship."[15]

Common Sense and the popular response to it emboldened the Continental Congress. In June, members of that body established a committee, which included Franklin and Thomas Jefferson, and charged it to write a declaration of independence. Early the next month, that manifesto announced to the world that the people of America would assume "the separate and equal station to which the laws of nature and of nature's god entitle them." That phrase remarkably echoed Polly Baker's claim that her steady production of bastards obeyed "The Command of Nature, and of Nature's God, *Encrease and Multiply*." (If Franklin fed Thomas Jefferson the line, he never confessed it.)

The authors of the Declaration of Independence, like Polly Baker and Tom Paine, leaned hard on the argument that nature itself proclaimed truths that humans needed only to follow. Indeed, either Franklin or Jefferson (the draft's handwriting is not clear) defined these "Truths to be self-evident." By the last quarter of the eighteenth century, this Newtonian language was thoroughly familiar and, more to the point, a thrilling bit of rhetoric. The laws of nature, nature's God, self-evident truths—the Declaration of Independence shows perfectly how the sciences had permeated public culture, even in provincial places on the far side of the Atlantic.[16]

Science even helped promulgate the Declaration of Independence. When Philadelphians assembled to hear it read for the first time, they gathered around the platform that the American Philosophical Society had built to observe the 1769 transit of Venus. Here again was the eighteenth century's distinctive blend of science and politics: a document read from an astronomical observatory insisted that nature was above politics—it simply proclaimed truth. Yet the sciences were always political, embedded in contemporary debate. Like their president, Franklin, the members of the APS had literally lent their platform—and their authority—to a political cause.[17]

To found a nation on unwritten laws of nature was bold, albeit debatable. If Americans were "entitled" to anything "by any law of God," snorted English moral philosopher Jeremy Bentham, "they had only to produce that law," meaning something in writing. Bentham's dismissive remarks were typical of the international reaction to the Declaration of Independence. Natural science did not, most people believed, generate a human science of comparable authority. Not a single monarch or head of state was willing to recognize the United States. Military force would have to prove what the laws of nature did not—the Americans would have to fight for their freedom.[18]

That much was evident to Franklin. His worry over the impending, all-out war affected even the national icons he proposed. He sketched a design for the national currency that featured, in Latin, his oft-repeated warning that "the waves never rise but when the winds blow." For the front of the seal of the United States, he suggested more Latin, the cheerful motto "E Pluribus Unum" (Out of Many, One). For the reverse of the seal, he suggested an image of Moses "extending his Hand over the Sea, thereby causing the same to overwhelm Pharoah." This image was to bear the motto "*Rebellion to Tyrants Is Obedience to God.*" Congress adopted the Latin motto but not the comparison of George III to Pharoah.[19]

But unless they created a navy, the Americans would be the ones overwhelmed by the sea. Others labored to create the Continental Army; Franklin, the former aspiring sailor, worried over the colonies' "Want of a naval Force." He had spent years decrying Americans who smuggled—now he wanted Congress to sponsor American privateering against the British. He wrote a fiery preamble to a resolution, never passed (and possibly never presented), in which he observed that Britons had already "proceeded to open Robbery" on the sea. They were "manifesting themselves to be *hostes humani generis*," or enemies of humanity, and should expect "Reprisals." "Nothing will give us a greater Weight and Importance," Franklin insisted, "than a Conviction that we can annoy, on Occasion, their Trade, and carry our Prizes into safe Harbors."[20]

The Committee of Secret Correspondence scrambled in July 1776 to obtain or commission ships. To one captain, members of the committee emphasized, "You must Ship as many Seamen as you can possibly get, especially American Seamen." But anyone would do—"We are in Want of Seamen and you may bring People of all Countrys or Nations" willing to serve the United States. In another of the committee's letters later that year, Franklin and Robert Morris hoped that measures "to encourage the breeding [training] of seamen amongst ourselves, will in a few Years make us respectable on the Ocean."[21]

Breeding in the usual sense was what Americans did best as far as Franklin was concerned, and he introduced it as a political factor during debates over the Articles of Confederation, predecessor of the U.S. Constitution. Franklin wanted a system of political representation based on the population of each state. He rarely opened his mouth, even in committees, so he surprised fellow delegates when he rose to speak in the full Congress three times, always on questions of representation and taxation. Leaders of small states, who feared their citizens would be outvoted by those in more populous states, wanted the same number of representatives for each state. Franklin protested. "To sett out with an unequal Representation is unreasonable," he said, given the long-standing colonial complaint against Britain's system of virtual representation. Franklin had made too much of America's burgeoning population for him to concede that it did not matter, politically.[22]

Franklin's tag—E Pluribus Unum—heralded the federal system (many states joined into one nation) but also celebrated that nation's multiplying citizens. It was an oddly erudite motto for a man who boasted his lack of Greek and Latin. But it made perfect sense for a political arithmetician such as Franklin, who believed that a state's power ultimately derived from its productive members. For this reason, too, Franklin ventured into the combustible debate over whether slaves should be counted as part of the population that would determine each state's contribution to the common treasury.

Southern delegates protested, one of them saying that slaves were not citizens to be taxed any more than sheep were. Franklin replied sharply. "Slaves rather weaken than strengthen the state," he declared, "there is therefore some difference between them and Sheep. Sheep will never make any Insurrections." He moved an amendment, "that Votes should be in Proportion to Numbers" of people, but was outvoted. (A similar proposal for assessment, which included slaves and free people, also failed.) Franklin would have to wait until the Constitutional Convention of 1787 to raise the question again.[23]

But he would keep reminding anyone who would listen that America's large population mattered. And he could not resist telling the British so. He served on a committee that, after the Battle of Long Island in 1776, met with Lord Howe on Staten Island, in yet another last-ditch effort at reconciliation. During the talks, Howe swore that the British did not seek merely to draw revenue from America—they esteemed "her Commerce, her Strength, her Men." Franklin evidently gave Howe "rather a sneering Laugh" and then said that America indeed had "a pretty considerable Manufactory of *Men.*" Americans' constant growth in numbers was a formidable weapon against the British. The meeting ended without any reconciliation.[24]

The breach was now permanent. Franklin must have felt himself torn away from Britain's centers of learning. His fellow Revolutionaries did not offer much consolation. On their way to meet Howe on Staten Island, Franklin and John Adams had shared a room—and bed—at an inn in New Brunswick, New Jersey. Nursing a cold, Adams ventured to shut the bedroom window. "Oh!" cried Franklin. "Dont shut the Window. We shall be suffocated." When Adams objected that the night air would make him worse, Franklin insisted that the air inside was "worse than that without Doors," meaning full of Adams's effluvia. "Come!" he invited Adams, "open the Window and come to bed, and I will convince you." In they tucked themselves. "The Doctor then began a harrangue," Adams made sure to record in his diary, "upon Air and cold and Respiration and Perspiration, with which I was so much amused that I soon fell asleep, and left him and his Philosophy together."[25]

That must have been rather how Franklin felt—surrounded by fellow patriots yet alone with his philosophy. Pressed into service by the new nation and the new state of Philadelphia, he was both celebrated as a philosopher and neglected as one, too. He would have better luck abroad. The United States was lucky as well. Desperate for help from France, continental Europe's most powerful nation, it had Benjamin Franklin, the internationally renowned natural philosopher, to make its appeal. At the trickiest court in Europe, where the politics were as dazzling and disorienting as the mirrored hall at Versailles, Franklin was the key to a lasting, important alliance between France and the United States.[26]

AT THE END OF 1776, the delegates to Congress decided to send embassies to the different European courts. Congress needed material support for the war and wanted international recognition of U.S. independence. The diplomatic mission would require someone well known abroad, and Franklin was really the only candidate. Earlier efforts to create a much-needed Franco-American alliance had been rather desperate. Congress had been depending on their man in France, Silas Deane, who barely knew French and who was realizing he was in over his head. Congress gained more from Pierre-Augustin Caron de Beaumarchais. By force of character, the French playwright managed to charm some of his compatriots, including the king, into a guarded sympathy for the American rebels. Zealous in the cause of American independence, Beaumarchais almost single-handedly organized a small and unofficial flow of materiel to America. But without any official connection to the United States or any great influence at the French court, he was unable to secure formal alliance.

Deane was greatly relieved to discover that two men, Franklin and Virginian William Lee, were about to join him. The three American commissioners would represent the United States in France during the first full year of the nation's independence. (In 1778, Congress would recall Deane and replace him with John Adams.)

On October 27, Franklin sailed on the aptly named *Reprisal*, having first scooped up his two grandsons, William Temple Franklin (sixteen years old) and Benjamin Franklin Bache (seven). Temple had been in New Jersey with his father, Benny with his parents in Philadelphia. The youngsters were delighted to be headed to France, but Temple's embarkation represented a family rupture: Franklin had just renounced his loyalist son, William Franklin. By appropriating his son's son, he made clear that he did not wish him raised in a household loyal to George III. Even a Catholic nation with a foreign king was better. Franklin also insisted on a European education for young Benny—American learning was, he implied, too limited for his grandson. The three Franklins had no idea how long they would be away or whether France would welcome them (or throw them out), but off they went.[27]

The journey began well but ended in misery, at least for Franklin. His grandsons were hardy, handy attendants at sea, and he evidently got along with the *Reprisal*'s captain and crew, to whom he made a shrewd gift of wine. But the thirty-day passage was agonizing. The *Reprisal* was faulty (it later sank), and conditions were rough. Even in good weather, Franklin suffered. The seventy-year-old developed boils and another skin condition, possibly psoriasis, both of which had begun to plague him during his mission to Canada. The old man still had a few teeth in his head, but he could not manage the ship's hard biscuits and tough fowls. He made do with salt beef. Even hashed into something like lobscouse, a savory sea dish, the beef might have been hard to chew—or keep down. Salt beef little resembled its fresh counterpart—suspicious sailors greeted it with the cry "salt horse."[28]

Yet within the ravaged body, the fierce intellect still burned. As the sea buffeted Franklin, he studied it. He made (or, from his berth, weakly directed his grandsons to make) a second set of temperature readings in the Atlantic in order to determine the position of the Gulf Stream. This set was more extensive than the data he had collected the previous year, twenty-nine days as against the thirteen from 1775. Clearly, Franklin realized he was on to something. This time, he did not mention his results to anyone, not even Priestley, perhaps because when he arrived in France on December 3, he was even busier than when he had disembarked in Philadelphia. And he was in extremely poor health.

Starved and pustular when he arrived, Franklin "had scarce strength to stand." (Much later, he admitted to his family that the trip "almost demolish'd" him.) Of course, nearly dying after crossing the Atlantic was a little tradition for Franklin. So too was his fond reliance on a comforting piece of travel clothing, a warm woolen gown on the 1764 passage and a soft fur cap in 1776. The latter was necessary because Franklin's skin conditions made a scratchy wig unbearable. The cap was a Canadian souvenir, useful in the chilly north when his skin had first erupted and useful again when winter wind clawed the Atlantic. The headgear drew cries of admiration—and inspired a brief fashion among the coastal French-women who first learned of it.[29]

It took some two weeks more, traveling overland and on coastal ships, for Franklin's party to reach Paris. They then settled into a wing of a grand private house, the Hôtel de Valentinois, at Passy, on the main road between the city and the court at Versailles. Now it was on to business.[30]

But when Franklin was ready for business in early 1777—housed and somewhat healthier—France did not officially recognize the United States. He could not be presented at court nor have official contact with French foreign minister Charles Gravier, Comte de Vergennes, or anyone else in the government. Franklin was frantically busy reminding the French that he was there and assuring Congress that he did so, but his official invisibility gave him incentive and opportunity to restate his authority in philosophical and political realms.

He already had an inkling that his fame in France would serve him and his nation quite well. In December 1776, he gloated to his sister, "You can have no Conception of the Respect with which I am receiv'd and treated here by the first People, in my private Character; for as yet I have assum'd no public One." He had also learned that his Canadian cap was a selling point. "Figure to yourself," he asked Polly Hewson, "an old Man with grey Hair appearing under a Martin Fur Cap, among the Powder'd Heads of Paris."[31]

Just as in 1757, when he had his miniature painted from a London sickbed, Franklin used his recovery period in 1777 to have a portrait done, yet another iconic Benjamin Franklin. This, the first important French image, a drawing of 1777, featured the fur cap. The drawing became a widely reproduced and circulated engraving, among those of Franklin that one French newspaper proclaimed "the fashionable New Year's gift." Franklin wears a good suit to offset the rustic headgear, but the escaping strand of hair emphasizes his informality. Cap and lack of wig became trademarks, which was just as well, as Franklin's skin disorders continued until his death and caused him to abandon wigs.[32]

The portrait shows Franklin at his wariest. He seems thinner and drawn (perhaps from the recent illness)—and watchful. His older trademark, his spectacles, draw attention to his sidelong gaze. See

The first fur-cap portrait.
Augustin de Saint-Aubin, *Benjamin Franklin* (1777).
FOGG ART MUSEUM, HARVARD UNIVERSITY ART MUSEUMS.

and be seen: he was examining the French examining him. (He was also listening to them, as bifocals helped him learn French by focusing precisely on "the Movements in the Features.") The portrait was a two-way image, but what did the French see in it? And what did Franklin see in them?[33]

The French saw a philosopher—his cap proclaimed him one. Generations of American schoolchildren (and historians) have celebrated the "American" quality of Franklin's hat. The cap did signal a plain style, as noted in a January 1777 account of Franklin's arrival, strengthening the Barbeu-Dubourg myth of a Quakerish Franklin. But Franklin also resembled fur-capped French philosophes. These included the moral philosopher Jean-Jacques Rousseau and the Newtonian theorist Pierre-Louis Moreau de Maupertuis. Maupertuis had gone to Lapland to help settle the dispute about the earth's axis; an engraving showed him in Laplander gear, including elegant fur cap, and with a pointing right index figure. In France, Franklin's fur cap was the badge not so much of a frontiersman as of a new kind of philosopher, the explorer-naturalist. Cap and bifocals together signaled his learned and adventurous quality.[34]

The French also saw in Franklin a dreaded possibility: the Seven Years' War all over again. Few thought that the Americans had a chance of winning their war against Britain. French leaders feared that, if they allied with the colonists, their presence in the conflict would reignite global combat. (Britons feared this, too.) Franklin offered an opportunity to the French to settle old scores—but at what appalling cost? In his charming cap and spectacles, he cut a dangerous figure.[35]

What, in turn, did the bifocal-wearing Franklin see in France? The Old Regime, as it would be known after the French Revolution of 1789, was an intensely hierarchical society with glittering and squalid extremes. The king was at the center and apex—the nobles and church clerics around him enjoyed considerable privilege. The Catholic Church was protected by the state; so, too, were the comprehensive taxes that raked wealth from land and commerce. No aspect of learning was unregulated because nothing could be legally published without first clearing a board of censors.[36]

All in all, France was somewhat like Franklin's beloved Britain but greatly unlike his native Pennsylvania. Britain had aristocrats and taxes, as well as an established church; Pennsylvania had none of these things. Both places lacked the busy censors and nosy police who made sure that argument over the constituted order of things never got out of hand.

But in France, people spoke two languages: French and code. Despite the censors, people could say and write nearly anything, if they were clever enough. Banned books were often best-sellers; coded commentary enabled a broader range of conversation than the law officially sanctioned. Playwrights, publishers, newspaper printers, and even ragged ballad-singers made fun of the church and court and often got away with it. And nearly everyone had something to say about France. The nation hovered in a palpable state of historic transition—or perhaps indecision. It had survived one war but might face another; its society had to change, but no one yet knew it would take a revolution to do so. The French endlessly discussed the possibilities and were particularly fascinated with the American struggle, which dominated political reporting. But they had to be more careful than ever—the censors cracked down on the press precisely because of speculation about the American war.[37]

So on top of everything else, Franklin would have to learn both the French language and the native mode of expression, clever yet elliptical. That wary glance in the fur-cap portrait of early 1777 already evoked a strategic silence. During his stay in France, Franklin generated fewer personal papers than in any other part of his life.

His actions, at least, made clear that he carefully picked his way through this foreign landscape with guides from the republic of letters. He especially relied on his old friends Jacques Barbeu-Dubourg and Jean Baptiste Le Roy. His first letter in France went to Barbeu-Dubourg; his residence in Passy was near the royal laboratory, which Le Roy directed. The two Frenchmen were eager to help—minor figures, they gained by association with the master electrician. Franklin convinced several other men of science to support the American cause. Rotterdam printer Reinier Arrenberg, who published the proceedings of the Batavian Society of Experimental Science (Franklin had been a member since 1771), helped Franklin distribute propaganda in the Netherlands. Even Thomas-François Dalibard, who had first done the "Philadelphia experiment," contracted to supply the United States with muskets, from the royal manufactory, no less.[38]

Next, Franklin inserted himself into the culture of learning in Paris, quickly replacing his British activities in the sciences with their French counterparts. He began attending meetings of the Académie Royale des Sciences, to which he had been elected *associé étranger* in 1772. His memoir on pointed electrical conductors had been read at the Académie in 1773, but to welcome him, the Académie published it in 1777. Chemical experimenter Antoine-Laurent Lavoisier invited him to the Académie, also in 1777, to observe experiments repeating Joseph Priestley's on air. No idle onlooker, Franklin served on an Académie committee, with Le Roy and the Marquis de Condorcet, to initiate a general correspondence among men of learning, *Nouvelles de la république des lettres et des arts*. Lavoisier admired

Franklin's ability to contemplate any philosophy amid the ongoing political whirlwind (*tourbillon de la politique*).[39]

Franklin could not, in fact, separate his political and philosophic reputations. His writings were widely read in France, perhaps more so there than in Britain and definitely more than in the United States. So close was his association with science that some correspondents addressed him as of the Académie, rather than of the United States. And people assumed that he, the Prospero of the new republic, enlisted science into the service of the United States. In Britain, rumors flew in 1777 that the electrical ambassador had a device, "the size of a toothpick case," that could reduce St. Paul's Cathedral "to a handful of ashes." He was also thought to be on the brink of erecting a battery of deflecting mirrors at Calais that would incinerate the British fleet.[40]

Franklin's status as a Newtonian experimenter in physics had particular cachet among French men of science. As in England, chemical experimentation had replaced physics as the hot topic. But in France, this meant that physics was regarded as a rather grand preserve of the old guard of the Académie Royale. And Franklin was doubly honored as a Newtonian veteran of the momentous battle against the Cartesians.

His work had helped rout the Cartesians, and this fact associated him powerfully with François-Marie Arouet de Voltaire, the mocking conscience of the Old Regime. In the 1730s, Voltaire had allied himself with French Newtonians, including Maupertuis and Gabrielle Émilie le Tonnelier de Breteuil, Marquise du Chatelet, the French translator of Newton's *Principia*. (Du Chatelet was mistress to both her fellow Newtonians.) Voltaire had published popularized interpretations of Newton that helped win the day. The frontispiece to Voltaire's *Elémens de la philosophie de Neuton* (1737) shows Newton presiding from the clouds as heavenly light bounces off a mirror, held by du Chatelet, to illuminate the French philosophe. It helped that Voltaire was neither mathematician nor natural philosopher; even more than Franklin, his Newtonianism seemed impartial because it was untutored. From the 1740s onward, Cartesianism faded. The death of the last "Cartesian" in the Académie des Sciences was proclaimed in 1771. With superb timing, Franklin arrived at the Académie just when Newton's triumph was complete.[41]

In France, however, French Newtonianism bore a dangerous subtext: Newton, an Englishman, had seen the light because he lived in

Voltaire as Newtonian philosopher. [François-Marie Arouet]
Voltaire, *Elémens de la philosophie de Neuton* (1738).
HOUGHTON LIBRARY, HARVARD UNIVERSITY.

a better place, a polity that protected person, property, and free debate. Voltaire had said as much—and not always in a sufficiently
coded fashion. For this and other criticisms, he had suffered arrest,
imprisonment, and exile. By the time Franklin arrived, Voltaire
lived in the country and had not seen Paris for years.[42]

French officials might have banished Voltaire but not demands for reform. The Physiocrats were the foremost group of reformers. *Physiocracy* meant "rule of nature." The economic theorists' very name indicated their determination to model society on scientific principles. They believed that agriculture was the source of all wealth and so sought changes in landholding, land use, and taxation. Even more radically, the mathematician Marie-Jean-Antoine-Nicolas Caritat, Marquis de Condorcet, proposed an entire human science modeled on natural science. More practically, Anne Robert Jacques Turgot, Baron de Laune, tried to implement plans to loosen government regulation of economic affairs during an extremely brief tenure as a government minister. Finally, there were the Freemasons, including Claude-Adrien Helvétius. The Masons stood for an alternate social order, based on the equal exchange of ideas. They were positioned against the church, even as they were well stocked with aristocrats who were otherwise comfortable with the status quo.[43]

The proposals to change France, particularly to pry the church out of public affairs and to reform taxes, were no small things. They clearly provided the liveliest points of debate within France, and a famous American man of science was highly coveted for his opinion on them. Franklin was eventually to be found not only at the Académie but also within Physiocratic circles (which included Barbeu-Dubourg and Turgot), in the Masonic Loge des Neuf Soeurs, and at the salon of Helvétius's widow.

At first glance, Franklin resembled the reformers found in those places. As a man of science and of politics, he seemed akin to the French pioneers of the human sciences. The Physiocrats regarded the crisply sapient *La science du Bonhomme Richard* as a remarkable analysis of rural life. A new edition of "Bonhomme Richard" appeared in 1777, the year when Franklin was busy crafting his image as American emissary. Because it was not packaged among philosophic essays (unlike the 1773 Barbeu-Dubourg edition of Franklin's work), the version of 1779 became a popular best-seller. It ran through four editions in two years, and Franklin bestowed copies on social callers, patrons, and clients.[44]

But his wide-ranging essays and opinions did not fit into any single school. He agreed with the Physiocrats that agriculture was the foundation of national wealth, but he had also written a great deal on trade and credit. He had criticized taxes in his 1766 interview in

Parliament but had elsewhere conceded that the British Navigation Acts were necessary. The Physiocrats saw what they wanted to see and claimed Franklin as one of their own in their journal, the *Ephémérides*. Franklin offered writings to the journal but was careful not to side openly with any distinct opinion, lest he alienate its opponents. Turgot scolded a fellow Physiocrat who had claimed Franklin's support for suffering from "a sectarian spirit."[45]

Franklin also disapproved of the sectarianism, and in 1778, he put a little distance between himself and the Physiocrats. He wrote a "Lettre à Madame B." Madame Brillon was his beautiful neighbor, inconveniently married (and faithful) to another man. The letter offered Brillon a history of mayflies. Franklin had just seen the insects swarm in the country, and his letter became known as "The Ephemera," the French name for mayflies. "You know I understand all the inferior Animal Tongues," Franklin assured Brillon. (This was his rueful acknowledgment of his inability to master the human language of French.) Buffon had theorized that the world would end when the sun went out and everything died of cold. Remarkably, Franklin's tiny, winged informants endorsed the French naturalist's idea. Their knowledge of the world's impending doom amplified their melancholy over their own brief lives, over in a day. "What now avails all my Toil and Labour," demanded one fly, who was 420 minutes old, so quite "greyheaded." "What the political Struggles . . . or my philosophical Studies for the Benefit of our Race in general!"[46]

Thus, Franklin hinted to the Physiocrats, who published *Ephémérides*, that their theories were even more ephemeral than they thought. He had gone native. He had yet to learn French, but already he had mastered France's clever, elliptical code. The gentle rebuke said much about Franklin. He ceaselessly scanned nature for pattern, for predictability, for truth. But he did not, and would not model a whole science of humanity on the physical sciences. As a younger generation explored the frontiers of a comprehensive human science, Franklin stopped at political arithmetic. He may even have begun to repent his firmer statements, as in the Declaration of Independence, about nature's laws imparting political truths.

However elegantly, Franklin was ducking the question of how exactly "the Laws of Nature" explained the human condition. Was it absurd that the United States based its independence on natural law? Bonhomme Richard found profundity within absurdity. He proposed another way to derive wisdom from nature: eavesdrop on insects.

THOUGH Franklin did not produce any new work in natural science, his reputation continued to grow. Just as he had once frequented a London coffeehouse hoping to spot Newton, so fans now stalked him. One admirer paid for a place at a window so he could see Franklin "pass by in his coach" but then barely saw the great man. Correspondents submitted corroboration of his work on electricity and on stilling fluids with oil. Everyone wanted Dr. Franklin for their learned societies; he would eventually be affiliated with organizations from Padua to St. Petersburg. It was all very heady—and not just for Franklin. Seeing French people mob his fellow commissioner, Silas Deane confessed his "Joy and Pride . . . for I considered it an honor to be known to be an American and his Friend."[47]

Others were irritated. When one French noblewoman would not stop rhapsodizing about Franklin, Louis XVI presented her with a chamber pot imprinted with the American's portrait—inside. John Adams, the American commissioner who replaced Deane, hated that the same French people who scorned his attempts at their language would hang on Franklin's every mispronounced, ungrammatical utterance. William Lee sarcastically wrote his commissioner brother, Arthur, that Franklin was listed among the "M.D.'s lately incorporated by his most Christian Majesty for examining and licensing all quack medicines."[48]

These criticisms were important: French adulation of Franklin was irrational. His self-taught prowess in science was highly unusual in France. As with the rest of French society, learning was more centralized and hierarchical than it was in Britain (let alone America). The crown took an active role in the Académie Royale des Sciences, where aristocrats were also prominent. Personal or state-granted privileges afforded French men of science steady funding, so they were able to specialize more than their British counterparts. Lavoisier, for instance, could focus on chemical work because he was a "rent farmer," a tax official supported by the very taxes that worried political reformers. The self-made generalist who rigged up experiments with his fireplace or with bits of cork, glass, and metal—a man such as Matthew Boulton or John Canton or Benjamin Franklin—

was rare in France. For some of the French, Franklin's lowly origins and self-creation added to his mystique. Other Parisians questioned that a mere printer, a craftsman who did not even know the proper way to eat asparagus, should rise so high.[49]

But Franklin was a *genius* and could eat his asparagus however he pleased. The French did not commonly use the word *génie* as a noun for a person, as the English were doing with *genius,* yet the French term did imply an almost inhuman gift, which was the key to understanding Franklin. Barbeu-Dubourg had set the pattern in the preface to Franklin's French *Oeuvres*: "La fécondité de son génie" made Franklin peerless. The term appeared again and again—mostly used, it should be said, to flatter him. Thus, Pierre Turini extolled the "Sublimité" of Franklin's "Genie" in a letter designed to get the busy American to write back.[50]

To honor his genius, the French ushered Franklin—alive, mortal, and a commoner—into the company of the glorious dead, the gods, and crowned heads. These images of an almost divine Franklin were often modeled on those of Newton. Indeed, one correspondent promised to install in his home Franklin's portrait alongside those of "Newton, Voltaire, Rousseau, Montesquieu et l'Imperatrice de Russie." One verse made the crucial connection between Franklin's wisdom about nature and his wisdom over human affairs: "He made in Philadelphia / a temple for philosophy / and a throne for liberty."[51]

And then there was that famous claim about Franklin. *"Eripuit coelo fulmen, sceptrumque tyrannis"*: he snatched lightning from heaven, and the scepter from the tyrants. Attributed to Turgot, the phrase followed Franklin everywhere. Jean Antoine Houdon inscribed it on his important marble bust of Franklin, and Jean Baptiste Nini wrote it on his myriad terra cotta profiles.[52]

The Franklin mania peaked after news of the American victory at Saratoga arrived in December 1777. Now, the French thought the Americans were worth helping. They also needed help—Saratoga was only one of many battles, most of which the Americans had lost. Vergennes invited the American commissioners to resubmit Congress's petition for a Franco-American alliance. France signed treaties of alliance and of amity and commerce with the United States in February 1778. After nearly two years of uncertainty, another nation had acknowledged the Declaration of Independence and recognized the existence of the United States. Military assistance followed, along with the recognition and alliance of other nations. The American commissioners had accomplished the primary goal of their mission. Yet again, Franklin emerged from a collaborative venture with most of the credit. In September 1778, Congress dissolved the collaborative mission and appointed him sole minister plenipotentiary, or ambassador.

He enjoyed the moment conspicuously, by attending balls and other entertainments. But though they did not look like work, these appearances were efforts to promote the American cause and opportunities for Franklin to advertise his learned image. He was careful, for instance, to redisplay his place in the republic of letters. After he had claimed a place at the Académie des Sciences early in 1777, diplomatic work dragged him away. In December, after the glorious news of Saratoga, he reappeared. Even social events let him showcase himself as a philosopher. After the alliance was signed, Franklin celebrated by attending a ball and kissing a great many obliging ladies. They dodged his scholarly "besicles" (spectacles) and he their elaborate rouge and powder. Then, in March, he was finally presented to the king and queen. One witness noted Franklin's bare head and "besicles," and "his manner, as if patriarch and founder of a nation, joined to his fame as discoverer of electricity, legislator for thirteen united provinces, and his wisdom"—the full scientific-political package.[53]

Amid the joy in 1778, a dying Voltaire returned from exile, and he and Franklin cheerfully used each other to promote their celebrity. With Temple, Franklin called on Voltaire, who, carefully arranged in his sickbed, blessed the young man in English: "God and Liberty." (It became Temple's motto.) Then Voltaire was admitted to the Loge des Neuf Soeurs on April 7, assisted by Franklin, Philadelphia brother. The men met again in April at the Académie des Sciences, where they were urged to embrace; when the two triumphant Newtonians and critics of tyranny did so, they were applauded. (Witnessing the embrace at the Académie, John Adams dismissed the "two Aged Actors upon this great Theatre of Philosophy and frivolity.") In late May, Franklin was himself admitted to the Loge des Neuf Soeurs and would inherit from Voltaire the Masonic apron of Helvétius, the lodge's founder.[54]

Then, as everyone had been expecting, Voltaire died. His body had to be smuggled out of Paris, lest it end in a pit of quicklime, the fate of suspected atheists in France, who could not be buried in a manner befitting Christians. It was acceptable to express sorrow at this loss (the queen did) but not to go on and on about it. Yet in November, Franklin joined an elaborate Masonic memorial service for Voltaire. At the Loge des Neuf Soeurs, he and others laid crowns below a painting of the apotheosis of Voltaire; a verse about defeating thunder, an unmistakable allusion to Franklin's defiance of tyranny, drew applause. It was almost designed to annoy the Paris police. Franklin may not have comprehended their disapproval, or perhaps, with his new confidence, he did not care. Irate government officials threatened to close the lodge. They backed down one day before Franklin took over a high position as the lodge's *vénérable*.[55]

The timing of the lodge's reprieve indicated Franklin's unassailable status within Franco-American affairs. Once an official alliance between the United States and France had been forged, his place in Franco-American affairs and cultural life was too important to create any scandal by censuring him. The modern Prometheus could indeed defy gods and tyrants.

And so, the images of Franklin as immortal sage piled up. At the top of the heap was the first portrayal of his apotheosis, "To the Genius of Franklin." In 1779, Marguerite Gérard produced this etching, based on a design by Jean-Honoré Fragonard. Clad in flowing robes and seated on clouds, Franklin points at menacing figures, and Mars repels them. Knowledge, personified by Minerva, shields Franklin from lightning; America (her fasces represent the United States) leans in a daughterly way on Franklin. And underneath it all is the famous phrase about defying heaven and tyranny. Note the resemblance to the Newton of Voltaire's frontispiece: both philosophers sit on clouds, point meaningfully, and are attended by females who direct heavenly effusions.[56]

Franklin marveled at his proliferating likenesses. "Pictures, busts, and prints," not to mention medallions, snuffboxes, and other knick-knacks, brought the famous Philadelphian into hundreds of public and private chambers in Paris and beyond, even in Britain. His face, as he told his daughter, was "as well known as that of the moon." He reveled in the impiety of it all. "It is said by learned etymologists that the name *Doll*, for the images children play with, is derived from the word IDOL; from the number of *dolls* now made of him[self], he may be truly said, *in that sense*, to be *i-doll-ized* in this country."[57]

As the Franklin trinkets poured out of workshops, people began to worry. Was an inhuman power over nature necessarily a good

Franklin almighty. Marguerite Gérard, "Au génie de Franklin" (1779).
DAVISON ART CENTER, WESLEYAN UNIVERSITY.

thing? Suddenly, the American Merlin was a menacing figure, not so much idol as demon. Franklin had been the first to benefit fully from the idea that genius in science made a man a genius in all realms. Now, he would be first to suffer from the suspicion that his genius made him dangerous.

Franklin appeared in fiction for the first time in 1778, in Jean Jacques Le Roux des Tillets's *Dialogue entre Pasquin & Marforio* (1778), a satire on a contemporary medical dispute. Le Roux des Tillets bestowed on Franklin the magical power to end quarrels at the Société Royale de Médicine. At the end of the piece, Franklin, to the accompaniment of thunder, waved a wand to transform each partisan into the animal that best represented his character. Other images of Franklin as a magician were less benign. A farce of 1779 claimed that he "forced the thunder to fall where he ordered it" and had "electrified a dog on the opposite bank of a river, making him howl like a martyr," a rather dark reading of Franklin's electrical picnic in Philadelphia. His crowning achievement was said to come when "he electrified the minds of all the Americans and made them believe that all the pain they suffered came directly from the Palace of Saint James in London."[58]

Not surprisingly, the English were equally attentive to the politics of Franklin's science. When lightning struck the Board of Ordnance at Purfleet on May 15, 1777, Franklin's not-so-protective system prompted questions. A Royal Society committee recommended modifications, but Benjamin Wilson cried foul: Franklin said lightning did not strike pointed rods, but it had. The king commanded Wilson to do further experiments; he complied by conducting elaborate ones in a London dance hall and again urged rods with rounded ends. The king found Wilson convincing.[59]

Yet again, Franklin declined to comment. Instead, in a private letter, he grandly pronounced his status as a gentleman, someone who did not have to work for a living. "I have no private Interest in the Reception of my Inventions by the World" he proclaimed, because he had never arranged "to make the least Profit by any of them." Moreover, he said, "I have never entered into any Controversy in defence of my philosophical Opinions; I leave them to take their Chance in the World."[60]

George III next ordered—at least, the French whispered he did—blunt rods installed atop the queen's palace and supposedly asked the president of the Royal Society, Franklin's old friend Sir John Pringle, to order that kind of rod for Purfleet. Pringle responded (again, as it was rumored) that the king might change human law but not the laws of nature. Of the king's preference, Franklin could not resist observing, "It is only since he thought himself and Family safe from the Thunder of Heaven, that he dared to use his own Thunder in destroying his innocent [American] Subjects." In Britain, some faintly disloyal verses made the rounds:

> While you great George for knowledge hunt
> And sharp conductors change for blunt,
> The Empire's out of Joint:
> Franklin another course pursues,
> And all your thunder heedless views,
> By keeping to the point.

Franklin liked the poem so much that he kept a copy.[61]

However these images of Franklin and science may amuse us, they revealed a deep ambivalence among his contemporaries. In the context of an unprecedented war against empire, the major combatants were using ideas about the sciences to portray power but also to argue about power. What was the point of the war? Each nation's use of Franklin indicated its answer. When conflict had begun between the United Colonies and Britain, Franklin's Promethean reputation had reemerged in order, it seems, to assure the Americans that they had a secret weapon. Indeed, Franklin's paradoxical authority resembled that of his new nation—it seemed contrary to nature, though it in fact used the laws of nature.

The French were not so sure. After the Franco-American alliance, they busily crafted images of Franklin as semidivine philosopher but also as evil sorcerer. Those images showed France's own uneasy ambition. The French hoped a war against Britain would help them recoup their losses in the Seven Years' War, yet they feared the new conflict might bring them even more devastating losses. Not surprisingly, they obsessed over the spell Franklin seemed to have cast on them.

Interestingly, the British were most conflicted. Some of his former fellow British subjects thought Franklin was now an enemy of the nation, someone who mischievously recommended invalid technology; others believed in Franklin's genius and considered him an astute critic of the monarch, perhaps even wiser than George III.

Franklin did not contest that notion. Once, as he played a game of chess with a French noblewoman, he seized her king. "We do not take kings so," the lady protested. "We do in America," Franklin replied.[62]

LIFE IN PARIS was not all poetry and board games—it was work. If Edinburgh had constituted Franklin's densest happiness, Paris was his densest busyness. Winning French recognition and alliance was only one of his tasks. He also had to make the United States a power in the world, which meant on the sea. His long, complicated relations with maritime people entered their final stage. So too did his long devotion to circulation, in both its physical and social forms.[63]

Congress had created the delightfully oxymoronic Continental Navy in late 1775, but it still (and always) lacked ships and supplies. When asked in early 1777 what America needed most, Franklin promptly replied, "bronze cannon and warships." He installed his grandnephew, Jonathan Williams Jr. (the Yankee merchant who had considered working for the East India Company) at Nantes, an important port where Williams procured everything from boots and blankets to entire ships. His uncle's famous name helped initially— "I am treated here with as much Respect as if I were the Nephew of a prince." Williams ran a lucrative private trade on the side and was a hands-on maritime expert. In one typical letter to his granduncle, Williams related his modifications to a French vessel to "make her a compleat Ship of War."[64]

America's hastily assembled navy began to harry British shipping. Franklin cheered that "our Privateers and Cruisers in the Channel have rais'd the Insurance in London." The American commissioners estimated in February 1777 that the British West Indies trade had lost almost 2 million pounds sterling, which pushed shipping insurance to 28 percent, higher than during the Seven Years' War. Meanwhile, British stocks fell, including those for the Bank of England and East India Company. Franklin must have enjoyed the news that a privateer named the *Franklin* took three British prizes in the spring of 1777.[65]

And he vengefully promoted attacks on the packets of the Post Office that had recently sacked him. British postal losses during the Revolution exceeded those of the Seven Years' War. In 1777, the Americans nabbed a British packet to the Netherlands and the 2,000 pieces of mail it carried. The American commissioners made a point of forwarding the letters that belonged to noncombatants, despite French protests that all the mail should be turned over to them. The action gave evidence both of America's military power and of its independence as a political actor.[66]

U.S. privateering offered an exciting start to the naval struggle with Great Britain. But it ignited a suspicion, which smoldered even through the Napoleonic Wars, that Americans were nothing but pirates. Vergennes counseled Franklin to recall privateers' commissions in midsummer 1780, and Franklin took the advice. But it was too late. Franklin would ever after have to defend everyone, sailors and officers alike, from the charge of piracy, and he never erased the stigma. Given that naval maneuvers never really advanced the American military cause, it was a high price to pay.[67]

In the long run, the Continental Navy was chiefly important for ferrying things and people. That assignment was dangerous enough, as Beaumarchais could have warned the American commissioners. Until the 1778 alliance, France did not officially allow its ships to convoy military supplies directly to the United States. Williams regretted that the choices were to use American ships or send French ones via the West Indies; "the first is too hazardous," he said, "the other too far round." Transporting peaceful items, such as mail, was no easier. Entrepreneur and American supporter Jacques-Donatien Le Ray de Chaumont, Franklin's landlord, contracted to supply a packet service, which failed after only one ship sailed. Williams then hired another French firm to send materiel. The company was diligent, sending sixty ships to America within the first eighteen months of service. But its losses mounted until the spring of 1778, when Louis XVI allowed it to take prizes, meaning capture enemy vessels and their contents for profit.[68]

Mere navigation was a problem. At the start of the war, the Revolutionaries were desperate for maps of land and charts of the sea. As Williams reported from Nantes, "nothing is more difficult than to procure Charts of our Coast"; William Bingham, holding down a U.S. outpost on Martinique, warned that "very few French Masters of Vessels are acquainted with the Coast of America." Williams could only refer the alliance's mariners to "the general Charts (Mercators &c.)." One American captain, Lambert Wickes (who had carried Franklin to France), protested that an order to cruise the Baltic would be a challenge without "proper Charts for those Sea's." On another occasion, Wickes offered to loan his precious "quarter Waggoner" to Williams, who pleaded with Franklin for proper "Charts from Paris."[69]

Franklin ordered what maps he could. He even received some English maps of the Great Lakes region from Benjamin Vaughan, an obligingly disloyal friend in London. (Vaughan sent the maps in January 1777, just as the Americans were digging in around Fort Ticonderoga and Lake Champlain—it was no idle gift.) And Franklin and the other commissioners advised captains unfamiliar with the western Atlantic. Perhaps drawing on Franklin's own knowledge of Atlantic winds, they cautioned one man "to keep well on the West on account of the North and westerly winds on the Coast of America."[70]

British cartographers were busy creating maps to help their own troops and commanders. In 1776, London mapmakers Sayer and Bennett published the capaciously named *American Military Pocket Atlas . . . of the British Colonies; Especially Those Which Now Are, or Probably May Be the Theatre of War.* The work drew on existing maps and charts done by William Gerard De Brahm, Surveyor General Samuel Holland, and Franklin's old associate Thomas Pownall, a colonial adminstrator. The biggest cartographic project had started before the war. In the 1770s, Joseph F. W. DesBarres had begun to survey the North American coastline, islands, and soundings for his *Atlantic Neptune.* He had produced the first part of this atlas in 1774. In 1776, it became clear that war would interrupt DesBarres's surveying but also make his work critical to military operations. In the end, he produced five volumes, the last appearing in 1781. The charts in the *Atlantic Neptune* were mainly valuable for their detailed depictions of the coastline, essential information for the British invasion and control of territory. DesBarres's charts did not, however, add much to knowledge of the open ocean.[71]

French cartographers also sensed a good moment to expand their market, and French officials, mindful of a possible war with Britain and a hoped-for trade with the Americans, encouraged the entrepreneurship. Georges-Louis Le Rouge, *géographe royale* and Franklin's eventual collaborator, played a major role in this burgeoning industry. Le Rouge had long produced French editions of British maps and atlases, and Franklin knew of his work as early as March 1778. That year, the Paris firm began to produce a large maritime atlas, *Pilot amériquain septentrional,* a French version of the London-produced *North American Pilot,* completed in 1779. But the French atlas turned British maps against Britain. The very first plate showed the channel and England's south coast, which hinted at a possible invasion of the latter via the former. The French launched just such an attack in 1779.[72]

The atlas moved from the channel across the North Atlantic, surveyed the coast of North America, passed through the West Indies, and then entered the Gulf of Mexico. The charts of the Gulf of Florida and of the Caribbean emphasized, with arrows, the gulf currents that flowed north—long a feature of sea charts. Likewise, northeasterly currents on either side of the Bermudas were described as the strongest because they were "coming from the Gulf of Florida" (*venant du Golfe de Floride*). All charts that included the North Atlantic were marked with lines to indicate the 1769 voyage of Charles-Pierre Claret de Fleurieu along the Gulf Stream. The largest chart, a two-sheet representation of the Atlantic, was also marked with the "voyage de Gerard de Brahm's en 1771." Thanks to De Brahm, among others, the northern part of the Gulf Stream was, at last, featured prominently on sea charts, just in time for the Revolutionary War.

But charts and ships were useless without sailors. The Continental Navy overflowed with officers but lacked able seamen. Franklin was so desperate to increase their ranks that he welcomed French convicts; some enterprising British smugglers offered to freelance. What a lively place an American warship must have been.[73]

The shortage of sailors challenged Franklin's conviction that the United States was bursting with people. He estimated the population of the country at 3 million and breezily promised that, were this an overestimate (it was), "rapid Increase" would soon make it true: "Men will not be wanting [lacking] to continue this War." To a member of the British Parliament, he claimed that "America adds to her Numbers annually 150,000 Souls. She therefore grows faster than you can diminish her."[74]

He gave the same message to his many petitioners, the thousands who requested military commissions, commercial favors, or assistance in removing to America. Scores of European families had strong, intelligent sons or nephews who were anxious to render service to the United States; countless people loved liberty and had peerless skills they offered to the new republic. Requests came from on high and from friends, as when Turgot asked for help with a relative. (Some petitioners offered proposals with their pleas—Franklin suffered through descriptions of numerous inventions, including an "Electrical Pistol.") After a few months of this, he never wanted to see a "begging" letter again. His sleep, Franklin complained to one supplicant, held the "only Hours of Comfort" away from the din of requests; "for God's sake, my dear Friend, let this your 23d Application be the last."[75]

Franklin made an important exception for sailors, whom his nation always needed. He quickly responded to pleas for help when the British tried to impress Americans onto Royal Navy vessels and imprisoned those who refused. Franklin fumed—such actions affronted human liberty and denied Americans' political independence. (He had less to say about the fact that the Continental Navy and various state navies also stooped to impressment.) The British government even refused to release American officers on parole, lest that imply any recognition that they fought for a real nation. But this was so much against the usual practice that, once publicized in British papers, even Britons were outraged. Within fifteen days, around Christmastime in 1777, British subscribers had raised £3,700 to comfort their nation's captive enemies. Freeing imprisoned sailors became Franklin's pet cause, so much so that he cited the financial needs for this effort as a reason not to fund other official projects.[76]

By equating impressment with slavery, Franklin joined the protests, mounting since the Seven Years' War, against all forms of captivity. Imprisonment, critics argued, was appropriate only for those within a legal system and convicted of crimes against it. It was an unjust penalty for people outside the legal system, meaning foreigners, European or otherwise. This argument was useful in a number of ways: to criticize the Indians who took war captives, the North Africans who enslaved Europeans, and the Europeans who enslaved black Africans. Now, during the American Revolution, simmering unease over the slave trade, impressment, and abuse of prisoners of war exploded into a propaganda war between Britain and the United States. If Americans were friends of liberty, why did they hold slaves? If the English championed legal rights, why did they trample on those of Americans?[77]

In 1779, Franklin and the Marquis de Lafayette assembled a list of British atrocities, which they planned to illustrate as a children's book (a primer for little patriots). They compared the British treatment of prisoners of war to the handiwork of Indians and Africans who abused their captives. Two of the twenty-five "British Cruelties" involved British-sponsored attacks by "negroes," and five others outlined the barbarities of British-allied Indians (one showed George III contentedly receiving an "*Acct. of Scalps*"). Nine of the projected illustrations would represent British mistreatment of American prisoners, whether soldiers or sailors, officers or ordinary men.[78]

Franklin demanded an exchange of American and British prisoners. The measure would promote "that mutual Confidence, which it would be for the Good of Mankind that Nations should maintain honourably with each other, tho' engag'd in War." He expressed empathy for the "poor Prisoners on both Sides" and, to honor the Franco-American alliance, insisted that French sailors taken from American ships were equivalent to American-born seamen. Franklin protested British impressment of Americans into the Britons' merchant trades, as if they were slave labor. (Britain impressed its own men into naval service, not commercial service.) "If we had sold your People to the Moors . . . as you have many of ours to the African and East India Companies, could you have complained?" The American commissioners petitioned Lord North on behalf of the American prisoners, some of whom had been lashed with "Stripes," others "now groaning in bondage in Africa and India." In 1779, Franklin learned that sixteen Americans who had been taken in the assault on Quebec two years earlier were among English-speaking prisoners released from Senegal.[79]

Once the British agreed, in 1778, to prisoner exchanges, Franklin asked the alliance's naval leaders to capture as many Britons as possible. They would then have men to swap for Americans. To Lafayette, Franklin proposed invading coastal towns in England and Scotland, seizing "ready Money and Hostages." He also commissioned French privateers to take British prisoners. And Franklin instructed the Revolution's famous naval captain, John Paul Jones, "to bring to France all the English Seamen you may happen to take Prisoners, in order to compleat the good Work . . . of delivering by an Exchange the rest of our Countrymen now languishing in the Gaols of Great Britain."[80]

Jones was diligent, if not obsessed. He took his ship, the *Ranger*, to Scotland in 1778 in an attempt to kidnap the Earl of Selkirk, a hostage expected to yield many Americans in exchange. (As it turned out, Selkirk was away at a spa; Jones looted the family silver, felt guilty, and returned it with an apology to Lady Selkirk.) Next, Jones tried to capture for ransom the Scottish town of Leith. When that effort failed, he resolved on a naval prize. To honor Franklin and Franklin's mission to save imprisoned seamen, he renamed the ship under his command in 1779 the *Bonhomme Richard* and used it to lead his brilliant moonlit attack on the *Serapis* and *Countess of Scarborough*, ships returning to Yorkshire from the Baltic. In the battle, Jones lost almost half his men, and after a French ally mistakenly (he said) fired into it, he lost the *Bonhomme Richard*, too. But Jones gained 504 prisoners and bore them back to France.[81]

Franklin expected this haul to sweep American sailors from British prisons; the British drove him mad with a slow series of exchanges, not always for Americans. To speed things up, he claimed there were more British prisoners of war in France than Americans in Britain. It was perhaps an exaggeration but one consistent with his repeated claim that, in terms of population, America always had the edge.[82]

The war entered its final, critical stage after the spring of 1780, and the exchange scheme collapsed. Franklin shifted his energies to improving conditions in the British prisons where sailors languished. Several Britons, especially Member of Parliament David Hartley, assisted him. But so closely was Franklin identified with sailors' welfare that even British prisoners petitioned him for help. He responded by working to improve their rations. He was appalled when one assistant absconded with relief funds, breaking a "sacred Trust" to help the helpless.[83]

In one of Europe's most hierarchical societies, Franklin defended some of the lowliest of workers. It was an astonishing contrast to the disgust he had felt for the striking sailors who had supported John Wilkes in London several years earlier. Franklin refused to consider seamen, even those he rescued, as subordinate workers. No one else treated sailors this way. When the crew of the *Ranger* muttered against him, John Paul Jones angrily insisted on his authority, whatever the cost. Franklin, by contrast, recommended that Jones release command of the *Ranger* to someone else and then start afresh with another crew and ship. Franklin also rejected attempts to draft former prisoners into specific tasks. He cautioned against "ordering them to go on board one Ship or another." "They are Freemen as soon as they land in France," he insisted, "and may inlist with which Captain they please."[84]

Word spread that Franklin was the seaman's friend. (One prisoner anxiously noted in his diary a 1781 rumor that Franklin had died.) Even fellow commissioners, such as Adams and Lee, who criticized nearly everything else Franklin did respected his commitment to prisoners of war. At Passy, bushels of letters arrived from seamen, and Franklin never complained of these "begging" letters. He also welcomed fugitive sailors; his accounts show small sums given to men who somehow made their way to Passy. Whatever they privately thought of the old landsman, seamen treated Franklin as their superior and patron and, if they were American, insisted on their patriotism. In one typical letter, addressed to "Dr. Franklin Sir," the authors asked "the favour to Come Before your honour" in order to prove themselves "amaricans," not Englishmen.[85]

The plight of American sailors was an excellent propaganda tool—all of Franklin's writings about imprisoned seamen reflected his partisan view of their ordeal. In an age of revolution, slavery had become a catchphrase for tyranny, and maritime workers benefited. If sailors, once valued for their heads, had become hands—mere workers—Franklin's patronage gave them hearts. He helped to consolidate a new stereotype: the patriotic American tar, scourge of tyrants.

But Franklin weakened his case when he favored members of his maritime family, especially those whose political loyalties were inventively broad. He knew he was suspected of nepotism (he employed a son-in-law, a grandnephew, and a grandson in official U.S. business). And he probably worried for his maritime kin; the British detained one relation, Isaac All, and briefly imprisoned another, Peter Collas. Above all, Franklin was painfully aware that his mother's home, Nantucket, was notorious for collaboration with the British. The island's Quakers refused as a matter of principle to take a side in the war; its merchant mariners were reluctant to do so, lest it reduce profits.[86]

Franklin's family troubles had begun in 1775, when an American privateer seized the ship of one Nantucket relative, Captain Seth Jenkins, thinking it a British vessel. At a Philadelphia prize court in 1776, Franklin had testified that Jenkins was American, and his cousin got his ship back. But Franklin must have warned his relations that he did not trust them, as became clear in 1777 when his "most Effectionate Kinsman," Seth Paddack (or Paddock), requested "a Comission for me in my Country's Service." "I will Tell you this," Paddack emphasized, "I will never Bring Disgrace on my Self or the family I Belong Too." His "attachment to [their] Country" was "well Known," he reminded Franklin, "altho you once

Douted it," perhaps referring to a conversation or lost letter in which Franklin had questioned his patriotism.[87]

The Nantucket swarm then followed Franklin to France. Both Seth Paddack and Timothy Folger ended up there at different points. And another relation, John Folger, managed to compromise Franklin when he lost some U.S. dispatches. Folger had agreed to carry the correspondence to Congress but was tricked into leaving his official package with a British spy who, after extracting the documents, replaced them with blank paper and then resealed the bundle. The theft was discovered only when Folger trustingly delivered the packet. After an embarassing inquiry, Folger was acquitted of spying. Again, a family connection survived a crisis; Folger thereafter transmitted Franklin's private letters, including at least one to Tom Paine.[88]

The accusation of loyalism particularly dogged America's whalers, who themselves became wartime prey. Whaling was extremely valuable—Americans, Britons, and the French all wanted whale products. Whale oil and bone served many of the functions petroleum and plastic do now, and demand for them was growing rapidly. Most experienced whalers came from the Maritime Provinces in Canada and from New England—including Nantucket, where Franklin had so many relatives. The industry was moving to the South Atlantic, down to Brazil, on its way to the Pacific of Herman Melville's era, and Americans, particularly Nantucketers, led the way.

The war in fact fostered battle over whaling and fishing. The president of Congress instructed American ships to attack "the British Fishery." The American commissioners championed their own sea hunters; of the prey off the coasts of Brazil, they claimed that "none but the Americans" had "learned the Art of killing that sort of Whales." But "American" whalers started turning up on non-American ships, even British ones. Did they voluntarily serve? Had they been impressed? Franklin received several letters from Nantucketers who presented themselves as loyal Americans. They swore that if they served on British whalers, they did so to avoid a worse fate: serving on British warships and fighting fellow Americans.[89]

For the moment, Franklin chose to believe them. Consider a remarkable contrast. He was partial toward seamen and regarded them as patriots even if there was evidence to the contrary, but he was indifferent to his loyalist son, William Franklin. The former royal governor of New Jersey was imprisoned for two years; his father never said or wrote a word on his behalf. Meanwhile, the elder Franklin lavished time, words, and money on the ordinary tars who were, for him, the truer patriots.

———————

GIVEN his political preoccupations, it is amazing that Franklin had any time to think of science. That he made time showed his genuine interest but also a grim determination to keep his hand in somehow. War and philosophy were, however, even stranger bedfellows than Benjamin Franklin and John Adams.

Certainly, nation and nature competed for Franklin's attention. Except to a favored few, he gave up answering all letters on science, instead writing "Answers in the Margin," as he did with one among a paralyzing number of inquiries about lightning rods. He was nonetheless able to cram in a remarkable amount of reading. He attended lectures and experiments when he could and discussed new theories with his friends. At one point, Le Roy reminded his "Dear friend" of "almost a cart Load of Books of the Royal academy for you here, at my House."[90]

Franklin's critics—including his fellow commissioners—complained that he spent too much time on philosophy. He entertained and enjoyed the French, they grumbled; meanwhile, he neglected to tell them, his colleagues, of key developments, and his papers were a jumble. Adams declared that Franklin's life was "a scene of continual discipation." Franklin spent his mornings, Adams relayed, being visited by "Phylosophers, Accademicians and Economists," then took tea at various ladies' salons. Some of this was true—Franklin himself confessed his untidiness. But whatever his haphazard methods of diplomacy, he worked at it steadily, in contrast to his experiments and observations. Therein lies an excellent and irrefutable measure of Franklin's patriotism: the growing obsolescence of his work in science.[91]

Bad news arrived in 1777 when Alessandro Volta (for whom the *volt* would be named) challenged Franklin's theory of electricity. In 1775, Volta, an Italian correspondent of Beccaria and Priestley, had perfected a device that Johannes Wilcke had invented in the 1760s. Volta's "electrophore" sandwiched an electrostatic cake (a blend of turpentine, resin, or wax) between a fixed metal plate below and a rotating wooden shield covered with tinfoil above. When the cake was rubbed (while the lower plate was grounded), it generated and condensed a charge (like a Leyden jar), but its fixed metal plate also *retained* a charge—it did not decay.[92]

The device defied Franklin's definitions of electricity as a fluid that slipped in and out of an equilibrium. Jan Ingenhousz carefully broached the news to Franklin in November 1776, noting that "as the present troubles may possibly have prevented you getting some knowledge of this discovery, I think it may [my] duty to give you a Slight idea of its nature." This was the main subject of Ingenhousz's letter—only toward the end did he add, "You will be surprized to hear that I am maried," which apparently hardly mattered in comparison.[93]

Ingenhousz sent his letter to Philadelphia after Franklin had left for France. It caught up with him in January 1777, around the time a Frenchman rushed to deliver the same news. Soon thereafter, Georgiana Shipley, an earlier recipient of Franklin's pet squirrels, wrote him that Sir William Hamilton (volcanologist and, nominally, Emma Hamilton's husband) had told her all about it at a London dinner party. Franklin really was the last to know about the attack on his theories, and he could not believe it, anyway. "I thank you for the Account you give me of M. Volta's Experiment," he wrote Ingenhousz. He dismissed it as "only another Form of the Leiden Phial" but confessed himself "puzzled by one Part of your Account." This was the critical part: "'Thus the electric Force once excited may be kept alive Years together'; which perhaps is only a Mistake."[94]

It was no mistake, as many others kept eagerly telling Franklin. But he was too busy to do experiments with the electrophore to test his theories of electricity on it. Matters were made worse in May 1777, four months after Ingenhousz's news of the electrophore had reached Franklin, when lightning struck the Purfleet gunpowder magazine and Benjamin Wilson started his assault on Franklin's theory of lightning rods. Franklin had insisted that he would and could let his ideas fend for themselves. His friends in London, however, thought he and his ideas might need a little help.

Ingenhousz tackled the electrophore. In 1775, Henry Baker had endowed an annual lecture on physical science at the Royal Society. (The Bakerian Lecture is still the society's premier lecture in physics.) Ingenhousz was invited to give the lecture in 1778, and quite generously, he used the opportunity to defend what he described as Franklin's "almost generally received theory" of positive and negative electrical charges. Ingenhousz had tested an electrophore. He noted that when its electrostatic cake was charged, so was the metal plate below it. Yet if the two were separated, one could not add charge to the other—each was more or less stable. From this finding, Ingenhousz deduced that each of the two charged parts of the electrophore bore a different charge, positive in the metal and negative in the cake. The two kinds of electricity were known to repel each other—that must explain why the metal plate and the cake could not transfer their charges to each other. These findings confirmed that Franklin's definition of electricity as an "inherent quality" of matter still held.[95]

Ingenhousz's lecture appeared in the volume of the *Philosophical Transactions* that appeared in 1779. That volume also contained "Sundry Papers relative to an Accident from Lightning at Purfleet." These papers included Benjamin Wilson's long account of his experiments to prove blunt and short lightning rods more effective than the long, pointed variety Franklin still recommended. In his essay, Wilson did not shrink from naming and attacking his adversary. "Behold!" he wrote, lightning had struck, "contrary to Dr. FRANKLIN's assertion." In his account of his experiments, Wilson included some diagrams and a plea to the king. Then followed a shorter statement signed by the society's president, John Pringle, as well as Joseph Priestley and others. The statement championed Franklin's pointed rods.[96]

The Royal Society thoroughly examined challenges to Franklin's most important ideas about electricity, and the fellows who were Franklin's friends came down firmly on his side. And no one, not even Wilson, stated the obvious—the philosopher at the center of the fracas was formally an enemy. Not even the *Gentleman's Magazine*, which synopsized the *Philosophical Transactions*, stooped to mentioning the political context. Instead, that London periodical simply noted that "when philosophers thus differ, many will think themselves safest with no conductors [lightning rods] at all." Though he was distant from London and unable to do his own experiments, Franklin maintained his place in the heart of its learned community.[97]

To make his own contribution to the republic of letters, Franklin had to reuse earlier ideas and writings, some of them decades old. For his circle at Passy, he reworked an essay, "The Morals of Chess," that he had probably written for the Junto. He continued to extol pointed lightning rods and coauthored a 1780 paper with Le Roy that advocated gilded points for the Strasbourg Cathedral. This was also the year Franklin wrote his flatulent assessment of the Newtonian-Cartesian debate. That bagatelle may have expressed some irritation over the busy self-importance of philosophers who did not have new and unprecedented republics to tend.[98]

The oldest idea out of which Franklin got the most mileage was that of America's fast-growing population. His French friends must have been impressed with Americans' sexual diligence. Franklin's "Observations Concerning the Increase of Mankind" had been circulating, in French, since Barbeu-Dubourg had published it in his 1773 edition of the Franklin *Oeuvres*. And Franklin never missed a chance to claim that the busily breeding Americans were thoughtfully forming a prize consumer market for any Europeans who took them on as trading partners. In his widely reprinted "Comparison of Great Britain and America as to Credit, in 1777," he restated that "natural Propagation" doubled the American population every twenty-five years. "Accession of Strangers" would speed the rate to every twenty years, but it was not necessary.[99]

And Franklin finally confessed that Polly Baker was none other than he. Although many French readers (including Voltaire) knew Polly was a fiction, some people still thought Miss Baker existed. Perhaps she was now a grandmother. The credulous Abbé Raynal had included her story, as authentic, in his *Histoire philosophique et politique des . . . deux Indes* (1770). The truth came out in a three-way conversation between Franklin, Raynal, and Silas Deane. Deane knew the story was a hoax (though he did not know its author). He tried to convince Raynal that Baker did not exist, and Franklin listened to the two men argue until, doubtless bursting with laughter, he told all. "My word," Raynal conceded to Franklin, "I am more pleased to have included your tales in my work than the truths of others."[100]

Franklin continued to play the teasing and even flirtatious American political arithmetician. To his charming but chaste Madame Brillon, he confessed belief in not ten commandments but twelve, far more generous in number and moral intent than what Moses bore down from Sinai. "The *first* was, *Increase and multiply*" and the twelfth "*that ye love one another.*" Franklin professed himself "always willing to obey them both whenever I had an Opportunity," which he hoped

offset his sin of "Coveting my Neighbour's Wife," meaning his correspondent. When the Lafayettes had a daughter in 1782, christening
her Virginie to honor the American republic, Franklin congratulated their "Acquisition of a Daughter" and their choice of America's
"most antient State" for her name. He hoped the Lafayettes would
"go thro the Thirteen" states to complete their family. Franklin did
worry, though, for the souls destined to bear the names "Massachusetts & Connecticut . . . too harsh even for the Boys."[101]

As he tossed over his stock of old ideas, nature itself saved Franklin. Shortly after six o'clock in the evening on December 3, 1778, he
and other amazed Parisians could be found outside, staring up at
the sky. The aurora borealis, a brilliant celestial display, was illumi-
nating France. The flashes were brightest for a surreal fifteen minutes, but the effects lasted over three hours, glowing even after
midnight. Nature was kind—only after the Franco-American treaties
were signed in 1778 could Franklin have ventured back into natural
philosophy.

The northern lights had fascinated Franklin for most of his life.
In 1737, he reported on them in the *Pennsylvania Gazette* and continued to ponder them over the succeeding decades. Le Roy and
Franklin discussed what they had seen on that spectacular evening
in Paris. They agreed that others (including Denis Diderot) had
supplied only "ridiculous Explanations," such as the idea that the
earth's core was made of a glass that affected its atmospheric magnetism, somehow making electrical rays shoot through the sky.[102]

Convinced he could do better, Franklin stole four days from
diplomacy and produced an essay and two diagrams. He drafted his
thoughts in English and then translated them, with clumsy literal-
ness, into French. Two friends, the Abbé de La Roche and then Le
Roy, corrected the French, and Le Roy read the essay to a public ses-
sion of the Académie des Sciences in April 1779.[103]

Franklin explained the aurora borealis as the result of atmospheric density in northern regions, where cold kept electricity from
entering the earth, as it could in warmer places. Imagine, he asked
his readers, "a Room" heated "by a Stove." Heated air rose to the
ceiling, spreading down as it accumulated. This could be "render'd
visible" in a real room by introducing smoke, which would "rise &
circulate with the Air." And "a Similar Operation is perform'd by
Nature on the Air of this Globe." The tropics were the stove within
the globe's "Atmosphere" and sent warm air rising, replaced by

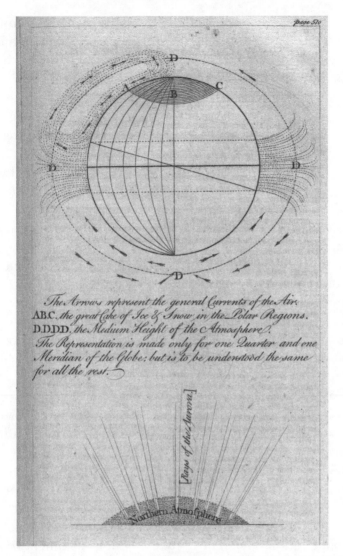

Franklin's illustration of the aurora borealis. Benjamin Franklin,
Political, Miscellaneous and Philosophical Pieces (1779).
HARVARD COLLEGE LIBRARY.

cooler air from the poles: "Thus a Circulation of Air is kept up in
our Atmosphere as in the Room above mentioned." To verify this
motion, one could watch clouds move in "Currents of different &
even opposite Direction," according to thermal variation, or use a
candle to see the different air currents in a heated room, with cool
air (below) bending the flame in one direction and hot air (above)
in the other.[104]

This atmosphere created differences in the earth's receptivity to electricity. The vapor arising in the tropics created motion in the air, which generated electricity; in warm climates, where the earth was "a good Conductor," atmospheric electricity could easily discharge in the form of lightning. Frozen earth was less receptive; an electrified cloud was unable to discharge in cold climates, where it became "as a bottle [Leyden jar] overcharg'd." Moreover, the cold air refracted the bursting electricity's light. The electric rays would converge and diverge depending on whether a "Conducting Body" could receive them, so the light they emitted darted about in characteristically auroral patterns—thus, the light show on December 3.[105]

Poor Richard would have admired Franklin's thrifty use of old materials: his first experiment on heating systems is here, as well as chunks of his meteorologic work, all garnished with his fundamental discovery that lightning was a form of atmospheric electricity. In English and French, he had made clear that his "Suppositions and Conjectures" were just that. He made statements about thermal trends in the atmosphere but posed questions on the auroral lights themselves. It would be charitable to call the essay old-fashioned; Franklin's image of a dangerously overcharged Leyden jar was outdated, meaning it ignored Volta's electrophore, which placidly stored electricity for long periods. Yet he also bolstered his important claim that heat and electricity behaved similarly, each in relation to the physical "conductors" of its fluid motions.[106]

Praise for the essay was rapturous, and Franklin received many solicitations for publication. The piece appeared in the June issue of the *Journal de Physique,* a new publication that reflected, in contrast to the Académie's *Mémoires,* a more specialized focus on physical science. In a London version of 1779, the editor's comment was three times as long as Franklin's six-page thesis. All the praise—or flattery really—generally noted Franklin's ability to comment on nature while attending to the fates of nations. The periodical *Mémoires secrets* marveled that the minister of a new republic found time to "amuse himself with physics." This was the tenor of all American, French, and even British admiration.[107]

Franklin was aware that experimental science remained beyond his reach—Ingenhousz's reports of his painstaking experiments made that clear. Ingenhousz still divided his time between Vienna and London (he was now Lord Shelburne's client, as Priestley had returned to his ministry) and was turning from electrical to chemi-

cal experiments, indeed following in Priestley's path. Priestley's tri-
als of mice and mint had established that plants did something that
sustained life in animals. He had hypothesized that plants somehow
purified the tainted air that animals exhaled.

Ingenhousz decided to investigate what plants did to air. He
planned and executed an experiment that eventually required a
prodigious 500 tests. In each, Ingenhousz put a plant, foliage end
down, into a glass vessel, filled the vessel with water, and then inverted it into a larger container of water so the plant was upright yet
still submerged. He then set everything in the sun and watched air
bubbles gradually displace the water in the glass vessel. Plants kept
in the dark did not do this, even if warmed as if by the sun. Assisted
by light, plants produced air of their own accord; they did not even
need gasping mice to exhale tainted air they would then purify. As
Ingenhousz put it, common plants thus generated "common air,"
the "invisible fluid which surrounds the whole earth." "One of the
great laboratories of nature for cleansing and purifying the air of
our atmosphere," Ingenhousz declared, "is placed in the substance
of the leaves."[108]

Ingenhousz published his findings as *Experiments upon Vegetables*
. . . (1779). He sent a copy to Franklin in late 1779, asking, in his
lovely, approximate English, "whether I spended my time
alltogeather useless." Franklin hardly thought so. He extolled Igen-
housz's exhaling vegetables to a fellow of the American Philosophical Society as "the greatest discovery made in Europe for some time
past." Later scientists would claim that Ingenhousz had provided
the first evidence of photosynthesis, a term Ingenhousz never used
(and was no longer alive to assess). But at the time, Priestley disputed the findings—he found a direct chemical action, in which
plants performed something on mephitic air, more convincing than
Ingenhousz's idea that light somehow stimulated plants to produce
air. If this was possible, Priestley asked, should not Ingenhousz be
able to define the physical process that achieved it? Franklin cautioned Ingenhousz not to weary the public and strain a friendship
with a direct refutation of Priestley's objections. He instead recommended his own strategy of allowing ideas to fend for themselves.[109]

That approach was ingenuous, if not ungrateful. It had been Ingenhousz, among others, who had, in fact, defended Franklin's
ideas against critics. And Ingenhousz lured Franklin back to experimentation. He hoped Franklin was "not lost to the world of Nature,

tho many of your old friends thinck so"—it was very nearly a threat. The Dutchman proposed to Franklin to "steal from your political occupations consecrated only to the service of your own country, some hours for the benefit of whole mankind," a cunning pitch.[110]

At some point, Franklin had devised experiments to test the speed at which various metals conducted heat. He sent a written protocol and materials to Ingenhousz, who did the tests. These experiments built on Franklin's earlier observations, as during Philadelphia's hot summer of 1749, that different materials conducted heat (and electricity) differently. Ingenhousz dipped wires made of various metals into melted wax, cooled them, and then dipped their unwaxed ends in hot oil; the faster a wire shed its wax, the faster it must transfer heat down its length. He reported the results to Franklin, who assured his friend that the distant experiments gave him "a great deal of Pleasure."[111]

Perhaps Franklin and Ingenhousz busied themselves as much as they did with science in order to avoid corresponding about the war. Ingenhousz favored the Americans. He could state this in Vienna, murmur it at his patron's house (Lord Shelburne had his own doubts about the war), but would have been unwise to proclaim it on the streets of London or write about it. In late 1780, he riskily wrote Franklin that he deplored Britain's "cowardly, shameful, and unmanly" tactics and stressed "how necessary it is for the tranquillity of Europe that your Country should remain free." It then dawned on Ingenhousz that Franklin might not be the only one to see the letter. He saw spies everywhere. (They were.) Early in 1781, he panicked when a letter from a mutual friend in Paris arrived only after it had been slit open. Ingenhousz resolved that his correspondence with Franklin should go via his French bankers, and he recommended against entrusting letters to servants, who might pocket the postage and discard the letters or pass them to the Paris police.[112]

Was it so hard to keep philosophy and politics apart? Franklin had to make an effort. Once the United States retreated from privateering, he took the high ground, insisting that everyone respect the neutrality of letters and ships unrelated to the war. In December 1777, he issued a passport for Ingenhousz to travel between England and Austria; Ingenhousz was "not an Enemy of the said States, nor a Subject of Great Britain" but rather "a Person of distinguished Merit" traveling on "private" business. Franklin likewise forbade captains of American ships to "meddle with the Pacquets between

Dover and Calais" while they still ran. And he commanded the captains not to attack ships engaged in peaceful pursuits. He first did so to protect supply ships bound for a Moravian mission on Labrador in 1778.[113]

Franklin made an even grander gesture in March 1779, when he ordered protection for James Cook's third Pacific voyage. The Duc de Croÿ had been pressing Franklin to issue such protection; finally, the American exclaimed, "with his sublime brevity, 'It shall be done!'" Franklin issued letters to all U.S. and allied ships: let pass Cook's vessels, devoted as they were to "the benefit of Mankind in general" and the exploration that "facilitates the Communication between distant Nations." Franklin learned later that his passport postdated, by a month, Cook's death in the Sandwich Islands— Pacific islanders proved deadlier than Atlantic privateers.[114]

So science and politics could enjoy somewhat separate spheres. Franklin got letters to many of Britain's men of science even after France closed its coast to British traffic in May 1779. The British stopped the Dover-Calais packet boat a month later, yet men of science still communicated, often via neutral Catholics. Spaniards delivered to Franklin publications from the Royal Society of Arts in 1778, before Spain entered the war. Two months after Priestley published his *Experiments and Observations . . .* (1778), he had a Catholic priest deliver a copy to Franklin. The same year, John Fothergill got a text on Linnaean botany to Franklin, and Franklin requested back issues of the Royal Society's *Philosophical Transactions*, published since his departure from London in 1775. "I do not suppose that Politicks have so far taken the Lead of Philosophy" as to deny him the volumes, he declared. The society granted the request without discussion. Receiving later volumes, Franklin presented them to the Académie.[115]

Indeed, Franklin's philosophic reputation in Britain was flourishing. Ingenhousz easily published his defense of Franklinist electricity in the *Philosophical Transactions* in 1778, not otherwise a good year for Anglo-American relations. James Cook, in his *A Voyage Towards the South Pole, and Round the World . . .* (1777), praised Franklin as the author of "the most rational account I have read of water spouts."[116]

In London, Benjamin Vaughan produced a major edition of Franklin essays, *Political, Miscellaneous, and Philosophical Pieces* (1779). Franklin's political position deterred neither the volume's production nor its favorable review in the British press. Indeed, Vaughan did not even feel compelled to disguise his subject's contributions to political affairs. He estimated that "no man ever made larger or bolder guesses than Dr. Franklin from like materials in politics and philosophy." He opened the volume with "Observations on the Increase of Mankind," Franklin's first and most aggressive challenge to Britain. "Can *Englishmen* read these things," Vaughan asked, "and not sigh at recollecting that the *country* which could produce their author, was once without controversy *their own!*" (Remember that Vaughan had, in 1777, sent Franklin those useful maps of the Great Lakes region.)[117]

Even amid pronouncements about knowledge belonging to all humanity, Franklin employed science in an openly partisan manner. Once his nation was formally allied with France, he used his expertise to advise France's military experts. One of Lavoisier's official duties was to serve as keeper of the nation's gunpowder. This task, as in England, involved both men of science and state officials. In 1779, a new powder magazine needed to be constructed. Franklin joined Lavoisier and Le Roy on an Académie committee to advise the project's leaders. He and Lavoisier also tried to get chemical materials that were essential to the American war effort to the beleaguered states.[118]

In addition, Franklin used the press to promote the American cause. He exulted to Richard Price that the printing press allowed modern people to "speak to nations; and good books and well written pamphlets have great and general influence." But the press could also produce propaganda. As early as 1777, Franklin considered setting up a press at Passy for official U.S. purposes, and he began to buy French type. He later acquired a full press and even a British copying machine, which he described to customs officials, falsely, as a scientific instrument. (It was illegal to import printing machinery.) While Franklin used the press for personal writings, notably his bagatelles, he also turned out U.S. documents, including passports. His first product was an invitation to a triumphant Fourth of July party at Passy in 1779.[119]

Franklin's patriotism only partly masked a growing disillusionment with the war. When Priestley joked that his chemical experiments might discover "the Philosopher's Stone" that would transform base materials into gold, Franklin made "a Request, that when you have found it you will take care to lose it again." If not, he said, people would "continue slaughtring one another as long as they can find Money to pay the Butchers." Five wearying years later, he told Joseph Priestley that he longed for "Leisure to search with you into the Works of Nature; I mean the *inanimate*, not the *animate* or moral part of them, the more I discover'd of the former, the more I admir'd them; the more I know of the latter, the more I am disgusted with them." Franklin then teased the Reverend Priestley for his interest in saving human souls: "Perhaps as you grow older, you may look upon this as a hopeless Project, or an idle Amusement, repent of having murdered in mephitic air so many honest, harmless mice, and wish that to prevent mischief, you had used Boys and Girls instead."[120]

Franklin hoped that peace would return him and his friends to the convivial learning he had enjoyed in London. In a letter to Joseph Banks, he expressed his longing "for a Return to those peaceful Times, when I could sit down in sweet Society with my English philosophic Friends, communicating to each other new Discoveries, and proposing Improvements of old ones; all tending to extend the Power of Man over Matter." By 1782, that prospect seemed to him infinitely sweeter than his life as one of "the Grandees of the Earth projecting Plans of Mischief."[121]

AND THEN, peace came. On November 11, 1781, Vergennes sent Franklin the news of the American victory at Yorktown, Virginia. The message arrived at eleven o'clock at night; it would have been welcome at three in the morning. The Franco-American defeat of the British vindicated the alliance and guaranteed a truce. It also demanded one final test of Dr. Franklin as a grandee not of the earth but of the ocean.

To Franklin's joy, the truce opened prison doors and made free communication between Americans and Britons possible again. In 1782, Parliament conceded that captive Americans had the formal status of prisoners of war. Franklin was pleased that British newspapers and parliamentary speeches used the word *reconciliation*—"it certainly means more than a mere peace. It is a sweet expression." He hoped the war would end with a show of humane principles. When American prisoners were exchanged for imprisoned Britons, he ventured, "it would be well, if some Kindness were mix'd in the transaction, with regard to their comfortable accommodation on shipboard." Franklin rejoiced when, in May 1782, David Hartley related the "*general* and *absolute*" British order to release all American prisoners. For his part, Hartley praised Franklin's wish for "*sweet reconcilation*" between their countries.[122]

But actual reconciliation proved difficult. It would require intricate procedures and arrays of carefully recruited diplomats. John Adams had his moment of glory—Congress appointed him minister plenipotentiary to negotiate with Britain and charged four other men, including Franklin, to help him.[123]

Franklin was mostly sidelined. Attacks of gout and a kidney stone often left him prostrate. But even in absentia, he overshadowed his colleagues. The British peacemakers included Lord Shelburne, Ingenhousz's patron, and Benjamin Vaughan, who had published Franklin's *Political, Miscellaneous, and Philosophical Pieces*. Shelburne reopened correspondence with Franklin in April 1782, recalling their work on American affairs fifteen years earlier. He complimented Franklin on the "Compass of your Mind and of your Foresight" and offered greetings to "Madame Helvetius and the Abbé Morellet" before he remembered himself and deleted reference to these French advocates of American independence.[124]

Polite greetings notwithstanding, it was the Seven Years' War all over again. The interested parties disputed some of that war's contested pieces of land and water in America, Africa, India, and Europe. As ever, Franklin worried about room for his nation's teeming people but also about their access to the Mississippi River and to the Atlantic. Fishing and whaling raised particular problems that defied national boundaries. Britain regarded the fishing banks off Canada as essential places where they could get not only fish but also men bred to the sea—potential seamen. The French king and ministers wanted to expand French whaling, perhaps in cooperation with the dubiously American Nantucketers. And extraordinarily, Congress passed a resolution in early 1783 permitting British ships to protect Nantucket.[125]

These unstable bargains could accumulate indefinitely, especially if the peace negotiations made several treaties rather than one. That was Franklin's worst fear and one of long standing. As early as 1778, rumors had flown that Britain might offer independence to the United States if it signed a separate peace. Franklin protested that the Franco-American treaty made such a bargain impossible: "An obligation of *Gratitude and Justice*" bound the United States to "a Nation which is engaged in a War on her Account." Without one binding document, he warned, Britain might continue a vindictive war against France, the most faithful ally of the new United States. Any "honest American would cut off his right hand rather than Sign an Agreement with England contrary to the spirit of it." Yet even in 1781 and 1782, when honest Americans held the upper hand, Great Britain threatened to recognize U.S. independence only if it could continue war against the Republic's allies, particularly the French and Spanish.[126]

Franklin, who had no spare hours to do anything unless he had good reason, picked this moment to chart the Gulf Stream a second time. This chart would assert, once and for all, America's sovereignty over the North Atlantic. But it would also offer the ocean to France. No longer an eyebrow over an imperial British smirk, the Gulf Stream would become a hand across the sea.

For Franklin, the chart was a personal diplomatic statement, a promise to honor the special relationship between the United States and France that he had helped create in 1778. To produce the chart, he collaborated with French publisher Le Rouge, with whom he had already made a wartime map of North America's embattled western territories. Le Rouge's participation indicated some expectation of French demand for such a chart. And Franklin hoped it would help establish a Franco-American packet-boat system.[127]

The Franklin/Le Rouge chart got to the point by shrinking the Atlantic. It reproduced the northwest corner of the 1768 Mount and Page chart, the section that focused on the Gulf Stream proper. The imperial rivalry over North America, evident in the 1768 Folger and Franklin chart (and the 1772 De Brahm chart), was updated, slightly, in the 1782 chartwork. But for a sprinkling of Spanish names in the south, the landscape was peppered with English (as with the "English Factori" on "James Baye") and French names. The names of the thirteen states designated the coast as U.S. territory, but "CANADA OU NOUV^LE FRANCE" revealed France's hope of regaining some of the territory it had lost in the Seven Years' War.

Franklin clearly wanted the chart to be used because he included sailing instructions on it. These were Timothy Folger's directions but rendered into a French so gropingly literal that one pities the mariners who tried to follow them. In fact, Franklin worried that they could not follow the instructions at all. When Michel Guillaume de

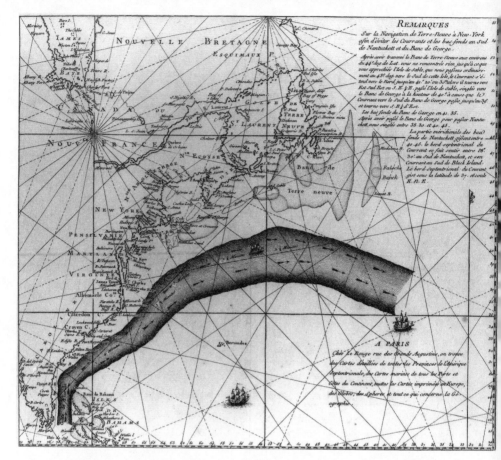

Franklin's second chart of the Gulf Stream. George-Louis Le Rouge
(c. 1782). FRANKLIN COLLECTION, YALE COLLEGE LIBRARY.

Crèvecoeur (alias J. Hector St. John de Crèvecoeur) was put in
charge of U.S. affairs at the French Ministry of the Marine, he
helped draft a March 1783 proposal for a packet-boat service between the two allies. Crèvecoeur gave Franklin a copy of his sugges-
tion, and Franklin returned it with comments and a copy of the Le
Rouge chart. He noted that the chart's "directions" were "imper-
fectly translated" (they were crossed out) and rendered them again
in English. His secretary entered most of these notes on the left and
bottom margins of the chart; Franklin wrote a note, to the right, on
the Gulf Stream's temperature, his first statement of his research on
this matter. The bottom notes referred to Nantucket whalers, the local experts.[128]

Franklin did not, however, name his cousin as an informant. In fact, the chart marked the end of the friendship between the two men, a casualty of war. Folger had visited Franklin in July of 1781, evidently to obtain a U.S. passport so he could return to America. Several pieces of paper might have changed hands: Folger gave Franklin a bond of £3,000 and a written oath of loyalty to the Republic. He may then have handed over a manuscript chart of the Gulf Stream (or a copy of the 1768 chart)—he got his passport, and Franklin got a prototype for the Le Rouge chart. But something had already altered their personal connection. This possible exchange (quid pro quo?) then ended contact between the two cousins. The stiff note in which Folger requested the passport was his last extant letter to Franklin and came after a telling eleven-year gap in their correspondence. The note was addressed simply "Sir" and signed "Yr. Most Obedt. Servt," nothing like the affectionate and rambling tone of their earlier letters.[129]

What had happened? Franklin may have worried that a Nantucketer was unlikely to be a loyal American, whatever he swore; he may have conveyed his concern to his cousin. And indeed, in the autumn of 1781, Jonathan Williams warned his uncle that Timothy Folger stood accused of "illicit Trade with the Enemy with your knowledge & support." Folger, it was said, operated with the awkwardly simultaneous protection of the British and of Franklin—an expansive interpretation of Nantucket's divided sovereignty. Surely, Franklin regretted his decision to favor a kinsman with an American passport.[130]

He had stood by many a sailor during the war, but now, Franklin briskly disowned his cousin. Should Folger use his passport to trade with the British, he said, "let our People catch him and hang him with all my Heart . . . for I always think that a Rogue hang'd out of a Family does it more Honour than ten that live in it." If anyone found him guilty of anything illicit, Franklin added, "they are welcome to hang me into the Bargain." There is no sign that the cousins ever met again. Folger's hydrographic collaboration with a famous natural philosopher had ended.[131]

The war may have made it difficult for Franklin to pursue the sciences, but it had destroyed Folger's attempts to do so. The family crisis showed too well how science and war may have stimulated each other yet could damage each other as well. The break between

Folger and Franklin also made clear that work and status affected a person's aspiration to philosophy. Within the republic of letters, genteel natural philosophers could fret, if not dissemble, over their wartime political ties. Those who depended on nature for a livelihood had no such leeway. The sea gave Folger his living, and its commercial activities compromised him. Franklin had long thought that the Atlantic would connect people, not divide them. In 1768, he had created an unprecedented chart of the Gulf Stream to make that point. But in 1781, he discarded the very person who had helped him make the chart. He was charming and ruthless, that fur-capped American philosopher.

Chapter 9

FINAL ACCOUNTS

I MAGINE Franklin on his terrace at Passy—head tilted back, double reflection of a globe floating over the lenses of his spectacles,
delighted smile underneath. He was seeing his first balloon. On November 21, 1783, the Passy terrace was crowded with onlookers.
John and Sarah Jay were visiting; two weeks earlier, their daughter
Ann had been born in the Franklin household. John Adams's
teenage son, John Quincy, was also on hand. They were fortunate in
their access to a prime viewing spot—thousands of Parisians had
desperately elbowed their way into any and all promising places.
Everyone had waited for hours as the launch was repeatedly de-
layed. Then, as the sun sank, the balloon finally rose—the first aerial flight to carry human beings successfully. Someone at Passy asked
what possible good the device might serve. Franklin shot back, "À
quoi sert un enfant qui vient de naître?" (What good is a newborn
baby?). It was a remarkable compliment, perhaps, to tiny Ann Jay.[1]

And it was a somewhat surprising declaration for a seventy-seven-
year-old natural philosopher. Franklin was well aware that he was
quite the opposite of a newborn baby. He would live seven years
more, but not knowing that, of course, he assumed he might die any
day. His newborn baby comment revealed his ambivalence over his
stage of life. He expressed hope for the future—immediate utility
was no measure of anything, let alone science. Yet even old things—
or people—had their value. In his late years, Franklin had, after all,
managed to master French, the language in which he made his celebrated retort about balloons and babies.

In this late phase of his life, Franklin hoped to be free, finally and
completely, from public affairs. U.S. independence and the end of
the mission in France offered him a return to private life. Many
friends urged him to use the reprieve to finish his autobiography—
they knew the world would want a record of his amazing rise to
celebrity. But however flatteringly put, these pleas reminded

Premier Voyage Aérien
Experience faite
Sous la Direction
Par M.ᵉ le Marquis d'Arlandes

En présence de M.ᵉ le Dauphin.
dans le Jardin de la Muette,
de M.ᵉ Montgolfier,
et M.ᵉ Pilâtre du Rosier, le 21. 9.ᵇʳᵉ 1783.

Vue de la Terrasse de M.ᵉ Franklin à Passi.

First manned aerial flight, seen from Franklin's terrace.
Bartelemy Faujas de Saint-Fond, *Première Suite* . . . (1784).
HOUGHTON LIBRARY, HARVARD UNIVERSITY.

Franklin of his mortality. "I have begun to write two or three Things which I wish to finish before I die," he wrote Ingenhousz in early 1785, "but I sometimes doubt the possibility."[2]

Franklin seemed determined to spend as much effort on living his life, whatever remained of it, as he did on telling the story of it. Why write about past accomplishments if future ones were still possible? Yet the past accomplishments were definitely the bird in the hand, the things worth advertising to the world. Franklin tried to do a bit of everything—cover his past, do something with his remaining days, consider the future. The results reveal an attention divided, even as the new prospects for science particularly enchanted the old man of letters.

———————————

IT MAY SEEM APT that the United States achieved its independence just as the sciences were entering a new phase. Recognizable fields of inquiry—chemistry and physics in particular—were emerging, as were men who specialized in them. The world now had a new republic and new ways of thinking, for a new age. Too much was occurring; looking back, we can only quickly review some of the highlights, much as Franklin did.

Chemical investigators were turning "air," in its multiplying forms, into different *gases*. Franklin followed the major developments, which included Lavoisier's eclipse of Priestley. The Frenchman coolly redefined many of Priestley's findings, as when he dismissed the concept of phlogiston. Priestley had argued that combustion burned phlogiston away from substances; in 1772, Lavoisier demonstrated that combustion made the substances heavier and so must be joining something (oxygen) to them, not taking something (the ultimately phantom phlogiston) away. Then, in 1782, Lavoisier redid some of Priestley's experiments with different states of air and demonstrated that water was a compound of inflammable air (hydrogen) and oxygen. Lavoisier concluded that no form of matter was ever lost; it only changed its configuration in relation to other materials.[3]

These and other experiments began to transform heat, that slippery fluid, into caloric units. Caloric measurements determined the amount of heat generated or transferred in different material reactions. These units could be standardized, from one demonstration to another. Explanations of the cause of heat also multiplied; experimenters examined chemical reactions, as well as physical causes such as friction. Again, Franklin followed these developments. (His theories of heat as a specific, fluid substance that could be conducted through various materials had indeed informed some of the relevant research that followed.) He discussed Joseph Black's theory of latent heat with a correspondent. And he probably also knew of Lavoisier's widely discussed *Mémoire sur la chaleur* (1783), or report on heat, a calorimetric study of animal heat and of combustion.[4]

Like heat, electricity took on a new form as well. It became less subtle substance than measured phenomenon. Volta had, with his electrophore, prompted men of science to define electricity in standard units. Electrical equipment became both more complicated and more precise, with electrometers and new electrophores appearing regularly. Experimenter Robert Symmer did some surprising things with two electrostatically charged stockings (one black and one white). Independently, each garment showed signs of electricity; for instance, they repelled other objects. But the charged socks had no such effect on each other—they simply hung there, limply. How, Symmer asked, could they be thought to each have a different charge? Franklin's two quantities of electricity, positive and negative, again were suspect. Electrical and chemical experiments intersected; demonstrators discovered that electricity could, when it sparked the right gas, cause combustion. Medical practitioners tested electricity's effects on animals and humans. Electricians, including Franklin, were fascinated by electric eels. The wriggling creatures were perhaps more evidence of electricity's constitutive place within matter, including living matter.[5]

The science starts to look familiar to us. Chemical demonstrations identified what we would regard as real elements (oxygen and hydrogen), as well as their actual combinations (water). We also glimpse more precision in experimentation, hence all those caloric and electric units. The subtle fluids of Franklin's day were modernized, assigned qualities that strike us today as more "scientific." The beautiful circulations of Franklin's fluids were in retreat, replaced by precision and control over heat, gases, and electricity. Discrete questions began to dominate scientific discussion and publications. Polymaths were vanishing, and specialists were emerging.

Was this progress? Maybe not. At the time, no one, including Franklin, could have known whether these new ideas would carry the day. Consider three possibilities they considered: the microscope could help identify the nature of heat, magnets might have therapeutic value, and aerial travel was perfectly possible. Early on, Franklin and his contemporaries regarded the first two notions as plausible and only subsequently labeled them nonsense and quackery. And they were stunned that the final concept turned out to be valid. As we review Franklin's engagement with the sciences after a long lapse, it is useful to remember this context—the wonderful yet bewildering new era that opened up at the end of his life, which would offer an opportunity for him to decide which camps he would be in.[6]

First, consider the microscopic heat. In the late 1770s, Jean-Paul Marat had trained sunlight through a microscope and onto heated objects. He claimed that the projected wavelike pattern was visible evidence of the *fluide igné* (igneous fluid) that Lavoisier had defined. The Académie Royale endorsed this work in 1778, which inspired Marat to launch a more ambitious essay on light, attacking Newton's theory of color. Marat courted Franklin, sending him essays under an alias and inviting him to demonstrations. When Franklin finally turned up in 1779, Marat focused the solar microscope on the American's notoriously unwigged head. The light that reflected off the philosopher's brainpan supposedly resembled the rays attributed to "Genius." The genius himself was too careful (or busy) to render any judgment on Marat's new ideas about light. But other academicians decreed Marat's experiments inconclusive and his critique of Newton unconvincing.[7]

Second, consider the medical magnets. They were the tools of Franz Anton Mesmer, who originated the idea of "animal magnetism." Mesmer was a healer from southern Germany whose therapy—dubbed mesmerism—was supposed to encourage the circulation of magnetic fluid into and within the body. Blockage of this magnetism was said to cause a variety of ailments, which Mesmer cured by touching patients with rods or his hands. At his clinic in Vienna, he arranged private treatments as well as collective sessions. In the latter, patients (or curiosity seekers) gathered around a trough filled with metal. Participants would grasp rods sunk into the trough, and magnetism, Mesmer claimed, would then flow into them. These séances featured soothing music, often emanating from a pressure-sensitive instrument such as a piano or glass armonica. Mesmer was a gifted performer on the armonica, which emphasized the delicate power of his hands.[8]

When he opened shop in Paris in 1778, he was initially friendly with Franklin. But Ingenhousz had informed Franklin that his friends in Vienna doubted Mesmer's powers. Franklin strategically took an interest in the healer's armonica playing, not his therapy. And when Mesmer demonstrated his medical talents at the Académie, he failed to gain its endorsement. But his patients were undeterred, and he soon had a cult following, even among academicians. Some doctors and men of science found it odd that Mesmer kept his procedures mysterious—no man of science was supposed to do that. And many people found it odd that, when Mesmer treated female patients, he sat very close to them and stroked them very attentively, eliciting responses remarkably like those of sexual climax—certainly, no gentleman was supposed to do *that*. To his critics, Mesmer had (or pretended to have) the wicked power over nature that others had suspected in Franklin.[9]

Those fascinating, armonica-playing natural philosophers. In hindsight, we believe that Franklin was a benevolent genius and Mesmer an opportunistic quack. But at the time, each man dodged some of the same criticisms. They were labeled charlatans, magicians, and seducers. True, Franklin had only kissed the ladies (maybe some of the very same ladies) whom Mesmer stroked. Both, however, were known as charmers of the fair sex. Moreover, Franklin had also been using his charms to seduce the French into a new war against Britain; nothing Mesmer did was quite that dangerous.

The lurid gossip surrounding Mesmer prompted an official inquiry in 1784. Both the Académie and the Société Royale de Médicine formed committees to investigate him, but the Académie contingent, which included Franklin, Lavoisier, and Joseph-Ignace Guillotin (the advocate of the guillotine), took charge. The tests they administered compared separate groups: people who thought they were being magnetized but were not, and those who thought they were not but were. The investigators also agreed to be magnetized to see what, if anything, it felt like. At Passy, Franklin assembled a group of subjects. He, his grandsons, and an officer, possibly John Paul Jones, were all mesmerized.

The results indicated that people who *thought* they were being magnetized, whether they were or not, had the strongest therapeutic responses. Expectations, not magnets, had medical value. In a published report, the committee denounced Mesmer. But the investigators noted the curative powers of the human imagination, what

Franklin routs the mesmerists. "Le magnétisme dévoilé."
BIBLIOTHÈQUE NATIONALE DE FRANCE.

is known today as the placebo effect. And an unpublished report, submitted to the king, showed concern mostly over Mesmer's behavior toward his female patients, not over the therapy. The investigators were using science to denounce conduct. Franklin himself had admitted, in a 1784 letter, that "Expectation" and even "Delusion" could harmlessly cure people. Yet he sat in judgment on Mesmer and decided against him. "It is surprising," Franklin clucked to Ingenhousz, "how much Credulity still subsists in the World." A print showed Franklin leading the academicians against Mesmer and the demons of ignorance—note Franklin's spectacles and his finger pointed at the committee's report, the one that was published. One notorious charmer routed another and quite possibly had his own reasons for doing so.[10]

Finally, consider the aerial travel. The delightful globe Franklin saw from his terrace was spawned by the late war as well as the ongoing chemical experiments. In 1777, Joseph Montgolfier, from a family of paper manufacturers, had quizzed a doctor cousin about the new chemistry. From him, Montgolfier learned of the varying weights and qualities of different gases. Then, in 1782, Montgolfier pondered the long, unsuccessful, and bloody Spanish siege of the British at Gibraltar. Could the fortifications not be taken by air? he wondered. A device to carry bombs would be a remarkable, albeit dangerous, invention. Since ancient times, people had attempted aerial travel, which usually ended quite badly.[11]

Chemicals were the answer. In 1782 and 1783, Joseph Montolfier and his brother Étienne made containers (usually of cloth reinforced, appropriately, with paper) and filled them with air heated by a fire. They first tried box-shaped kites, but when they attempted to make them bigger, these rectangles proved perilously rigid. Bouncy bubbles, they discovered, would distribute the interior tension more evenly—and this has remained the classic shape for hot-air balloons. In June 1783, the Montgolfiers unveiled their invention—the *Montgolfière*—before an audience, sending a globe up about 3,000 feet to "general astonishment."[12]

Imitators were quick to follow, and soon, many balloons soared over France. Some were filled with hydrogen made from iron filings and "vitriol" (sulfuric acid). These so-called *Charlières* were the creations of J.-A.-C. Charles and Barthélemy Faujas de Saint-Fond. (Earlier, Faujas had raised a subscription for Charles's popular demonstrations of physics.) Hydrogen had greater lifting power, lasted longer, and interested chemical experimenters—all of which represented a big threat to the Montgolfiers. The Montgolfiers responded by launching the first manned flight (in November 1783), the one Franklin saw.[13]

Suddenly, balloons were the rage of Paris. They inspired everything, including (this being France, after all) fashionable clothing, interior decoration, and tableware. Soon, it was no longer sufficient to send a balloon aloft—it had to be gorgeously decorated and released to prove some new point. The subsequent contest between heated-air Montgolfières and inflammable-air Charlières brought about the first instance of inner-ear pain due to abrupt change in pressure (in December 1783), the first hijacking (in January 1784), the first air crash (in January 1785), and the first commercial flight (in January 1786). Each of the Montgolfier brothers received the title *savant,* or learned one, from the Académie Royale, though Charles received more attention from men of science. He shared the glory. At his own December 1783 liftoff, Charles respectfully asked Étienne Montgolfier to release a little pilot balloon to test the wind—and he gallantly toasted the crowd with champagne.[14]

Franklin, a former kite enthusiast, avidly watched these ventures into the sky, knew most of the balloonists, and was a touchstone for them. During the war, he had corresponded with the Montgolfier family patriarch about stationery and about getting letters to a Montgolfier relative in Canada. When Joseph and Étienne had requested an official Académie demonstration of their balloon, they remarked that it enabled the observation of electricity in clouds, science's Franco-Franklinian topic. One Masonic admirer compared Joseph Montgolfier to Franklin. And before Charles turned to ballooning, Franklin had been one of his patrons. He had encouraged Charles's chemical demonstrations, some of which used a glass armonica. (Seeing Franklin at a Charles lecture, an observer commented that it was like spotting Jupiter amid the mortals.) And it was as a designated witness of the Académie Royale that Franklin saw the ascent of the first successful aeronauts.[15]

He marveled at aerostatics. He declared that "a few months since[,] the idea of witches riding thro' the air upon a broomstick, and that of philosophers upon a bag of smoke, would have appeared equally impossible and ridiculous." Le Roy sent him descriptions of the Montgolfiers' work; he and Franklin, among others, wrote an official report on the Montgolfière as a technical device.[16]

Franklin immediately grasped that balloons were not only tremendous fun but also boons for philosophy. Their construction and motion confirmed the significance of temperature to fluid dynamics. As the first manned flight "went over our Heads," he reported, "we could see the Fire [it carried,] which was very considerable. As the Flame slackens, the rarified Air cools and condenses, the Bulk of the Balloon diminishes and it begins to descend." Of Charles's little pilot balloon, Franklin concluded that its "falling at Vincennes shows that mounting higher it met with a current of air in a contrary direction, an observation that may be of use to future aerial voyagers." Franklin appreciated that balloons were even airborne laboratories, with gondolas outfitted for philosophical aeronauts: "There is room in this car for a little table to be placed between them, on which they can write and keep their journal; that is, take notes of everything they observe, the state of their thermometer, barometer, hygrometer, etc." One aeronaut even took samples of upper air for chemical analysis. (It was similar to air at sea level.)[17]

It was clear that ballooning was a young person's activity—as when Cook had headed to the Pacific, Franklin could not hope to embark. But he enjoyed playing with miniature balloons, the fad in France in 1783. In September, he wrote Richard Price that "they make small Balloons now of the same material with what is called Gold-beater's Leaf. Inclos'd I send one, which being fill'd with inflammable Air by my Grandson [Temple], went up last Night, to the Cieling in my Chamber, and remained rolling about there for some time. Please give it also to Sir Joseph Banks." Yet again, an interior room or atmosphere gave Franklin all the experimental space he needed.[18]

Happily, balloons were invented too late to be used in the recent War of Independence. Instead, they symbolized the nascent peace. Frenchman Jean-Pierre François Blanchard and loyalist American John Jeffries made this point when they ballooned from England to France in 1785. Four years earlier, a big, unearthly globe approaching France would have seemed menacing, destined to be incinerated by Dr. Franklin's rumored mirrors at Calais.

The craft barely made it across the channel, but that probably increased public interest in its intrepid mission. The balloon's barometer is now considered the oldest surviving flight instrument; a portrait of Jeffries shows him, in a splendid fur cap, holding the barometer. And the Charlière bore mail. Jeffries called at Passy with the world's first airmail letter, from loyalist William Franklin. Only in this way did William dare to contact his father and son. It was a "sweet reconciliation" indeed: an Anglo-Franco-American venture sailed over national boundaries and reconnected a family divided by war. Sadly, an excursion crossing from France to England in June 1785 ended horribly when its Montgolfière-Charlière hybrid exploded and its gondola plummeted to the rocks below. Its two aeronauts "were both found dashed to pieces," as Franklin warned a would-be imitator.[19]

———————

DESPITE the breathtaking tableaux all around him—science in midair!—Franklin found it hard to restart his own efforts. The casualty rate (Mesmer discredited, aeronauts dead) might have been a deterrent, but the real problem was the continued demand of public affairs. In October 1783, Franklin had discovered an incomplete letter on hygrometers to London instrument maker Edward Nairne, one that he had begun three years earlier. He finished and sent it, accepting Nairne's forgiveness in advance: "You are so good as to consider how much my time has been taken up." As during the war, he read and corresponded widely. He read the electrical work of others but did not attempt any himself; neither Volta's electrophore nor Symmer's socks tempted him back into experimentation. His rooms at Passy accumulated chemical books and equipment, but they were probably for his grandson, Temple.[20]

As he had done decades earlier, with Cadwallader Colden, Franklin used letters to ease himself into philosophy. From 1782 to 1785, he wrote several long letters on topics in science, addressing them to old friends such as Jan Ingenhousz or Benjamin Vaughan or to minor figures such as the Abbé Jean-Louis de Giraud-Soulavie, none of whom were likely to be overly critical. Franklin usually took up topics he already knew a great deal about, for instance, meteorology. If he discussed subjects that were new to him, he tended to focus on fields in which he would not be expected to do experiments, such as geomorphism.[21]

Franklin's 1782 "Conjectures Concerning the Formation of the Earth" was characteristic. When he sent the essay to Soulavie, he confessed he had "given loose to imagination" because "actual observation" of nature was "out of my power." In his essay, he reviewed the theories of others—Gottfried Wilhelm Leibnitz's idea that the earth's core might be fluid and Isaac Newton's theory that gravity made matter converge on a common center. The "internal parts" of the resulting earth were, Franklin concluded, a "fluid more dense, and of greater specific gravity than any of the solids we are acquainted with; which therefore might swim in or upon that fluid." The "surface of the globe" was a mere "shell, capable of being broken and disordered" by its fluid center, which probably held a great deal of iron. "The iron contained in the substance of this globe," Franklin speculated, had "made it capable of becoming as it is a great magnet." Further, "the fluid of magnetism exists perhaps in all space," giving the "universe" a "magnetical North and North" and making interstellar travel possible.[22]

In his "Meteorological Imaginations and Conjectures" of 1784, Franklin was on even better form. In this letter, he addressed one of his oldest interests, the weather. Once again, he took up the idea that the atmosphere contained layers of warmth and cold. He hypothesized "a Region high in the Air over all Countries, where it is always Winter." He believed that cold zone formed hail and snow and counterbalanced warmth from the sun and the heat-absorbing earth. (The fact that balloonists got colder as they ascended might have made him remember his earlier speculation.)[23]

Then Franklin noted, almost in passing, the "constant Fog over all Europe" in the summer of 1783. This oddly "dry" fog had occluded the sun and made the summer milder, and it brought winter on earlier than usual. Everyone noticed it, and everyone was mystified by it—except Franklin. A dry fog must be a form of smoke, he reasoned, but why was there so much smoke in the atmosphere? Maybe the earth had encountered one of "those great burning Balls or Globes," he posited. In other words, a big comet might have entered and been destroyed by "our Atmosphere," which then retained the smoke from the explosion. Or the fog might have come from a volcano. Mount Hecla in Iceland had recently erupted, as well as another "Volcano which arose out of the Sea near that Island, which Smoke might be spread by various Winds, over the northern Part of the World." Lacking time to do experiments, scrambling to keep up with new discoveries, and recycling old conjectures, Franklin had hit on an important, if rare, aspect of climate change.[24]

So far, so good—and it is interesting that Franklin was finding his feet not in the electrical material that had catapulted him to fame but in the natural history he had first examined in his twenties and thirties. Luckily for him, he had salted away some data—his measurements of sea-surface temperature from his 1775 and 1776 crossings of the Atlantic. Unluckily, many other people shared his interest in the sea, which meant that Franklin would have to hurry to make anything of his findings.

His fame made it likely that colleagues and even competitors would seek his attention. A train of British guests at Passy (Polly Hewson came with her sons) included Thomas Pownall, an old friend and servant of empire. Pownall had been writing a piece entitled "Hydraulic and Nautical Observations on the Currents in the Atlantic Ocean," and he sought Franklin's opinion of it. On October 7, 1784, Franklin read the essay, a narrative description of the Gulf Stream and of investigations of it, including Franklin's and those of others as well. He marked comments in the margins.

Franklin did not correct and so presumably agreed with Pownall's statements that he had, with Folger, produced a chart "at London in 1768," had since had it "copied & Printed at Paris by Mr de Chaumont," but had found it "not perfectly exact." Franklin then gave Pownall "some notes" of his own on the subject. In these, he confirmed that he had made "several experiments with the Thermometer" to locate the Gulf Stream.[25]

From this visit, Pownall got Franklin's imprimatur on his essay, and Franklin got credit in it for his own chart and for the first thermometric investigation of the Gulf Stream. But Franklin, ever attentive to the state of his scientific reputation, must have gotten the message that it was high time for him to publish his own study of the Gulf Stream. Neither of his two charts enjoyed wide circulation, and both bore another man's description of the current—Timothy Folger's sailing instructions were their only narrative material. Fortunately, developments in hydrography were not nearly as daunting as those in chemical or physical experiments. And of course, Franklin had been following innovations in maritime cartography and technology through the war. His patriotic diligence now came in handy.

Throughout the 1770s and 1780s, Franklin had steadily gathered information about affairs of the sea. Johann Reinhold Forster, one of the naturalists who had accompanied James Cook on his second Pacific journey, sent Franklin his *Observations Made During a Voyage Round the World* . . . (1778), with a final chapter containing "useful Directions for preserving the lives of mariners on long Voyages." Le Roy and Franklin discussed Forster's account. Le Roy noted that the lightning rod and chain on one ship had protected it during a storm at "Tahity." Meanwhile, some of Franklin's many "begging letters" had offered maritime inventions to the United States, in exchange for money or assistance in getting to America. Stephen Sayre sent several accounts of improved naval architecture, for example, and Franklin received promises to develop submarine vessels, none of which quite worked.[26]

Franklin's patronage of the Continental Navy had, however, taught him which maritime innovations did work. The standout was copper sheathing. Placed over the hull of a ship, corrosion-resistant sheets of copper repelled the sea growths that sprouted on wooden vessels and made them slow and difficult to maneuver. The result was greater stability, or "stiffness." It seems that the British Admiralty had begun sheathing its ships around 1778, and the Post Office soon followed suit. John Paul Jones had lobbied to command two captured, copper-bottomed ships. Pierre Landais, the Frenchman who commanded the *Alliance*, pleaded to have it sheathed: "She would still sail better, and be *stiffer under sail at sea, which is what she wants to be.*" Franklin had assented to Landais but regretted that funds did not allow for routine sheathing. "For God's sake be sparing," he had told Jones in 1780, "unless you mean to make me a Bankrupt."[27]

Peace brought yet more maritime news. Of Franklin's passport for Captain Cook, Sir Joseph Banks confessed, "I could not but rejoice at the triumph which such an indisputable proof afforded me over those who warp'd by politicks or party wish'd to entertain a different opinion of your character." To thank Franklin, the Royal Society had, in 1780, nominated him for its gold medal bearing Cook's image. Banks bestowed the medals on the monarchs of France, Britain, and Russia; Franklin did not get his until 1784, once peace was a firm fact. The same year, the Royal Society sent him a copy of Cook's three-volume *Voyages.* Franklin was frustrated that the thank-you gift had been mispacked: the set lacked its first volume but had a duplicate of the third. That he cared about the missing volume showed that he remained interested in hydrography.[28]

He had no time just yet for even a speculative letter on maritime matters. Instead, he turned back to political arithmetic. His firm declarations on this long-gestating topic stood in marked contrasts to his diffident speculation on other areas of science—he knew exactly what he wanted to say about the population of a now independent United States.

He still assumed that America's population was growing so fast that immigrants would not be needed. Yet no sooner did British troops stack their arms at Yorktown than petitions for assistance in emigrating to America stacked up on his desk. Tired of answering each appeal, Franklin instead refashioned the bits of advice he had been dispensing since 1777 into "Information to Those Who Would Remove to America" (1782).[29]

Steadily and cheerfully, he gave would-be migrants the same advice: think twice. Franklin meant his essay to quash "mistaken Ideas and Expectations" about America. "[It] is the Land of Labour," he cautioned, "and by no means what the English call *Lubberland,* and the French *Pays de Cocagne,*" where houses were "til'd with Pancakes, and where the Fowls fly about ready roasted, crying, *Come eat me!*"

Though various colonies had formerly encouraged settlers "by Paying their Passages" or providing land, the current government did not. No one was worth the cost of importation. "Strangers" should go to the United States for its "good Laws and Liberty," Franklin said, and because there was "room enough for them all." He also warned any man who had "no other Quality to recommend him but his Birth" to stay put. Inherited rank was "a Commodity that cannot be carried to a worse market than that of America." The United States had instead "a general happy Mediocrity."[30]

Even men of learning and accomplishment were advised to think carefully before packing up. Few Americans were rich enough to "pay the high Prices given in Europe for Paintings, Statues, Architecture." "The natural Geniuses, that have arisen in America with such [artistic] Talents," he explained, "have uniformly quitted that Country for Europe." Things were slightly better for those talented in "Letters and Mathematical Knowledge." The nation's "nine Colleges or Universities," plus many small academies, promised a number of academic positions. The professions—divinity, law, and medicine—were also a good bet: "The quick Increase of Inhabitants everywhere gives them a Chance of Employ." But European clerics, lawyers, and doctors would have to compete "with the Natives."[31]

Americans appreciated, above all others, people with practical talents. "The People have a saying, that God Almighty is himself a Mechanic [artisan], the greatest in the Univers[e]." His material creation, the universe itself, was the ultimate practical invention.[32]

This America suited Franklin quite well. He had been an artisan. He was a deist who believed in the argument from design, which deduced God's existence from his marvelous Creation. He prized learning, though he admitted that the United States offered only limited institutional support for it; universities, academies, some libraries, and one learned society—the American Philosophical Society—were its only berths. Above all, people had to work—Americans labored with their heads but also with their hands. Leisure of the grandly aristocratic variety was impossible in the new country. Even wealthy Americans had farms, plantations, merchant houses, or professions to tend.

Franklin wanted to keep America as it was, characterized socially by that happy mediocrity he described. He feared that postwar Americans might welcome the reintroduction of aristocracy; he wished instead to abolish what inherited privileges remained in the country. To antislavery advocate Granville Sharp, Franklin deplored the custom of primogeniture, which gave property to the firstborn child or son. He agreed with Sharp that the law of "*gavelkind,*" which divided estates equally among all children, was entirely preferable and should spread.[33]

For the same reason, Franklin despised the new Society of the Cincinnati, which passed its membership to male descendants of officers of the Continental Army. To his daughter (his *female* heir, since he had effectively disinherited his loyalist son), Franklin sneered that the Cincinnati's only value was that it demonstrated that "the Absurdity of *descending Honours*" was "capable of mathematical Demonstration." A person had too many ancestors to treasure the blood of one. "A Man's Son, for instance, is but half of his Family, the other half belonging to the Family of his Wife. His Son, too marrying into another Family, his Share in the Grandson is but a fourth." "Thus in nine Generations," Franklin concluded, "(no very great Antiquity for a Family), our present Chevalier of the Order of Cincinnatus's Share in the then existing Knight, will be but a 512th part." A total of 1,022 men and women had created the "knight"— how could one male ancestor matter most?[34]

Franklin's denunciation of inherited status might have surprised his French friends, many of whom were aristocrats, but his was a common American sentiment in the 1780s. He emphasized his views in his autobiography after a British friend, Benjamin Vaughan, urged him, in 1783, to finish it. The work would be, Vaughan claimed, an "efficacious advertisement" for America and "tend to invite to it settlers of virtuous and manly minds." When Franklin resumed writing in 1784, he indeed picked up at his and his fellow workingmen's creation of the Library Company and his struggles to make his printing business a success. He insisted that he had "spent no time in Taverns, Games, or Frolicks"—an implicit warning to migrants who expected to be idle or frolicsome in America. Franklin seemed nostalgic. As he wrote, he decided to go home.[35]

———————

HE HAD SPENT ten years in France and had seriously considered staying there. (In fact, he had contemplated marriage, both for himself and for Temple.) But Franklin ultimately chose to spend his last years in Philadelphia. The long journey back would have severely tested any seventy-nine year old, but this one had gout and a kidney stone so big he felt it migrate when he turned in bed. He could not have endured a jolting coach all the way to the coast—that would have been screamingly painful. So the king and queen sent a royal litter and smoothly paced mules. The loan was kind. And it was shrewd—the royals doubtless wished to avoid the bad publicity that might result should the famous American die in agony on a French roadside. On July 12, 1785, Benny Bache reported that his grandfather "ascended his litter" while a crowd at Passy kept "a mournful silence . . . only interrupted by sobs." Once at Le Havre, Franklin and the entourage would take a channel boat for Southampton and then begin a sea passage for Philadelphia.[36]

It was quite an operation: a famous invalid, his two grandsons and grandnephew, their two tons of baggage—one disassembled printing press, one miniature of Louis XVI surrounded by diamonds (the king's standard parting gift to an ambassador), three Angora cats, one crate of fruit trees, twenty-three of books, four of scientific instruments, and so on. There was also a hanger-on, Jean-Antoine Houdon, the sculptor who had rendered Franklin in marble.

Why was Houdon heading for the United States? Franklin had said Americans could not afford fine art. And Houdon, acknowledged as the best sculptor of the day and a fine talent indeed, was exactly the kind of person Franklin had said would be as out of place in America as silk sheets on a camp bed. Yet Houdon would execute several American commissions, including a daringly shirtless George Washington. The sculptor's presence in the entourage showed Franklin's conviction that he and those around him were exceptional. America was no haven for geniuses, unless they were on the order of Benjamin Franklin, who could go where he pleased with whoever pleased him.[37]

On July 24, the Franklin party crossed the channel. That notoriously choppy body of water did not disappoint: "All sick except my Grandfather," Temple reported. Benny repeated the line—it must have been a rueful, much-repeated joke on everyone else. The old would-be sailor had sea legs. Franklin then refreshed himself at a saltwater bathing establishment in Southampton where the waters were so soothing that he floated and napped for almost an hour, remarking that it was "a thing I never did before."[38]

From Southampton, Franklin and his grandsons went up to London. Several of Franklin's oldest friends visited him there, and they promised to write or visit Philadelphia. But the Atlantic remained a formidable barrier. A very dear friend, Jonathan Shipley, the Bishop of St. Asaph, knew he would never see Franklin again; he stayed with him in London until the last minute. There was also a cool but cordial meeting with William Franklin, for whom Temple intended one of the Angoras. Alas, a servant managed to lose the cat (or sold it on the side) before the transfer. That pretty much summed up the family's lack of sweet reconciliation: there were some rather oddly expressed good intentions but no resolutions. And then, on July 29, it was time to go back to America.

The westward passage, Franklin's last Atlantic crossing, was probably his easiest. One can imagine that everyone on board took tender care of the famous passenger. He may even have conferred with the captain about their route. When the ship encountered another, Benny Bache recorded that it "proposed going to the no[r]th of the Azores and we to the south[, we] fearing the gulf stream, and he, the Algerines." Certainly, Franklin traveled like an aristocrat, with attendants and plenty of comforts—none of the inedible food or peremptory mariners of previous voyages. The journey took forty-nine days but, to understand what this meant, we should review all of Franklin's Atlantic crossings.

EAST	WEST
1724: 49 days	1726: 83 days
1757: 28 days	1762: 38 days
1764: 33 days	1775: 45 days
1776: 39 days	1785: 49 days

His average westbound voyage lasted almost 54 days, whereas the average going the other way was only 37, a difference of 16.5 days, over two weeks. (The extremes were the agonizingly slow return from London in 1726 and the amazingly fast wartime crossing in 1757.) Franklin's experience verified his point that something in the North Atlantic made its westbound traffic slower than the eastbound. Only the westward journey via Madeira, in 1762, beat the overall trend by avoiding the northernmost waters. And that route had been possible only because a truce prevented Spanish or French attacks on British ships.[39]

Franklin took advantage of the 1785 voyage to make his third set of readings of ocean temperature. His data were extensive. Clearly, he was determined not to lose the opportunity, deferred since 1776, to make a general statement about the Gulf Stream. He took readings for the forty-four days from July 29 to September 10, including the temperature of the air and water at eight in the morning and six in the evening. He also always noted the ship's position. On August 12, Franklin's party must have noticed (or someone pointed out to them) that a ship's officer calculated their position at noon, when the sun was at its zenith; Franklin thereafter made temperature readings three times a day, including noon.[40]

For his measurements, he surely relied on his spry grandsons, on his grandnephew (who recorded the data), and possibly on Houdon. Grandson Benny reported that he and the Frenchman braved the deck during an August gale, "contemplating the beauty of this spectacle." Benny would "now and then" go below "to tie down the sick who were turned upside down" in their hammocks or berths. Bursting with the unsympathetic health of youth, alert, and maybe getting under foot as the crew fought the gale, Benjamin Franklin Bache now resembled an earlier incarnation of his grandfather.[41]

The young Benjamin Franklin could never have imagined the welcome Philadelphia gave him on September 14, 1785. As he sailed in, the ships in the harbor, even the British ones, showed their colors. Hundreds of people crowded the docks, church bells rang, and cannon roared. It was quite a contrast to Franklin's first arrival in the city as an unkempt, hungry runaway. It rivaled the crowds and excitement he had seen for the Reverend George Whitefield, who had preached on the Court House steps in the 1740s, and for the Declaration of Independence, read on an astronomical platform before the State House in 1776. This time, the hullabaloo was all for him.

It was a relief to be home. Franklin described himself as "one, who, although he has crossed the Atlantic eight times, and made many smaller trips, does not recollect his having ever been at sea without taking a firm resolution never to go to sea again." He was delighted to see friends and family, especially Sally Bache and her children.[42]

Yet Philadelphia must have been a shock to Franklin. He had spent not quite two of the preceding twenty years in America, and his idea of a city was London or Paris. He surely noticed that the mass of Philadelphians who had greeted him was dwarfed by the thousands of assembled Parisians with whom he had watched the ascent of the first manned balloon. Franklin had worked so hard to establish himself in the centers of European knowledge. What did home mean for him?

Philadelphia's main advantage was its peace and quiet. Like his puritan ancestors, Franklin had crossed the ocean to get away from it all. In Paris, he had delighted in his importance. But his fame came at the old cost of the relentless demands of public service, and that was, in Paris, time-consuming. "Celebrity may for a while flatter one's Vanity," he had admitted to Ingenhousz, "but its Effects are troublesome"[43]

Franklin would be less troubled by fame at home. In the United States, he was not quite the idol he was in France. Nor, ironically, did he have as great a reputation in the new republic as he enjoyed in its vanquished enemy, Great Britain. Franklin would learn of his diminished importance when he requested reimbursement for his expenses in Paris. None ever came, nor did any official praise or thanks for his service. As in 1776, when he was ignored by his bedfellow John Adams, Franklin was remarkably alone with his philosophy.

Because science was becoming somewhat more specialized, it was being divided from other realms of knowledge, including politics. Adams had already made this distinction when he conceded that Franklin was "a great philosopher" but denied that he was a true "legislator" for the Republic. By the 1780s, young Americans, even if concerned with the human sciences, did not assume they had to learn about physics and chemistry—or nature in any form—in order to talk about politics. And politics were the focus of American life in the 1780s. Propertied men were very busy reworking state constitutions. Other pursuits, including the sciences, were pushed aside. Men with legal training and an extensive knowledge of political systems—such as Adams—were the center of attention.[44]

But the world had not changed altogether. The result was that, even though he was slighted in his home country, Franklin was still called on to serve his state and nation. He was annoyed that the political frenzy prevented his retirement yet again. From Paris, he had told a British friend, "I am going home *to go to bed!*" But someone or other kept hiding his nightshirt. He had scarcely unpacked before he was drafted as head of Pennsylvania's Executive Council—the governor, in effect. "I had on my return some right," Franklin complained to other friends, "to expect repose; and it was my intention to avoid all public business." Pennsylvanians had other plans. "I find myself harnessed again in their service. . . . They engrossed the prime of my life. They have eaten my flesh, and seem resolved now to pick my bones."[45]

And most of them ignored his strong suit, natural philosophy. As Franklin himself had predicted, the nation's happy mediocrity did not support learning. Americans had renounced the complex, hierarchical society that Britain had extended over the Atlantic. They now had neither monarch nor aristocrats to act as patrons. Until 1789, there was no central government that could invest in anything other than the basics, such as warships or postal riders. And the individual states, particularly after the war, had no resources for luxuries. "Philosophy," Philadelphia physician Benjamin Rush lamented, "does not here, as in England, walk abroad in silver slippers."[46]

In America, philosophers found refuge in two learned societies. The American Philosophical Society took seriously its status as the oldest learned society in the United States. Created in 1768 under colonial law, it had been incorporated anew in 1780 as part of a new political order. Meanwhile, John Adams had been the prime mover for the creation of Boston's American Academy of Arts and Sciences (AAAS) in 1780. But neither society shone very brightly. After its brilliant first volume of *Transactions*, showcasing colonial observations of the 1769 transit of Venus, the APS had produced nothing. The fledgling AAAS was even further behind.[47]

The inertia confirmed Old World prejudice. Europeans may finally have recognized the political independence of the United States, but they still rightly assumed its cultural dependence on the Old World. In 1774, the Abbé Raynal had come out and said what everyone was thinking, that it was "astonishing that America has not yet produced a good poet, an able mathematician, a man of genius in a single art, or a single science." A few years later, Raynal met Franklin, who disproved his words but proved his point: geniuses defied categorization. If Franklin was an exception, he was the exception who proved the rule.[48]

Americans resented European criticism, and members of U.S. learned societies tried to refute it. The United States had one significant advantage—North America's natural bounty. If they were willing to make the effort, Americans could use science to prove themselves twice over: they lived amid nature of stunning expanse and variety, and they could intellectually master that natural array, informing the world of new species and new phenomena.

In their 1780 act of incorporation, members of the APS defiantly claimed that the land "offers to these United States one of the richest subjects of cultivation, ever presented to any people upon earth." With less justification, the APS asserted that the "public spirited gentlemen" who founded the society, "to the great credit of America, have extended their reputation so far, that men of the first eminence in the republic of letters in the most civilized nations in Europe, have done honour to their publications, and desired to be enrolled among their members." This claim pretended that the singular gentleman who actually had done these things—Benjamin Franklin—was somehow representative of the plural gentlemen who, by and large, stood in his shadow.[49]

Members of the APS continued to keep in touch with European centers of learning. Indeed, the society's main business was processing news from abroad. In June 1784, the APS fellows had considered the Montgolfier description of balloons and hoped to send up an "*Air Ballon* by subscription." The society politely noted, on August 12, 1784, that "the marquis la Fayette entertained" it with an account of mesmerism. (Unfortunately for Lafayette, the Académie des Sciences's denunciation of the theory of animal magnetism arrived four months later.) The society was also gearing up to solicit new corresponding members. One was the Comte de Vergennes, who expressed his "Honour" at being rewarded for his assistance to the Republic by being selected. Such members were essential both as conduits of information and as potential donors—lacking American aristocrats, American men of science had to seek notables abroad.[50]

Franklin was, usefully, both an American and a European. The APS fellows had faithfully reelected him president in each year of his absence. They were ecstatic, incredulous that he had finally returned to them. Two days after his return, the APS formed a committee "to invite the Honourable *Doctor Franklin*, to take his Seat as *President*." On September 27, two weeks and a day after his arrival in Philadelphia, Franklin went to the society. "It reflects Honour on Philosophy," declaimed the official address to him, "when one, distinguished for his deep Investigations and many valuable Improvements in it, is known to be equally distinguished for his Philanthropy, Patriotism, and liberal attachment to the Rights of human Nature." By returning to the society, Franklin added "to the

Institution much Lustre in the eyes of all the World." He gave "grateful Acknowledgments" of the society's compliments.[51]

Then, everyone settled down to hear some letters and reports. Rather marvelously, these included a communication on "the East India manner of writing" and John Fitch's model and drawing of a boat powered by a "Steam Engine." Empire and expansion remained at the heart of the sciences. Americans were even interested in the British empire from which they had just removed themselves. Distant India could not but continue to fascinate them. Distance itself remained a compelling problem, though steam power offered a new way to conquer it.[52]

Franklin patronized each of the new nation's learned societies— the APS, in his adopted state, and the AAAS, in his native city. He kept in touch with James Bowdoin, an AAAS organizer. And he was extremely generous to the APS, using his diplomatic skills, money, and influence within Philadelphia to help the society produce its second volume of *Transactions* and to build a new meeting place. He also solicited new and important foreign members. In Paris, he had met Princess Ekaterina Romanovna Daschkova of Russia. When he learned that Catherine the Great had made Daschkova president of St. Petersburg's Academy of Sciences, he wrote to congratulate her and send a copy of "the second Volume of the Transactions of our Philosophical Society." Wheels were set into motion, and the princess became the first female member of the APS, indeed, of any U.S. learned society. In return, Daschkova invited Franklin to become a member of the St. Petersburg society, as he surely must have expected.[53]

But the brilliant European world of debate and demonstration was now only a memory for Franklin. Lamenting his agonizing kidney stone, Franklin wished he "had brought with me from France a balloon sufficiently large to raise me from the ground. In my malady it would have been the most easy carriage for me, being led by a string held by a man walking on the ground." What a comedown for the person who had sent an airborne "Philadelphia experiment" to France.[54]

But perhaps the absence of spectacle would let Franklin concentrate, as he had just managed to do at sea. He assured Louis-Guillaume Le Veillard that, en route, he had "written three pieces, each of some length; one on Nautical matters, another on Chimneys;

and a third a Description of my Vase [stove] for consuming smoke."
He intended all of these for "the Transactions of our Philosophical
Society." (Franklin neglected, however, the memoirs Le Veillard
wanted. He claimed he could write the essays "out of my own head,"
whereas "the little history" of his life required him to consult documents in Philadelphia.) Franklin had also promised Ingenhousz
that, via letters, they would continue to do "Plenty of Experiments
together." In Philadelphia, he had his old "Instruments if the Enemy did not destroy them all."[55]

It was a false hope. British officers had occupied the Franklin
home in 1777 and 1778, and Franklin's son-in-law had already
warned him of considerable losses. All of the musical instruments
(including the armonica), some of the "electric Aparatus," and
many of the books were taken, as well as Benjamin Wilson's oil
painting of Franklin (which was not recovered until 1906). Worse,
troops had ransacked a friend's house in Bucks County where
Franklin had stored a chest of papers, which has never been recovered. It would be hard for Franklin either to write about his life or
to do the experiments he had promised Ingenhousz.[56]

If he had gone home to "*go to bed*," Franklin must surely have
wanted to pull the covers over his head at times. He hinted as much
when he lamented his idleness to Mary Hewson. By idleness, he
meant that he was playing cards with his family. He relieved his guilt
by telling himself, "*You know that the soul is immortal; why then should
you be such a niggard of a little time, when you have a whole eternity before
you?*" He would then "shuffle the cards again, and begin another
game."[57]

FRANKLIN'S idleness was another person's diligence. As he shuffled
his cards, the American Philosophical Society finally produced the
second volume of its *Transactions*, which contained Franklin's final
philosophical efforts.

With some understatement, the editors explained in their preface that "the peculiar circumstances of America, since the publication of the first volume of the Transactions of this Society, will be a
sufficient apology for the long delay in publishing a second." If the
theme of the first volume had been Venus's transit over the sun, that
of its second was Franklin's career in the sciences. Anyone who

wants a crash course in Franklin's range of scientific interests can begin here, at the end. Of its forty-five essays, four were the ones Franklin had just completed on hygrometers, smoky chimneys, his vase stove, and maritime affairs—no electricity. Eleven essays by other authors were on topics Franklin had addressed earlier: thunder and lightning, waterspouts, electric eels, the aurora borealis, chimneys, meteorology, and maritime concerns. In total, a third of the essays were related to Franklin, and three out of the volume's four illustrations appeared in his contributions.[58]

When members of the APS publications committee stated that they had discovered "materials more than sufficient for a second volume of Transactions," they hinted that the selection of Franklin-related material had been deliberate. Franklin was the society's foremost patron; of the nine pages that listed donations (books, money, instruments), two came under his name. The list of foreign members likewise showed his influence, including as it did Barbeu-Dubourg (a posthumous honor), Lafayette, Lavoisier, Le Roy, and Vergennes, as well as Joseph Priestley and Richard Price, two British men of science who had criticized Britain's war against the former colonies. In a way, Franklin had become the new James Logan, his old friend who had, decades earlier, been Philadelphia's premier patron of learning.[59]

Franklin's essays got pride of place within the *Transactions*. His piece on smoky chimneys opened it—very fitting, given that his essay on Pennsylvania fireplaces was his first experimental piece. And of all the volume's essays, Franklin's "Maritime Observations" was the most elaborate, comprising the essay, tables of data, illustrations, and a chart.

It was a gift. Franklin could have published the essay in Europe, as he had done with others quite recently. Had it appeared abroad, the piece might have circulated even more widely and been recognized for what it was, the most extensive study of sea-surface temperatures to date. Instead, Franklin used the essay patriotically, to anchor a U.S. publication and to proclaim the virtues of his nation and its people.

He had originally composed the piece as a letter to Julien-David Le Roy, architect and ship-building brother of his steadfast friend. The epistolary genesis shows. Even in published form, the piece drifts over a variety of salty topics, mostly on existing problems of navigation and nautical technology. All were harvested from Franklin's extended engagement with the sea.[60]

Franklin pleaded with sailors to entertain "the advice of land-men," and he poured out over thirty-one pages of it. He offered his own ship and sail designs and had, of course, tested his model sails with an "experiment." (He subjected a ship's model to a "steady current of air" from a hole in his "kitchen chimney.") Franklin recommended ways of loading ships. He advised captains to carry lightning rods and a sailcloth brake to be used in the water "on almost the same principles with those of a paper kite used in the air. Only as the paper kite rises in the air, this is to descend in the water" and slow the ship. He commented on a design to use a jet of water to propel a boat and proposed a steam engine to assist the water's force. He also recommended ways to prevent a ship being flooded (lessening insurance costs) and considered William Petty's seventeenth-century design for a double-hulled ship, much like the "outriggers" of "the islanders in the great Pacific."[61]

An ominous amount of the essay recommended ways to preserve lives at sea. During his many passages, Franklin must have thought about this subject a great deal. He extolled the ways in which Captain Cook had secured "the health of the sailors" he commanded on his Pacific voyages and how he had, on his final voyage, followed Franklin's advice on preserving breadstuffs. Franklin outlined how a shipwreck survivor could make an emergency compass with a needle in a cup of water. If facing a "long traverse" to swim, the survivor could also rig a kite from a handkerchief to help drag his or her body through the water. He told passengers how to keep and prepare food at sea, warning that ships' fowls and biscuit were "tough" and "too hard for some sets of teeth." And he stressed the importance of selecting, whenever possible, a "sociable, good natured" captain.[62]

Parts of the essay were surprisingly moralizing. Franklin restated his convictions that Atlantic migration should be voluntary and should lift up the deserving. He recommended that private passengers take extra stores, not merely for their own comfort but to relieve the "poorer passengers." These "superfluities distributed occasionally may be of great service, restore health, save life, make the miserable happy, and thereby afford you infinite pleasure." Conversely, Franklin deplored the "pillaging [of] merchants and transporting slaves" from Africa; both, he implied, were forms of piracy. The slave trade was "clearly the means of augmenting the mass of human misery." Its common end product, sugar, was "thoroughly dyed scarlet" in human blood.[63]

Then, deep within the "Maritime Observations," Franklin devoted about three pages to the Gulf Stream, appending, as well, four pages of data and the fold-out chart. Here, he finally offered an authoritative account of the current, one he had not provided on either of his earlier charts. In this piece, he established that he had used a thermometer to investigate the Atlantic before anyone else. By embedding his discussion within some impressive slabs of knowledge about ships and the sea, he made clear that he had thought long and carefully about his topic.

Franklin began with his faulty recollection that his first cartographic effort came "about the year 1769 or 70," when the Boston Board of Customs had complained about different travel times across the Atlantic. (Had he forgotten his 1784 discussion, with Pownall, of the 1768 publication of his chart?) Franklin explained that, to solve the problem, he had consulted "a Nantucket seacaptain of my acquaintance," who told him of "the gulf stream," marked it on a chart, and added "directions for avoiding it in sailing from Europe to North-America." This information was then "engraved" for the Post Office "on the old chart of the Atlantic, at Mount and Page's."[64]

Franklin concluded that the gigantic Atlantic current was "probably generated by the great accumulation of water on the eastern coast of America between the tropics, by the trade winds which constantly blow there." The winds "heaped up" water that then issued "through the gulph of Florida, and proceeding along the coast to the banks of Newfoundland, where it turns off towards and runs down through the Western islands." He listed the three aspects of the stream he had seen in his several voyages: its gulfweed, its being "always warmer than the sea on each side of it," and its failure to "sparkle in the night" with phosphorescence. Franklin also noted the warmth of the air above the stream; when it collided with colder air from the north, it would "form those tornados and water-spouts frequently met with, and seen near and over the stream."[65]

If Franklin was restating his many efforts to study the Atlantic's winds, waterspouts, and currents, it was a restatement with a difference. This time, he slighted global causes in favor of local ones. Decades earlier, he had speculated that the earth's rotation must matter. And in his manuscript version of the "Maritime Observations," he likewise stated that the globe's "Diurnal Motion" helped explain "the expediting and retarding [of] the Voyages between N.

America and England." But Franklin deleted this phrasing at the last minute. He explained to Jonathan Williams Jr. that he was "on Consideration convinc'd that its Effect is equal both ways," eastward and westward. Franklin's preference for the local was evident, as well, in his new reticence to trace Atlantic circulation past the "Western Islands."[66]

It is significant that he was not forsaking the larger world entirely, just in this one essay. He had speculated on the composition of the globe and on global weather patterns as recently as 1784. And he wrote Ingenhousz in 1785, "with regard to the Tides, I doubt the Opinion of there being but two High Waters and two Low Waters existing at the same time on the Globe. I rather think there are many, and those at the Distance of about 100 Leagues from each other." Observations of the Pacific would "confirm or refute" the idea and allow the eventual charting of tidal patterns over the entire globe. The world retreated, however, as Franklin found one final meaning for the Gulf Stream—as evidence of the United States' independence.[67]

The chart that illustrated "Maritime Observations" shows just how much Franklin was shrinking his world for this essay. He had given Philadelphia engraver James Poupard a copy of his Le Rouge chart, but the result was a free interpretation of the original. Poupard was no cartographer, and his limited abilities showed, especially in his crude rendition of the American coastline, with a drooping Florida. Yet Poupard captured quite well the politics of mapping in the early Republic. Only the territory of the United States was in sharp focus.

The arrangement of land and water was the key to the map—and to the nation. Poupard placed a landmass, the territory of the United States, between two fluid crescents, the Mississippi River in the west and the Gulf Stream in the east. Each waterway led the citizens of the United States out to the rest of the world. In this cramped space, Poupard could barely include the Mississippi—a bend of the river announces that it is indeed there, though the rest of it runs off the map. This rendition was a contrast to the two charts Franklin had produced earlier. The first, Mount and Page's of 1768, had gloried in distance, recklessly representing entire oceans, whole continents, and a vast British empire. The second, Le Rouge's of circa 1783, had emphasized the whole ocean between the United States and France, though it had excluded the Mississippi, probably because it was the object of contention at the Paris peace negotiations.

Franklin's third chart of the Gulf Stream. *Transactions of the
American Philosophical Society* 2 (1786). PRIVATE COLLECTION.

The Poupard illustration omitted the larger ocean and territories
that had dominated its two predecessors. It implied a specific and
continental destiny for the United States. Clearly, Franklin had the
fate of the continent on his mind. As he saw his "Maritime Observations" to press, he scoffed at Spanish offers to allow the United
States free ascent of the Mississippi. "The Use of the River for *ascending* with Ships is worth very little," he reminded a friend; "but for *descending*, it is of great Importance to all our Country beyond the
Mountains."[68]

It is surprising, however, that Franklin did not try to represent the
Gulf Stream, either in words or in Poupard's picture, as part of a
larger oceanic circulation. He forsook not only a global explanation
of the Gulf Stream but also and even more remarkably the concept
of equilibrium. Why was Benjamin Franklin, the connoisseur of

balances (hot and cold, negative and positive), still not worried about where all the Gulf Stream's water *went?* Why did he accept a chart that did not make any of the big claims about oceans and empires that he had been pondering for decades?

Thrift may be part of the explanation. The APS had limited funds—American learning indeed lacked silver slippers or silver anything. The Poupard illustration served two essays, Franklin's "Maritime Observations" and John Gilpin's piece on the migration of herring (they are busy swimming in the upper left corner). It only included as much Atlantic as was needed to show the main crescent of the Gulf Stream, leaving the rest of the ocean to the viewer's imagination. Yet nearby, all those determined fish swim a rebukingly circular pattern in the whole North Atlantic.[69]

His tight focus on the Gulf Stream revealed Franklin in a final guise: romantic nationalist. Long before, when he had produced his 1768 chart of the Gulf Stream, he had assured Anthony Todd that Americans had maritime skills that the British should admire. Now, in 1786, Franklin published an even longer version of this claim. He lauded American mariners, especially those plucky Nantucketers. He did not name Timothy Folger, but the cast-off loyalist cousin might have been surprised to see that Franklin ventriloquized him to rebuke British captains: "We have informed them that they were stemming a current, that was against them to the value of three miles an hour; and advised them to cross it and get out of it; but they were too wise to be counselled by [a] simple American fisherman." Franklin also announced that British packet captains had "slighted" his 1768 chart. (There is no evidence for this.) The French were wiser, he implied to his French correspondent, Le Roy, to whom he had written the letter on which the essay was based. The chart was "since printed in France, of which edition I hereto annex a copy."[70]

So in the end, Franklin credited mariners, *American* mariners, for knowing about the Gulf Stream, though (as during the war) he cloaked them in sentimental patriotism—and he still did not name them. Alongside the Poupard chart, he ran a version of Folger's sailing instructions and gushed about the "whalemen" who knew all about the tricky Gulf Stream. But the name and the initials that accompany the directions are "B. Franklin" and "B. F." Franklin named only one mariner, the (American) "Captain Truxton" on whose vessel he had sailed in 1785, the man who promised to test, on a voyage to China, a canvas anchor of Franklin's design.[71]

Franklin also defined the thermometer as a new hydrographic instrument. His "Maritime Observations" presented three pages of thermal data, from the three years he had collected them (1775, 1776, and 1785). The spread of numbers amply made the points that Franklin had been among the very few naturalists who used thermometers to study the sea's surface and that he had more and more elaborate measurements of temperature than anyone else. Henceforth, he claimed, "the thermometer may be an useful instrument to a navigator."[72]

Franklin was criticizing the existing techniques of navigation. At that point in history, mariners still had to stand on heaving decks, whatever the weather, and use fairly complicated instruments, such as sextants, to figure out where they were. In addition, sailors needed cumulative experience—both as individuals and as a community—of the sea and of ships. Technology, including chronometers and newly detailed charts, would enable them to read the state of nature more quickly. Thermometers would also, Franklin implied, lessen the need for experience or careful training—drop one in the water, and you knew where you were. He predicted a future in which men of science would design the instruments and sailors would then use them. The division between head and hands would widen.

The thermometer was just the beginning. On Franklin's 1785 voyage, his grandnephew, Jonathan Williams, had tested two other devices. Franklin had probably advised Williams and certainly found the results worth discussing in his "Maritime Observations." One instrument was "an empty bottle, corked very tight," that was sent down deeper and deeper until, at thirty-five fathoms, the water pressure "forced in the cork." Williams hauled up the resulting water sample from that depth, "six degrees colder than [water] at the surface." Then Williams deployed a sea gauge modeled on Stephen Hales's instrument, described in the *Philosophical Transactions* that had contained one of Franklin's early electricity pieces. Williams's version was a keg with "a valve at each end, one opening inward, the other outward." The bottom valve leaked, but the imperfect sample from eighteen fathoms was nevertheless "12 degrees colder than at the surface." It was an early example of deep-sea exploration. The technology remained little improved until the second half of the nineteenth century.[73]

Ocean currents, physical circulation, seaborne observations, Atlantic weather, charts, definitions of place and distance—by returning to some of the oldest questions of his career, Franklin had come full circle. His earliest ambitions had been either to attend college or run away to sea. The "Maritime Observations" shows that, in a remarkable way, he had done both—he had combined natural philosophy with engagement in the public affairs of the Atlantic world. (He inspired others to think of the Gulf Stream in political terms. In 1790, Tom Paine declared the French Revolution "as fixed as the Gulf Stream." Jonathan Williams claimed the current's waters were as distinct as "the colours of red, white and blue.")[74]

The Poupard engraving illustrates Franklin's engagement in Atlantic affairs. In the lower right-hand corner, Franklin points at the sea, personified as Neptune. Moreover, he appears to be haranguing Neptune, perhaps enlightening the god on some aspect of his own watery medium. And why not? In many earlier paintings and engravings, Franklin extends an insistent finger and consorts with deities. The Poupard engraving is less polished than the British and European images that had created these ideas of Franklin. In a charming way, however, it brings to America a grand Old World tradition of celebrating Franklin's power over the physical and social worlds of the Atlantic.[75]

But however brilliant its insights and however ambitious its collection of data, the "Maritime Observations" seems unfinished. The temperature readings are all there, but they remain substantially unanalyzed; the patriotic focus on a small corner of the Atlantic world seems forced, given Franklin's ongoing interest in the whole planet. Perhaps, had Franklin had more time, he could have followed up with another and more synthetic essay.[76]

Perhaps . . . the word lingers over Franklin's life in science. One political crisis after another, from the Seven Years' War to the formation of the United States, had prevented his full-time pursuit of natural philosophy. The "ifs" proliferate: if he had had time to do more experiments, if he had accepted patronage from Britain's great and good, if he had stayed in England even after the colonies broke away.

Then there's the biggest if. What if the American Revolution had never happened? Franklin is so associated with that event that it may seem improper for anyone—and unpatriotic for an American—to ask the question. But Franklin's hallowed status as Revolutionary and Founder may obscure how the Declaration of Independence and War of Independence did a kind of damage to his life. What if, instead, he had been able to settle permanently in London? He would have become a fixture among British men of letters and followed all the new developments in electrical and chemical demonstrations. Might he have bequeathed to later "scientists" still other insights? Would we still have a sense that the electrical experiments of the 1740s were his intellectual peak? Or might he have continued to develop, fully, as a natural philosopher? The evidence from the 1760s through the 1780s points in too many directions.

Without the American Revolution to distract him, perhaps Franklin might have been an even greater figure in the sciences; perhaps not. Every great life should have a mystery at its center—this is Benjamin Franklin's.

IN THE SPRING of 1787, one year after his "Maritime Observations" appeared in the APS *Transactions*, Franklin was longing yet again for the one thing he lacked—repose. He hoped to get it either by resigning his gubernatorial office or, failing that, "by ceasing to live." But just then, a convention met in Philadelphia to discuss the writing of a new constitution for the United States. There was no escape: Franklin became the convention's oldest delegate.[77]

He was not always perceived as its most diligent. (He was literally caught napping.) Characteristically, he refrained from addressing the full assembly and instead worked more quietly in committees and with private conferences. And at least some of Franklin's fellow delegates were not sure he was qualified as a legislator. A Georgia delegate stated that "Dr. Franklin is well known to be the greatest philosopher of the present age . . . the very heavens obey him. . . . But what claim he has to be a politician, posterity must determine."[78]

Franklin did make some contributions to the U.S. Constitution. Moreover, those contributions were interesting evidence of how he thought science would assist politics and how it would not or even should not.

Franklin was revealingly silent on the clause of the constitution that actually mentioned science. Article I, Section 8 gave the federal government power "to promote the Progress of Science and useful Arts, by securing for limited Time to Authors and Inventors the exclusive Right to their respective Writings and Discoveries." The section was the origin of U.S. patent law, and Franklin disapproved. Other delegates drafted, argued, and revised the clause; the convention's most famous "Author and Inventor" did not help them.[79]

Franklin thought authors and inventors should get credit for their creations but not benefit financially. Certainly, he wanted credit for what he had invented. Having worn his bifocals for decades, he had made sure to tell a London friend, in 1785, exactly what they were and how they worked. He had even provided a diagram and corrected the opinion of an eminent London instrument maker and optician about their function. But he claimed no right to any reward for his "double Spectacles." And he had even earlier stated, in his autobiography, that he had never wished to patent his Pennsylvania fireplace. He had allowed another man to do so (he got "a little Fortune by it") because he believed *that as we enjoy great Advantages from the Inventions of others, we should be glad of an Opportunity to serve others by any Invention of ours.*[80]

Nor did Franklin assist two rival patent seekers who were trying to develop a working steamboat as the Constitutional Convention met. The steamboat would play a major role in the new nation. Steam power, like ballooning, represented another attempt to conquer distance. Vehicles powered by steam could move faster and against powerful currents. As Americans threatened to take over at least part of a continent and to find the means to ascend the Mississippi River, the promise of steam power was immense. It was not yet clear, however, if the new inventions would fulfill their promise.

James Rumsey and John Fitch had each designed steam engine–powered boats, and each sought support anywhere he could find it. They both curried favor from the various states. Fitch also angled for federal help. He demonstrated his boat on the Delaware River while the Constitutional Convention met—it was a pleasant diversion for the delegates and invaluable advertising for Fitch. Both Rumsey and Fitch approached the APS and solicited its fabled president. Franklin let Fitch copy the part of his manuscript "Maritime Observations" that discussed using a jet of water to power boats. But he worried that the steamboat's construction and operation were far too expensive. In the end, Rumsey got APS support to go to England, where he could buy a Watt and Boulton steam engine for his experiments and, if they were successful, apply for a British patent. Franklin's letter of introduction for Rumsey explained his emigration as necessary because "another Mechanician of this Country is endeavouring to deprive him of such Advantage, by pretending a prior Right to the Invention."[81]

Franklin still assumed that knowledge was cumulative and collaborative, that it should be made public for the good of all. Newton had modestly claimed that he could see further than others only because he "stood on the Shoulders of Giants." Franklin, Newton's acolyte, continued to see things that way. But even he, the old Newtonian, accepted that older and wealthier countries, such as England, should have patent law. That was why he encouraged Rumsey to go there to work on his steam engine. In the more complicated and wealthier countries of Europe, patent laws encouraged innovation—and the state could pay for the encouragement. But the happy mediocrity of the United States could not support anything comparable. Younger Americans saw things differently. The constitution's clause on intellectual property was approved and still exists.[82]

Maybe the nation could not yet help science, Franklin thought, but science could help the nation. The field of political arithmetic gave him one last chance to define his new nation, particularly its system of representation.

The drafters of the Articles of Confederation had not accepted political representation based on population, as Franklin had recommended. But the men who drafted the Constitution considered the possibility more carefully. At the convention, debate over systems of representation reached an impasse. There was agreement that two houses, upper and lower, should represent the states. But how should representation—and contributions to national finances—be apportioned among the states? Delegates from big states proposed that population should determine numbers of national representatives in both houses, upper and lower; delegates from small states feared they and their descendants might, within such a system, be trampled on.

Franklin urged compromise yet insisted that "the number of Representatives Should bear some proportion to the number of the Represented." He proposed a ratio of one member of the lower house for every 40,000 inhabitants. This idea died in committee. But a ratio between population and representatives in the lower house, balanced by a fixed number of senators for each state, eventually passed. This "Great Compromise" finally rejected the "virtual representation" that had precipitated the Revolution. The size of a state's population would determine its political power in the House of Representatives, as well as its contribution to national taxes. The delegates also proposed a national census, to be taken every ten years. The first was done in 1790, eleven years before the former home country, Great Britain, managed to do the same.[83]

Franklin had long believed that population—a growing body of producers and consumers—was the true measure of America's power. The U.S. Constitution enshrined that idea. The document is an excellent example of how the science of political arithmetic, in which Franklin had been a pioneer, had become, at the end of his life, an accepted tool of politics.

The constitutional debate also gave Franklin an opportunity to argue for the value of all workingmen, including sailors. They were still considered the lowest of the low because they were among the least likely to own property. Other delegates in Philadelphia proposed property requirements for the franchise. Franklin rose in protest and uncharacteristically addressed the entire convention. A property requirement would, he lamented, disqualify the maritime heroes of the Revolution, who had received little enough for their efforts. (Congress had offered land bounties to many people during the war but never to sailors, not even naval officers.) Franklin insisted that workers were, no less than property holders, qualified to vote. "The late war is a glorious Testimony in favor of plebian Virtue," he lectured. "I know that our Seamen prisoners in England refused all Allurements to draw them from their Allegiance—they were threatened with Halters but refused."[84]

Franklin's claim was not strictly true. (Some seamen had defected.) And it did not convince the other delegates, who went on to draft property requirements for voters. But it was an amazing preview of the momentous debates that would occur in the age of Andrew Jackson over extending the franchise to all free white men. Franklin's argument marked his long series of debts to sailors and his even longer memory of the value of ordinary working people. True, sailors were no longer as valuable for their knowledge as they had once been. Scientific expertise was changing that. But Franklin did not believe that this demotion meant that working men were any less capable as political actors—he continued to wrap sailors in the sentimental patriotism he had used in wartime to denounce their imprisonment. Above all, he held true to his old idea that the ability to work defined a person's value.

He had been quiet and even sleepy during parts of the convention. But Franklin managed to get in the last word. As the moment arrived for a final vote on the document, he delivered the convention's final speech. He did so out of fear that disagreements among the delegates might drag debate out even further and eventually prevent a strongly favorable vote for the Constitution.

In his September 17 oration, Franklin distinguished between opinion and system. He confessed himself unable to agree with each word of the constitution. But that was not the point. "When you assemble a Number of Men, to have the Advantage of their joint Wisdom," he told his fellow delegates, "you inevitably assemble with those Men all their Prejudices, their Passions, their Errors of Opinion." *Opinion* inescapably characterized the human condition, as Franklin had emphasized in his 1731 "Apology for Printers" and had reiterated in his 1766 interview in Parliament on the Stamp Act.[85]

As he had on those occasions, Franklin insisted that opinion did not need to divide people. Indeed, he said, it might help the delegates see their handiwork as contingent, necessarily and productively contingent. Franklin acknowledged that political theorists might wish to create within the United States a "System." He thus used a word associated with natural science, one that implied a theoretically coherent scheme for human governance. But this goal was an impossible one. Unlike the laws of nature, the constitution would never elicit universal assent. It could never be perfect. But Franklin was pleased to find "this System approaching so near to Perfection as it does." He urged any who, like himself, believed "in his own Infallibility" to vote to accept the document. A unanimous vote would be far more authoritative than a divided outcome. By confronting their opinions, the measures of their infallibility, delegates could achieve consensus.[86]

It was Franklin's final public statement on the connections between science and human affairs. Throughout his life, he had considered many definitions of knowledge. He had considered the place of opinion in public life. He had used probability to examine questions of life and death. He had sometimes used a Newtonian language of nature's laws. In the 1740s, Franklin had made Polly Baker declare her belief in the laws of nature and nature's God; in 1776, he may have helped Thomas Jefferson put similar words into the Declaration of Independence. But a few years later, surrounded by French Physiocrats, Franklin had overheard French mayflies, ephemera, declare the futility of any political system. Those short-lived, garrulous insects had evidently followed him back to Philadelphia, where they buzzed in his ears yet again.

Franklin, the first scientific American, argued that the United States should be founded on a reasonable acceptance of doubt. He questioned whether certainty had any place in public affairs and pleaded for toleration of a variety of opinions. People would always disagree with each other, as he had explained in his "Apology for Printers," but their differences did not have to prevent civil exchange with each other. By restating the idea in 1787, Franklin cleverly acknowledged the disagreements among the delegates yet identified a way for them to transcend them honorably. He thus guaranteed that the U.S. Constitution would gain the acceptance of all those who had helped write it. Immediately after his speech, his motion was carried with the unanimous vote he had wanted.

But Franklin let opinion overrule him in another and more tragic way. However admirably he had deployed political arithmetic to defend ordinary white people, he did not use it to champion the rights of the truly oppressed. The final constitution, on which the signature of "Benj. Franklin" appeared, included the notorious "three-fifths" clause. Until the Civil War wiped it away, that clause meant that each slave would count as three-fifths of a free person for the purposes of representation and taxation. A related clause declared that unless they paid taxes, Indians did not count at all. There is reason to believe Franklin was critical, even regretful, about the three-fifths clause. But he may have agreed that Indians should be excluded from the new nation.

He was very careful not to mention slavery at the Constitutional Convention—of all issues discussed there, it was the one most likely to threaten the equanimity and compromise he sought. But in the year the convention met, he made a public statement against slavery when he agreed to serve as president of the Pennsylvania Society for Promoting the Abolition of Slavery, and the Relief of Free Negroes Unlawfully Held in Bondage. As the organization's president, Franklin helped prepare a mission statement. In this document, he went well beyond criticism of the slave trade and attacked slavery itself.

Moreover, the statement insisted that people of African descent had the capacity to acquire not just liberty but also "civil liberty."

This wording implied that they or their descendants might become citizens. The Republic could not, Franklin believed, contain populations doomed to permanent inferiority and exclusion. So slaves had to be freed. But their mere manumission could not undo the effects of slavery, "an atrocious debasement of human nature." Education and other assistance had to "promote the public good, and the happiness of these our hitherto too much neglected fellow-creatures." It was the most radical opinion Franklin ever expressed, one that only a handful of his white contemporaries shared.[87]

Nor did it match Franklin's thoughts on other non-European peoples, especially Indians. In the wake of the Seven Years' War, he had defended their rights. Now, he assumed that they would and should vanish from the land. Like many of his contemporaries, he believed that Indians did not use the land to its full capacity. "The World is large," he told an English friend, "and a great Part of it still uncultivated," which would have surprised the thousands of Indians who now found themselves under U.S. control. Franklin was not, in this matter, a disinterested party. He had retained his shares in the Walpole Company, one of many groups that had claimed western land after the Seven Years' War. Even during the War of Independence, Franklin had sought information about the British company under the pseudonym Mr. Moses, for whom North America was the Promised Land.[88]

Franklin nevertheless hoped the states and the Republic would avoid conflict with Indians. In late 1787, he wrote Samuel Elbert, the governor of Georgia, that "almost every War between the Indians and Whites has been occasion'd by some Injustice of the latter toward the former." This statement was a nod toward the defense of Indians he had made after the Paxton Massacre.[89]

Yet in a section of his autobiography, composed just after he wrote to Elbert, Franklin was less conciliatory. Remembering a 1753 treaty ceremony at Carlisle, Pennsylvania, Franklin described how the Indians got drunk afterward. "Their dark-colour'd Bodies, half naked" and "their horrid Yellings," he had stated, resembled "our Ideas of Hell." Franklin had forgotten what he had actually written about the incident in 1753: that the fault lay with the traders who plied Indians with liquor, threatening all the careful diplomacy. His selective memory served his opinion, circa 1788, that "if it be the Design of Providence to extirpate these Savages in order to make room for Cultivators of the Earth, it seems not improbable that Rum may be the appointed Means." It had already "annihilated all the Tribes who formerly inhabited the Sea-coast."[90]

Franklin was not alone—many white Americans made this mordant, self-interested prediction. Certainly, it supported his vision of a settler population inexorably filling North America. Through his antislavery activities, Franklin significantly modified his earlier racism against people of African descent. But he did not reassess Indians in the same way. Indeed, he continued to see their bodies as significantly weaker than those of rum-resistant whites. He had always used political arithmetic aggressively to champion white Americans as North America's true inhabitants. He never lost a taste for doing so.

RETIRED from the Pennsylvania Executive Council in the fall of 1788, Franklin told a French friend, "I begin to feel myself a Freeman, and to enjoy the little Leisure that the Remnant of Life may afford me." This time, he was right. At the age of eighty-two, Franklin left public service.[91]

He used his "little Leisure" to work on his memoirs. He had written a long section of them in 1774, then a shorter one starting in 1784. Beginning in 1788, he wrote another section, similar in length to the first. He enjoyed the task: "Calling past Transactions to Remembrance makes it seem a little like living one's Life over again." He relived one of the best parts. In the penultimate section of his autobiography, Franklin summarized his electrical experiments. He began with Collinson's gift of the electric "Tube," recalled the breathless months of experimentation, and detailed his eventual success in France (including the old battle with the Abbé Nollet). Finally, he noted his "sudden and general Celebrity" and "infinite Pleasure" over his successes.[92]

But he had waited too long. The autobiography ends in 1759. Franklin had just time to get to his experience aboard Walter Lutwidge's *General Wall* in 1757. He recounted how Ludwidge fiddled with his ship until it proved "the best Sailer in the Fleet." From this experience, he recommended uniformity in ships' construction, rigging, lading, and sailing. "I think a Set of Experiments might be instituted" to discover optimal standards for all this, much as Cadwallader Colden had long ago recommended. "Erelong,"

Franklin hoped, "some ingenious Philosopher will undertake it: to whom I wish Success."[93]

This passage is the autobiography's final reference to the sciences, falling within a dozen pages of its end. Its placement and Franklin's leaving it to others are valedictory, very much in the spirit of his admonition to "enjoy great Advantages from the Inventions of others."

Franklin laid aside his autobiography (as he had done his philosophical work) and would write his final thoughts in letters. As he had done at the start of his life, Franklin mixed personal letters with ones to fellow men of letters and ones written under pseudonyms. His second to last letter was a March 23, 1790, diatribe against the slave trade, published in the *Federal Gazette*. Significantly, it was an indication both of Franklin's abolitionist resolve and of the heated public debate over the slave trade. With this letter, he invented one last alias, Sidi Mehemet Ibrahim. Ibrahim parodied southern pro-slavery arguments in the guise of refuting protests against North African enslavement of Europeans. Mere hypocrisy, Ibrahim declared: "Even England treats its Sailors as Slaves." (Around this time, Franklin signed his last public document, a Pennsylvania Abolition Society petition to Congress.)[94]

Franklin also used letters to say good-bye to his scattered family, especially his beloved sister, Jane Mecom, who still lived in Boston. He asked her whether she knew anything of their Nantucket relations and gingerly noted his estrangement from them. For years, he said, none "were disposed to be acquainted with me, except Captain Timothy Foulger." The war had divided Franklin from his loyalist kin, and he had, of course, broken with his last connection to Nantucket, Folger. Franklin had invited some other of the island cousins to dinner a year earlier: "Their answer was, that they would, if they could not do better." "I admire," he wryly allowed, "their honest plainness of Speech." They never showed up. Franklin's penultimate letter, of March 24, 1790, was again to Jane and was again a plea for news of their extended family.[95]

Franklin's very last letter was to a fellow man of letters. Thomas Jefferson had asked about the boundary between British and U.S. territories in the northern maritimes. Jefferson reported that British settlers had been appearing on what U.S. officials considered the wrong side of the line. On April 8, 1790, Franklin wrote that he "was perfectly clear in the remembrance" of the map used in the peace deliberations in Paris. He assured Jefferson that Congress probably had a copy of the map. Also, John Adams would surely remember this point of the Paris deliberations, and Jefferson could consult him. Franklin apologized for his delay in answering Jefferson— "your letter found me under a severe fit of my malady."[96]

It was amazing that Franklin could still write or even dictate letters. Gout and the kidney stone were still his companions. The appetite-suppressing opiates he took against the pain had reduced him to skeletal frailty. But the critical problem was congestion in his lungs, his old weakness. On April 2, fifteen days before he died, he grew feverish and his breathing was more labored—he wrote his letter to Jefferson just in time. Six days before his death, an abscess in his lungs burst, releasing fluid. That ended the chest pains, but Franklin could no longer speak. Lucid before, he became lethargic and was unconscious for his last half day. We have no way of knowing his final thoughts—whether of family, philosophy, eternity. He died at about eleven o'clock at night on April 17, 1790.[97]

Franklin perished, John Adams jibed, as "a Sacrifice" to "his own theory; having caught the violent Cold, which finally choaked him, by sitting for some hours at a Window." At the Constitutional Convention, Franklin had claimed to abjure theory, in the form of political "system." Adams, however, had not forgotten Franklin's earlier career, in which the natural philosopher had made his name by theorizing about forms of circulation. Adams claimed his version of events came from Franklin's own doctor. But the story bore a nasty similarity to accounts of the death of Francis Bacon in 1625. According to rumors, Bacon had wanted to test his theory that cold would preserve meat. Equipped with a dead chicken, out he went into the snow. He stuffed the bird with snow and, while he did so, caught a cold. The cold turned into pneumonia, and he died—thus the folly of natural philosophers. Franklin's interest in theories of nature, Adams mocked, had been his death.[98]

At the least, Adams had neatly diagnosed Franklin's lifelong dread of "colds." Work backward through Franklin's health crises: his death from pleurisy in 1790, the severe "cold" that confined him to bed in London in 1757, the bout of pleurisy in 1735 (when another lung abscess had burst), and then the possible root of the problem, the "Pleurisy that nearly carried me off" at twenty-one in 1727, after the longest and most grueling of his Atlantic passages. Now work forward through Franklin's persistent analysis of "colds" and of the circulation of breathable air: his fascination with Hales, his 1732 *Pennsylvania Gazette* discussion of colds, his imagining a way to heat rooms that would prevent cold- and pleurisy-producing drafts, his wandering examination of the causes of colds as he faced disgrace in the Cockpit in 1774, his dispute with the window-closing Adams two years later, his concern for Priestley's gasping mice, and his delight with Ingenhousz's air-emitting plants.

He had made his body his first object of study, and Franklin, a gifted student of nature, had figured out that body's fatal flaw. Unlike his eyesight, this flaw could not be repaired. Circulation of air, his first problem in the sciences, was his last problem in life.

About his physical mortality, Franklin had always been suitably philosophical. He and his weak lungs had, after all, managed to elude death for eighty-four years. And Franklin had always counted on immortality. His epitaph of 1728 had predicted his body would be "Food for Worms" but his soul bound to appear in "a new & more perfect Edition." He was no less hopeful in his first surviving will, of 1750. He imagined himself in death—"reposing my self securely in the Lap of God and Nature as a Child in the Arms of an affectionate Parent." He would become, again, a newborn baby.[99]

Chapter 10

AFTERLIFE

W HAT is Franklin's monument? In 1790, when he delivered a eulogy on Franklin for the Commune of Paris, the Abbé Claude Fauchet imagined a monument in the middle of the Atlantic Ocean. There, a pyramid would bear Franklin's image and would be inscribed, on the sides facing Europe and America, "Men, love humanity; be free and open the doors of the nation to all." Fauchet's idea for a memorial celebrated the centrality of the Atlantic to Franklin's life. And it suggested that it would take a whole ocean to provide a sufficiently impressive backdrop for that life. Certainly, Franklin would have enjoyed the idea of being commemorated in the middle of the North Atlantic, the ocean that he had crossed eight times, had studied, and had put at the center of his life. But the monument would have had a kind of built-in obsolescence. In the age of sail, travelers would have seen it as they crossed the Atlantic. In the age of steam, even more people could have paid it a visit. But in the age of flight, the pyramid would have much less visibility. Most people would hear about it but could not actually examine it themselves. It would have become like Franklin himself, who was first monumental, then overlooked.[1]

Franklin hoped to be remembered and in quite specific ways. Attentive to his legacy, he had been writing and rewriting his will since 1750. In the final version of 1788, he traced his upward rise. Opening his will with "I, Benjamin Franklin, of Philadelphia, printer, late Minister Plenipotentiary from the United States of America to the Court of France, now President of the State of Pennsylvania," he celebrated his progress from his head-and-hands trade to his glory in Paris and command over his home state. But in death, he would return to simplicity. In the 1789 codicil to his will, Franklin requested that his and Deborah's grave be covered with "a marble stone" engraved only with their names.[2]

The monument was frugal—Franklin was saving his money for his heirs. He ordered that most of his wealth go to his family, especially his daughter and son-in-law, Sarah and Richard Bache; he excluded his loyalist son. He then made two bequests of £1,000 sterling apiece to the cities of Boston and Philadelphia. Franklin specified that these sums should be loaned "upon interest" to "young married artificers," such as he had been. After one hundred years, the trustees in each city were to lay out most of the accumulated money in "public works" (which was indeed done); after two hundred years, Franklin left it to each city (and its state government) to spend the funds as needed. He also left a small sum to Boston's public schools, perhaps proportionate to his brief education there.[3]

Then Franklin distributed the artifacts of his life. The books required careful division, starting with how-to guides and compendia. The folio *Arts et métiers* went to the American Academy of Arts and Sciences in Massachusetts, the quarto version of that work went to the Library Company, and the "History of the Academy of Sciences" in Paris went to the American Philosophical Society. Franklin designated books for his young companions in France, Benny, Temple, and Jonathan Williams. One of Polly Hewson's sons received a bound set of London newspapers, including the *Spectator*, from which Franklin had learned to write. He gave all his "philosophical instruments" to Francis Hopkinson (son of his electrical collaborator), his press and printing materials to Benny, and his London-made telescope to Philadelphia astronomer David Rittenhouse. There were provisos. Sarah Bache received the miniature of Louis XVI (after whom she had named a son), but Franklin asked her never to use its diamonds as jewelry—aristocratic extravagance—for herself or her daughters. Sarah's husband, Richard, owned a slave, "Bob," whom Franklin specified had to be freed for Bache to claim his inheritance.[4]

It is all there: reading, writing, printing, wealth (and moderation), science, public service, social reform. Any good will should document the life that has just ended; Franklin's will remarkably restated his life's events and ambitions. It was a fitting memoir.

But Franklin could not quite believe he would really die. His faith in immortality was a testament to his Christian belief, which had survived his youthful irreligion and mature deism. But his conviction also revealed his ideas about matter itself, which, he thought, never ended but only changed. And his fame, which continued after death, has certainly given him a kind of immortality. Franklin's afterlife has its own rich history, one that poses a fundamental question: What good is science, anyway?

FRANKLIN'S friends and admirers had kept telling him he would live on after death. In a 1769 letter, later published in the *Philosophical Transactions* of the Royal Society, Richard Price had assured Franklin that "the world owes to you many important discoveries; and your name must live as long as there is any knowledge of philosophy among mankind." Boston minister Samuel Fayerweather had likewise written the living Franklin, in devout and devoted capitals, that "So long As Natural and Experimental Philosophy have Any footing in the Understanding, [I] will Bless GOD ALMIGHTY THE INFINITE AUTHOR of all Wisdom for Raising Up So Great And So Good A Man As DOCTOR FRANKLIN." Fayerweather hoped Franklin would "be Dignified with a Lawrell in Heaven."[5]

Heavenly laurels did not satisfy Franklin—he wanted an earthly afterlife, too. He fantasized that he would be able to witness the future, perhaps through resurrection or the preservation of his body. Franklin expected that the improvements he had witnessed would continue, if not accelerate. In a 1783 letter to Joseph Banks, he confessed, "I begin to be almost sorry I was born so soon, since I cannot have the happiness of knowing what will be known 100 years hence." Five years later, Franklin told the Reverend John Lathrop of his faith in "the growing felicity of mankind, from the improvements in philosophy, morals, politics, and even the conveniences of common living." Again, there is a tone of regret: "I have sometimes almost wished it had been my destiny to be born two or three centuries hence." It seems an odd wish—hadn't Franklin seen (and created) marvels enough? But "invention and improvement are prolific," he believed," and beget more of their kind"; "many of great importance, now unthought of, will before that period be produced."[6]

Maybe science could conquer even death. Franklin had a teasing correspondence with his sister's neighbor in Boston, the Reverend Samuel Danforth, in which the two men discussed the philosopher's stone, which would transform base matter into gold and cure all human ills. In 1773, a year of tremendous uncertainty for all colonists,

Franklin thanked Danforth for his "kind Intentions of including me in the Benefits of that inestimable Stone, which curing all Diseases, even old Age itself, will enable us to see the future glorious State of our America, enjoying in full Security her own Liberties." That same year, Franklin wrote Jacques Barbeu-Dubourg that he wished to know the future state of America; perhaps he could be preserved "with some friends in hogsheads of Madeira," until such time that he (and they) could be "restored to life by the heat of the sun of my beloved country."[7]

But if alchemy or fortified wine failed Franklin, perhaps matter itself might guarantee his immortality. "Finding myself to exist in the World," he told George Whatley, "I believe I shall, in some Shape or other, always exist." When Linnaeus named a plant for Cadwallader Colden, Franklin offered congratulations. "No Species or Genus of Plants was ever lost, or ever will be while the World continues," he assured Colden, "and therefore your Name, now annext to one of them, will last forever." Learning that Linnaeus had named a plant for him, Peter Collinson declared that he had been granted "a species of eternity." Franklin himself received the honor when John Bartram named the *Franklinia altamaha*, a fragrant flowering tree from the southern part of North America, for him.[8]

Eternity was a comforting hypothesis—nothing in nature would end. To Danforth, Franklin claimed that matter simply underwent metamorphosis, as when wood "dissolved" by fire would "again become Air, Earth, Fire, and Water." He declared that "the natural Reduction of compound Substances to their original Elements" was perfectly evident; "when I see nothing annihilated, and not even a Drop of Water wasted, I cannot suspect the Annihilation of Souls."[9]

This was quite a claim. Christians typically believed that the soul was immortal because it was insubstantial and therefore invulnerable to the decay that afflicted matter. Franklin did not go as far as his friend Joseph Priestley, who believed that the soul was actually material. Instead, his views resembled the ancient Christian tenet that human bodies would, at the end of the world, be resurrected and reunited with their souls. But Franklin's statement about the continual transformation of matter reflected his private faith that material change (including decay) did not signify death as such but rather a transmigration of the soul to a new material condition. It was an unconventional idea, though altogether fitting for a deist and natural philosopher who wished to peer into the future.

AN ENDLESS SOURCE of fascination during his lifetime, Franklin was even more compelling immediately after death. His surviving contemporaries eulogized, monumentalized, criticized, misremembered, and—at least sometimes—mourned him. But his memory held very different meanings in the three nations where he had lived. His afterlives in France, Britain, and the United States reveal a great deal about the status of science in each country, as well as Franklin's very different legacies in their political realms.

The French lamented the loudest. Franklin died nine months after Parisians had stormed the Bastille. During this early phase of the French Revolution, the reformers who had befriended Franklin believed they were creating a new society. It was the perfect moment to reclaim their American brother, a fellow enemy of tyrants and himself a Revolutionary figure of wisdom.[10]

On June 11, 1790, the Comte de Mirabeau officially announced to the National Assembly: "Franklin is dead . . . the genius who freed America and shed torrents of light upon Europe." Mirabeau continued with a eulogy—"Antiquity would have raised altars to this mighty genius," who had managed "to conquer both thunderbolts and tyrants." Then he proposed a remarkable tribute, "that the National Assembly for three days wear mourning for Benjamin Franklin." It was decreed. With this unprecedented honor for Franklin, a new French custom was invented: national mourning. Previously, court mourning had been reserved for aristocrats in line to the throne. By commemorating Franklin in this way, the French set aside hierarchies of birth and rank, as they were doing in many other Revolutionary activities. They celebrated a commoner solely for his remarkable accomplishments. The only objection seems to have come from someone who wanted confirmation that the long-lived and irrepressible Philadelphian was in fact dead.[11]

French commoners as well as counts mourned Franklin's passing. The street criers who announced his death refused payment. At one Paris ceremony of 1790, as a printer delivered a eulogy on Franklin, others busily set type for its text. Once done, the text was printed and distributed to the onlookers. It was perhaps the perfect way to celebrate the life of a man of letters.[12]

The French also appreciated that Franklin's life had held so many connections between science and public affairs. It was, appropriately, the Marquis de Condorcet, the mathematician and social reformer, who offered a November 1790 eulogy in which he compared Franklin to Pythagoras. Both had used "the laws of nature" to establish truth about the world and about humanity. But the American, unlike the ancient philosopher, had sought to "purify" rather than "subdue" nature—Franklin's efforts were themselves natural. Condorcet also extolled Franklin's electrical and political theories, which, he believed, exemplified the spirit of inquiry and progress that had characterized Franklin's entire era.[13]

Condorcet spoke too soon. During the radical phase of the Revolution that began in 1791 and culminated in the violent Terror of 1793–1795, science and the learned academies were criticized as nests of elite privilege. Jean-Paul Marat, the experimenter who had begun a second career as a radical journalist, remembered too well that the Académie Royale des Sciences had dismissed his analyses of light and color (which Franklin had so studiously ignored). Marat made a point of attacking learned societies and academicians such as Lavoisier. In late 1792, the Revolutionary Legislative Assembly halted elections to fill vacant seats in learned societies. Academicians began to shun meetings, lest they appear too elitist. The Académie itself closed in 1793. Lavoisier was imprisoned under a general arrest of all farmers general, those who had administered and benefited from the Old Regime's taxes. He was convicted and guillotined. An observer remarked, "It took them only an instant to cut off that head, and a hundred years may not produce another like it."[14]

The French academies recovered, and the monarchy was later restored. Yet even after the Terror, the French (and other Europeans) were less eager to apply scientific principles to human society. Condorcet's science of humanity and Condorcet himself (who died in prison) were discredited. Natural science was no longer quite so central to public life. It instead occupied the academic sphere, in universities and learned societies. Franklin's reputation survived all the troubles. A Frenchman remarked in 1864 that "even today Franklin exists as a demi-god." And Paris still has a "rue Benjamin Franklin," explained as honoring the "physicien et homme d'état" (physicist and statesman), science, and politics in that order, as they had appeared in Condorcet's eulogy.[15]

One would look in vain for such a street in London. Franklin's post-1775 politics rendered him a far more complicated figure in Britain than in France. (In 1976, the British did commemorate the bicentennial of the American Revolution—rather sporting of them—with a series of postage stamps, including one of Franklin.) To embrace him, Britons had to disconnect Franklin's natural philosophy from his political career. Jonathan Odell, an American whose loyalty to Britain had made him a refugee during the American Revolution, praised Franklin as a philosopher—"Like Newton sublimely he soared . . . And the palm of philosophy gained"—and as someone who used science to improve the human lot:

> With a spark which he caught from the skies,
> He displayed an unparalleled wonder;
> And we saw with delight and surprise,
> That his rod could secure us from thunder.

But Franklin had erred when he entered politics:

> To covet political fame
> Was in him a degrading ambition;
> The spark that from Lucifer came
> Enkindled the blaze of sedition.[16]

Throughout Europe, the idea that men of science should enlist in public affairs was on the wane at the turn of the nineteenth century. If anything, genius was now thought to separate a person from the world. Consider William Wordsworth's verses on Newton: "A mind for ever / Voyaging through strange seas of Thought, alone." This romantic characterization, done circa 1805, after the shock, debate, and disillusionment over the French Revolution, would have puzzled anyone in Newton's or Franklin's era. But nineteenth-century poets, politicians, and philosophers tended to characterize genius as impractical, if not dangerous. The fantasy of a fiendish philosopher who could subject matter to his will—already evident during the American Revolution—persisted. Thus Mary Shelley's creation, in 1818, of an electrically adept Dr. Frankenstein (Franklin-stein?) whose tragedy it was to master life and death.[17]

Franklin's afterlife in the United States was similarly fraught, although there was tremendous grief over his death. On April 21,

1790, 20,000 people formed a long procession to the Christ Church burial ground in Philadelphia. (Remarkably, this crowd was as big as the gathering that had watched Buffon's burial in Paris, two years earlier.) The clergy led the procession. Mayor and governor were pallbearers; so was astronomer Rittenhouse. Fellows of the American Philosophical Society and printers mournfully trailed behind.[18]

One group of Philadelphians was notable for its absence: Freemasons. In Franklin's European absence, American Masons had rediscovered their workers' origins. Masonic lodges, including Franklin's old lodge, now welcomed the craftworkers they had earlier rejected. Franklin the upstart leather apron had become, by the time of his death, too grand for the Masons, so they stayed away from his funeral. He might have appreciated the irony.[19]

For different reasons, politicians were also reluctant to express sorrow over Franklin's passing. Congress, prompted by James Madison, voted to wear badges of mourning for a month. The members of the lower house did so, but the senators refused. Thomas Jefferson suggested that members of the executive branch should wear mourning; George Washington declined. Franklin had, after all, died neither in office nor on the battlefield—if mere celebrity prompted national mourning, where would things end? And when official statements of condolence arrived from France, no one in the brand-new federal government knew quite what to do. Should they be answered? Somehow, the messages were ignored. Finally, members of Congress arranged for a formal eulogy. Almost a year after Franklin's death, William Smith—the vice president of the American Philosophical Society and one of his political enemies—read before both houses of Congress an assessment of Franklin that was an uninspired list of his life's events.[20]

John Adams made a good case for forgetting Franklin. During Franklin's last weeks, Adams had complained that "the history of our revolution will be one continued lye from one end to the other." People would assume *"that Dr Franklins electrical Rod smote the earth, and out sprung General Washington. That Franklin electrised him with his rod—and thenceforward these two conducted all the policy, negotiation, legislation, and War."* True, Adams was still envious of Franklin, but he had a point: many people, including ordinary ones, had fought and won the war. Why should Franklin be the supernatural hero of the story? The Revolutionaries had founded the Republic, after all, to vindicate the rights of ordinary people.[21]

The price of that Revolutionary goal was suspicion of elites, including intellectual elites. Franklin had never doubted that ordinary people could read, think, and argue with the best of them. And he had, through his own powerful example, demonstrated that those who worked with their hands could also use their heads. But after his death, Americans would grow increasingly critical of the men who did most of the reading of books and arguing of ideas. That was one thing, but they would also begin to reject the books and ideas themselves. Just as Freemasons were now celebrating their stoneworkers' heritage, so Americans generally extolled practical knowledge over book learning. When Jefferson seemed destined for the presidency, his opponents attacked his learned status. In 1793, one South Carolinian remarked that "the great WASHINGTON was, thank God, no philosopher." In contrast to a man of action, such as Washington, a philosopher such as Jefferson had "timidity, whimsicalness . . . a proneness to predicate all his measures on certain abstract theories."[22]

The distrust of philosophy, theory, and learning left its mark on antebellum America. Well past the moment of the nation's founding, state-sponsored learning, which was the standard in western Europe, remained unusual in the United States. Universities, learned societies, and interested individuals (not least Jefferson) kept natural philosophy simmering at a low level. Occasional American publications drew attention from Europeans. But citizens of the new nation still depended on overseas talent for scientific stimulus. In cultural terms, they remained colonial subjects of Europe.[23]

To celebrate Franklin, Americans had to make less, not more, of his gift for science. So in their statements of praise for their electrical founder, nineteenth-century Americans demoted science from his leading characteristic to, at best, one item on a long list of achievements. Americans were far less interested in the cosmopolitan character that Franklin had worked so hard to develop. Instead, they celebrated how Franklin was typically American, meaning intelligent, hardworking, politically shrewd—civic responsibility had become his primary virtue. One entrepreneur made a point of reinventing Franklin along these lines. Mason Locke Weems, the "Parson" Weems who would craft Washington's posthumous image (cherry tree, axe, "cannot tell a lie"), did the same for Franklin. Weems peddled extracts from Franklin's *The Way to Wealth* and *Autobiography* and constructed Franklin, first and foremost, as a patriot.[24]

The Weemsian image stuck. Subsequently, historians and national propagandists presented this version of Franklin to immigrants, working people, young men on the make. His life was a series of civic deeds that led up to his starring role as a founder of the United States. By 1906, the 200th anniversary of Franklin's birth, Philadelphia's Masonic Lodge described its former brother as "the distinguished statesman, scientist, diplomat and Mason." He was "not a man of letters but a man of affairs."[25]

Science began to fall out of the picture, quite literally. A stream of nineteenth-century images, including commemorative medals and state or federal coins and bills, presented Franklin as equally statesman and scientist. In the second half of the nineteenth century, both the federal government and state banks issued bills that presented Franklin with his electric kite. He became indelibly associated with the kite and lightning rod, but people were beginning to forget what those inventions signified. In their famous engraving of 1876, Currier and Ives proposed that the kite "identified lightning with electricity" and helped develop the lightning rod, which protected humanity from lightning. The kite and lightning rod were symbols of a clever, civic-minded American practicality. Franklin's serious investigation of electricity as a form of matter slipped away.[26]

And then science vanished altogether from many images of Franklin. Should you have one handy, look at a $100 bill. One side bears Franklin's head, a portrait based on Siffrèd Duplessis's 1778 oil painting. The other side bears an image of Independence Hall, Pennsylvania's old State House. Not a lightning rod or kite is in sight—nor is there any hint that this was the site of Franklin's earliest experiments with electricity. First issued in the 1910s, the bill was intended to honor Franklin as a Founder. It perhaps unintentionally honors his early commitment to the circulation of money. But it ignores entirely his interest in all other kinds of circulation, natural and social.[27]

Not even famous Founding Fathers can control their legacies. The present-day images of Franklin hardly resemble the historical character. In his own time, he enjoyed—even exploited—a society in which the sciences were still at the center of things, including public affairs. He and his contemporaries worried over how politics might affect science, even as they were not above using the political context to promote science or the reverse. They defined matter in ways that made sense to them, in terms of particles, fluids, and forces. Never mind that these ideas no longer have the life they once did—neither does Franklin. Under a plain marble slab, he rests beside his wife.

But he wanted to see the way we live now. If we could rouse him from his rest, we could take him on a whirlwind tour of the developments in science and technology that came after his death. Is this wise? Remember what Franklin said: "I have sometimes almost wished it had been my destiny to be born two or three centuries hence." He asked for it.

———————————

MANY of Franklin's biographers play this almost irresistible game— they imagine him living in our age. Franklin involved himself in so many activities that seem modern to us. How eager Silence Dogood would have been to blog "her" advice, or the Pennsylvania postmaster to check his e-mail. How delighted the master electrician would have been to see Paris, the City of Lights, electrically illuminated at night; how entranced the inventor of the glass armonica would have been to hear the Theremin or Moog synthesizer, and how intrigued the Gulf Stream investigator would have been to examine infrared images of the Atlantic Ocean. To imagine Franklin doing these things is to make him one of us.

In part, we enjoy these fantasies because we like to imagine that we, the true moderns, have perfected his work. Franklin embarked on many projects that we (or our recent ancestors) then completed. He advocated inoculation against smallpox; twentieth-century doctors and health workers managed, through a global effort at vaccination, to eradicate naturally occurring smallpox. He recommended that Parisians, during the summer, go to bed earlier, which would give them more daylight hours and therefore reduce the expense of buying candles; we now credit him with the idea of daylight saving time.[28]

Scientists have likewise claimed their continuity with Franklin. At the turn of the nineteenth century, when J. J. Thomson described the electron, some enthusiasts announced it as ultimate vindication of Franklin's idea that electricity existed in particles. Others have pointed out that Franklin's experiment, using oil to still waves, could have determined the size of a molecule. (Measure the amount of oil, measure the amount of water it covers; use the ratio between them to determine the "depth" of the thin film, meaning the diameter of a molecule). Scientists have lamented that Franklin himself failed to follow through. Oceanographers who study the Gulf Stream hail the 1768 Franklin and Folger chart as the first, if partial, representation of a clockwise system of circulation in the North Atlantic.[29]

This rather self-congratulatory game permits us to judge Franklin by our own standards of achievement. We like to think he would admire us for building on his and other eighteenth-century accomplishments. If he liked the Leyden jar, he would marvel that we, surrounded by electric lights and electronic devices, are permanently bathed in electrical emissions. If he thought the Atlantic postal system speeded communication, he would adore the telegraph and Internet.

But we distort Franklin's work in science when we see it as a flawed or incomplete version of our own. He held many ideas we no longer accept. It is an insult to him and to his contemporaries to diminish their theories of particulate matter with such terms as *wrong* or, even more patronizingly, *headed in the right direction.*

If Franklin could have what he wanted, a deathless view of the future, he surely would have been delighted and dismayed in equal measure. We delude ourselves when we imagine that the march of years is invariably a march of progress. So let us consider the things that would have upset Franklin and also the things that might upset us if we thought about how he would have assessed them. That version of Franklin's imagined afterlife would give a truer sense of the significance of modern science. Science would become, after Franklin's death, highly specialized, very expensive, and non-Newtonian. It would first lose its place in public life, then regain it. Let us take Franklin through these developments and see how and when they might have challenged his ideas of science and of nature, starting with the people and ideas that he almost encountered.

First, we should introduce him to Alexander von Humboldt (1769–1859). Humboldt, a stupendously talented Prussian naturalist, nearly equaled Franklin as an iconic natural philosopher and public figure—he was the only person remotely capable of doing so. He made contributions to most of the sciences. And in the tradition of fur-capped explorer-naturalists, Humboldt combined his research with travels, particularly in the Andes. He collected temperature readings for the South Atlantic current that now bears his name, as Franklin had done with the Gulf Stream. He composed some of the

first natural histories of entire sections of South America and effort-
lessly mastered revolutions in thought as they exploded around him.
At the height of his fame, he placed a newspaper advertisement asking admirers please not to write—he was drowning in letters.
Franklin would have sympathized.[30]

At times, Humboldt did lend his talents to the state, but for the
most part, he and his brother, Wilhelm, divided the territory: Alexander studied nature and stayed out of politics, and Wilhelm did
the reverse. Had he met Humboldt, Franklin would have seen that
science was becoming specialized. Its practitioners no longer
seemed qualified to contribute to other realms, as Franklin himself
had done.

Over the course of the nineteenth century, the practice of science
required more and more specialized education, moving still further
from the knowledge of ordinary working people. And by the early
twentieth century, scientific research came to require unprecedented funding, increasingly from government sources. Scientists
no longer contributed to politics (unless their expertise and political needs coincided exactly) and became instead the beneficiaries
of political institutions.

In the United States, however, those institutions gave little to scientists. From the 1790s until the early twentieth century, the only
educational establishments that received federal support were the
military academies, starting with West Point. That was where a man
had to go to study the latest in science and mathematics. Otherwise,
until World War II, the United States would remain a backwater, particularly in the areas of physical science in which Franklin had made
his name but that now required instruments much more expensive
than those he had used. In contrast, natural history and the fields
that would become the life sciences remained less specialized and
less expensive. These were subjects that Americans could address.

This was the case for hydrography, where our resurrected Franklin would have met many of his own friends and relatives. Two of
these were his younger contemporaries. Thomas Truxton (or Truxtun), the captain who had carried Franklin home in 1785, and
Jonathan Williams Jr., Franklin's grandnephew, both published
analyses of oceans and navigation that included material on the
Gulf Stream. In his 1794 piece, Truxton wrote as a naval captain
and emphasized the value of Franklin's work to navy men. He had
been "attentive," he claimed, to temperature variation in water and

air, "as recommended by that great philosopher, the late Dr Franklin."[31]

In contrast, Williams used his *Thermometrical Navigation* to distinguish between men of learning and ordinary tars. He had made his own claim to learning when he published parts of his essay in the third volume of the APS *Transactions* (1790). Men of rank and with titles litter Williams's narrative: "Captain Ellis," "Doctor Franklin," "Don Cipriano Vimercati," "Captain William Billings," "Sir George Staunton." None of Franklin's old sea captains or intelligent whalemen make appearances. Williams, like his granduncle, believed that navigators could use the thermometer to detect dangerously shallow water, which tended to be colder. But this belief differentiated learned men from mere sailors. Because the latter tested sea temperature "with the hand" rather than instruments, "they think [it] merely a matter of curiosity." So much for the human hand as a sensitive instrument of science.[32]

As Williams (and Franklin) had predicted, technical instruments began to dominate hydrography. Armed with new devices, such as chronometers and improved thermometers, investigators sought larger patterns in ocean circulation and offered explanations. Benjamin Thompson, Count Rumford, hypothesized in 1798 that if there was thermal variation at the sea's surface, the same must occur below; cold water must sink as warm water spread above it. The cold water would also be denser, meaning it would contain more salt. Humboldt presented a similar theory of circulation. The idea of a general oceanic circulation would not, however, be widely accepted until well into the twentieth century. In the meantime, hydrographers continued to trace surface currents, as Humboldt did in the South Atlantic.[33]

Scientists and even travelers collected a variety of data on the world's oceans. The accumulation of information occurred, in large part, because ocean travel was becoming more common. European empires spread; naval and commercial shipping expanded; steam power (and then fossil fuel) made ocean travel faster; and ocean cruises, which more than once had nearly killed Franklin, actually became enjoyable. Ships' logs, diaries, letters, and data sets abounded. Collating all this new marine information was a formidable task. Franklin might have been pleased that a great-grandson, Alexander Dallas Bache, did some notable collecting and collating. He might also have been surprised that Bache was the gentlemanly nemesis of a self-made naval hydrographer, Matthew Fontaine Maury.[34]

Bache attended West Point, where he gained the best education in science and mathematics then to be had in the United States. In 1843, he became second superintendent of the U.S. Coast Survey, which undertook a fifteen-year study of the Gulf Stream. This analysis of thermal variation was a clear descendant of Franklin's pioneering work. Bache enjoyed his pedigree. He was fond of quoting Poor Richard, admonishing one of his assistants that "a man who was good at making excuses was good for little else." One of Bache's admirers observed a "striking parallel between the great Philosopher and Statesman, Benjamin Franklin, and his illustrious descendant Alexander Dallas Bache."[35]

While Bache collected data with instruments, his rival, Maury, studied ordinary ships' logs. With these, Maury tracked patterns of winds and currents, publishing his results as guides to navigation. One of these guides was sold with a packet of blank forms, enlisting navigators in an ongoing project to which they submitted further information. Maury also tried his hand at hydrographic theories in *The Physical Geography of the Sea* (1855), in which he memorably described the Gulf Stream as "a river in the ocean." In addition, he paid careful attention to the configurations of the seabed and created the first bathymetric chart of the North Atlantic. The *Oxford English Dictionary* credits Maury with the first printed use (in 1859) of the word *oceanography*.[36]

But it was navigators, not scientists, who most valued Maury's work. Notably, Bache snubbed him. Maury's charts of wind and currents were respected but not his theories of circulation. The contempt he suffered from better-educated men of science reflected the growing fissure between scientists and amateurs. (The split existed in Franklin's own family: the Philadelphia Baches studied the sea, whereas the Nantucket Folgers continued to be seafarers. In 1808, it had been Mayhew Folger who, commanding the *Topaz* in search of seals, discovered the famous *Bounty* mutineers hiding on Pitcairn Island in the Pacific.) From the Victorian era onward, hydrographers would steadily adopt instruments and gather data. Each development made it more difficult for nonspecialists to make a contribution.[37]

It was even more difficult in other areas of natural history. Americans continued to produce descriptive work, to gather specimens

and data, and to write narrative accounts of the natural world—
these activities came together in the fabled Merriwether Lewis and
William Clark expedition of 1804 to 1806. But in Europe, universities and learned societies that had government support and connections provided a superior environment for naturalists, whose claims
were getting bigger and bolder.[38]

So it was wealthy, Cambridge-educated Charles Darwin, with the
support of the Royal Navy in the form of HMS *Beagle*, who radically
redefined humanity's place within nature. In his work in paleontol-
ogy, geology, and natural history and particularly with his ideas of
extinction and evolution, Darwin attacked many ideas Franklin
(and others) had held dear. Darwin presented evidence that species
changed or even went extinct. He argued that these processes had
happened frequently and were ongoing. And he insisted that
changes in species had eventually given rise to humans, who were
descended from animal ancestors.

Many people shrank from these conclusions (many still do), and
Franklin, had he lived to meet Darwin, might have been similarly
chagrined. Franklin knew Darwin's grandfather—Erasmus Darwin
had been a Birmingham Lunar Society friend. And Franklin met
Charles's father, Robert Waring Darwin, who visited him in Paris.
But Franklin rejected the idea of the annihilation of species that the
later Darwin would be famous for. He believed that material things,
created by a divine power, could only be destroyed by that power. In
1767, Franklin had seen what turned out to be fossilized mastodon
tusks and teeth. But he thought they were evidence that the animals
had found one region uninhabitable and had moved on. And he
had long believed in the argument from design, which Darwin
firmly rejected. Darwin's evolution either showed the lack of a divine creator or revealed a malevolent deity who extinguished as
much as he created.[39]

Would Franklin have been appalled or flattered to learn that he in
fact had a place in evolution's intellectual genealogy? Darwin had
formed his idea of the struggle for existence after reading Thomas
Malthus's work in political arithmetic. Malthus argued that populations of plants and animals (including humans) would increase until
they ran out of the means of subsistence. Subsequent survival depended on a struggle for access to subsistence. Malthus cited Franklin's own political arithmetic to make this point: in his "Observations
Concerning the Increase of Mankind," the American had said that

plants and animals could breed until they ran out of ground. Franklin had not moved on to Malthus's gloomy conclusion, but British America's burgeoning inhabitants were for Malthus the first evidence of the phenomenon that would later convince Darwin that nature truly was red in tooth and claw.[40]

It is a sign of the complexity of both the theory of evolution and Franklin's mind that it is impossible to say what his reaction to Darwin might have been. At the very least, the evolutionist Victorian would have given him pause. Franklin would probably have been dismayed to learn that after Darwin, religion and science were pitted as adversaries. Following his youthful and brief flirtation with libertinism, Franklin had always sought to reconcile the two forms of belief.

Contemporary work in physical science might have been less dismaying to Franklin. Indeed, he would have recognized many of its premises, which remained Newtonian. Nineteenth-century scientists still accepted that elementary particles, forces, subtle fluids, and even the aether were useful concepts for their work. Had Franklin turned up in their laboratories, physical scientists might have begun their conversation with him with a polite acknowledgment of the law of the conservation of charge. Franklin had never used that phrase, but it did reflect his idea that electricity had two quantities, positive and negative, and that it occurred when both these charges were present.

Physical scientists still focused on heat and electricity as central properties of inorganic matter. But nineteenth-century experimenters also investigated magnetism. They examined the interplay of electricity and magnetism, assuming that the forces had a constitutive role in matter itself. In the parallel field of thermodynamics, scientists studied the nature and significance of heat, and they began to define energy as a central property of matter. Experimenters explained that light and other forms of radiation created waves in the aether. By the middle to late part of the century, they used new ideas—subatomic matter, chemical structure, and radiation (especially X rays)—to challenge the older concepts of particles and forces. But they did so mostly to elaborate on what was still a fundamentally Newtonian view of the world. Scientists continued to believe they could measure, in absolute terms, material properties and connections, as when they defined the mass of different particles and the speeds of their motion.[41]

Franklin might have recognized aspects of these experiments, but he would have been confused by others. The study of electromagnetism required ever more elaborate equipment and would eventually demand a rigorous command of mathematics. The classic experiments in physics were done in Europe. At best, learned societies and universities in the United States could repeat the experiments, if they could afford the necessary apparatus. Had he visited laboratories abroad, Franklin could have admired their thrumming electromagnetic apparatuses. But even the politest of laboratory hosts would eventually have had to show Franklin some equations that the colonial electrician could not possibly have understood.

When it came to electricity, nineteenth-century Americans distinguished themselves with its practical applications. New devices stored and released electricity in a finely controlled manner. Most notably, technicians sent pulses of electricity through metal wires or cables, creating the telegraph. In fact, the invention of the telegraph united two of Franklin's favored fields, electricity and hydrography.

It all came together in the Atlantic Ocean. In 1842, Samuel Morse first submerged a cable in New York harbor to demonstrate electrical communication through the sea. A grand, transnational project to lay an Atlantic cable commenced. (Matthew Maury's investigation of the Atlantic seabed was, in part, meant to help lay that cable.) In 1856, a coin struck to commemorate the unveiling of a Franklin statue in Boston featured Morse along with a bust of Franklin. "SCIENCE UNITED THEM," the coin proclaimed, along with Morse's own Shakespearean claim, "I'LL PUT A GIRDLE AROUND THE EARTH IN FORTY MINUTES," a Puckish defiance of distance Franklin would indeed have admired. Two years later, the completed cable carried the first official telegraphic message—Queen Victoria sent greetings to President John Buchanan. In his reply, Buchanan stated his wish that the cable be "forever neutral even should hostilities arise." The director of the Atlantic Telegraph Company in England added: "Europe and America are united by telegraphic communication." Although the cable failed a short time later, it was replaced, and others were laid under other seas. Nations—and the republic of letters—had a new and much faster means of communication.[42]

Subsequent developments in physics kept those telegraph wires humming. Above all, many new discoveries challenged the Newtonian view of nature that Franklin had taken for granted. By the end of the nineteenth century, experimenters in quantum physics were stating that particles of matter did not have absolute mass. The masses instead changed, depending on where the particles were positioned or were moving, in relation to other material entities.

What quantum mechanics did for matter, relativity did for time. In 1905, Albert Einstein put forward his special theory of relativity. He proposed that there was no single, unified temporal flow but only moments of time that existed relative to each other. Einstein assumed that the speed of light was constant but that no other motion (or the time it took) was. He thus scuttled the idea of an aether. Newton had cheated, Einstein believed, by positing an absolute frame of reference that was not actually there; light did not need a medium to move through space. Einstein also suggested that mass and energy could be understood in relation to each other: $E = mc^2$. In his famous 1905 equation, he expressed the relation between mass and energy mathematically. The equation summarized his hypothesis that the energy (E) needed to accelerate a mass (m) to the speed of light (c) would be infinite (an amount of energy divisible by the speed of light squared).[43]

Taken together, quantum mechanics and relativity demolished the Newtonian view of the cosmos. The new view of nature was relational, not absolute. Matter *could* be destroyed—that was how energy was created. Franklin would have found these ideas unfamiliar, if not deeply unsettling. He had believed himself to be observing and explaining forms of matter and their effects on each other. He would never have thought that the particulate configuration of matter and its movement (measured over time) could be a matter of relative position, either of the particles or of the person who observed them. Nor did Franklin think that matter itself could be annihilated—instead, he believed it changed form without ever ceasing to exist.

In a world without universally true physical form, can anything be certain? Einstein did not believe that nature necessarily lacked absolutes—he simply concluded that that was the way humans experienced it. Quantum mechanics alarmed even him. He rejected the conclusion that there was no real pattern in physical reality. "God does not play dice with the Universe," Einstein would begin to proclaim. (Franklin would have agreed with that.) Universal patterns might still exist in the natural world, but they were beyond the human ability to perceive, let alone reason about them. Other scientists were not as sure as Einstein that this might be true. And in the popular imagination, the new physics seemed like a philosophy of radical uncertainty.[44]

The popular view matched the era, unfortunately. With World War I, the global depression that followed, the reconfiguration of European empires, and the rise of political extremism, the center no longer held. Meanwhile, scientists were dismantling long-standing assumptions about nature's unity and stability. Yet the scientific ideas were arresting. Einstein became a muse to a variety of artists and writers; his theory of relativity was widely reported, though not always accurately.[45]

At the start of the twentieth century, science reemerged into the public sphere. It was a surprising development. Science had been becoming more specialized, more abstract and mathematized—and inaccessible to outsiders. But the use of chemical gases in World War I gave scientists a public, if disturbing, role. World War II did so again with the famous race to develop nuclear weapons. At that point, the center of scientific learning was shifting westward. Many brilliant scientists (including Einstein) fled from National Socialism and to the United States. The war and the infusion of talent were essential to the U.S. government's new sponsorship of scientific research. In 1939, physicists Edward Teller and Leo Szilard managed to convince Einstein to sign a letter to President Franklin D. Roosevelt advocating the development of an atomic bomb. Roosevelt complied by creating several collaborative and heavily funded projects. Scientists involved in the Manhattan Project developed much of the foundation of the atom bomb; they built and tested one in New Mexico on July 16, 1945.[46]

And so, the idea of the scientist as political conscience was reborn. Einstein had played this role when he wrote to Roosevelt. His inspirer, Leo Szilard, now worried over the unguarded use of nuclear weapons and pleaded for a slow, deliberate consideration of the bomb's use. Szilard organized reports and petitions and gathered signatures—a sign that other scientists also worried about their new status as weapon makers. In their actions, the physicists made clear that they knew they were stepping outside their usual domain. It was a contrast to Franklin's easy migration, even during war, between science and politics. Moreover, the scale of destruction that the twentieth-century scientists could now achieve was devastatingly greater than anything the American Founder might have imagined.[47]

This new, big science transformed hydrography into modern oceanography. The world wars and the ensuing Cold War gave the United States incentive to study oceans. Submarine vessels presented both military and scientific challenges—how could they be kept on course? How might their approach be detected? Sonar made it possible to track submarine traffic. But variations in seawater's temperature, depth, and velocity affect sonar. Oceanographers at the Woods Hole Oceanographic Institute, on Cape Cod, developed a bathythermograph. This instrument would measure water temperature variation as depth increased—information that was essential to the accurate operation and reading of sonar—and postwar oceanographers would use this instrument to investigate ocean currents, including the Gulf Stream.[48]

Over the second half of the twentieth century, the amount of material available for physical oceanography exploded. Current meters and neutrally buoyant floats tracked major currents and eddies; electronic sensors and satellites gathered millions of pieces of data about the sea—temperature at every level, surface and subsurface motion, fine shades of salinity, and so on. Computers eventually allowed the quick processing of all this information. The Gulf Stream is now understood as part of a general pattern of oceanic circulation that has tremendous implications for climate. And the Atlantic is now the world's most studied ocean. This is not necessarily because it is the most interesting ocean; rather, it has become one of the most protected bodies of water in the world because of U.S. security concerns.[49]

By the middle of the twentieth century, science had a public profile it had not enjoyed since the eighteenth century. The idea that scientists such as Einstein and Szilard could make wise interventions into public life survived the war. In 1964, Americans ranked three occupations as most prestigious: Supreme Court justices, physicians, and nuclear physicists, in that order. As the United States became the world's only superpower and the center of the most lavishly funded science—a complete historical turnaround—scholars began to examine the history of American science. In 1941 (just before the United States would enter World War II), a scholarly edition of Franklin's *Experiments and Observations on Electricity* appeared for the first time in the United States.[50]

Franklin might finally have felt at home. He would not have fully understood the actual science of the mid-twentieth century, but he might have recognized the popular appreciation of it. He might have felt kinship with the scientist who, above all others, became the era's popular icon: Einstein. The iconography of fame (now displayed on coffee mugs rather than snuffboxes) showed an odd affinity between the two men, both presumed geniuses. Their work in the sciences was nothing alike—Einstein questioned everything Franklin had assumed. And Einstein was the more important figure in science, precisely because he challenged rather than accepted Newton. But the eras in which Franklin and Einstein lived and the uses to which their images were put had some similar contours.[51]

Perhaps the Seven Years' War, American Revolution, debates over slavery, and developments in Newtonian science were not equivalent to the two world wars, the Holocaust, quantum mechanics, and the theory of relativity. Maybe the eighteenth-century developments were not quite so earth-shattering, in the long term. But at the time, they shocked people in a way not seen again until the twentieth century. The context of global upheaval mattered—it definitely gave an edge to discussions of science. Thus, it is all the more striking that the nineteenth century lacked any global cataclysms, despite the localized carnages of the American Civil War and of the Crimean War. Had his theory of evolution come onto the scene during a period of massive global conflict, might Darwin have faced a different reception?

In both the eighteenth and twentieth centuries, people responded to the upheavals in a similar way. They created a hero, a genius in science who could decode the cosmos. In the popular imagination, both men acquired a slightly rumpled quality. The "bohemian" Einstein matched the informally wigless Franklin. Both were transformed into kindly if eccentric uncles, improbably twinkly of eye. What accounted for the desire to domesticate each great intellect? The words *genius* and *genial* come from the same root but are rarely applied to the same person. Perhaps the latter word can defuse the impact of the former. That may be why their contemporaries rendered Franklin and Einstein as geniuses—but charming ones.

None of this hero worship effectively represented either Franklin's or Einstein's science—or science at all, which involves much more than individual personalities. Apart from their similar places in popular culture, Franklin and Einstein did not have much in common. And it is a bit sad that each genius was eventually assigned a symbol whose scientific meaning few people truly understood. Franklin is endlessly flying his kite in some fictitious rainstorm; Einstein will forever be writing $E = mc^2$ on some fictitious blackboard. Ask anyone what they know about either "scientist," and you'll probably get some kind of statement about the kite or the equation; ask the follow-up question, "what does it *mean*," and you're unlikely to get a response that explains a Newtonian view of particulate matter and friction or a relation between energy and mass.

We could bring Franklin completely up to date by introducing him to string theory and complexity theory. Had he been shocked at the demolition of the Newtonian worldview, he could then reel from new assaults on Einstein's view of the cosmos. (And he could see how discovery of the DNA double helix and human genome have reignited arguments over race and racism.) But perhaps the point is already clear: Franklin does not belong to our era. The revolutions in thought and society between his death and the present day are vast; his response to those changes is something we can never know.

But really, Franklin stood not for a specific theory but for a kind of curiosity—a way of being in the world. He was endlessly fascinated by nature and wanted others to be so, as well. Had he been kept alive in his barrel of Madeira and then revived to witness our era, it is likely that he would have been most surprised not by any particular invention or theory but by our lack of curiosity. The gap between experts in science and the general public continues to widen. In Franklin's own country, science education has declined dramatically, along with the reading public's grasp of scientific terms and theories.[52]

What would Franklin have made, for instance, of the debates over climate change? Earth scientists, including oceanographers, have been arguing for the past few decades that there is strong evidence that the globe's climate is changing. They point to extreme weather patterns, now more common than they were a century ago. Oceanographers analyze data that indicate that the warm waters of the Gulf Stream are now not so apparent because the rest of the ocean's surface is heating up. If that warming trend continues, oceanographers claim, the ocean's system of circulation will not transfer heat from equator to poles as effectively. The warming trend in ocean and climate would become even worse. But even as scientists have presented data to support these claims, Americans, including political leaders, have tended to ignore them.[53]

Franklin certainly would have been interested in the subject. Climate was, after all, a topic he had considered throughout his life, starting with his observations at sea in 1726 and continuing through his almanacs and subsequent work in the sciences. And his first scientific work had been on the circulation of heat. Above all, he was a pioneer observer of the Gulf Stream, which is now regarded as a key indicator of climate change. Surely, Franklin would have been dismayed at current predictions that the Gulf Stream may cease to exist as the ocean warms up around it? Surely, he would have been amazed, if not appalled, at projections that the warming of polar zones will open up the Northwest Passage he had long sought?

But perhaps the aspect of the debate that would most alarm Franklin would be the divide between scientists and nonscientists. Why do the latter ignore the former? He had never imagined a division of this sort. And, indeed, why should it exist?

It does not exist in another area, one that might have delighted Franklin. At several points in his life, he had encouraged other Americans to participate in astronomical observations. They still can. Big science notwithstanding, there has been a renaissance of backyard astronomy. Mere aficionados with telescopes and access to the Internet have been collaborating with astronomers to generate a battery of useful observations of the heavens, far more than the specially trained astronomers could ever collect themselves. It is not necessarily the gadgetry—telescopes and laptops—that would delight Poor Richard. Instead, it is the assumption that any person with a basic education can participate in science and examine the natural world. Franklin had many faults; he had tried to cultivate many virtues. But his best qualities were perhaps his endless curiosity about the natural world and his determination that others learn to share it.[54]

WHEN he was a young printer, Franklin had experimented with nature prints, in which he imprinted the leaves of plants onto paper. As a youth in London, he may have learned about the technique of stereotyping. Printers who produced stereotypes used a soft material, usually papier-mâché, to make an impression of an object, perhaps something from nature such as a leaf, flower, or feather. When the impression dried, printers could use it to mold lead; in this way, they created very specialized pieces of type, or characters, as they called them. Around 1731, Franklin's Library Company colleague, Joseph Breintnall, had started to produce nature prints—some exquisite examples survive at the Library Company today. Then Franklin tried

Nature counterfeited (*front*). Franklin and Hall's nature print
on Philadelphia currency, 1764. PRIVATE COLLECTION.

his hand. He used one nature print, of a leaf of the "Rattle-Snake"
plant, in *Poor Richard* for 1737; he touted the herb's power against
pleurisy. At least as early as 1737, he began to use nature prints on
paper currency. When Franklin produced bills for New Jersey, Delaware, and Pennsylvania, he used plants—willow or blackberry leaves,
fern pinnules—to print designs on their reverse sides.[55]

It was a brilliant way to prevent counterfeiting. The print on each
bill was unique. Franklin could pluck a leaf or fern, use it to produce a carefully guarded impression, and then discard it. The bills
he printed would bear images impossible to reproduce. People
would gain greater confidence in the paper money, which would
foster its broad circulation, one of Franklin's cherished goals. Many
of the surviving bills he printed have creases in them. His contemporaries had clearly used them and perhaps folded them to put
away for safekeeping. Inspired by Franklin's example, printers who
produced currency for the United Colonies and the later United

Nature counterfeited (*back*). Franklin and Hall's nature print
on Philadelphia currency, 1764. PRIVATE COLLECTION.

States also used nature prints. Nature itself would protect the republic's credit and finances.

"To Counterfeit is DEATH," a common phrase on early American
currency warned. The admonition had many meanings when it appeared above a nature print. A nature print was unique; only God
could create the living things that were unique. But was a nature
printer thereby counterfeiting the works of the divine Craftsman?
Or, was the printer instead reverently observing his power? Certainly, Franklin was aware of the power of his craft. He was careful
not to reveal his technique of nature printing to anyone he thought
untrustworthy. He must have told his business partner, David Hall.
Hall continued to use nature prints on currency into the 1760s.
And Franklin evidently explained the process to Cadwallader
Colden, but loyally, Colden kept his friend's secret. In 1743, Colden
wrote William Strahan that he could not describe how Franklin produced his nature prints: "As printing is this mans trade and he

makes a Benefite of it I do not think my self at liberty to communicate it." We still do not know how Franklin created his nature prints.
Did he use plaster, or papier-mâché, or damp earth? How did he
manipulate any of these sticky substances into a useful stereotype?
The trade secret died with its inventor, the Philadelphia master
printer.[56]

Mastery and mystery. As with the nature prints, so with all of
Franklin's science. Throughout his life, Franklin sought to understand and control natural phenomena. But he never lost his faith
that nature was, in the end, wonderful, a vast scene of marvels. To
counterfeit Creation—who but Benjamin Franklin, that unique
eighteenth-century character, the first scientific American, could
have made the act one of both the highest arrogance and of the
greatest reverence?

NOTES

For further information on the events of Franklin's life, see the chronologies in each volume of Leonard W. Labaree et al., eds., *The Papers of Benjamin Franklin,* 37 vols. to date (New Haven, 1959–), and in *The Autobiography of Benjamin Franklin,* ed. Leonard W. Labaree et al., 2nd ed. (New Haven, 2003), 303–322. Carl Van Doren's *Benjamin Franklin* (New York, 1938), is still the best comprehensive biography.

To emphasize the sociable and collaborative nature of eighteenth-century science, I have not used the published versions of Benjamin Franklin's *Experiments and Observations on Electricity;* instead, I cite the versions of the essays as they originally appeared, as letters. *The Papers of Benjamin Franklin* publishes the letters but also specifies which edition of Franklin's *Experiments and Observations* they appeared in and what changes were made to them when they were published.

Abbreviations

The following abbreviations are used throughout the notes. Each work listed here is cited in full at first appearance in the the Notes section.

People

BF: Benjamin Franklin
CC: Cadwallader Colden
DF: Deborah Franklin
JB: Jacques Barbeu-Dubourg
JI: Jan Ingenhousz
JL: Jean-Baptiste Le Roy
JP: Joseph Priestley
MS: Mary "Polly" Stevenson (later Mary Hewson)
PC: Peter Collinson
WF: William Franklin
WS: William Strahan

Books and Periodicals

Autobiography: Leonard W. Labaree et al., eds. *The Autobiography of Benjamin Franklin.* 2nd ed. (New Haven, 2003).
AWM: American Weekly Mercury
BFP: Charles Coleman Sellers, *Benjamin Franklin in Portraiture* (New Haven, 1962).

BFS: I. Bernard Cohen, *Benjamin Franklin's Science* (Cambridge, Mass., 1990).

CHS: The Cambridge History of Science, vol. 4, *Eighteenth-Century Science,* ed. Roy Porter (Cambridge, 2003).

F&N: I. Bernard Cohen, *Franklin and Newton: An Inquiry into Speculative Newtonian Experimental Science and Franklin's Work in Electricity as an Example Thereof* (Philadelphia, 1956).

JA: L. H. Butterfield et al., eds., *Diary and Autobiography of John Adams,* 4 vols. (Cambridge, Mass., 1961).

NEC: New-England Courant

NEQ: New England Quarterly

PBF: Leonard W. Labaree et al., eds., *The Papers of Benjamin Franklin,* 37 vols. to date (New Haven, 1959–).

PG: Pennsylvania Gazette

PR: Poor Richard

PRI: Poor Richard Improved

SFF: I. Bernard Cohen, *Science and the Founding Fathers: Science in the Political Thought of Thomas Jefferson, Benjamin Franklin, John Adams, and James Madison* (New York, 1995).

WBF: Albert Henry Smyth, ed., *The Writings of Benjamin Franklin,* 10 vols. (New York, 1905–1907).

WMQ: William and Mary Quarterly, 3rd ser.

Archives

APS: American Philosophical Society, Philadelphia
PO: Post Office Archives, London
RS: Royal Society, London
TNA: The National Archives, London

Chapter 1

1. BF to Sarah Bache, June 3, 1779, Leonard W. Labaree et al., eds., *The Papers of Benjamin Franklin,* 37 vols. to date (New Haven, 1959–), 29:613; Charles Coleman Sellers, *Benjamin Franklin in Portraiture* (New Haven, 1962), ill. 5–44; *PBF,* 36:fig. facing p. 11 and 11n (on Jacques Bianchi's silk portrait).

2. *Oxford English Dictionary,* 2nd ed. (Oxford, 1989), s.v., "genius"; Penelope Murray, "Introduction," in *Genius: The History of an Idea,* ed. Penelope Murray (New York, 1989), 1–8; L. P. Smith, *Words and Idioms: Studies in the English Language* (London, 1925), 108–112; Simon Schaffer, "Genius in Romantic Natural Philosophy," in *Romanticism and the Sciences,* ed. Andrew Cunningham and Nicholas Jardine (New York, 1990), 82–98; "B. B." [BF], *A Modest Enquiry into the Nature and Necessity of a Paper-Currency* (1729), *PBF,* 1:148; Penuel Bowen to BF, Nov. 6, 1771, *PBF,* 18:244.

3. The literatures on Franklin are enormous, and what appears below is necessarily selective, focusing on monographic studies.On science as public culture, the main works are Margaret C. Jacob, *The Cultural Meaning of the Scientific Revolution* (New York, 1988); Larry Stewart, *The Rise of Public Science: Rhetoric, Technology, and Natural Philosophy in Newtonian Britain, 1660–1750* (Cambridge, 1992); Jan Golinski, *Science as Public Culture: Chemistry and Enlightenment in Britain, 1760–1820* (New York, 1992). These works have only scattered references to Franklin and do not consider imperial or transatlantic contexts for science.The best studies of

Franklin's science are specialized and tend to stress the electricity. See especially the foundational work of I. Bernard Cohen: "Introduction," in *Benjamin Franklin's Experiments: A New Edition of Franklin's Experiments and Observations on Electricity*, ed. I. Bernard Cohen (Cambridge, Mass., 1941), 3–161; *Franklin and Newton: An Inquiry into Speculative Newtonian Experimental Science and Franklin's Work in Electricity as an Example Thereof* (Philadelphia, 1956); and *Benjamin Franklin's Science* (Cambridge, Mass., 1990). Another essential source is J. L. Heilbron, *Electricity in the Seventeenth and Eighteenth Centuries: A Study of Early Modern Physics* (Berkeley, 1979). Many other studies have also stressed Franklin's electrical work, most recently Michael Brian Schiffer, *Draw the Lightning Down: Benjamin Franklin and Electrical Technology in the Age of Enlightenment* (Berkeley, 2003), and Philip Dray, *Stealing God's Thunder: Benjamin Franklin's Lightning Rod and the Invention of America* (New York, 2005). There is very little material on other aspects of Franklin's sprawling work in science, but see Charles Tanford, *Ben Franklin Stilled the Waves: An Informal History of Pouring Oil on Water with Reflections on the Ups and Downs of Scientific Life in General* (Durham, N.C., 1989). Excellent studies of Franklin and public affairs (which nevertheless do not explain the place of science within his life) include Gerald Stourzh, *Benjamin Franklin and American Foreign Policy* (Chicago, 1954); Paul W. Conner, *Poor Richard's Politics* (New York, 1965); Robert Middlekauff, *Benjamin Franklin and His Enemies* (Berkeley, 1996); Edmund S. Morgan, *Benjamin Franklin* (New Haven, 2002); David Waldstreicher, *Runaway America: Benjamin Franklin, Slavery, and the American Revolution* (New York, 2004); Gordon S. Wood, *The Americanization of Benjamin Franklin* (New York, 2004); and Stacy Schiff, *A Great Improvisation: Franklin, France, and the Birth of America* (New York, 2005).The "catalog of a life" approach is exemplified by Carl Van Doren, *Benjamin Franklin* (New York, 1938); H. W. Brands, *The First American: The Life and Times of Benjamin Franklin* (New York, 2000); Walter Isaacson, *Benjamin Franklin: An American Life* (2003); and J. A. Leo Lemay, *The Life of Benjamin Franklin: Journalist, 1706–1730*, and *The Life of Benjamin Franklin: Printer and Publisher, 1730–1747* (Philadelphia, 2005), the first two of a projected seven-volume study of Franklin.

4. *Oxford English Dictionary*, s.vv., "science" and "scientific."

5. Ibid., "scientist"; Steven Shapin, "The Image of the Man of Science," in *The Cambridge History of Science*, vol. 4, *Eighteenth Century Science*, ed. Roy Porter (Cambridge, 2003), 159–183.

6. BF to PC, Sept. 1753, *PBF*, 5:69.

Chapter 2

1. *The Autobiography of Benjamin Franklin*, ed. Leonard W. Labaree et al., 2nd ed. (New Haven, 2003), 43, 268.

2. Ibid. 50–51; Perry Miller, "Errand into the Wilderness," *William and Mary Quarterly*, 3rd ser., 10 (1953), 3–19; Virginia DeJohn Anderson, "Migrants and Motives: Religion and the Settlement of New England," *New England Quarterly* 58 (1983), 339–383.

3. Ian K. Steele, *The English Atlantic, 1675–1740: An Exploration of Communication and Community* (New York, 1986), 14–15; Martin W. Lewis, "Dividing the Ocean Sea," *Geographical Review* 89 (1999), 188–214.

4. *Autobiography*, 52–53. The best overview of Franklin's life in Boston is in Arthur Bernon Tourtellot, *Benjamin Franklin: The Shaping of Genius, 1706–1723* (Garden City, N.Y., 1977).

5. BF to Samuel Mather, May 12, 1784, Albert Henry Smyth, ed., *The Writings of Benjamin Franklin*, 10 vols. (New York, 1905–1907), 9:208.

6. Samuel Eliot Morison, *Three Centuries of Harvard* (Cambridge, Mass., 1936), chaps. 1 and 2; William Eamon, *Science and the Secrets of Nature: Books of Secrets in Medieval and Early Modern Culture* (Princeton, 1994), 93–94.

7. *Autobiography*, 53; Nian-Sheng Huang, *Franklin's Father Josiah: Life of a Colonial Boston Tallow Chandler, 1657–1745*, APS Transactions 90 (2000), 73–74; Gary B. Nash, *The Urban Crucible: Social Change, Political Consciousness, and the Origins of the American Revolution* (Cambridge, Mass., 1979), 60–65, 111–118 (on Boston's economy).

8. Huang, *Franklin's Father Josiah*, 15–86; "Feb. 5, 1702/03," *The Diary of Samuel Sewall, 1674–1729*, ed. M. Halsey Thomas, 2 vols. (New York, 1973), 1:482.

9. Steven Shapin, *The Scientific Revolution* (Chicago, 1996), 30–46; Stephen A. Epstein, *Wage Labor and Guilds in Medieval Europe* (Chapel Hill, N.C., 1991), esp. chap. 3; W. J. Rorabaugh, *The Craft Apprentice: From Franklin to the Machine Age in America* (New York, 1986), 4–5, 8.

10. Elizabeth L. Eisenstein, *The Printing Press as an Agent of Change: Communication and Cultural Transformations in Early-Modern Europe* (Cambridge, 1976), esp. chap. 6 (but cf. Adrian Johns, *The Nature of the Book: Print and Knowledge in the Making* [Chicago, 1998], chap. 1); Eamon, *Science and the Secrets of Nature*, 94–133.

11. Rorabaugh, *Craft Apprentice*, 6–7; Huang, *Franklin's Father Josiah*, 60–62.

12. *Autobiography*, 53.

13. Genealogical notes, *PBF*, 1:lviii, lx; N. A. M. Rodger, *The Command of the Ocean: A Naval History of Britain, 1649–1815* (London, 2004), 205–206, 636–639; Marcus Rediker, *Between the Devil and the Deep Blue Sea: Merchant Seamen, Pirates, and the Anglo-American Maritime World, 1700–1750* (Cambridge, 1987), 30–33, 80–81, 290; Daniel Vickers, "Beyond Jack Tar," *WMQ* 50 (1993), 418–424; Dava Sobel, *Longitude: The True Story of a Lone Genius Who Solved the Greatest Scientific Problem of His Time* (London, 1995).

14. *PBF*, 1:liv, lv (on Starbucks); Nathaniel Philbrick, *Away Off Shore: Nantucket Island and Its People, 1602–1890* (Nantucket, Mass., 1994), 79 (on Starbuck store), chap. 11 (on Peleg Folger); Edward Byers, *The Nation of Nantucket: Society and Politics in an Early American Commercial Center, 1660–1820* (Boston, 1987); Edouard A. Stackpole, *The Sea-Hunters: The New England Whalemen during Two Centuries, 1635–1835* (Philadelphia, 1953), 37 (on Peleg).

15. Herman Melville, *Moby-Dick*, ed. Harrison Hayford and Hershel Parker (New York, 1967), 101.

16. *PBF*, 1:liv, lv; Folger genealogy, *PBF*, 10:397–399; BF to Abiah Franklin, Oct. 16, 1747, *PBF*, 3:179–180; BF to Keziah Coffin, Aug. 29, 1765, *PBF*, 12:247; BF to [Jonathan Folger], Aug. 29, 1765, *PBF*, 12:248; BF to Jane Mecom, July 7, 1773, *PBF*, 20:290.

17. BF to Jane Mecom, Jan. 9, 1760, *PBF*, 9:18.

18. *PBF*, 1:lvii, lix, lx; Peter Franklin to BF, Feb. 21, 1765, *PBF*, 12:77; *Autobiography*, 79; *PBF*, 8:120 and illustrations that follow.

19. *Autobiography*, 53–54; Benjamin Franklin (the elder), "Sent to My Name upon a Report of His Inclineation to Martial Affaires," 1710, *PBF*, 1:4.

20. N. A. M. Rodger, *The Wooden World: An Anatomy of the Georgian Navy* (New York, 1996), 45; Rediker, *Between the Devil and the Deep Blue Sea*, 155–156, 163–169, 186–193.

21. *Autobiography*, 57.

22. Rorabaugh, *Craft Apprentice*, 11–14.

23. Johns, *Nature of the Book*, 74–108.

24. Possible BF poetry, *PBF*, 1:6–7; *Autobiography*, 58–60.

25. *Autobiography*, 62.

26. Ibid., 61n; Edward A. Bloom and Lillian D. Bloom, *Joseph Addison's Sociable Animal: In the Marketplace, on the Hustings, in the Pulpit* (Providence, R.I., 1971).

27. William Clark, Jan Golinski, and Simon Schaffer, eds., *The Sciences in Enlightened Europe* (Chicago, 1999), 5–29; *Spectator* 1, no. 10, p. 54.

28. *Spectator*, 7, no. 554 (1713), 543, and 8, no. 635 (1715), 424.

29. *Autobiography*, 64.

30. Ibid., 113–114.

31. Ibid., 63–64.

32. J. D. Davies, *Gentlemen and Tarpaulins: The Officers and Men of the Restoration Navy* (Oxford, 1991); Richard Ollard, "The Navy," in *The Diary of Samuel Pepys*, vol. 10, *Companion*, ed. Robert Latham (Berkeley, 1983), 285–287; Daniel A. Baugh, *The British Naval Administration in the Age of Walpole* (Princeton, 1965), 100–102.

33. Rediker, *Between the Devil and the Deep Blue Sea*, esp. chaps. 3 and 4; Ira Dye, "Early American Merchant Seafarers," APS *Proceedings* 120 (1976), 331–360; Rodger, *Command of the Ocean*, 127–130, 312–316; Christopher Lloyd, *The British Seaman, 1200–1860: A Social Survey* (Rutherford, N.J., 1970), chaps. 6, 7.

34. *Autobiography*, 64; Samuel Sturmy, *The Mariners Magazine* (London, 1669), poem by Henry Phillippes on p. 1.

35. *Autobiography*, 64.

36. Robert Darnton, *The Great Cat Massacre and Other Episodes in French Cultural History* (New York, 1984), 75–104; *Autobiography*, 62–63.

37. Tourtellot, *Benjamin Franklin*, 233.

38. *New-England Courant*, Aug. 7–Aug. 14, 1721; Perry Miller, *The New England Mind: From Colony to Province* (Cambridge, Mass., 1953), 345–366; James W. Schmotter, "William Douglass and the Beginnings of American Medical Professionalism: A Reinterpretation of the 1721 Boston Inoculation Controversy," *Historical Journal of Western Massachusetts* 6 (1977), 23–36; Maxine Van de Wetering, "A Reconsideration of the Inoculation Controversy," *NEQ* 58 (1985), 46–67; Margot Minardi, "The Boston Inoculation Controversy of 1721–1722: An Incident in the History of Race," *WMQ* 61 (2004), 47–76.

39. *NEC*, Nov. 27–Dec. 4, 1721.

40. Silence Dogood, no. 1, *NEC*, Apr. 2, 1722, *PBF*, 1:9–10; Douglas Anderson, *The Radical Enlightenments of Benjamin Franklin* (Baltimore, 1997), 16–33.

41. *NEC*, Dec. 3, 1722.

42. Silence Dogood, no. 13, *NEC*, Sept. 24, 1722, *PBF*, 1:42.

43. *Autobiography*, 69.

44. Ibid., 68–70.

45. Ibid., 71.

46. Ibid., 71–73, 81.

47. Ibid., 75–76.

48. Ibid., 77–78.

49. Ibid., 81–83, 92–93.

50. Ibid., 93.

51. Ibid., 93–94.

52. Ibid., 96, 99–101; Johns, *Nature of the Book*, 62–99.

53. BF to Benjamin Vaughan, July 31, 1786, *WBF*, 10:531; *Autobiography*, 101.

54. Roy Porter, *London: A Social History* (London, 1996), 98, 132–133.

55. *Autobiography*, 96, 97.

56. Ibid.; Anderson, *Radical Enlightenments*, 33–53.

57. *Autobiography*, 97, 97n; Anderson, *Radical Enlightenments*, 33–53.

58. Shapin, *Scientific Revolution*, 1–29; Roy Porter, *The Greatest Benefit to Mankind: A Medical History of Humanity, from Antiquity to the Present* (London, 1997), 56–58, 60.

59. Shapin, *Scientific Revolution*, 30–117; Porter, *Greatest Benefit to Mankind*, 201–244; Mordechai Feingold, *The Newtonian Moment: Isaac Newton and the Making of Modern Culture* (New York and Oxford, 2004); Richard S. Westfall, *Never at Rest: A Biography of Isaac Newton* (Cambridge, 1980).

60. Feingold, *Newtonian Moment*, 118–141; Mary Fissell and Roger Cooter, "Exploring Natural Knowledge: Science and the Popular," *CHS*, 134–139.

61. *Autobiography*, 97; Margaret C. Jacob, *The Cultural Meaning of the Scientific Revolution* (New York, 1988); Larry Stewart, *The Rise of Public Science: Rhetoric, Technology, and Natural Philosophy in Newtonian Britain, 1660–1750* (Cambridge, 1992).

62. Michael Hunter, *Establishing the New Science: The Experience of the Early Royal Society* (Woodbridge, Suffolk, UK, 1989); James E. McClellan III, *Science Reorganized: Scientific Societies in the Eighteenth Century* (New York, 1985), chap. 2; Raymond Phineas Stearns, *Science in the British Colonies of America* (Urbana, Ill., 1970), chap. 4.

63. BF to Sir Hans Sloane, June 2, 1725, *PBF*, 1:54.

64. *Autobiography*, 97–98.

65. Ibid., 103–104, 105–106.

66. Ibid., 106; "Plan of Conduct," *PBF*, 1:99, 100.

67. BF, "Journal of a Voyage," 1726, *PBF*, 1:73, 98.

68. Ibid., 83, 89, 94–95.

69. Ibid., 85–90.

70. Ibid., 93–95.

71. Ibid., 95.

72. *Oxford English Dictionary*, s.v., "gulf-weed."

73. BF, "Journal of a Voyage," 89, 90, 93, 94, 95.

74. Chronology, *PBF*, 1:lxxxvii; BF, "Journal of a Voyage," 90.

75. BF, "Journal of a Voyage," 84–85, 88, 91.

76. Ibid., 92, 93.

77. Ibid., 95–96.

78. Ibid., 97–99.

79. *Autobiography*, 106.

Chapter 3

1. BF, "Journal of a Voyage," 1726, *PBF*, 1:99.

2. *Autobiography*, 107.

3. BF epitaph, *PBF*, 1:111.

4. *Proceedings of the Right Worshipful Grand Lodge . . . at Its Celebration of the Bi-centenary of the Birth of Right Worshipful Past Grand Master Brother Benjamin Franklin* (Philadelphia, 1906), 55–56; *Autobiography*, 116.

5. *Autobiography*, 109, 116–118.

6. "Standing Queries for the Junto," *PBF*, 1:258–259.

7. Ibid., 257; "Proposals and Queries to Be Asked the Junto," *PBF*, 1:259.

8. *PBF*, 1:113–114; *Autobiography*, 120.

9. "The Busy-Body," no. 1, *American Weekly Mercury*, Feb. 4, 1728/1729, *PBF*, 1:115–116.

10. Letters of "Martha Careful" and "Caelia Shortface," *AWM*, Jan. 28, 1728/ 1729, *PBF*, 1:111–113.

11. Ian K. Steele, *The English Atlantic, 1675–1740: An Exploration of Communication and Community* (New York, 1986), 145–167; Charles E. Clark and Charles Wetherell, "The Measure of Maturity: *The Pennsylvania Gazette*, 1728–1765," *WMQ* 46 (1989), 279–303; *PG*, Oct. 23, 1729.

12. Gary B. Nash, *Quakers and Politics: Pennsylvania, 1681–1726* (Princeton, 1968).

13. *PG*, Apr. 22, 1731, and Dec. 14, 1731.

14. *Autobiography*, 96, 96n.

15. Richard S. Westfall, *Science and Religion in Seventeenth-Century England* (New Haven, 1958); Neal C. Gillespie, "Natural Order, Natural Theology and Social Order: John Ray and the 'Newtonian Ideology,'" *Journal of the History of Biology* 20 (1987), 1–49; William B. Ashworth, "Natural History and the Emblematic World View," in *Reappraisals of the Scientific Revolution*, ed. David C. Lindberg and Robert S. Westman (Cambridge, 1990), 305–308.

16. BF, "On the Providence of God in the Government of the World" [1732], *PBF*, 1:265; BF, "Articles of Belief and Acts of Religion, Nov. 30, 1728, *PBF*, 1:104, 105.

17. BF, "Apology for Printers," *Pennsylvania Gazette*, June 10, 1731.

18. Ibid.

19. *PG*, Dec. 8, 1737, Apr. 6, 1738, and May 18, 1738.

20. Gary B. Nash, "Up from the Bottom in Franklin's Philadelphia," *Past & Present*, no. 77 (1977), 57–83.

21. *PG*, June 15, 1732, Oct. 29, 1741, Aug. 4, 1748, and Sept. 7, 1749.

22. Clark and Wetherell, "*Pennsylvania Gazette*," 289–291; David Waldstreicher, "Reading the Runaways: Self-Fashioning, Print Culture, and Confidence in Slavery in the Eighteenth-Century Mid-Atlantic," *WMQ* 56 (1999), 243–272.

23. David Waldstreicher, *Runaway America: Benjamin Franklin, Slavery, and the American Revolution* (New York, 2004), 3–26, 87–114.

24. *PG*, July 31, 1735 (on coffee), Sept. 8, 1737 (on oil), Nov. 16, 1734 (on soap). On advertisements of projects, see the discussion of Pennsylvania Academy below.

25. *PG*, Mar. 21, 1734.

26. *PG*, Dec. 12 and 26, 1734.

27. *PG*, Dec. 29, 1730, and Jan. 5, 1731.

28. *PG*, May 14, 1730 (on Boston), May 28, 1730 (on inoculation), Mar. 4 and 11, 1731 (on *Philosophical Transactions*), and July 8, 1731.

29. *PG*, Nov. 30, 1732.

30. *PG*, Jan. 6, 1737.

31. Hugh Meredith, Dissolution of Partnership, [July 14, 1730], *PBF*, 1:175.

32. *PG*, June 30, 1737; Deborah Franklin advertised other missing religious books in *PG*, Aug. 13, 1741.

33. Margaret C. Jacob, *Living the Enlightenment: Freemasonry and Politics in Eighteenth-Century Europe* (New York, 1991), esp. 3–22, 31–35; Steven C. Bullock, *Revolutionary Brotherhood: Freemasonry and the Transformation of the American Social Order, 1730–1840* (Chapel Hill, N.C., 1996), 16–17 (for quotation), 25–41.

34. Jacob, *Living the Enlightenment*, 36–38, 41–43, 47–50, 56–57, 137; Bullock, *Revolutionary Brotherhood*, 3–4, 9–25, 36–41, 55.

35. Bullock, *Revolutionary Brotherhood*, 46–47; Accounts for Printing Business, 1748–1766, *PBF*, 3:271.

36. *PG,* Dec. 8, 1730; Report of a Committee on By-laws for St. John's Lodge, [June 5, 1732], *PBF,* 1:232.

37. Bullock, *Revolutionary Brotherhood,* 50–52, 66–68.

38. *Autobiography,* 130, 142.

39. [BF], "A Short Account of the LIBRARY," *PBF,* 2:308–309; Rules for Library Co. of Philadelphia, Dec. 12, 1763, *PBF,* 10:387.

40. *Autobiography,* 143; Directors of Library Co. to John Penn, Aug. 8, 1738, *PBF,* 2:207; BF to WS, July 4, 1744, *PBF,* 2:412, 412n; *PG,* June 5, 1740 (see also *PBF,* 2:286n).

41. Rudolph M. Bell, *How to Do It: Guides to Good Living for Renaissance Italians* (Chicago, 1999); Eamon, *Science and the Secrets of Nature,* 342–346; Frank A. Kafker, ed., *Notable Encyclopedias of the Seventeenth and Eighteenth Centuries: Nine Predecessors of the Encyclopédie* (Oxford, 1981); John Lough, *The Encyclopédie* (London, 1971), 1–19; E[phraim] Chambers, *Cyclopedia; or, An Universal Dictionary of Arts and Sciences* (London, 1728), xxix, 202, 358. Franklin even reprinted Chambers's description of Masons; see *Proceedings of the Right Worshipful Grand Lodge,* 61–62.

42. Charles Coulston Gillispie, *Science and Polity in France at the End of the Old Regime* (Princeton, 1980), 337–356; Lough, *Encyclopédie,* 17–60, 85–91.

43. BF to WS, Apr. 29, 1749, *PBF,* 3:379; BF to WS, May 9, 1763, *PBF,* 10:261; BF to Thomas Becket, Dec. 17, 1763, *PBF,* 10:393; BF to Charles Thomson and Thomas Mifflin, July 7, 1769, *PBF,* 16:171–172; Library Co. Committee to BF, Jan. 25, 1771, *PBF,* 18:17; JP to BF, Apr. 19, 1771, *PBF,* 18:69–71 (on price list); BF to Library Co. Committee, *PBF,* 18:117–118; Library Co. to BF, Apr. 27, 1772, *PBF,* 19:117.

44. Dena Goodman, *The Republic of Letters: A Cultural History of the French Enlightenment* (Ithaca, 1994).

45. *PG,* Dec. 28, 1732; *Poor Richard,* 1734, *PBF,* 1:311; *Autobiography,* 145; Sheila Skemp, "Family Partnerships: The Working Wife, Honoring Deborah Franklin," in *Benjamin Franklin and Women,* ed. Larry Tise (University Park, Pa., 2000), 19–36.

46. Marion Barber Stowell, *Early American Almanacs: The Colonial Weekday Bible* (New York, 1977), 17, 25, 80–82.

47. Bernard Capp, *English Almanacs, 1500–1800: Astrology and the Popular Press* (Ithaca, 1979); Stowell, *Early American Almanacs,* 13–25, 76, 80–82.

48. *PR,* 1733, *PBF,* 1:314, 315; *PR,* 1735, *PBF,* 2:9; *PR,* 1736, *PBF,* 2:137, 141.

49. *PR,* 1744, *PBF,* 2:396; Martin Davies, *Aldus Manutius: Printer and Publisher of Renaissance Venice* (London, 1995), 39, 63.

50. *PR,* 1733, *PBF,* 1:311. Richard Saunder, Franklin's English prototype, had scoffed at astrology; see Capp, *English Almanacs,* 239.

51. Anderson, *Radical Enlightenments,* 99–101. Confusingly, there was a real Titan Leeds, whose alamanacs Jerman was claiming to publish; see Stowell, *Early American Almanacs,* 69, 72.

52. *PR,* 1745, *PBF,* 3:3–4.

53. *PG,* Sept. 17, 1747 (*PR*), *PBF,* 3:236.

54. *Poor Richard Improved,* 1748, *PBF* 3:250–251; *PRI,* 1749, *PBF,* 3:335; Franklin similarly regarded Francis Bacon as "the father of the modern experimental philosophy," *PBF,* 3:339. See Anderson, *Radical Enlightenments,* 120–123.

55. *PRI,* 1748, *PBF,* 3:250, 251; *PRI,* 1749, *PBF* 3:336; Alan D. McKillop, "Some Newtonian Verses in Poor Richard," *NEQ* 21 (1948), 383–385; Anderson, *Radical Enlightenments,* 55–60.

56. *PRI,* 1751, *PBF,* 4:90, 91; Edwin Wolf, 2nd, ed., *The Library of James Logan of*

Philadelphia, 1674–1751 (Philadelphia, 1974), 5; Directors of Library Company to John Penn, Aug. 3, 1741, *PBF,* 2:312.

57. Alan Macfarlane and Gerry Martin, *Glass: A World History* (Chicago, 2002), chap. 5; Catherine Wilson, *The Invisible World: Early Modern Philosophy and the Invention of the Microscope* (Princeton, 1995), esp. chap. 5.

58. Isaac Newton, *Opticks; or, A Treatise of the Reflections, Refractions, Inflections and Colours of Light,* 4th ed. of 1730 (New York, 1952), 15–16; J. L. Heilbron, *Elements of Early Modern Physics* (Berkeley, 1982), 5, 43–47; Shapin, *Scientific Revolution,* 112–117; I. Bernard Cohen, *Franklin and Newton: An Inquiry into Speculative Newtonian Experimental Science and Franklin's Work in Electricity as an Example Thereof* (Philadelphia, 1956), 118–127.

59. Charles E. Letocha, "The Invention and Early Manufacture of Bifocals," *History of Opthalmology* 35 (1990), 226–235; *AWM,* Dec. 9, 1736.

60. *PG,* Apr. 28, 1743, and Dec. 9, 1746; *PRI,* 1753, *PBF,* 4:406–408.

61. *PR,* 1734, *PBF,* 1:358.

62. *PRI,* 1757, *PBF,* 7:86.

63. *PRI,* 1753, *PBF,* 4:408. The signature is from *PRI,* 1745, *PBF,* 3:4.

64. Raymond Phineas Stearns, *Science in the British Colonies of America,* 575–593; Thomas P. Slaughter, *The Natures of John and William Bartram* (New York, 1996).

65. *PR,* 1741, *PBF,* 2:298–299; *PG,* Mar. 17, 1742; *PG,* Apr. 26, 1744.

66. Wolf, *Library of James Logan,* xvii–xlv; Stearns, *Science in the British Colonies,* 535–536; *PG,* Nov. 3, 1737 (see also *PBF,* 2:188n).

67. Stearns, *Science in the British Colonies,* 536–539.

68. BF to James Logan, [1737?], *PBF,* 2:184–185; Logan to BF, Feb. 26, 1744, *PBF,* 2:401–402; BF's preface to Logan's *Cato Major* (1744), *PBF,* 2:405.

69. Smyth, "The Life of Benjamin Franklin," *WBF,* 10:489n; *Proceedings of the Right Worshipful Grand Lodge,* 90; BF, *Some Observations on the Proceedings against the Rev. Mr. Hemphill* (1735), *PBF,* 2:38; BF, afterword to [John Tennent], *Every Man His Own Doctor* (1736), *PBF,* 2:155–158.

70. *PG,* Dec. 30, 1736.

71. BF to PC [1752?], *PBF,* 4:392–403; Paul C. Pasles, "The Lost Squares of Dr. Franklin: Ben Franklin's Missing Squares and the Secret of the Magic Circle," *American Mathematical Monthly* 108 (2001), 489–511.

72. Howard Robinson, *Carrying British Mails Overseas* (New York, 1964), chap. 4; John Haskell Kemble, "England's First Atlantic Mail Line," pt. 1, *Mariner's Mirror* 26 (1940), 33–54.

73. Robinson, *Carrying British Mails Overseas,* 39–46.

74. *Autobiography,* 126, 127; editorial note, *PBF,* 2:178.

75. Distribution of the mail, Apr. 1743, *PBF,* 2:377–378; BF to PC, May 21, 1751, *PBF,* 4:135.

76. John Clyde Oswald, *Benjamin Franklin, Printer* (New York, 1917), chap. 13; Frank Lambert, "'Pedlar in Divinity': George Whitefield and the Great Awakening, 1737–1745," *Journal of American History* 77 (1990), 812–837.

77. *Autobiography,* 179.

78. "A PROPOSAL for Promoting USEFUL KNOWLEDGE," May 14, 1743, *PBF,* 2:381; *Autobiography,* 193, 193n.

79. [BF], *Proposals Relating to the Education of Youth in Pensilvania* (Philadelphia, 1749), *PBF,* 3:415–417. The key Christian-naturalist works were John Ray's *Wisdom of God Manifested in the Works of the Creation* (1691) and William Derham's *Physico-*

Theology; or, A Demonstration of the Being and Attributes of God from His Works of Creation (1713).

80. BF to WS, July 10, 1743, *PBF,* 2:383–384; BF to WS, July 4, 1744, *PBF,* 2:409–410.

81. Editorial note, *PBF,* 2:383n–384n; BF to WS, Jan. 31, 1757, *PBF,* 7:116; BF to WS, Aug. 19, 1784, *WBF,* 9:262.

Chapter 4

1. *PR,* 1747, *PBF,* 3:100; James N. Green, "Benjamin Franklin as Publisher and Bookseller," in *Reappraising Benjamin Franklin: A Bicentennial Perspective,* ed. J. A. Leo Lemay (Newark, Del., 1993), 99.

2. *PR,* 1747, *PBF,* 3:100.

3. Simon Schaffer, "Golden Means: Assay Instruments and the Geography of Precision in the Guinea Trade," in *Instruments, Travel, and Science: Itineraries of Precision from the Seventeenth to the Twentieth Century,* ed. Marie-Noëlle Bourguet, Christian Licoppe, and H. Otto Sibum (London, 2002), 37–39.

4. *Autobiography,* 63.

5. Thomas Tryon, *The Way to Health, Long Life and Happiness; or, A Discourse of Temperance,* 3rd ed. (London, 1697), 33, 43, 325.

6. Ibid., 237–238, 247, 264, 265, and chap. 14; Keith Thomas, *Man and the Natural World: Changing Attitudes in England, 1500–1800* (New York, 1983), 291–292.

7. Philippe Rosenberg, "Thomas Tryon and the Seventeenth-Century Dimensions of Antislavery," *WMQ* 61 (2004), 609–642.

8. Alfred Owen Aldridge, *Franklin and His French Contemporaries* (New York, 1957), 208 (Abiah Folger seemed suspiciously conversant with the Pythagorean trope about mad philosophers and their mad diets); *Autobiography,* 63. It is also possible, given that Franklin would eventually author a tract called *The Way to Wealth,* that he at some point read Tryon's *Way to Make All People Rich* (1685) or his *England's Grandeur, and Way to Get Wealth . . .* (1699).

9. *Autobiography,* 87–88.

10. Ibid., 101.

11. Ibid., 99–100.

12. Ibid., 149, 150; W. J. Rorabaugh, *The Alcoholic Republic: An American Tradition* (Oxford, 1979); Peter Thompson, *Rum Punch and Revolution: Taverngoing and Public Life in Eighteenth-Century Philadelphia* (Philadelphia, 1999).

13. Steven Shapin, "How to Eat Like a Gentleman: Dietetics and Ethics in Early Modern England," in *Right Living: An Anglo-American Tradition of Self Help Medicine and Hygiene,* ed. Charles E. Rosenberg (Baltimore, 2003), 21–58.

14. Ralph H. Major, "Santorio Santorio," *Annals of Medical History* 10 (1938), 373–375.

15. *Autobiography,* 73; [BF], *Proposals Relating to the Education of Youth in Pensilvania* (Philadelphia, 1749), *PBF,* 3:417, 417n (on Arbuthnot and Sanctorius).

16. *Oxford English Dictionary,* s.vv., "circulate" and "circulation"; Jerome J. Bylebyl, ed., *William Harvey and His Age: The Medical and Social Context of the Discovery of the Circulation* (Baltimore, 1979).

17. Everett Mendelsohn, *Heat and Life: The Development of the Theory of Animal Heat* (Cambridge, Mass., 1964), 29–34; S. Todd Lowry, "The Archaeology of the Circulation Concept in Economic Theory," *Journal of the History of Ideas* 35 (1974), 429–444; I. Bernard Cohen, "Harrington and Harvey: A Theory of the State Based

on the New Physiology," *Journal of the History of Ideas* 55 (1994), 187–210; Thomas Hobbes, *Leviathan* (1651), ed. Richard Tuck (Cambridge, 1996), 174.

18. Richard Striner, "Political Newtonianism: The Cosmic Model of Politics in Europe and America," *WMQ* 52 (1995), 583–608; I. Bernard Cohen, *Science and the Founding Fathers: Science in the Political Thought of Thomas Jefferson, Benjamin Franklin, John Adams, and James Madison* (New York, 1995), 204–210, 215–230, 243–257. In this last work, Cohen cautioned against equating equilibriums with Newtonianism; assumptions about political balance had multiple sources.

19. BF to JB, [Mar. 10, 1773], *PBF*, 10:103.

20. J. L. Heilbron, "Franklin as an Enlightened Natural Philosopher," in *Reappraising Benjamin Franklin*, 207; BF to JP, Sept. 19, 1772, *PBF*, 19:299–300.

21. Terence Hutchison, *Before Adam Smith: The Emergence of Political Economy* (New York, 1988), chaps. 1–3 (for background), 245–247; John Brewer, *The Sinews of Power: War, Money, and the English State, 1688–1783* (Cambridge, Mass., 1990), 223–230; Patricia Cline Cohen, *A Calculating People: The Spread of Numeracy in Early America* (Chicago, 1982).

22. Barbara J. Shapiro, *Probability and Certainty in Seventeenth-Century England: A Study of the Relationships between Natural Science, Religion, History, Law, and Literature* (Princeton, 1983); Lorraine Daston, *Classical Probability in the Enlightenment* (Princeton, 1988), esp. chaps. 2 and 3.

23. Geoffrey Clark, *Betting on Lives: The Culture of Insurance in England, 1695–1775* (New York, 1999).

24. Silence Dogood, no. 10, *NEC*, Aug. 13, 1722, *PBF*, 1:33.

25. B. B. [BF], *A Modest Enquiry into the Nature and Necessity of a Paper-Currency* (1729), *PBF*, 1:144, 147, 149, 150.

26. Ibid., 150; *Autobiography*, 124.

27. "Articles of the Union Fire Company," 1736, *PBF*, 2:150. See also Hutchison, *Before Adam Smith*, 139–140; W. A. Wetzel, *Benjamin Franklin as an Economist* (Baltimore, 1895), 18–22; Lewis J. Carey, *Franklin's Economic Views* (Garden City, N.Y., 1928), esp. chaps. 1 and 6; Tracy Mott and George W. Zinke, "Benjamin Franklin's Economic Thought: A Twentieth Century Appraisal," in *Critical Essays on Benjamin Franklin*, ed. Melvin H. Buxbaum (Boston, 1987), 114, 116–118.

28. "Queries to Be Asked the Junto," [1732], *PBF*, 1:260; *PG*, July 8, 1731.

29. Ivan Hannaford, *Race: The History of an Idea in the West* (Baltimore, 1996), chaps. 1–6, quotation on p. 171.

30. Ibid., chap. 7; Winthrop D. Jordan, *White over Black: American Attitudes Toward the Negro, 1550–1812* (New York, 1969), chaps. 2 and 5, Petty quotation on pp. 224–225; Joyce E. Chaplin, "Race," in *The British Atlantic World, 1500–1800*, ed. David Armitage and Michael J. Braddick (New York, 2002), quotation on pp. 162–163.

31. S.v. "La Condamine, Charles-Marie de," in Charles Coulston Gillispie, ed., *Dictionary of Scientific Biography* (New York, 1978), 15:217–272; *PR*, 1745, *PBF*, 3:5; *PRI*, 1750, *PBF*, 3:445.

32. BF, *Account of the New Invented Pennsylvanian Fire-Places* (1744), *PBF*, 2:425; Samuel Y. Edgerton Jr., "The Franklin Stove," in I. Bernard Cohen, *Benjamin Franklin's Science* (Cambridge, Mass., 1990), 199–211; John E. Crowley, *The Invention of Comfort: Sensibilities and Design in Early Modern Britain and Early America* (Baltimore, 2004), 171–174, 180–183.

33. BF, *Pennsylvanian Fire-Places*, 422, 425.

34. Ibid., 422–423, 432.

35. Ibid., 435, 438.

36. *PR*, 1733, *PBF*, 1:312.

37. BF, *Pennsylvanian Fire-Places*, 422, 441.

38. The six works were: Nicolas Gauger, *La méchanique du feu* (Paris, 1713), trans. J. T. Desaguliers as *Fires Improv'd* (London, 1715); Martin Clare, *The Motion of Fluids, Natural and Artificial* (London, 1737); Luca Antonio Porzio, *De militis in castris sanitate tuenda* (The Hague, 1739); [Hermann Boerhaave], *Boerhaave's Aphorisms* (London, 1735); J. T. Desaguliers, *A Course of Experimental Philosophy* (London, 1734–1744); Robert Boyle, *Philosophical Works*, ed. Peter Shaw (London, 1725).

39. BF, *Pennsylvanian Fire-Places*, 422, 423.

40. In his various letters and essays, Franklin discussed Boyle but not the other barometric expert, Evangelista Torricelli.

41. J. L. Heilbron, *Elements of Early Modern Physics* (Berkeley, 1982), 22–35; Steven Shapin, *The Scientific Revolution* (Chicago, 1996), 46–57

42. Heilbron, *Early Modern Physics*, 38–43, 47–50.

43. *F&N*, pt. 3.

44. See esp. J. L. Heilbron, *Electricity in the Seventeenth and Eighteenth Centuries: A Study of Early Modern Physics* (Berkeley, 1979), 63–73, chap. 14.

45. BF, *Pennsylvanian Fire-Places*, 423; *F&N*, 366–368.

46. *Oxford English Dictionary*, s.v., "atmosphere"; D. G. King-Hele, "The Earth's Atmosphere: Ideas Old and New," *Quarterly Journal of the Royal Astronomical Society* 26 (1985), 237–238, 247–253.

47. BF, *Pennsylvanian Fire-Places*, 426, 440.

48. *F&N*, 254–261, 269–276.

49. Joyce E. Chaplin, "The Secret Lives of Plants," *Environmental History* 10 (2005), 127–131; Heilbron, *Early Modern Physics*, 57–59; Mendelsohn, *Heat and Life*, 75–80; D. G. C. Allan and R. E. Schofield, *Stephen Hales: Scientist and Philanthropist* (London, 1980), 10–19, 30–64, 122, 140; *F&N*, 278–279.

50. BF to Josiah and Abiah Franklin, Sept. 6, 1744, *PBF*, 2:414.

51. Simon Schaffer, "Natural Philosophy and Public Spectacle in the Eighteenth Century," *History of Science* 21 (1983), 1–43; *BFS*, 40–60, quotations on p. 44; *Autobiography*, 240.

52. *Autobiography*, 117; Raymond Phineas Stearns, *Science in the British Colonies of America* (Urbana, Ill., 1970), 516.

53. Editorial note, *PBF*, 2:379n; Stearns, *Science in the British Colonies*, 515–516, 577–579.

54. Brooke Hindle, *The Pursuit of Science in Revolutionary America, 1735–1789* (Chapel Hill, N.C., 1956), chap. 2; Michael Warner, *The Letters of the Republic: Publication and the Public Sphere in Eighteenth-Century America* (Cambridge, Mass., 1990); Alfred O. Aldridge, "Benjamin Franklin: The Fusion of Science and Letters," in *American Literature and Science*, ed. Robert J. Scholnick (Lexington, Ky., 1992), 39–57; Dena Goodman, *The Republic of Letters: A Cultural History of the French Enlightenment* (Ithaca, 1994).

55. CC to BF, Oct. 1743, *PBF*, 2:386, 387n.

56. Stearns, *Science in the British Colonies*, 494–497, 559–567; E[phraim] Chambers, *Cyclopedia; or, An Universal Dictionary of Arts and Sciences* (London, 1728), list of subscribers.

57. Hindle, *Pursuit of Science*, 67–73; Francis D. West, "John Bartram and the American Philosophical Society," *Pennsylvania History* 23 (1956), 463–466, Bartram quotation on pp. 465–466; BF to CC, Nov. 4, 1743, *PBF*, 2:388; BF to CC, Apr. 5, 1744, *PBF*, 2:406.

58. BF to CC, Oct. 16, 1746, *PBF,* 3:92n (on Gronovius).

59. CC to BF, Sept. 17, 1744, *PBF,* 2:416; BF to CC, Oct. 25, 1744, *PBF,* 2:417–418.

60. Stearns, *Science in the British Colonies,* 567–575; Brooke Hindle, "Cadwallader Colden's Extension of the Newtonian Principles," *WMQ* 13 (1956), 459–475.

61. BF to CC, Nov. 28, 1745, *PBF,* 3:46.

62. BF to CC, Aug. 15, 1745, *PBF,* 3:33.

63. *Autobiography,* 196; BF to CC, Aug. 15, 1745, *PBF,* 3:34–35; BF to CC, Nov. 28, 1745, *PBF,* 3:47.

64. BF to CC, Aug. 15, 1745, *PBF,* 3:35 (on heart), 37 (on warmth).

65. BF to John Lining, Apr. 14, 1757, *PBF,* 7:188; BF to DF, Feb. 19, 1758, *PBF,* 7:380.

66. BF to CC, [Feb. 1746], *PBF,* 3:67–68.

67. Ibid., 69, 70.

68. Ibid., 67.

69. BF to WS, Feb. 12, 1745, *PBF,* 3:13.

70. T. H. Breen, *The Marketplace of Revolution: How Consumer Politics Shaped American Independence* (New York, 2004), pt. 1.

71. "A Tradesman" [BF], *Plain Truth* (Philadelphia, 1747), *PBF,* 3:195, 197, 199.

72. Ibid., 190, 204.

73. *Autobiography,* 183, 187; "Form of Association," *PBF,* 3:205–212.

74. "The Speech of Miss Polly Baker," 1747, *PBF,* 3:123, 124, 125.

75. *PR,* 1735, *PBF,* 2:7.

76. Mary Poovey, *A History of the Modern Fact: Problems of Knowledge in the Sciences of Wealth and Society* (Chicago, 1998); Barbara J. Shapiro, *A Culture of Fact: England, 1550–1720* (Ithaca, 2000), esp. chap. 5.

77. BF to PC, Mar. 28, 1747, *PBF,* 3:119; Bernard Cohen, *Benjamin Franklin's Experiments: A New Edition of Franklin's Experiments and Observations on Electricity,* ed. I. (Cambridge, Mass., 1941), intro., 57–77.

78. Heilbron, *Early Modern Physics,* 160–171.

79. Ibid., 171–174.

80. Ibid., 179–182.

81. *F&N,* 290–299; Heilbron, *Early Modern Physics,* 159–179.

82. James Delbourgo, *A Most Amazing Scene of Wonders: Electricity and Enlightenment in Early America* (Harvard University Press, forthcoming).

83. *BFS,* 40–65; BF to PC, Mar. 28, 1747, *PBF,* 3:115–117, 118–119; Cohen, *Benjamin Franklin's Experiments,* intro., 57–61.

84. Cohen, *Benjamin Franklin's Experiments,* 60n, 62n, 401–408; J. A. Leo Lemay, *Ebenezer Kinnersley: Franklin's Friend* (Philadelphia, 1964), esp. chaps. 3 and 4.

85. *PG,* June 5, 1740; "A Short Account of the Library," [July 13, 1741], *PBF,* 2:309; on West Wing of the State House, now Independence Hall, personal communication of Karie Dicthorn, chief curator, Independence National Historical Park, Dec. 22, 2005; Edwin Wolf, 2nd, *"At the Instance of Benjamin Franklin": A Brief History of the Library Company of Philadelphia, 1731–1976* (Philadelphia, 1976), 6.

86. BF to PC, May 25, 1747, *PBF,* 3:127.

87. Ibid.

88. Ibid., 128–129.

89. Ibid., 130–132; Heilbron, *Early Modern Physics,* 187–190.

90. BF to PC, May 25, 1747, *PBF,* 3:131–132.

91. BF to PC, July 28 1747, *PBF,* 3:157–162; Heilbron, *Early Modern Physics,* 187–192; Jessica Riskin, *Science in the Age of Sensibility: The Sentimental Empiricists of the French Enlightenment* (Chicago, 2002), 88–91.

92. BF to PC, May 25, 1747, *PBF,* 3:131; BF to PC, July 28, 1747, *PBF,* 3:158. Franklin had used images of balance earlier; see BF to [Thomas Hopkinson?], Oct. 16, 1746, *PBF,* 3:85–86.

93. BF to PC, May 25, 1747, *PBF,* 3:131–132; BF to PC, July 28, 1747, *PBF,* 3:157–158; "Opinions and Conjectures," [July 29, 1750], *PBF,* 4:16.

94. BF to PC, Apr. 29, 1749, *PBF,* 3:362.

95. *Autobiography,* 241; BF to Thomas Darling, Mar. 27, 1747, *PBF,* 3:114–115; BF to PC, May 25, 1747, *PBF,* 3:133–134, 133n.

96. BF to PC, Mar. 28, 1747, *PBF,* 3:118, 119; BF to PC, May 25, 1747, *PBF,* 3:132–133.

97. BF to PC, May 25, 1747, *PBF,* 3:132; BF to CC, June 5, 1747, *PBF,* 3:143.

98. "Articles of Agreement with David Hall," [January 1, 1748], *PBF,* 3:263–267.

99. John Brewer, *The Pleasures of the Imagination: English Culture in the Eighteenth Century* (London, 1997), 531–535, quotation on p. 532.

100. Simon Schaffer, "Experimenters' Techniques, Dyers' Hands, and the Electric Planetarium," *Isis* 88 (1997), 456–483; BF to PC, May 25, 1747, *PBF,* 3:127.

101. BF to PC, July 28, 1747, *PBF,* 3:158; BF, "Opinions and Conjecture," *PBF,* 4:17 (on knuckle) and 33 (on purgative); BF to [John Franklin?], Dec. 25, 1750, *PBF,* 4:82–83 (on "Blow").

102. BF to John Mitchell, Apr. 29, 1749, *PBF,* 3:365–367, 369–370.

103. Ibid., 369–372, 376.

104. BF to PC, Apr. 29, 1749, *PBF,* 3:364, 365; BF to CC, Aug. 30, 1754, *PBF,* 5:427 (on winter as season for electrical experiments).

Chapter 5

1. BF to John Lining, June 17, 1758, *PBF,* 8:110.

2. *Autobiography,* 185.

3. Matthew H. Edney, *Mapping an Empire: The Geographical Construction of British India, 1765–1843* (Chicago, 1990), chaps. 1–3, quotations on p. 51; David N. Livingstone and Charles W. J. Withers, eds., *Geography and Enlightenment* (Chicago, 1999), 1–31; J. B. Harley, *The New Nature of Maps: Essays in the History of Cartography,* ed. Paul Laxton (Baltimore, 2001), chaps. 2 and 3.

4. Harley, *New Nature of Maps,* chaps. 4 and 6.

5. Martin W. Lewis, "Dividing the Ocean Sea," *Geographical Review* 89 (1999), 188–214; Martin W. Lewis and Karen E. Wigen, *The Myth of Continents: A Critique of Metageography* (Berkeley, 1997), 21–31.

6. Walter Klinefelter, "Lewis Evans and His Maps," *APS Transactions,* n.s., 61 (1971), 5, 7–8; BF to WS, May 22, 1746, *PBF,* 3:77.

7. Editorial notes, *PBF,* 3:48n, 116–117, 392n–393n; Klinefelter, "Lewis Evans and His Maps," 9, 12, 17.

8. Klinefelter, "Lewis Evans and His Maps," 3–16.

9. Ibid., 21, 30–31.

10. William E. Lingelbach, "Franklin and the Lewis Evans Map of 1749," *American Philosophical Society Yearbook 1945* (Philadelphia, 1945), 63–73.

11. BF to Jared Eliot, July 16, 1747, *PBF,* 3:149.

12. BF to Eliot, Feb. 13, 1750, *PBF,* 3:463–464.

13. Ibid., 464, 465.

14. BF to James Bowdoin, Jan. 24, 1752, *PBF*, 4:257, 258; BF to Jared Eliot, Apr. 12, 1753, *PBF*, 4:466; BF to PC, Sept. 1753, *PBF*, 5:68.

15. *BFS*, chap. 6; editorial note, *PBF*, 4:360–366; BF, "Opinions and Conjectures," [July 29, 1750], *PBF*, 4:19–20.

16. J. L. Heilbron, *Elements of Early Modern Physics* (Berkeley, 1982), 194–195; PC to BF, July 11, 1750, *PBF*, 4:5–6; editorial note, *PBF*, 4:126.

17. Heilbron, *Early Modern Physics*, 50–55; John Gascoigne, "Ideas of Nature: Natural Philosophy," *CHS*, 295–302; Mary Terrall, *The Man Who Flattened the Earth: Maupertuis and the Sciences in the Enlightenment* (Chicago, 2002).

18. Heilbron, *Early Modern Physics*, 195–196.

19. *Gentleman's Magazine*, June 1752 (Franklin would mention in his *Autobiography*, p. 243, that Nollet had considered him to be an imagined person—this was perhaps a faulty memory of the London article); editorial note, *PBF*, 4: 360–366; Jessica Riskin, *Science in the Age of Sensibility: The Sentimental Empiricists of the French Enlightenment* (Chicago, 2002), chap. 3.

20. [BF], "To the Royal Academy of * * * * *," [after May 19, 1780], *PBF*, 32:399–400.

21. BF to James Logan, [Nov. 7, 1748], *PBF*, 3:325.

22. BF to CC, Jan. 1, 1754, *PBF*, 5:185–186, 186n.

23. *BFS*, 98–99.

24. *PG*, Oct. 19, 1752, *PBF*, 4:367.

25. Cited in *BFS*, 69.

26. BF to John Mitchell, Apr. 29, 1749, *PBF*, 3:374.

27. *PRI*, 1753, *PBF*, 4:408–409.

28. Ibid.

29. BF to PC, Sept. 1753, *PBF*, 5:69–76; BF to John Lining, Mar. 18, 1755, *PBF*, 5:524–525; BF to PC, Nov. 22, 1756, *PBF*, 7:24; BF to Ebenezer Kinnersley, Feb. 20, 1762, *PBF*, 10:37–38.

30. Charles Coulston Gillispie, ed., *Dictionary of Scientific Biography* (New York, 1970–1990), 3:51.

31. Heilbron, *Early Modern Physics*, 200–202.

32. BF to John Mitchell, Apr. 29, 1749, *PBF*, 3:372; BF to John Perkins, Feb. 4, 1753, *PBF*, 4:433.

33. BF to CC, Apr. 23, 1752, *PBF*, 4:298–299.

34. BF to CC, Feb. 26, 1763, *PBF*, 10:204.

35. BF to CC, Apr. 23, 1752, *PBF*, 4:299, 300. He would restate this many times.

36. Bernard Cohen, *Benjamin Franklin's Experiments: A New Edition of Franklin's Experiments and Observations on Electricity*, ed. I. (Cambridge, Mass., 1941), chap. 4.

37. BF to PC, July 29, 1750, *PBF*, 4:9.

38. Alfred Owen Aldridge, *Franklin and His French Contemporaries* (New York, 1957), 22.

39. Raymond Phineas Stearns, *Science in the British Colonies of America* (Urbana, Ill., 1970), 625–626.

40. BF to President and Council of the Royal Society, May 29, 1754, *PBF*, 5:334.

41. Ezra Stiles, "Oratio," [Feb. 5, 1755], *PBF*, 5:500; James Turner's words of 1758 are cited in *PBF*, 8:59n.

42. Charles Woodmason, "To Benjamin Franklin Esq.," *PBF*, 5:60; Richard Brooke to BF, June 27, 1755, *PBF*, 6:95; "Musing near a Cool Spring," [1756?], *PBF*, 7:74; Ebenezer Kinnersley to BF, Mar. 12, 1761, *PBF*, 9:293.

43. Ezra Stiles to BF, Feb. 26, 1766, *PBF*, 13:175; John Walsh to BF, July 1, 1773, *PBF*, 20:267.

44. Immanuel Kant, *Gesammelte Schriften* . . . (Berlin, 1902–[1997]), 1:472; Peter Hinrich Tesdorpf, "Poem in Eulogy of Franklin," *PBF*, 16:122.

45. Woodmason, "To Benjamin Franklin Esq.," 60; Kinnersley to BF, Mar. 12, 1761, 285; Penuel Bowen to BF, Nov. 6, 1771, *PBF*, 18:244.

46. *PRI*, 1749, *PBF*, 3:339; BF to CC, Oct. 11, 1750, *PBF*, 4:68.

47. Word searches for "Lisbon" (none by Franklin relating to the 1755 earthquake) and "earthquake(s)" (six instances by Franklin, all as news, not commentary), Papers of Benjamin Franklin on CD-ROM, Yale University; editorial notes, *PBF*, 4:125, 317n; Elizabeth Hubbart to BF, Feb. 16, 1756, *PBF*, 6:404, 404n; Dennis R. Dean, "Benjamin Franklin and Earthquakes," *Annals of Science* 46 (1989), 481–495; Susan Neiman, *Evil in Modern Thought* (Princeton, 2002), 240–250.

48. BF to PC, Sept. 1753, *PBF*, 5:69–70; BF to PC, Apr. 18, 1754, *PBF*, 5:262.

49. BF to DF, June 10, 1758, *PBF*, 8:94. On Peter and Jemima, see David Waldstreicher, *Runaway America: Benjamin Franklin, Slavery, and the American Revolution* (New York, 2004), 25.

50. James Alexander to BF and BF to Alexander [1753?] (both read before the Royal Society in December 1756), *PBF*, 5:178–180.

51. Ibid.

52. BF to PC, May 21, 1751, *PBF*, 4:134, 135.

53. Ibid., 135; General Post Office: Appointment of BF and William Hunter, Aug. 10, 1753, *PBF*, 5:18, 18n.

54. *Autobiography*, 246, 246n.

55. See *PRI*, 1750, *PBF*, 3:438–441, and *PRI*, 1754, *PBF*, 5:182–183.

56. [BF], "To the Printers of the Gazette," *PG*, May 9, 1751. See also BF, petition to the House of Commons, [Apr. 12–15, 1766], *PBF*, 13:241–242.

57. [BF], "Observations Concerning the Increase of Mankind," 1751, *PBF*, 4:227–229, 233.

58. Linda Colley, *Captives: Britain, Empire, and the World, 1600–1850* (London, 2002), 8–9; Lewis J. Carey, *Franklin's Economic Views* (Garden City, N.Y., 1928), chap. 3; Carl Van Doren, *Benjamin Franklin* (New York, 1938), 216 (on the Iron Act); *SFF*, 156–164; Andrea A. Rusnock, "Biopolitics: Political Arithmetic in the Enlightenment," in *The Sciences in Enlightened Europe*, ed. William Clark, Jan Golinski, and Simon Schaffer (Chicago, 1990), 49–68.

59. "Increase of Mankind," 229, 233–234. Or, as Franklin emphasized in 1754, the colonies "being separated by the ocean" from the mother country, "they increase much more its shipping and seamen"; see BF to William Shirley, Dec. 22, 1754, *PBF*, 5:450.

60. *PRI*, 1751, *PBF*, 4:91, 93; "Increase of Mankind," 233–234.

61. "Increase of Mankind," 228, 230–231, 234. On Franklin's continuing antipathy to slaves, see Douglas Anderson, *The Radical Enlightenments of Benjamin Franklin* (Baltimore, 1997), 158–167, but also Waldstreicher, *Runaway America*.

62. "Increase of Mankind," 234.

63. Ibid., 234, 234n; BF to PC, [1753?], *PBF*, 5:160.

64. *PRI*, 1751, *PBF*, 4:97, 98.

65. BF to PC, May 9, 1753, *PBF*, 4:479–485.

66. BF to John Franklin, Jan. 2, 1753, *PBF*, 4:409; CC to BF, Nov. 29, 1753, *PBF*, 5:122.

67. BF to WS, Apr. 14, 1745, *PBF*, 3:21, 22n; BF to WS, Dec. 11, 1745, *PBF*, 3:49; book advertisements in *PG*, May 31, 1744, Oct. 2, 1746, and Apr. 9, 1747.

68. Mary Blewitt, *Surveys of the Seas: A Brief History of British Hydrography* (n.p. [Great Britain], 1957), 18–26.

69. Norman J. W. Thrower, ed., *The Three Voyages of Edmond Halley in the Paramore, 1698–1701* (London, 1981); Patricia Fara, *Sympathetic Attractions: Magnetic Practices, Beliefs, and Symbolism in Eighteenth-Century England* (Princeton, 1996), chap. 4; Alan Cook, *Edmond Halley: Charting the Heavens and the Seas* (Oxford, 1998), chaps. 3 and 10.

70. BF to WS, July 4, 1744, *PBF*, 2:410, 410n–411n; PC to BF, June 14, 1748, *PBF*, 3:300; editorial note and petition to king, [Nov. 18? 1752], *PBF*, 4:380–383; PC to BF, Jan. 26, 1754, *PBF*, 5:191; editorial note, *PBF*, 10:85–88.

71. Editorial note, *PBF*, 4:382–383; BF to John Pringle, May 27, 1762, *PBF*, 10:99.

72. BF to PC, [1751], *PBF*, 4:240, 241; BF to Eliot, May 3, 1753, *PBF*, 4:474 (on trade winds).

73. BF to John Perkins, Feb. 4, 1753, *PBF*, 4:esp. pp. 433–437, quotation on p. 434.

74. BF to PC, Aug. 25, 1755, *PBF*, 4:167.

75. Adolph B. Benson, ed., *Peter Kalm's Travels in North America: The English Version of 1770*, 2 vols. (New York, 1937), 1:155; BF to John Mitchell, Apr. 29, 1749, *PBF*, 3:376; BF to John Perkins, Feb. 4, 1753, *PBF*, 4:431.

76. BF to WS, Apr. 18, 1754, *PBF*, 5:264.

77. "A Letter to the Rev. Dr. Hales, F.R.S. from Captain Henry Ellis, F.R.S.," *Philosophical Transactions*, 1751–1752, 47 (1753), 211–213; "A Letter to the President, from Stephen Hales, D.D. and F.R.S.," June 8, 1751, *Philosophical Transactions*, 1751–1752, 47 (1753), 215.

78. "Letter to Hales from Ellis," 213.

79. Bruce A. Warren, "Deep Circulation of the World Ocean," in *Evolution of Physical Oceanography: Scientific Surveys in Honor of Henry Stommel*, ed. Bruce A. Warren and Carl Wunsch (Cambridge, Mass., 1981), 8; "Letter to Hales from Ellis," 213, 214.

80. "Letter to Hales from Ellis," 213.

81. BF to William Watson, Apr. 19, 1754, *PBF*, 5:265 (vol. 47 of *Philosophical Transactions*); BF to PC, July 27, 1750, *PBF*, 4:8 (Hales essay in *Philosophical Transactions*); Pennsylvania Assembly to Governor, [May 15, 1755], *PBF*, 4:40.

82. Diana and Michael Preston, *A Pirate of Exquisite Mind: Explorer, Naturalist, and Buccaneer—The Life of William Dampier* (New York, 2004).

83. William Dampier, *A Discourse . . .* , in Dampier, *A Collection of Voyages in Four Volumes* (London, 1729), 2:45, 100, 103–104, 105; Anna Neill, "Buccaneer Ethnography: Nature, Culture, and Nation in the Journals of William Dampier, *Eighteenth-Century Studies* 33 (2000), 165–180.

84. Thrower, *Voyages of Halley*, 60; Dampier, *Discourse*, 49–58.

85. BF to John Perkins, Feb. 4, 1753, *PBF*, 4:429, 431 (including notes 7 and 8), 441.

86. Pennsylvania Hospital: Report of the Weekly Committee, Nov. 24, 1753, *PBF*, 5:116–117; Charles Hargrave to BF, Mar. 6, 1761, *PBF*, 9:282 and 282n.

87. BF to Perkins, Feb. 4, 1753, *PBF*, 4:442; Falconer cited in Jonathan Raban, ed., *The Oxford Book of the Sea* (New York, 1993), 119–131.

88. BF to PC, June 26, 1755, *PBF*, 6:84.

89. Fred Anderson, *Crucible of War: The Seven Years' War and the Fate of Empire in British North America* (New York, 2000).

90. Carl Van Doren, "Introduction," in *Indian Treaties Printed by Benjamin Franklin, 1736–1762,* ed. Julian P. Boyd (Philadelphia, 1938); *Autobiography,* 209.

91. *Autobiography,* 234–235.

92. BF to PC, Nov. 5, 1756, *PBF,* 7:13; *Autobiography,* 238.

93. BF to Jared Eliot, Apr. 12, 1753, *PBF,* 4:466; William Shipley to BF, Sept. 1, 1756, *PBF,* 6:499.

94. PC to BF, [May 27, 1756?], *PBF,* 6:449.

95. Edgar L. Pennington, *Thomas Bray's Associates and Their Work among the Negroes* (Worcester, Mass., 1939); D. G. C. Allan and R. E. Schofield, *Stephen Hales: Scientist and Philanthropist* (London, 1980), 65–76.

96. BF, "A Plan for Settling Two Western Colonies," 1754, *PBF,* 5:458.

97. WS to DF, Dec. 13, 1757, *PBF,* 7:296–297; BF to DF, Jan. 14, 1758, *PBF,* 7:359–360.

98. Waldstreicher, *Runaway America,* 25, 144.

99. *Autobiography,* 252, 255–256.

100. Ibid., 256; Howard Robinson, *Carrying British Mails Overseas* (New York, 1964), 45.

101. Roy Porter, *London: A Social History* (London, 1994), 99, 147–148.

102. BF to DF, Nov. 22, 1757, *PBF,* 7:272–274.

Chapter 6

1. *BFP* (1962), 47–50, 236–250; Brandon Brame Fortune and Deborah J. Warner, *Franklin and His Friends: Portraying the Man of Science in Eighteenth-Century America* (Washington, D.C., 1999), chap. 4.

2. Chronology, *PBF,* 7:xxvi–xxvii; WF to BF, Mar. 2, 1769, *PBF,* 16:60.

3. James Douglas, 14th Earl of Morton, to BF, Nov. 24, 1766, *PBF,* 13:509-510; Morton to BF, [Dec. 11, 1766?], *PBF,* 13:518–519, 518n; Society of Arts to BF, June 10, 1761, *PBF,* 9:322.

4. Everett Mendelsohn, *Heat and Life: The Development of the Theory of Animal Heat* (Cambridge, Mass., 1964), 102–104.

5. BF to John Lining, Apr. 14, 1757, *PBF,* 7:184–185; BF to Lining, June 17, 1758, *PBF,* 8:108–109.

6. Ibid., 110, 111. Franklin proposed a device of connected pieces of wood and metal that would indicate the different materials' conductivity. See the sketch in the upper left corner of the illustration of page 169.

7. BF to Lining, June 17, 1758, PBF, 8:110–111; Raymond Phineas Stearns, *Science in the British Colonies of America* (Urbana, Ill., 1970), 595–596.

8. BF to Lining, June 17, 1758, *PBF,* 8:111.

9. William Watson to the Royal Society, Dec. 20, 1752, *PBF,* 4:390; BF to Ebenezer Kinnersley, Feb. 20, 1762, *PBF,* 10:52.

10. *F&N,* 537–543.

11. Ibid., 540.

12. Chronology, *PBF,* 8:xxiv; BF to DF, Sept. 6, 1758, *PBF,* 8:144–145.

13. Jenny Uglow, *The Lunar Men: The Friends Who Made the Future, 1730–1810* (London, 2002), 59–60.

14. BF to John Baskerville, [1760?], *PBF,* 9:257–260.

15. Uglow, *Lunar Men,* 264–265; BF to Matthew Boulton, May 22, 1765, *PBF,*

12:140; notes for JP, [1766], *PBF,* 13:542–543; Erasmus Darwin to BF, Jan. 24, 1774, *PBF,* 21:24–25.

16. Chronology, *PBF,* 8:431; BF to Kames, Jan. 3, 1760, *PBF,* 9:9; City of Edinburgh for BF, Sept. 5, 1759, *PBF,* 8:434; James Buchan, *Crowded with Genius: The Scottish Enlightenment* (New York, 2003).

17. BF to Kames, Oct. 21, 1761, *PBF,* 9:376; Kames to BF, Feb. 18, [176]8, *PBF,* 15:50–51; BF to Kames, Feb. 28, 1768, *PBF,* 15:61. See also BF to Sir Alexander Dick, Jan. 21, 1762, *PBF,* 10:14–16.

18. Editorial note, *PBF,* 10:62n; G. R. de Beer, "The Relations between Fellows of the Royal Society and French Men of Science When France and Britain Were at War," *Notes and Records of the Royal Society* 9 (1952), 244–299. Franklin was scrupulous and avoided writing Dalibard during the war; see BF to Dalibard, [Dec. 9, 1761], *PBF,* 10:396.

19. *BFP,* 53–57, 409–410, ill. 2.

20. Ibid., ill. 2.

21. Ibid., ill. 4.

22. Editorial note, *PBF,* 10:116–126.

23. Ibid., 119n, 123; BF to Giambatista Beccaria, July 13, 1762, *PBF,* 10:126–130.

24. BF to Giambatista Beccaria, July 13, 1762, *PBF,* 10:130; Stanley Sadie and John Tyrrell, eds., *The New Grove Dictionary of Music and Musicians,* 2nd ed. (London, 2001), s.vv., "Franklin, Benjamin," "musical glasses," and "pianoforte."

25. Jessica Riskin, *Science in the Age of Sensibility: The Sentimental Empiricists of the French Enlightenment* (Chicago, 2002); BF to Caleb Whitefoord, Dec. 9, 1762, *PBF,* 10:173 (on harp); BF to le Comte de Salmes, July 5, 1785, *WBF,* 9:361.

26. Editorial note, *PBF,* 10:118–123.

27. BF to MS, May 17, 1760, *PBF,* 9:118; MS to BF, [Aug.? 1760], *PBF,* 9:194–195; Claude-Anne Lopez, "Three Women, Three Styles," in *Benjamin Franklin and Women,* ed. Larry E. Tise (University Park, Pa., 2000), 51–63.

28. BF to MS, Sept. 13, 1760, *PBF,* 9:216; MS to BF, Sept. 16, 1760, *PBF,* 9:217; Geoffrey Sutton, *Science for a Polite Society: Gender, Culture, and the Demonstration of Enlightenment* (Boulder, 1995), esp. 144–157, 341–348; Londa Schiebinger, "The Philosopher's Beard: Women and Gender in Science," *CHS,* 184–210.

29. MS to BF, May 19, 1761, *PBF,* 9:319.

30. BF to MS, Sept. 13, 1760, *PBF,* 9, 212–217; BF to MS, [Nov.? 1760], *PBF,* 9:247–252.

31. BF to MS, Aug. 10, 1761, *PBF,* 9:339.

32. BF to MS, Mar. 30, 1761, *PBF,* 9:296–297; John Winthrop to BF, Mar. 5, 1773, *PBF,* 20:95; BF to Sir Alexander Dick, Jan. 21, 1762, *PBF,* 10:16.

33. Fred Anderson, *Crucible of War: The Seven Years' War and the Fate of Empire in British North America* (New York, 2000), pt. 5.

34. "A Briton" [BF], "Of the Meanes of Disposing the Enemie to Peace," *London Chronicle,* Aug. 11–13, 1761, *PBF,* 9:342–343; Gerald Stourzh, *Benjamin Franklin and American Foreign Policy,* 2nd ed. (Chicago, 1969), 80–81.

35. Anderson, *Crucible of War,* 503–506.

36. BF, *A Plan for Settling Two Western Colonies,* [c. 1754], *PBF,* 5:457; BF to Kames, Jan. 3, 1760, *PBF,* 9:7; Anderson, *Crucible of War,* 523–528, 594–597; Stourzh, *Benjamin Franklin and American Foreign Policy,* 61–65.

37. [BF], *The Interest of Great Britain Considered . . .* (1760), *PBF,* 9:78 (on manufactures), 81 (on waterways), 88–89 (on manufactures), 91 (on Russia).

38. Ibid., 94, 95.

39. Henry M. Stommel, *The Gulf Stream: A Physical and Dynamical Description*, 2nd ed. (Berkeley, 1965), chap. 1; Thomas Frohock Gaskell, *The Gulf Stream* (New York, 1973), 3–5.

40. J. H. Parry, *The Spanish Seaborne Empire* (London, 1966), 102–122.

41. Robert Bishop, *Instructions and Observations Relative to the Navigation of the Windward and Gulph Passages* (London, 1761), 48, 50 (for quotation), 51, 52 (on Spanish ships), 54 (on Gulf of Mexico and Mississippi).

42. Editorial note, *PBF,* 10:86–88; BF to Pringle, May 27, 1762, *PBF,* 10:94.

43. Ibid., 89.

44. Ibid, 90, 93–94.

45. Thomas Penn to Richard Peters, July 5, 1758, *PBF,* 7:363n–364n; BF to [Isaac Norris], Jan. 14, 1758, *PBF,* 7:362.

46. Penn and Richard Peters cited in *PBF,* 7:110n–111n

47. WS to David Hall, Aug. 10, 1762, *PBF,* 10:141; BF to Kames, Aug. 17, 1762, *PBF,* 10:147; David Hume to BF, May 10, 1762, *PBF,* 10:81–82.

48. BF to Kames, June 2, 1765, *PBF,* 12:159.

49. BF to Richard Jackson, Mar. 8, 1763, *PBF,* 10:208; BF to William Ponsonby, Earl of Bessborough, July 13, 1765, *PBF,* 12:208–209; BF to WF, Aug. 28, 1767, *PBF,* 14:243; Stourzh, *Benjamin Franklin and American Foreign Policy,* 42, 54–65.

50. BF and William Hunter to James Parker, Apr. 22, 1757, *PBF,* 7:196; Anthony Todd to BF and John Foxcroft, Mar. 12, 1763 (three letters), *PBF,* 10:217–224; BF and John Foxcroft, Tables of Rates of Postage, c. 1763, *PBF,* 10:417–420; Howard Robinson, *Carrying British Mails Overseas* (New York, 1964), 43–44, 46.

51. Chronology, *PBF,* 10:277–279.

52. Christopher L. Brown, "Empire without Slaves: British Concepts of Emancipation in the Age of the American Revolution," *WMQ* 56 (1999), 273–306.

53. BF to John Waring, Feb. 17, 1758, *PBF,* 7:377–379; Waring to BF, Jan. 4, 1760, *PBF,* 9:12; BF to Waring, Dec. 17, 1763, *PBF,* 10:395–396; David Waldstreicher, *Runaway America: Benjamin Franklin, Slavery, and the American Revolution* (New York, 2004), 194.

54. BF to Francis Hopkinson, Dec. 16, 1767, *PBF,* 14:340.

55. [BF], *A Narrative of the Late Massacres in Lancaster County . . .* (1764), *PBF,* 11:55; BF to Sir William Johnson, Sept. 12, 1766, *PBF,* 13:416; "A New England-Man" [BF], *Public Advertiser,* Mar. 16, 1773, *PBF,* 20:115–122.

56. A. B. [BF], *Cool Thoughts on the Present Situation of Public Affairs* (1764), *PBF,* 11:160, 172–173.

57. "To the Freeholders . . . ," *PBF,* 11:381; William B. Reed, ed., *Life and Correspondence of Joseph Reed* (Philadelphia, 1847), 1:36–37; *Autobiography,* 271.

58. BF to DF, Dec. 9, 1764, *PBF,* 11:517; BF to MS, [Dec. 12–16, 1764], *PBF,* 11:521; BF to DF, Dec. 27, 1764, *PBF,* 11:534; BF to DF, Feb. 14, 1765, *PBF,* 12:62 (on gown).

59. Stearns, *Science in the British Colonies,* 585; entry for Feb. 16, 1771, Benjamin Franklin Journal, 1764–1774, Franklin Papers, APS.

60. BF to WF, [Sept. 27, 1766], *PBF,* 13:425; BF to WF, Aug., 28, 1767, and [Nov. 13, 1767], *PBF,* 14:242–243, 302–303; Jack M. Sosin, *Whitehall and the Wilderness* (Lincoln, Neb., 1961); George E. Lewis, *The Indiana Company, 1763–1798: A Study in Eighteenth-Century Frontier Land Speculation and Business Venture* (Glendale, Calif., 1941).

61. Timothy Folger to Sir Jeffery Amherst, [1763], *PBF,* 10:429–431; BF to

Richard Jackson, May 1, 1764, *PBF,* 11:187; Privy Council, grant of land for BF, June 26, 1767, *PBF,* 14:202, 203.

62. BF, scheme for a western settlement, [1763–1764], *PBF,* 10:420–422; Grand Ohio Company petition to the king, [June? 1769], *PBF,* 16:167; editorial note, *PBF,* 21:31–33.

63. Brooke Hindle, *The Pursuit of Science in Revolutionary America, 1735–1789* (Chapel Hill, N.C., 1956), 174–177.

64. BF to Charles Morton, Oct. 29, 1765, *PBF,* 12:341–342; Thomas D. Cope, "Some Contacts of Benjamin Franklin with Mason and Dixon and Their Work," APS *Proceedings* 95 (1951), 232–238.

65. Nicholas Rogers, "Liberty Road: Opposition to Impressment in Britain during the American War of Independence," in *Jack Tar in History: Essays in the History of Maritime Life and Labour,* ed. Colin Howell and Richard J. Twomey (Fredricton, New Brunswick, Canada, 1991), 57. On Franklin's map purchases, see entries for Sept. 8, 1766, Mar. 1772, Aug. 1773, *Benjamin Franklin Journal,* 1764–74, APS.

66. Mary Blewitt, *Surveys of the Seas: A Brief History of British Hydrography* (n.p. [Great Britain], 1957), 29; W. R. Chaplin, "A Seventeenth-Century Chart Publisher . . .," *American Neptune* 8 (1948), 310–311; Thomas R. Adams, "Mount and Page: Publishers of Eighteenth-Century Maritime Books," in *A Potencie of Life: Books in Society — The Clark Lectures, 1986–1987,* ed. Nicolas Barker (London, 1993), 147–153; Victor Suthren, *To Go Upon Discovery: James Cook and Canada, from 1758 to 1779* (Toronto, Canada, 2000), 153.

67. *PG,* Jan. 31, 1765,

68. Dava Sobel, *Longitude: The True Story of a Lone Genius Who Solved the Greatest Scientific Problem of His Time* (New York, 1995); William J. H. Andrewes, ed., *The Quest for Longitude* (Cambridge, Mass., 1996); BF to John Winthrop, Dec. 23, 1762, *PBF,* 10:179, 179n–180n; BF to DF, June 21, 1767, *PBF,* 14:192; Winthrop to BF, Oct. 26, 1770, *PBF,* 17:264, 264n (on Maskelyne). Franklin also knew John Walsh, one of Maskelyne's cousins, who investigated the electrical torpedo fish or ray; see John Walsh to BF, [before June?, 1772], *PBF,* 19:160–163.

69. BF and John Foxcroft to Anthony Todd, Sept. 21, 1764, *PBF,* 11:341–346 (on postal rates); Table of Revised Postal Rates, c. 1764, *PBF,* 11:535–536; BF to Anthony Todd, [Jan. 16, 1764], *PBF,* 11:21 (for first quotation); Postmasters General to Lords of the Treasury, Jan. 28, 1764, *PBF,* 11:37–41 (second quotation on p. 38); Post Office commission to BF and John Foxcroft, Sept. 25, 1765, Franklin Papers, APS; Lords Sandwich and Le Despencer to Treasury Commission, Post Office, Dec. 14, 1768, Post 1/9, PO. West Florida was not included in the expanded service. See Robinson, *Carrying British Mails,* 45, 47–49; John D. Ware with Robert R. Rea, *George Gauld: Surveyor and Cartographer of the Gulf Coast* (Gainesville and Tampa, Fla., 1982), 115, 140.

70. Ian K. Steele, *The English Atlantic, 1675–1740: An Exploration of Communication and Community* (New York, 1986), chaps. 7 and 9.

71. Ibid., chap. 7; editorial note, *PBF,* 20:73n (on post horns).

72. BF to DF, Dec. 9, 1764, *PBF,* 11:517; BF to MS, July 18, 1770, *PBF,* 17:94–95; BF to MS, Mar. 14, 1764, *PBF,* 11:110.

73. On postal venison, 1766–1768, see: *PBF,* 13:529; *PBF,* 14:220; *PBF,* 15:182. On Falconer, see: BF to WF, July 14, 1773, *PBF,* 20:306; Falconer to BF, Dec. 2, 1773, *PBF,* 20:491; Library Company committee to BF, Dec. 28, 1773, *PBF,* 20:517; BF to Falconer, Feb. 14, 1773, *PBF,* 20:58; Falconer to BF, Nov. 15, 1772, *PBF,* 19:371; Falconer to BF, Nov. 15, 1772, *PBF,* 19:371.

74. Jane Mecom to BF, Nov. 7, 1768, *PBF,* 15:263; BF to Mecom, Nov. 20, 1768, *PBF,* 15:268; Jonathan Williams Sr. to BF, [Aug.? 1772], *PBF,* 19:291; BF to Richard Bache, Dec. 1, 1772, *PBF,* 19:394 (on Isaac All, see also *PBF,* 12:31n); Paddock to BF, [Dec.] 21, 1773, *PBF,* 20:512–513; BF to DF, Dec. 13, 1765, *PBF,* 12:400.

75. Falconer to BF, Apr. 5, 1765, *PBF,* 12:100–101; BF to DF, Dec. 15, 1766, *PBF,* 13:525; entries for Sept. 25, 1768 (on Harvard) and Jan. 4, 1770 (on Le Roy), Benjamin Franklin Journal, 1764–1774, APS; BF to Humphry Marshall, Mar. 18, 1770, *PBF,* 17:110.

76. *BFP,* 58, 221; Fortune and Warner, *Franklin and His Friends,* 77; BF to Jonathan Williams, Feb. 24, 1764, *PBF,* 11:89–90, 89n; John Bartram to BF, Nov. 5, 1768, *PBF,* 15:257; Mary Bache to BF, Feb. 5, 1772, *PBF,* 19:66; DF to BF, May 30, 1771, *PBF,* 18:63; Harvard College to BF, June 24, 1771, *PBF,* 18:138.

77. BF to DF, [Jan.? 1758], *PBF,* 7:369 (on Goodeys); BF to DF, June 10, 1758, *PBF,* 8:93 (on ham, apples, and cranberries); BF to DF, Feb. 27, 1760, *PBF,* 9:27 (on apples); BF to DF, June 27, 1760, *PBF,* 9:175 (on venison and bacon); DF expenses, 1762, *PBF,* 10:101 (on Goodeys); DF to BF, Oct. 8–13, 1765, *PBF,* 12:303 (on apples and cranberries); DF to BF, Apr. 2[0–25, 1767], *PBF,* 14:139 (on no-cake); Seth Paddock to BF, Nov. 29, 1769, *PBF,* 16:250 (on cod); BF to –, Apr. 3, 1772, *PBF,* 19:99 (on codfish tongues and "sounds").

78. Edmund S. Morgan and Helen M. Morgan, *The Stamp Act Crisis: Prologue to Revolution* (Chapel Hill, N.C., 1953); Bernard Bailyn, *The Ideological Origins of the American Revolution,* enlarged ed. (Cambridge, Mass., 1992), 161–175.

79. "Homespun," second reply to "Vindex Patriae," *Gazetteer and New Daily Advertiser,* Jan. 2, 1766, *PBF,* 13:7–8.

80. Benjamin Franklin's examination by the House of Commons, *PBF,* 13:135–136, 144.

81. Ibid., 135, 137, 144.

82. Ibid., 135, 158; Bailyn, *Ideological Origins,* 213–215.

83. Harvard College to BF, *PBF,* 16:6–7; *Autobiography,* 271; R. Hingston Fox, *Dr. John Fothergill and His Friends* (London, 1919); Page Talbott, ed., *Benjamin Franklin: In Search of a Better World* (New Haven, 2005), 203, fig. 6.2—the jug was made in 1765, though it is not clear whether Fothergill gave it to Franklin then.

84. *BFP,* 74–83, 328–340; Fortune and Warner, *Franklin and His Friends,* 26–29.

85. Chronology, *PBF,* 13:xxvii–xxviii; Chronology, *PBF,* 14:xxviii; Alfred Owen Aldridge, *Franklin and His French Contemporaries* (New York, 1957), 23–30.

86. BF to PC, Apr. 30, 1764, *PBF,* 11:182; "F. B." on smuggling, *London Chronicle,* Nov. 21–24, 1767, *PBF,* 14:317, 318.

87. Commissioners of Customs (Boston) to Lords Commissioners of His Majesty's Treasury, May 12, 1768, Treasury 1/465/60–61, TNA; Anthony Todd to Thomas Bradshaw, June 4, 1768, Treasury Letters, Post 1/9, PO.

88. BF to Anthony Todd, Oct. 29, 1769 [1768], *PBF,* 15:246–247.

89. Ibid.

90. Ibid., 247.

91. Ibid.; Chaplin, "Seventeenth-Century Chart Publisher," 309, 310; Lloyd A. Brown, "The River in the Ocean," in *Essays Honoring Lawrence C. Wroth,* ed. Frederich R. Goff (Portland, Me., 1951), 69–84; Philip Richardson, "Benjamin Franklin and Timothy Folger's First Printed Chart of the Gulf Stream," *Science* 207 (1980), 643–645; Ellen Cohn, "Benjamin Franklin, Georges-Louis Le Rouge and the Franklin/Folger Chart of the Gulf Stream," *Imago Mundi* 52 (2000), 130–132 (Cohn dated the chart at 1769, Franklin at 1768—see below).

92. Instructions to Deputies, Packet Captains and Surveyors, 1763–1811, Post 44/1, PO; Suthren, *To Go Upon Discovery*, 57–60, 97–102, 126–128, 147 (quotation), 154–155; James Cook, master, "A Journal of the Grenville," June 14, 1764–Dec. 31, 1765, 111r, 115r, 127r (for quotation), ADM 52/1263, TNA. These entries match those in Cook's logbook; later logbooks and journals contain nothing on currents.

93. Edouard A. Stackpole, *The Sea-Hunters: The New England Whalemen during Two Centuries, 1635–1835* (Philadelphia, 1953), 26, 31–32, 37, 42, 49–55. On the mistaken date, see *PBF,* 15:246n; the date of 1769 was carried forward in subsequent correspondence—see Thomas Gage to Hillsborough, Jan. 6, 1769, in *The Correspondence of General Thomas Gage with the Secretaries of State, 1763–1775,* ed. Clarence Edwin Carter, 2 vols. (New Haven, 1931), 1:213.

94. Adams, "Mount and Page," 153–155; Richardson, "First Printed Chart of the Gulf Stream," 645; Thomas Pownall, "Hydraulic and Nautical Observations on the Currents in the Atlantic Ocean . . . ," with annotations by Benjamin Franklin [c. 1787], title page, Royal Society Library, London; entry for Oct. 10, 1767, Incident Bills, 1766–1769, PO; Richard Mount and Thomas Page, *Atlas maritimus novus; or, The New Sea-Atlas* (London, 1702), 35. The truncated stream echoed other of Franklin's analyses of fluid circulation as occurring in discrete sections (BF to MS, Sept. 13, 1760, *PBF,* 9:213, 214; BF to MS, Nov.? 1760, *PBF,* 9:249) and his assertion, in a conversation with Lord Egmont, that Britain had "in its rightful Possession the *Turnpike of the Sea,*" a passage subject to the collection of tolls, reversing the usual understanding, as defined by Dutch jurist Hugo Grotius, that the sea was the free highway of nations (BF to Joseph Galloway, Jan. 9, 1769, *PBF,* 16:13).

95. Mount and Page, *Atlas maritimus novus,* compare the chart on p. 35 (used for the Franklin and Folger chart) with those on pp. 36 and 37, which do not include the full geography surrounding the Atlantic Ocean.

96. BF to Todd, Oct. 29 [1768], 247–248; [BF], *The Interest of Great Britain Considered . . . ,* 91.

Chapter 7

1. "F+S" [BF], *London Chronicle,* Jan. 5–7, 1768, *PBF,* 15:3.

2. George F. E. Rudé, *Wilkes and Liberty: A Social Study* (Oxford, 1962); John Brewer, *Party Ideology and Popular Politics at the Accession of George III* (Cambridge, 1976).

3. Jesse Lemisch, "Jack Tar in the Streets: Merchant Seamen in the Politics of Revolutionary America," *WMQ* 25 (1968), 371–407; Nicholas Rogers, "Liberty Road: Opposition to Impressment in Britain during the American War of Independence," in *Jack Tar in History: Essays in the History of Maritime Life and Labour,* ed. Colin Howell and Richard J. Twomey (Fredricton, New Brunswick, Canada, 1991), 57, 60–61; Adam Hochschild, *Bury the Chains: Prophets and Rebels in the Fight to Free an Empire's Slaves* (Boston, 2005), 222–225.

4. BF to WF, Apr. 16, 1768, *PBF,* 15:98–99; BF to John Ross, May 14, 1768, *PBF,* 15:129 (see also BF to Joseph Galloway, *PBF,* 15:127–128).

5. BF to Jane Mecom, July 7, 1773, *PBF,* 20:290.

6. BF to –, Nov. 28, 1768 (printed in *Gentleman's Magazine,* vol. 49), *PBF,* 15:273.

7. Brooke Hindle, *The Pursuit of Science in Revolutionary America, 1735–1789* (Chapel Hill, N.C., 1956), 122–138.

8. [Charles Thomson] to BF, Nov. 6, 1768, *PBF,* 15:262; William Smith to BF,

May 3, 1771, *PBF,* 18:95; James E. McClellan III, *Science Reorganized: Scientific Societies in the Eighteenth Century* (New York, 1985), chap. 4; Durand Echeverria, *Mirage in the West: A History of the French Image of American Society to 1815* (Princeton, 1968), 23–29.

9. *Autobiography,* 271.

10. BF to John Winthrop, July 2, 1768, *PBF,* 15:170–171.

11. Editorial note, *PBF,* 20:26n.

12. On rain, see BF to Thomas Percival, June 1771, *PBF,* 18:154, 154n, 156; William E. Knowles Middleton, *A History of the Theories of Rain . . .* (New York, [1966]), 98–99, 168–170. On water's compressibility, see BF to John Canton, Mar. 14, 1764, *PBF,* 11:98; Canton to BF, June 29, 1764, *PBF,* 11:244–246; Charles Coulston Gillispie, *Dictionary of Scientific Biography* (New York, 1970–1990), 3:52.

13. Editorial notes, *PBF,* 4:376n, 377n; Benjamin Franklin, *Experiments and Observations on Electricity* (London, 1769), 165. The fifth edition (of 1774) was essentially the same as the fourth.

14. Editorial note, *PBF,* 21:292–297; *Monthly Review* 42 (1770), 200.

15. Franklin to O[liver] N[eave], [before 1769], *PBF,* 15:295–297.

16. Contents of 1769 edition, *PBF,* 21:293–296. Despite his quarrels with Pennsylvania's proprietors, Franklin never omitted from any edition of his *Experiments and Observations* the stiff note of 1750 in which he acknowledged Thomas Penn's gift of an electrical apparatus to the Library Company.

17. Verner W. Crane, "The Club of Honest Whigs: Friends of Science and Liberty," *WMQ* 23 (1966), 210–233.

18. Roger Hahn, *The Anatomy of a Scientific Institution: The Paris Academy of Sciences, 1666–1803* (Berkeley, 1971), 77–78; BF to WF, Aug. 19 [–22], 1772, *PBF,* 19:259–260; BF to Académie Royale des Sciences, Nov. 16, 1772, *PBF,* 19:372; JL to BF, Apr. 22, [1770], *PBF,* 17:126, 126n; JL to BF, Sept. 30, 1772, *PBF,* 19:308, 308n; JL to BF, Apr. 19, 1773, *PBF,* 20:170; JL to BF, Nov. 29, [1773], *PBF,* 20:487.

19. JB to BF, May 8, 1768, *PBF,* 15:112–115, 115n.

20. BF to Beccaria, Aug. 11, 1773, *PBF,* 20:354–355; editorial note, *PBF,* 14:4n; Howard S. Reed, "Jan Ingenhousz, Plant Physiologist, with a History of the Discovery of Photosynthesis," *Chronica Botanica* 11 (1949), 291–294.

21. BF to JL, June 22, 1773, *PBF,* 20:240–241; BF to Kames, Feb. 21, 1769, *PBF,* 16:47–48; JL to BF, Nov. 29, [1773], *PBF,* 20:488.

22. Jan Golinski, *Science as Public Culture: Chemistry and Enlightenment in Britain, 1760–1820* (Cambridge, 1992); Archibald Clow and Nan L. Clow, *The Chemical Revolution: A Contribution to Social Technology* (London, 1952); Jenny Uglow, *The Lunar Men: The Friends Who Made the Future* (London, 2002), 229–239.

23. *Autobiography,* 43, 133.

24. Ralph H. Brown, "The de Brahm Charts of the Atlantic Ocean, 1772–1776," *Geographical Review* 28 (1938), 124–132.

25. Commission for Determining the New York–New Jersey Boundary, [June 26, 1767], *PBF,* 14:198; Louis De Vorsey, "Pioneer Charting of the Gulf Stream: The Contributions of Benjamin Franklin and William Gerard De Brahm," *Imago Mundi* 28 (1976), 111; De Vorsey, intro. to William Gerard De Brahm, *The Atlantic Pilot* (London, 1772), fac. (Gainesville, Fla., 1974), ix–xxiv.

26. "Mr Brahm's Observations on the American Coast," *Gentleman's Magazine* 41 (1771), 436.

27. De Brahm, *Atlantic Pilot,* iii, 13.

28. Ibid., xxx, 7.

29. Ibid., "The Ancient Tegesta, Now Promontory of East Florida," pp. 3, 8, 9.

30. De Brahm, "East Florida," notations above Cape Canaveral, sheet 1, CO 700/Florida 3, TNA; De Brahm, *Atlantic Pilot*, 13, 16; De Vorsey, "Pioneer Charting," 114.

31. Philip L. Richardson, "Benjamin Franklin and Timothy Folger's First Printed Chart of the Gulf Stream," *Science* 207, no. 8 (1980), 643–645.

32. On the supposed lack of contact between Franklin and De Brahm, see De Vorsey, "Pioneer Charting," 114. On their points of intersection, see BF to WF, Nov. 9, 1765, *PBF*, 12:362–364 (on Franklin's audience with Dartmouth); BF and William Bollan to Lord Dartmouth, Aug. 20, 1773, *PBF*, 20:368–369; De Vorsey, intro., *Atlantic Pilot*, xxvii–xxix (on Dartmouth and Royal Society), xxxvii (on reviews of De Brahm); Benjamin Franklin, "The Cravenstreet Gazette," Sept. 25, 1770, *PBF*, 17:225 (on untidy newspapers).

33. De Brahm, *Atlantic Pilot*, vii.

34. Ibid., iii; *Autobiography*, 271; "Twilight" [BF], "On Absentee Governors: II," *Public Advertiser*, Aug. 27, 1768, *PBF*, 15:195; Bernard Bailyn, *Faces of Revolution: Personalities and Themes in the Struggle for American Independence* (New York, 1990), 174.

35. De Brahm, *Atlantic Pilot*, iii, vi; Brown, "De Brahm Charts," 129; BF to Thomas Cushing, June 10, 1771, *PBF*, 18:122.

36. BF to JP, Sept. 19, 1772, *PBF*, 19:299–300.

37. Frederic George Stephens, *Catalogue of Prints and Drawings in the British Museum, Division One: Political and Personal Satires* (London, 1883), 4:649; James Delbourgo, "Political Electricity: The Occult Mechanism of Revolution," available at www.common-place.org, vol. 5, no. 1 (Oct. 2004), accessed on Dec. 30, 2004; David P. Miller, "'My Favourite Studdys': Lord Bute as Naturalist," in *Lord Bute: Essays in Reinterpretation*, ed. Karl W. Schweizer (Leicester, 1988), 213–239.

38. JP to BF, Sept. 21, 1766, *PBF*, 13:423–424; Joseph Priestley, *The History and Present State of Electricity*, 2nd ed. (London, 1769), 636–647.

39. DF to BF, [Oct. 6–13? 1765], *PBF*, 12:296; L. H. Butterfield et al., eds., *Diary and Autobiography of John Adams*, 4 vols. (Cambridge, Mass., 1961), 4:150–151.

40. [BF], "Prudential Algebra," [before Aug. 3? 1773], *PBF*, 20:337–338.

41. BF to Jane Mecom, Jan. 9, 1760, *PBF*, 9:18; BF to Jonathan Williams Sr., Mar. 5, 1771, *PBF*, 18:56; Jonathan Williams Jr. to BF, Apr. 20, 1773, *PBF*, 20:176; Williams to BF, [before Sept. 21, 1773], *PBF*, 20:408–410.

42. *Autobiography*, 145; C. A. Bayly, *The Birth of the Modern World, 1780–1914* (Oxford, 2004), 49–64.

43. BF to [Noble Wimberly Jones?], Mar. or Apr. 1771, *PBF*, 18:65; Jones to BF, Jan. 13, 1773, *PBF*, 20:24; Joyce E. Chaplin, *An Anxious Pursuit: Agricultural Innovation and Modernity in the Lower South, 1730–1815* (Chapel Hill, N.C., 1993), 137, 146–150, 249.

44. P. J. Marshall and Glyndwr Williams, *The Great Map of Mankind: Perceptions of New Worlds in the Age of Enlightenment* (Cambridge, Mass., 1982), 258–265.

45. Ibid., 268–276.

46. Ibid., 270 (quotation), 276–284; Rob Iliffe, "Science and Voyages of Discovery," *CHS*, 618–645; Larry Stewart, "Global Pillage: Science, Commerce, and Empire," *CHS*, 825–844.

47. BF to JP, May 4, 1772, *PBF*, 19:125–126; BF to Horace-Bénédict de Saussure, Oct. 8, 1772, *PBF*, 19:325–326.

48. Harry Woolf, *The Transits of Venus* (Princeton, 1959).

49. Hindle, *Pursuit of Science*, 98–101, 146–165; Raymond Phineas Stearns, *Science in the British Colonies of America* (Urbana, Ill., 1970), 653–668, 673–674.

50. Hindle, *Pursuit of Science,* 153, 157–159; BF to John Winthrop, June 6, 1770, *PBF,* 17:158.

51. BF to Cadwallader Evans, Sept. 7, 1769, *PBF,* 16:199; BF to John Ewing, Aug. 27, 1770, *PBF,* 17:212.

52. BF to Grey Cooper, June 24, 1768, *PBF,* 15:158; BF to Jonathan Shipley, Aug. 19, 1771, *PBF,* 18:209, 210; Richard Jackson to BF, [July 27? 1771], *PBF,* 18:191.

53. [BF], foreword to Alexander Dalrymple, *Scheme of a Voyage by Subscription to Convey the Conveniences of Life . . . to Those Remote Regions, Which Are Destitute of Them . . .* (London, 1771), *PBF,* 18:215, 216.

54. Ibid., 216. See also Williams and Marshall, *Great Map of Mankind,* 258–259.

55. David Brion Davis, *The Problem of Slavery in the Age of Revolution, 1770–1823* (Ithaca, 1975); Seymour Drescher, *Capitalism and Antislavery: British Mobilization in Comparative Perspective* (London, 1986).

56. Dr. Bray's Assoc. to BF, 1766, *PBF,* 13:516; on fees for associates, Jan. 4, 1770, Benjamin Franklin Journal, 1764–1774, Franklin Papers, APS; [BF], "A Conversation on Slavery," *Public Advertiser,* Jan. 30, 1770, *PBF,* 17:39, 43, 44; David Waldstreicher, *Runaway America: Benjamin Franklin, Slavery, and the American Revolution* (New York, 2004), 192–198.

57. Editorial note, *PBF,* 19:112–113; Anthony Benezet to BF, Apr. 27, 1772, *PBF,* 19:113–116; BF to Benezet, Feb. 10, 1773, *PBF,* 20:41; Benjamin Rush to BF, May 1, 1773, *PBF,* 20:193.

58. [BF] on the Somerset Case, *London Chronicle,* June 18–20, 1772, *PBF,* 19:188; Waldstreicher, *Runaway America,* 198–202.

59. BF to Jonathan Williams Sr., July 7, 1773, *PBF,* 20:291–292 (on Wheatley); BF to Anthony Benezet, July 14, 1773, *PBF,* 20:296.

60. BF to WF, July 14, 1773, *PBF,* 20:303; *"A Friend to the Poor"* [BF], [December? 1773], *PBF,* 20:523, 525.

61. Editorial note, *PBF,* 21:293–296; JB to BF, Feb. 12, 1773, *PBF,* 20:46; BF to JB, [Mar.? 1773], *PBF,* 20:131–133; BF to JB, June 29, 1773, *PBF,* 20:251; BF notes, [before Aug. 3? 1773], *PBF,* 20:337.

62. Barbeu-Dubourg, intro. to *Oeuvres de M. Franklin* (1773), *PBF,* 20:430 ("Je suis persuadé que beaucoup de peres de familles desireroient un semblable Mentor à leurs filles"), 431 ("son bain d'air").

63. Ibid., 431–432. Barbeu-Dubourg had published both, the latter as an appendix to John Dickinson's *Letters from a Farmer in Pennsylvania,* an important criticism of the Stamp Act.

64. [BF], *The Interest of Great Britain Considered* (1760), *PBF,* 9:62; Echeverria, *Mirage in the West,* chap. 1.

65. Barbeu-Dubourg, intro. to *Oeuvres de M. Franklin,* 423, 424.

66. Ibid., 429.

67. Ibid., 427.

68. BF to DF, Dec. 1, 1772, *PBF,* 19:395 (on apples and cranberries); BF to DF, Feb. 2, 1773, *PBF,* 20:34, 34n (on all those apples); BF to Nathaniel Falconer, Feb. 14, 1773, *PBF,* 20:58 (on nuts and apples); BF to WF, Feb. 14, 1773, *PBF,* 20:62 (on cranberries, meal, and dried apples); BF to Jonathan Williams Sr., Mar. 9, 1773, *PBF,* 20:101 (on cod sounds and tongues); WF to BF, Jan. 5, 1774, *PBF,* 20:11 (on pork and dried apples); "Cravenstreet Gazette," 221.

69. BF to Timothy Folger, Sept. 29, 1769, *PBF,* 16:208; BF to Folger, Aug. 21, 1770, *PBF,* 17:210.

70. BF to DF, Dec. 15, 1766, *PBF,* 13:525; BF to DF, Jan. 28, 1772, *PBF,*

19:43–44; BF to DF, Aug. 22, 1772, *PBF,* 19:275; BF to Georgiana Shipley, Sept. 26, [1776], *PBF,* 19:301–302.

71. "The Colonist's Advocate" [BF], eleven essays in the *Public Advertiser* (early 1770), *PBF,* 17:description on p. 5; "An American" [BF], *Public Ledger* (Nov. 19, 1774), *PBF,* 21:357.

72. "N. N." [BF], *London Chronicle,* Nov. 6–8, 1770, in *PBF,* 17:273.

73. BF to Henry Home, Lord Kames, Feb. 25, 1767, *PBF,* 14:69–70; BF's marginalia in [Matthew Wheelock], *Reflections Moral and Political on Great Britain and Her Colonies* (1770), *PBF,* 17:394–395; [BF], Remarks on Agriculture and Manufacturing, [late 1771?], *PBF,* 18:273.

74. BF to John Pringle, May 10, 1768, *PBF,* 15:115–118, 492–496.

75. François Willem de Monchy, May 15, 1767, *PBF,* 14:149–150, and plates following p. 150; Thomas Gilpin to BF, Oct. 10, 1769, *PBF,* 16:216–218; BF to Gilpin, Mar. 18, 1770, *PBF,* 17:103; Samuel Rhoads to BF, May 3, 1771, *PBF,* 18:94; Rhoads to BF, May 30, 1772, *PBF,* 19:158; BF to Rhoads, Aug. 22, 1772, *PBF,* 19:278–279; BF to Peter P. Burdett, Aug. 21, 1773, *PBF,* 20:371. See also Douglas S. Brown, "The Iberville Canal Project," *Mississippi Valley Historical Review* 32 (1946), 491–516.

76. Franklin's Account of His Audience with Hillsborough, Jan. 16, 1771, *PBF,* 18:15. Hillsborough had also nixed an American land scheme, the Grand Ohio Company, in which William and Benjamin Franklin were interested. See Peter Marshall, "Lord Hillsborough, Samuel Wharton and the Ohio Grant, 1769–1775," *English Historical Review* 80 (1965), 717–739; Bailyn, *Faces of Revolution,* 174–177.

77. Journal of Jonathan Williams Jr., with BF and others, 1771, *PBF,* 18:114–116; BF to DF, July 14, 1772, *PBF,* 19:207.

78. BF to WF, Aug. 19–22, 1772, *PBF,* 19:258, 259.

79. Alan Q. Morton and Jane A. Wess, *Public and Private Science: The King George III Collection* (Oxford, 1993).

80. Editorial note and BF to Richard Dawson, May 29, 1772, *PBF,* 19:153–156.

81. J. L. Heilbron, *Elements of Early Modern Physics* (Berkeley, 1982), 202.

82. Franklin sent copies of his letter to Dawson and the committee report and a sketch to Dubourg to include in the French edition of his writings. Editorial note and Committee of the Royal Society, *PBF,* 19:260–262, 262–265; BF to JB, May 28 [–June 1], 1773, *PBF,* 20:213–216.

83. BF to John Pringle, Dec. 1, 1762, *PBF,* 10:158–159; Pringle to BF, [May? 1763], *PBF,* 10:269.

84. BF to William Brownrigg, Nov. 7, 1773, *PBF,* 20:466, 468.

85. Ibid., 464–465.

86. Ibid., 464–465, 466, 467, 469; Brownrigg to BF, Jan. 27, 1773, *PBF,* 20:30–31. Stearns, *Science in the British Colonies,* 637; Charles Tanford, *Ben Franklin Stilled the Waves . . .* (Durham, N.C., 1989), chaps. 1–3.

87. BF to Brownrigg, Nov. 7, 1773, *PBF,* 20:471–474.

88. BF, preface to *The Votes and Proceedings of the Freeholders and Other Inhabitants of the Town of Boston . . .* (1773), *PBF,* 20:86; Fothergill to Dartmouth, [Feb. 6, 1775], *PBF,* 21:482.

89. WF to BF, Oct. 13, 1772, *PBF,* 19:333–334; BF to WF, Dec. 2, 1772, *PBF,* 19:416–417.

90. Bernard Bailyn, *The Ordeal of Thomas Hutchinson* (Cambridge, Mass., 1974), 221–238; editorial note, *PBF,* 19:399–409; BF to Thomas Cushing, Dec. 2, 1772, *PBF,* 19:411–413.

91. BF to Thomas Percival, [Oct. 15, 1773], *PBF,* 19:444, 445.

92. BF to JB, [Mar. 10, 1773], *PBF*, 20:103 (first quotation); BF to JL, June 22, 1773, *PBF*, 20:241–242; BF to Samuel Cooper, July 7, 1773, *PBF*, 20:270 (second quotation, Hutchinson letters); BF to Benjamin Rush, July 14, 1773, *PBF*, 20:315 (third quotation).

93. Uglow, *Lunar Men*, 229–241; BF to JP, [July 1772?], *PBF*, 19:215, 216.

94. BF, notes on colds, *PBF*, 20:529.

95. Ibid., 529–538.

96. Ibid., 533.

97. Final Hearing Before the Privy Council, *PBF*, 21:47, 49, 56, 59; William Temple Franklin, ed., *Memoirs of the Life and Writings of Benjamin Franklin*, 3 vols. (London, 1818), 1:185.

98. Anthony Todd to BF, Jan. 31, 1774, *PBF*, 21:74; BF to JI, Apr. 26, 1777, *PBF*, 23:613, 613n.

99. J. A. Leo Lemay, *Ebenezer Kinnersley: Franklin's Friend* (Philadelphia, 1964), 110; [BF], "A Letter from London," *Boston Gazette*, Apr. 25, 1774, *PBF*, 21:83.

100. W[illiam] Small to BF, Aug. 10, 1771, *PBF*, 18:199; Percival to BF, Jan. 10, 1775, *PBF*, 21:446.

101. BF to Jane Mecom, Sept. 26, 1774, *PBF*, 21:317; John Winthrop to BF, Mar. 28, 1775, *PBF*, 22:10.

102. Toby L. Ditz, "Shipwrecked; or, Masculinity Imperiled: Mercantile Representations of Failure and the Gendered Self in Eighteenth-Century Philadelphia," *Journal of American History* 81 (1995), 51–80; BF to WF, Mar. 22, 1775, *PBF*, 21:548.

Chapter 8

1. "Speculation on the Speed of Ships," Apr. 5, 1775, *PBF*, 22:16.

2. Ibid.; Margaret Deacon, *Scientists and the Sea, 1650–1900: A Study of Marine Science* (London, 1971), 186–188, 202.

3. "Observations at Sea on Temperatures of Air and Water," *PBF*, 22:17–18.

4. Ibid.

5. BF to [JP], May 16, 1775, *PBF*, 22:44 (he accidentally gave this 1768 letter the date of General Gage's similar letter, of 1769—see Chapter 6, above); BF to [JP?], May 1775, *PBF*, 22:55; JP to BF, Feb. 13, 1776, *PBF*, 22:349.

6. Editorial note, *PBF*, 22:204–205; J. B. Harley, Barbara Bartz Petchenik, and Lawrence W. Towner, *Mapping the American Revolutionary War* (Chicago, 1978), 91–92.

7. Editorial Note, *PBF*, 22:132–134; William Smith, *The History of the Post Office of British North America, 1639–1870* (Cambridge, 1920), 67; WS to BF, Oct. 4, 1775, *PBF*, 22:220, 221; BF to WS, July 5, 1775, *PBF*, 22:85.

8. BF to Anthony Todd, Mar. 29, 1776, *PBF*, 22:392–393.

9. Ibid., 299n (on letters from Hewson); MS to BF, Sept. 5, 1776, *PBF*, 22:589.

10. BF "to a Friend in London," [Oct. 3? 1775], *PBF*, 22:215–216 (see also BF to JP, Oct. 3, 1775, *PBF*, 22:218).

11. Commission from Congress, [Mar. 20, 1776], *PBF*, 22:386.

12. William Goforth to BF, Feb. 22–23, 1776, *PBF*, 22:359.

13. *New-Jersey Gazette*, Dec. 31, 1777.

14. BF to Richard Bache, Sept. 30, 1774, *PBF*, 21:325–326; Thomas Paine to BF, Mar. 4, 1775, *PBF*, 21:515–518; Eric Foner, *Tom Paine and Revolutionary America* (New York, 1976), 72.

15. Thomas Paine, *Common Sense and Other Writings*, ed. Gordon S. Wood (New York, 2003), 36. Franklin had considered the problem in 1754, with the Albany

Plan of Union, then recommending "small vessels of force" as colonists' contribution to imperial security; see "Reasons and Motives," [July 1754], *PBF*, 5:413.

16. I. Bernard Cohen, "The Empirical Temper of Benjamin Franklin," in *Benjamin Franklin: A Profile*, ed. Esmond Wright (New York, 1979), 70–71, but also *SFF*, 122, 329n, 127.

17. Brooke Hindle, *The Pursuit of Science in Revolutionary America, 1735–1789* (Chapel Hill, N.C., 1956), 233.

18. David Armitage, "The Declaration of Independence and International Law," *WMQ* 59 (2002), 53–54.

19. Design for Continental Currency, *PBF*, 22:facing p. 358; proposal for the Great Seal of the United States, before Aug. 14, 1776, *PBF*, 22:563.

20. BF to Silas Deane, Aug. 27, 1775, *PBF*, 22:184; Preamble to a Congressional Resolution on Privateering, *PBF*, 22:388–389; BF to [Samuel Cooper], [Oct. 25, 1776], *PBF*, 22:670.

21. William M. Fowler Jr., *Rebels under Sail: The American Navy during the Revolution* (New York, 1976), chaps. 3 and 4; Committee of Secret Correspondence to Peter Parker, July 10, 1776, *PBF*, 22:507; BF and Robert Morris to Silas Deane, Oct. 1, 1776, *PBF*, 22:644.

22. Editorial note, *PBF*, 22:536–538.

23. Ibid.

24. Lord Howe's Conference with the Committee of Congress, Sept. 11, 1776, *PBF*, 22:602.

25. *JA*, 3:418.

26. Gerald Stourzh, *Benjamin Franklin and American Foreign Policy* (Chicago, 1954), chaps. 4 and 5.

27. Sheila Skemp, *Benjamin and William Franklin: Father and Son, Patriot and Loyalist* (Boston, 1994).

28. Editorial note, *PBF*, 23:23; BF's Description of His Ailments, Oct. 17, 1777, *PBF*, 25:78–79; BF's Journal of His Health, Oct. 4, 1778[–Jan. 16, 1780], *PBF*, 27:497; Fowler, *Rebels under Sail*, 135.

29. Editorial note, *PBF*, 23:23n, 59n; BF to Richard and Sally Bache, May 10, 1785, *WBF*, 9:327, 696; Jonathan Williams Jr. to BF, Jan. 25, 1777, *PBF*, 23:232.

30. Chronology, *PBF*, 33:lviii–lix; Thomas J. Schaeper, *France and America in the Revolutionary Era: The Life of Jacques-Donatien Leray de Chaumont, 1725–1803* (Providence, R.I., 1995), 97.

31. BF to Jane Mecom, Dec. 8, 1776, *PBF*, 23:34; BF to MS, Jan. 12, 1777, *PBF*, 23:155; Alfred Owen Aldridge, *Franklin and His French Contemporaries* (New York, 1957), 42–43, 60.

32. *BFP*, 96–99; *Mémoires secrets* cited in Aldridge, *Franklin and His French Contemporaries*, 61; BF to Benjamin Vaughan, Sept. 18, 1777, *PBF*, 24:539; BF's Description of His Ailments, 79.

33. BF to George Whateley, May 23, 1785, *WBF*, 9:338.

34. Aldridge, *Franklin and His French Contemporaries*, 61; *BFP*, ill. on pp. 9–10; Mary Terrall, *The Man Who Flattened the Earth: Maupertuis and the Sciences in the Enlightenment* (Chicago, 2002), chaps. 4 and 5 (portraits on frontispiece and p. 162).

35. Durand Echeverria, *Mirage in the West: A History of the French Image of American Society to 1815* (Princeton, 1968), chap. 2.

36. Peter Gay, *Voltaire's Politics: The Poet as Realist* (New Haven, 1988), 69–79; Colin Jones, *The Great Nation: France from Louis XV to Napoleon, 1715–99* (London, 2002), chaps. 5–7.

37. Robert M. Isherwood, *Farce and Fantasy: Popular Entertainment in Eighteenth-Century Paris* (New York, 1986); Sarah Maza, *Private Lives and Public Affairs: The Causes Célèbres of Prerevolutionary France* (Berkeley, 1993); Robert Darnton, *The Forbidden Best-Sellers of Pre-Revolutionary France* (New York, 1995); Jeremy Popkin, "The *Gazette de Leyde* under Louis XVI," in *Press and Politics in Pre-Revolutionary France*, ed. Jack Censer and Jeremy Popkin (Berkeley, 1987), 94–98.

38. BF to JB, Dec. 4, 1776, *PBF*, 23:24–25; Reinier Arrenberg to BF, Mar. 31, 1777, *PBF*, 23:538–539 (also 538n–539n); editorial note, *PBF*, 24:171n; JB to BF, June 25, 1777, *PBF*, 24:222; Echeverria, *Mirage in the West*, 55–56; Schaeper, *France and America in the Revolutionary Era*, 98.

39. JL to BF, [June 24, 1777], *PBF*, 24:217–218; Antoine-Laurent Lavoisier to BF, June 8, 1777, *PBF*, 24:142; Report of a Committee of the Académie Royale des Sciences, May 23, 1778, *PBF*, 26:520–521; Lavoisier to BF, Aug. 9, 1778, *PBF*, 27:236; Echeverria, *Mirage in the West*, 59–60.

40. JL to BF, May 26, [1777], *PBF*, 24:84; Jean-François-Clément Morand to BF, Aug. 10, 1777, *PBF*, 24:405; Horace Walpole to William Mason, Feb. 27, 1777, in *The Letters of Horace Walpole*, ed. Paget Toynbee, 16 vols. (Oxford, 1903–1905), 10:22.

41. Gay, *Voltaire's Politics*, chap. 1; Charles Coulston Gillispie, *Science and Polity in France at the End of the Old Regime* (Princeton, 1980), 112–114; Mordechai Feingold, *The Newtonian Moment: Isaac Newton and the Making of Modern Culture* (New York and Oxford, 2004), 94–116; Roger Pearson, *Voltaire Almighty: A Life in Pursuit of Freedom* (New York, 2005), chaps. 7–12.

42. Gay, *Voltaire's Politics*, 309–328; Pearson, *Voltaire Almighty*, chaps. 14–20.

43. Gay, *Voltaire's Politics*, 328–333; Keith Michael Baker, *Condorcet: From Natural Philosophy to Social Mathematics* (Chicago, 1975), esp. chap. 2; Margaret C. Jacob, *Living the Enlightenment: Freemasonry and Politics in Eighteenth-Century Europe* (New York, 1991), chap. 9; Gillispie, *Science and Polity in France*, esp. 3–21; John Lough, *The Encyclopédie*, (London, 1971), chaps. 8 and 9.

44. Aldridge, *Franklin and His French Contemporaries*, 38–54. Antoine-François Quétant produced the 1777 edition.

45. Ibid., 15, 24–38; Jessica Riskin, *Science in the Age of Sensibility: The Sentimental Empiricists of the French Enlightenment* (Chicago, 2002), chap. 4.

46. BF to Madame Brillon, "The Ephemera," *PBF*, 27:430–435; Gilbert Chinard, "Random Notes on Two 'Bagatelles,'" APS *Proceedings* 103 (1959), 740–760. On Franklin's French social life, see Claude-Anne Lopez, *Mon Cher Papa: Franklin and the Ladies of Paris* (New Haven, 1966).

47. On fans, see *New-Jersey Gazette*, Dec. 31, 1777; Charles M. Andrews, "A Note on the Franklin-Deane Mission to France," *Yale University Library Gazette* 2 (1928), 63. On waves, see Achille-Guillaume Lebège de Presle to BF, Nov. 22, 1777, *PBF*, 25:183; William Carmichael to BF, May 14, 1778, *PBF*, 26:451. On electricity, see Abbé Jacob Hemmer to BF, Sept. 24, 1778, *PBF*, 27:457. On learned societies, see Société Royale de Médecine re. BF, June 17, 1777, *PBF*, 24:176; Padua Academy of Sciences, Letters, and Arts to BF, Dec. 20, 1781, *PBF*, 36:273; Princess Daskaw to BF, Nov. 4, 1789, William Temple Franklin, ed., *Memoirs of the Life and Writings of Benjamin Franklin*, 3 vols. (London, 1818), 1:408.

48. Echeverria, *Mirage in the West*, 50; Lopez, *Mon Cher Papa*, 26–27; Worthington Chauncey Ford, ed., *Letters of William Lee, 1766–1783*, 3 vols. (Brooklyn, N.Y., 1891), 2:505.

49. Roger Hahn, *The Anatomy of a Scientific Institution: The Paris Academy of Sci-*

ences, 1666–1803 (Berkeley, 1971), 3, 45–47, 58–83, 97–98, 119–120; Gillispie, *Science and Polity in France,* 78–99, 122; Aldridge, *Franklin and His French Contemporaries,* 108 (on asparagus).

50. Jacques Barbeu-Dubourg, preface to *Oeuvres de M. Franklin* . . . , 2 vols (Paris, 1773), *PBF,* 20:427; Pierre Turini to BF, Sept. 28, 1780, *PBF,* 33:339.

51. Dumas to BF, Oct. 23, 1778, *PBF,* 27:613; Jean-Gabriel Monaudoüin de la Touche to BF, Dec. 21, 1776, *PBF,* 23:61 ("il a fait a philadelphie / un temple a la philosophie, / [et] un Thrône pour la liberté").

52. Aldridge, *Franklin and His French Contemporaries,* 16, 124–129.

53. Editorial note, *PBF,* 25:lxiii; Journal of the Duc de Croÿ, *PBF,* 26:140 ("son air de patriarche et fondateur de la Nation, jointe à sa célébrité comme inventeur de l'électricité, législateur des treize provinces unies, et sa science"); Stourzh, *Franklin and American Foreign Policy,* 139–146.

54. Gay, *Voltaire's Politics,* 334–340; editorial notes, *PBF,* 26:697 (on Masonic ceremony); *PBF,* 35:frontispiece, xxii (on apron); Aldridge, *Franklin and His French Contemporaries,* 9–12; *JA,* 4:80–81.

55. Pearson, *Voltaire Almighty,* 387–390; editorial note, *PBF,* 28:286–287.

56. See also Bernard Bailyn, *To Begin the World Anew: The Genius and Ambiguities of the American Founders* (New York, 2003), 84–99.

57. BF to Sarah Bache, June 3, 1779, *PBF,* 29:613. Franklin was idolized at home, too. New Jersey celebrations on the first anniversary of the Franco-American alliance had featured "the American Philosopher and Ambassador extracting lightening from the clouds"; see *New-Jersey Gazette,* Mar. 3, 1779.

58. Aldridge, *Franklin and His French Contemporaries,* 105–106, 116–117.

59. J. L. Heilbron, *Elements of Early Modern Physics* (Berkeley, 1982), 202; Lebègue de Presle to BF, June 13 [1777], *PBF,* 24:162–164; Lebègue de Presle to BF, July 16, 1777, *PBF,* 24:325; editorial note, *PBF,* 25:5n–6n.

60. BF to [Lèbegue de Presle], Oct. 4, 1777, *PBF,* 25:26.

61. *PBF,* 25:5n–6n, 26; Heilbron, *Early Modern Physics,* 202–203.

62. Adrienne Koch and William Peden, eds., *The Life and Selected Writings of Thomas Jefferson* . . . (Indianapolis, Ind., 1944), 178.

63. William C. Stinchcombe, *The American Revolution and the French Alliance* (Syracuse, N.Y., 1969); Jonathan R. Dull, *The French Navy and American Independence: A Study of Arms and Diplomacy, 1774–1787* (Princeton, 1975); Ronald Hoffman and Peter J. Albert, eds., *Diplomacy and Revolution: The Franco-American Alliance of 1778* (Charlottesvilla, Va., 1981).

64. Fowler, *Rebels under Sail,* 78, chaps. 6 and 7; Schaeper, *France and America in the Revolutionary Era,* 199–200; Conde de Aranda to Marqués de Grimaldi, [Jan. 13, 1777], *PBF,* 23:178 (quoting Franklin); Jonathan Williams Jr. to BF, Jan. 25, 1777, *PBF,* 23:232; Williams to the American Commissioners, Aug. 2, 1777, *PBF,* 24:384–385. See also the American Commissioners to the Committee for Foreign Affairs, May 26, 1777, *PBF,* 24:79–82.

65. American Commissioners to Committee of Secret Correspondence, Feb. 6, 1777, *PBF,* 23:287; [Samuel Wharton] to BF, Jan. 17, 1777, *PBF,* 23:204–205; BF to Richard Bache, May 22, 1777, *PBF,* 24:64; American Commissioners to the Committee for Foreign Affairs, May 26, 1777, *PBF,* 24:79; Jonathan Williams Jr. to the American Commissioners, Apr. 12, 1777, *PBF,* 23:578 (on *Franklin's* prizes); Fowler, *Rebels under Sail,* 25, 57 (on *Franklin*).

66. Howard Robinson, *Carrying British Mails Overseas* (New York, 1964), 52–56; American Commissioners, May 10–11, 1777, *PBF,* 24:48–50.

67. William Bell Clark, *Ben Franklin's Privateers: A Naval Epic of the American Revolution* (Baton Rouge, La., 1956), 164–170; Jonathan R. Dull, "Was the Continental Navy a Mistake?," *American Neptune* 44 (1984), 167–170.

68. Jonathan Williams Jr. to BF, Apr. 8, 1777, *PBF,* 23:572–573 (see also similar statements on pp. 350, 410, 420n, 435); American Commissioners to Committee of Secret Correspondence, Mar. 12[–Apr. 9], 1777, *PBF,* 23:467; Reculès de Basmarein & Raimbaux to BF, Nov. 18, 1777, *PBF,* 25:172; Reculès de Basmarein & Raimbaux to American Commissioners, [before May 16, 1778], *PBF,* 26:472–474; Dull, *French Navy,* chaps. 3 and 4; Dull, "Continental Navy a Mistake?" 169; Fowler, *Rebels under Sail,* 93–95; Ellen Cohn, "Benjamin Franklin, Georges-Louis Le Rouge, and the Franklin/Folger Chart of the Gulf Stream," *Imago Mundi* 52 (2000), 133–134.

69. Jonathan Williams Jr. to BF, Jan. 25, 1777, *PBF,* 23:229; William Bingham to American Commissioners, Apr. 6, 1777, *PBF,* 23:561; Lambert Wickes to American Commissioners, Mar. 5, 1777, *PBF,* 23:428; Williams to American Commissioners, Mar. 11, 1777, *PBF,* 23:463; Williams to American Commissioners, Mar. 25, 1777, *PBF,* 23:520; Harley, Petchenik, and Towner, *Mapping the American Revolutionary War,* 91–93; Fowler, *Rebels under Sail,* 132–133.

70. Benjamin Vaughan to BF, Jan. 27, 1777, *PBF,* 23:242; American Commissioners to Williams, [Feb. 25, 1777], *PBF,* 23:380.

71. Robert Sayer and John Bennet, *The American Military Pocket Atlas . . .* (London, 1776); Joseph F. W. Des Barres, *The Atlantic Neptune* (London, 1774–1781); G. N. D. Evans, "Hydrography: A Note on Eighteenth-Century Methods," *Mariner's Mirror* 52 (1966), 248–249; Harley, Petchenik, and Towner, *Mapping the American Revolutionary War,* 87–91.

72. Jean-Pierre Bérenger to BF, Mar. 1, 1778, *PBF,* 26:6; Harley, Petchinik, and Towner, *Mapping the American Revolutionary War,* 92; Cohn, "Franklin, Le Rouge and Franklin/Folger Chart," 125; Dull, *French Navy,* 143–158. The first part of the *Pilot amériquain septentrional* (Paris, 1778) appropriated the 1775–1776 edition of *The North American Pilot*; the second part used the 1779 edition, which included James Cook's surveys.

73. Fowler, *Rebels under Sail,* 279–286; Vergennes to BF, Aug. 22, 1778, *PBF,* 27:289–290; Robert Henderson and John Smith to BF, Sept. 5, 1779, *PBF,* 30:297.

74. Memoir on the State of the Former Colonies, [before Jan. 5, 1777], *PBF,* 23:119, 120; BF to David Hartley, Mar. 21, 1779, *PBF,* 29:177.

75. BF to [Ann-Robert-Jacques Turgot, Baron de l'Aulne], Apr. 2, 1777, *PBF,* 23:551; Johann Rodolphe Valltravers to BF, Jan. 10, 1778, *PBF,* 25:464–466 (on pistol); BF to [JB?], [after Oct. 2, 1777?], *PBF,* 25:22. Each volume of the *PBF* for the period of Franklin's residence in Paris gives synopses of the bushels of petitions.

76. Fowler, *Rebels under Sail,* 286–289; Nicholas Rogers, "Liberty Road: Opposition to Impressment in Britain During the American War of Independence," in *Jack Tar in History: Essays in the History of Maritime Life and Labour,* ed. Colin Howell and Richard J. Twomey (Fredricton, New Brunswick, Canada, 1991), 72–75; Catherine M. Prelinger, "Benjamin Franklin and the American Prisoners of War in England during the American Revolution," *WMQ* 32 (1975), 261–264; Linda Colley, *Captives: Britain, Empire, and the World, 1600–1850* (London, 2002), 208–227.

77. Colley, *Captives,* 208–227.

78. Franklin and Lafayette's List of Prints to Illustrate British Cruelties, [c. May 1779], *PBF,* 29:590–593.

79. BF to David Hartley, Oct. 20, 1778, *PBF,* 27:575; American Commissioners to Sartine, Nov. 5, 1778, *PBF,* 18:35; BF to David Hartley, Oct. 14[–Dec. 11], 1777,

PBF, 25:67; American Commissioners to Lord North, Dec. 12, 1777, *PBF*, 25:275; BF to Sartine, May 8, 1779, *PBF*, 29:448.

80. Prelinger, "Franklin and Prisoners of War," 271–277; BF to John Paul Jones, June 10, 1778, *PBF*, 26:607; American Commissioners to David Hartley, June 16, 1778, *PBF*, 26:626; BF to Lafayette, Mar. 22, 1779, *PBF*, 29:186; BF to Jones, [Apr. 28, 1779], *PBF*, 29:387; BF to Committee for Foreign Affairs, May 26, 1779, *PBF*, 29:549.

81. Prelinger, "Franklin and Prisoners of War," 277–280; Fowler, *Rebels under Sail*, 154–169; Robert Gardiner, ed., *Navies and the American Revolution, 1775–1783* (London, 1996), 152–153.

82. Prelinger, "Franklin and Prisoners of War," 277–280; Colley, *Captives*, 210–211.

83. Prelinger, "Franklin and Prisoners of War," 282–289; BF to William Hodgson, Apr. 1, 1781, *PBF*, 34:507.

84. BF to Jones, June 10, 1778, *PBF*, 26:606–607; BF to John Adams, Apr. 8, 1779, *PBF*, 29:279.

85. Prelinger, "Franklin and Prisoners of War," 261, 269; example from Aug. 22, 1777 (money for sailors), Benjamin Franklin Waste Book, 1776–1779, Franklin Papers, APS; John Atwood, Jacob Vere, and Nathan Chadwick to BF, Aug. 7, 1778, *PBF*, 27:233.

86. Edward Byers, *The Nation of Nantucket: Society and Politics in an Early American Commercial Center, 1660–1820* (Boston, 1987), chap. 10; BF relatives, editorial notes, *PBF*, 26:38n, 259n–260n. On Franklin's awareness of the problem of nepotism, see Richard Bache to BF, Oct. 22, 1778, *PBF*, 27:602; BF to Jonathan Williams, Mar. 23, 1782, *PBF*, 37:41.

87. Testimony in a Prize Case, [Oct. 14, 1776], *PBF*, 22:657–658; Seth Paddack to BF, Aug. 2, 1777, *PBF*, 24:389.

88. Jonathan Williams Jr. to BF, Mar. 11, 1777, *PBF*, 23:465 (Paddack); [Silas Deane] to John Folger, Oct. 7, 1777, *PBF*, 25:48–50; Committee for Foreign Affairs to the American Commissioners, Jan. 12, 1778, *PBF*, 25:467–468; Thomas Paine to BF, Mar. 4, 1779, *PBF*, 29:44.

89. Richard Grinnell, memorandum [Oct. 7, 1778], *PBF*, 27:515; Tristram Barnard to the American Commissioners, [after Oct. 9, 1778], *PBF*, 27:528; Richard Grinnell to American Commissioners, [after Oct. 23, 1778], *PBF*, 27:608; American Commissioners to Antoine Raynaud Jean Galbert Gabriel de Sartine, Oct. 30, 1778, *PBF*, 27:659–660; Griffith Williams to BF, *PBF*, 27:666–667; Henry Laurens to BF, Oct. 26, 1778, *PBF*, 27:636; American Commissioners to Sartine, Nov. 17, 1778, *PBF*, 28:122 (for quotation); Elisha Clark to BF, Dec. 5, 1778, *PBF*, 28:189; Shubael Gardner to the American Commissioners, Dec. 22, 1778, *PBF*, 28:260; Edouard A. Stackpole, *The Sea-Hunters: The New England Whalemen during Two Centuries, 1635–1835* (Philadelphia and New York, 1953), 66–84.

90. BF to the Duc de Villequier, Oct. 1, 1779, *PBF*, 30:425; JL to BF, May 26 [1777], *PBF*, 24:84.

91. *JA*, 4:118; Stourzh, *Franklin and American Foreign Policy*, 150–169.

92. Heilbron, *Early Modern Physics*, 210–213.

93. JI to BF, Nov. 15, 1776, *PBF*, 23:10–11.

94. Prince de Gallitzin (Dimitri Golitsyn) to BF, Jan. 28, 1777, *PBF*, 23:250; Georgiana Shipley to BF, Feb. 11, 1777, *PBF*, 23:305; Johann Rodolphe Valltravers to BF, Sept. 21, 1777, *PBF*, 24:552; Henri Serre to BF, May, 29, 1778, *PBF*, 26:541–542.

95. John Ingenhousz, "Electrical Experiments, to Explain How Far the Phenomena of the Electrophorus May Be Accounted for by *Dr. Franklin's* Theory of Positive and Negative Electricity," *Philosophical Transactions* 48 (London, 1779), 1027–1048, quotation on p. 1027; JI to BF, May 25, 1779, *PBF,* 29:545.

96. "Sundry Papers Relative to an Accident from Lightning at Purfleet," *Philosophical Transactions* 48 (London, 1779), 232–317, quotation on p. 240.

97. *Gentleman's Magazine* 49 (1779), 556.

98. Editorial note on "The Morals of Chess," *PBF,* 29, 750–753; BF and JL on lightning rods, May 12, 1780, *PBF,* 32:373–376. On the continuing saga of lightning rods, see *BFS,* chap. 8; Riskin, *Science in the Age of Sensibility,* chap. 5.

99. American Commissioners to Vergennes, Jan. 5, 1777, *PBF,* 23:123; BF, "Comparison of Great Britain and America as to Credit, in 1777," *PBF,* 24:508n, 512.

100. Aldridge, *Franklin and His French Contemporaries,* 40–41, 95–104.

101. BF to Madame Brillon, Mar. 10, 1778, *PBF,* 26:85; BF to Lafayette, Sept. 17, 1782, *WBF,* 8:595–596.

102. Editorial note, *PBF,* 28:190–192; *PG,* Jan. 6, 1737; John Bartram to BF, [Nov. 12, 1757], *PBF,* 7:271–272; Isaac L. Winn to BF (and BF's response), Aug. 12, 1772, *PBF,* 19:236–239; JL to BF, [c. Dec. 1778], *PBF,* 28:309.

103. Editorial note, *PBF,* 28:191; editorial note, *PBF,* 29:323n–324n.

104. BF, "Suppositions and Conjectures on the Aurora Borealis," [before Dec. 7, 1778], *PBF,* 28:192–193.

105. Ibid., 193–195.

106. Ibid., 192–200.

107. *Mémoires secrets* cited in *PBF,* 29:323n–324n; Abbé François Rozier, Apr. 21, 1779, *PBF,* 29:353–354; Georgiana Shipley to BF, June 6, 1779, *PBF,* 29:636; Gillispie, *Science and Polity in France,* 188 (on Rozier's *Journal de Physique*); editorial note, *PBF,* 30:66n (on London ed.).

108. Howard S. Reed, "Jan Ingenhousz, Plant Physiologist, with a History of the Discovery of Photosynthesis," *Chronica Botanica* 11 (1949), 295–296, 301–302; Jan Ingenhousz, *Experiments upon Vegetables . . .* (London, 1779), in *Chronica Botanica* 11 (1949), 311, 313, 324 (for quotation), 338–340, 379–380.

109. JI to BF, Nov. 18, 1779, *PBF,* 31:122; BF to Francis Hopkinson, Mar. 16, 1780, *PBF,* 32:120; JI to BF, Apr. 24, 1782, *PBF,* 37:212; BF to JI, Oct. 2, 1781 [–June 21, 1782], *PBF,* 35:550.

110. JI to BF, May 3, 1780, *PBF,* 32:341–346 (quotations on pp. 341, 345).

111. BF to JI [after May 3, 1780], *PBF,* 32:346–349; JI to BF, Dec. 5, 1780, *PBF,* 34:121–123; BF to JI, Oct. 2–[June 21], 1782, *PBF,* 35:545–446; BF to JI [June 21, 1782], *PBF,* 37:504–512; *F&N,* 326–334.

112. JI to BF, Apr. 7, 1781, *PBF,* 34:522; JI to BF, May 23, 1781, *PBF,* 35:98–99.

113. BF's passport for JI, [Oct. 17, 1777], *PBF,* 25:80–81; BF to Baudouin, June 18, 1779, *PBF,* 29:700. On Moravians, see BF to captains and commanders, June 22, 1778, *PBF,* 26:667–668; BF to captains and commanders, [Apr. 11, 1779], *PBF,* 29:308–309.

114. Duc de Croÿ to BF, [Mar. 1, 1779], *PBF,* 29:5; Duc de Croÿ's account of a dinner with BF, [Mar. 1, 1779], *PBF,* 29:8 ("avec son laconisme sublime . . . 'Cela sera fait!'"); BF to captains and commanders, [Mar. 10, 1779], *PBF,* 29:86. See also John Gascoigne, *Science in the Service of Empire: Joseph Banks, the British State and the Uses of Science in the Age of Revolution* (Cambridge, 1998), 158.

115. Dull, *French Navy,* 149; [Joshua Steele] to BF, Oct. 18, 1778, *PBF,* 17:568–569, 568n (on RSA); JP to BF, May 8, 1779, *PBF,* 29:453; BF to JI, May

4[-5], 1779, *PBF*, 29:428 (for quotation); editorial note on Royal Society, *PBF*, 29:544n; Jean-Hyacinthe de Magellan to BF, May 13, 1779, *PBF*, 29:489; Joshua Steele to BF, June 25, 1779, *PBF*, 29:741; *PBF*, 31:lxii.

116. James Cook, *A Voyage towards the South Pole, and Round the World* . . . (London, 1777), 1:104–105.

117. Benjamin Vaughan, ed. *Political, Miscellaneous, and Philosophical Pieces* . . . *Written by Benj. Franklin* (London, 1779), in *PBF*, 31:210–218 (quotation on p. 214).

118. BF et al., report to the Académie Royale des Sciences, [Mar. 26, 1779], *PBF*, 29:209–211 (on gunpowder); Denis I. Duveen and Herbert S. Klickstein, "Benjamin Franklin (1706–1790) and Antoine Laurent Lavoisier (1743–1794)," *Annals of Science* 11 (1955), 271–278; Claude-Anne Lopez, "Saltpetre, Tin and Gunpowder: Addenda to the Correspondence of Lavoisier and Franklin," *Annals of Science* 16 (1960), 83–87.

119. BF to Richard Price, June 13, 1782, *WBF*, 8:457; Jean-François Fournier to BF, Sept. 4, 1777, *PBF*, 24:500–501 (on typefaces); invitation to an Independence Day celebration, [before June 24, 1779], *PBF*, 29:726–727; passport for Thomas Burdy (first passport), 1779, *PBF*, 30:181–182; Simon-Pierre Fournier le Jeune to BF, Sept. 16, 1779 (on order for type), *PBF*, 30:346–347; BF to Fizeaux, Grand et Cie., Oct. 29, 1779 (on orders for English equipment), *PBF*, 30:609–612.

120. BF to JP, Jan. 27, 1777, *PBF*, 23:238; BF to JP, June 7, 1782, *FW*, 8:451, 452.

121. BF to Joseph Banks, Sept. 9, 1782, *WBF*, 8:593.

122. Colley, *Captives*, 219; Stourzh, *Franklin and American Foreign Policy*, 186–192; BF to David Hartley, Apr. 5, 1782, *WBF*, 8:414; BF to Lord Shelburne, Apr. 18, 1782, *WBF*, 8:467–468; Hartley to BF, May 3, 1782, *WBF*, 8:499.

123. Stourzh, *Franklin and American Foreign Policy*, 167–169; Richard B. Morris, *The Peacemakers: The Great Powers and American Independence* (New York, 1965), chaps. 1 and 9–12.

124. Earl of Shelburne to BF, Apr. 6, 1782, *PBF*, 37:103–104, 104n; Morris, *Peacemakers*, chap. 14.

125. Stourzh, *Franklin and American Foreign Policy*, 169–179; Morris, *Peacemakers*, chap. 15; Dull, *French Navy*, 312–314; Orville T. Murphy, "The Comte de Vergennes, the Newfoundland Fishers, and the Peace Negotiations of 1783: A Reconsideration," *Canadian Historical Review* 46 (1965), 32–46; Stackpole, *Sea-Hunters*, chaps. 7 and 8.

126. BF and John Adams to the President of Congress, July 23, 1778, *PBF*, 27:146; BF to David Hartley, Oct. 26, 1778, *PBF*, 27:629; BF to Hartley, May 4, 1779, *PBF*, 29:427.

127. Cohn, "Franklin, Le Rouge, and the Franklin/Folger Chart," 125–128.

128. Ibid., 135–136.

129. Ibid., 135; Folger to BF, July 3 [1781], *PBF*, 35:217, 217n.

130. Jonathan Williams Jr. to BF, Nov. 10, 1781, *PBF*, 36:41.

131. BF to Williams, Nov. 19, 1781, *PBF*, 37:67; Williams to BF, Feb. 24, 1782, *PBF*, 37:611.

Chapter 9

1. *BFS*, chap. 12; Richard P. Hallion, *Taking Flight: Inventing the Aerial Age from Antiquity through the First World War* (New York, 2003), 51; Thomas J. Schaeper, *France and America in the Revolutionary Era: The Life of Jacques-Donatien Leray de Chaumont, 1725–1803* (Providence, R.I., 1995), 136–137.

2. BF to JI, Apr. 29, 1785, *WBF*, 9:318.

3. Henry Guerlac, *Lavoisier, the Crucial Year: The Background and Origin of His First Experiments on Combustion in 1772* (Ithaca, 1961); Charles Coulston Gillispie, *Science and Polity in France at the End of the Old Regime* (Princeton, 1980), 61–64.

4. Douglas McKie and Niels H. de V. Heathcote, *The Discovery of Specific and Latent Heats* (London, 1935); *F&N*, 334–340; William Alexander to BF, Sept. 26, 1778, *PBF*, 27:464; "Books Lent," Nov. 1778, *PBF*, 28:178; Benjamin Vaughan to BF, Sept. 20, 1779, *PBF*, 30:381–382.

5. J. L. Heilbron, *Elements of Early Modern Physics* (Berkeley, 1982), 213–240; James Delbourgo, *A Most Amazing Scene of Wonders: Electricity and Enlightenment in Early America* (Harvard University Press, forthcoming).

6. Patricia Fara, "Marginalized Practices," *CHS*, 485–507.

7. Gillispie, *Science and Polity in France*, 290–330; [Jean-Paul Marat] to BF, [before Mar. 13, 1779], *PBF*, 29:105–107; [Marat] to BF, Apr. 12, 1779, *PBF*, 29:311–312; François Sage, *Analyse chimique et concordance des trois règnes* (Paris, 1786), 1:118.

8. Robert Darnton, *Mesmerism and the End of the Enlightenment in France* (Cambridge, Mass., 1968), 10, 62–64; Gillispie, *Science and Polity in France*, 261–265; editorial note, *PBF*, 10:123 (on armonica).

9. JI to BF, Oct. 5, 1778, *PBF*, 27:506.

10. Gillispie, *Science and Polity in France*, 265–283; Jessica Riskin, *Science in the Age of Sensibility: The Sentimental Empiricists of the French Enlightenment* (Chicago, 2002), chap. 6; BF to La Sabliere de La Condamine, Mar. 19, 1784, *WBF*, 9:182–183; BF to JI, Apr. 29, 1785, *WBF*, 9:320.

11. Charles Coulston Gillispie, *The Montgolfier Brothers and the Invention of Aviation, 1783–1784* (Princeton, 1983), 15–17, 22; Hallion, *Taking Flight*, chaps. 1 and 2.

12. Gillispie, *Montgolfier Brothers*, 3–4, 27–33; Hallion, *Taking Flight*, chap. 3.

13. Gillispie, *Montgolfier Brothers*, 51–56; Hallion, *Taking Flight*, chap. 3.

14. Gillispie, *Montgolfier Brothers*, 75, 118–125; Hallion, *Taking Flight*, 53, 56–59.

15. Gillispie, *Montgolfier Brothers*, 7–10, 28; Hallion, *Taking Flight*, 48, 49; Alfred Owen Aldridge, *Franklin and His French Contemporaries* (New York, 1957), 135; Maurice-Augustin Montgolfier to BF, [before Jan. 28, 1782], *PBF*, 36:486–487; BF to Montgolfier, Feb. 4, 1782, *PBF*, 36:533–534; account from *Journal de Paris*, Dec. 26, 1781, *PBF*, 36:lxii; Faesch to BF, July 25, 1782, *PBF*, 37:676–677.

16. BF to Joseph Banks, Nov. 21, 1783, *WBF*, 9:117 (on witches and philosophers); Le Roy to BF, [1783] (two undated letters), Franklin Papers, APS.

17. BF to Banks, Nov. 21, 1783, *WBF*, 9:114 (on flame), 116 (on car); BF to Banks, Dec. 1, 1783, *WBF*, 9:122 (on Vincennes); Brooke Hindle, *The Pursuit of Science in Revolutionary America, 1735–1789* (Chapel Hill, N.C., 1956), 342.

18. Gillispie, *Montgolfier Brothers*, 51; BF to Richard Price, Sept. 16, 1783, *WBF*, 9:100.

19. Hallion, *Taking Flight*, 59–60; Brandon Brame Fortune and Deborah J. Warner, *Franklin and His Friends: Portraying the Man of Science in Eighteenth-Century America* (Washington, D.C., 1999), 122–123; BF to anonymous, June 20, 1785, *WBF*, 9:345.

20. BF to Mme. Lavoisier, Oct. 23, 1788, *WBF*, 9:669; BF to Richard Price, July 29, 1786, *WBF*, 9:529; BF to Edward Nairne, Oct. 18, 1783, *WBF*, 9:109.

21. Charles Coulston Gillispie, ed., *Dictionary of Scientific Biography*, 15 vols. (New York, 1975), 12, s.v. "Soulavie, Jean-Louis Giraud."

22. BF to Soulavie, Sept. 22, 1782, *WBF*, 9:597–600, 601; Rhoda Rappaport, "The Earth Sciences," *CHS*, 417–436; Dennis R. Dean, "Benjamin Franklin and Earthquakes," *Annals of Science* 46 (1989), 481–495.

23. BF, "Meteorological Imaginations and Conjectures," May 1784, *WBF*, 9:215, 217.

24. Ibid.

25. Thomas Pownall, "Hydraulic and Nautical Observations on the Currents in the Atlantic Ocean . . . ," t.p., 13, 14, RS.

26. Johann Reinhold Forster to BF, July 30, 1778, *PBF*, 27:181; JL to BF, [Aug. 1778?], *PBF*, 27:328–329; Stephen Sayre to BF, Mar. 21, 1779, and June 7, 1779, *PBF*, 29:181, 639; Benjamin Gale to BF, Aug. 7, 1775, *PBF*, 22:154–158. See also François-Marie Fyot to BF, Aug. 3, 1778, *PBF*, 27:209 (on longitude); Honoré-Sébastien Vial du Clairbois to BF, Aug. 14, 1778, *PBF*, 27:235 (on naval architecture); "Christin" to BF, Sept. 19, 1778, *PBF*, 27:425; Alexandre-Henry-Guillaume le Roberger de Vausenville to BF, June 29, 1779, *PBF*, 29:776–778.

27. John Paul Jones to BF, Sept. 18, 1778, *PBF*, 27:421; Jones to BF, Sept. 24, 1778, *PBF*, 27:458; intelligence from Havana and other places, Nov. 13, 1778, *PBF*, 28:109; Landais to BF, Feb. 26, 1779, *PBF*, 28:620–621; BF to Landais, Mar. 4, 1779, and Mar. 6, 1779, *PBF*, 29:41, 59; BF to Jones, Feb. 19, 1780, *PBF*, 31:499. See also Mauer Mauer, "Coppered Bottoms for the Royal Navy: A Factor in the Maritime War of 1778–1783," *Military Affairs* 14 (1950), 57–61; Howard Robinson, *Carrying British Mails Overseas* (New York, 1964), 51.

28. Banks to BF, Mar. 29, 1780, *PBF*, 32:176–177; William Bell Clark, "A Franklin Postscript to Captain Cook's Voyages," APS *Proceedings* 98 (1954), 400–405; BF to Vaughan, July 26, 1784, *WBF*, 9:241; BF to Andrew Strahan, May 6, 1786, *WBF*, 9:510.

29. Robert Glen, "Industrial Wayfarers: Benjamin Franklin and a Case of Machine Smuggling in the 1780s," *Business History* 23 (1981), 309–326.

30. "Information to Those Who Would Remove to America," c. Sept. 1782, *WBF*, 8:603–607. Franklin had in fact helped concoct a scheme to offer U.S. land to Hessians who would desert the British. See Lyman H. Butterfield, "Psychological Warfare in 1776: The Jefferson-Franklin Plan to Cause Hessian Desertions," APS *Proceedings*, 94 (1950), 234–241.

31. "Information to Those Who Would Remove to America," c. Sept. 1782, *WBF*, 8:604–605, 606.

32. Ibid., 606.

33. BF to Granville Sharp, July 5, 1785, *WBF*, 9:357.

34. BF to Sarah Bache, Jan. 26, 1784, *WBF*, 9:163–165; see also BF to Conde de Campomanes, June 5, 1784, *WBF*, 9:222.

35. *Autobiography*, 135, 141–244. Another Franklin protégé, "J. Hector St. John" de Crèvecoeur (the Michel-Guillaime Jean who had planned a Franco-American packet service), made the same point in his *Letters from an American Farmer* (1782). Franklin recommended the book to others. See BF to Crèvecoeur, c. Dec. 1783/Jan. 1784, *WBF*, 9:147–149; BF, "On Immigration," c. 1783, *WBF*, 9:149–150; BF to Crèvecoeur, Feb. 16, 1788, *WBF*, 9:636.

36. Claude-Anne Lopez, *Mon Cher Papa: Franklin and the Ladies of Paris* (New Haven, 1966), 91–96, 264–271; BF to John Jay and Mrs. Jay, Sept. 21, 1785, *WBF*, 9:466 (on litter); Benjamin Franklin Bache Diary, July 12, 1785, Bache Papers, APS.

37. Anne L. Poulet, *Jean-Antoine Houdon: Sculptor of the Enlightenment* (Washington, D.C., 2003).

38. B. F. Bache Diary, July 12 and 24; William Temple Franklin Diary, 1785, July 22, Franklin Papers, APS; Benjamin Franklin Diary, July 12–Sept. 14, 1785, July 25, Franklin Papers, APS.

39. B. F. Bache Diary, June–July 1785; chronologies in *Autobiography*, 303–320, and *PBF*, 1:lxxxvii. The number of days for 1724 is an estimate but is, if anything, on the high side.

40. "A Letter from Dr. Benjamin Franklin, to Mr. Alphonsus le Roy . . . Containing Sundry Maritime Observations," APS *Transactions* 2 (1786), 328–329.

41. B. F. Bache Diary, Aug. 23.

42. BF to John Lathrop, May 31, 1788, *WBF*, 9:650.

43. BF to JI, Apr. 29, 1785, *WBF*, 9:317–318.

44. *JA*, June 23, 1779, 2:391.

45. BF to David Hartley, July 5, 1785, *WBF*, 9:359; BF to John Bard and Mrs. Bard, Nov. 14, 1785, *WBF*, 9:476.

46. John C. Greene, *American Science in the Age of Jefferson* (Ames, Iowa, 1984), 3–12, quotation on p. 11.

47. BF to James Bowdoin, Jan. 1, 1786, *WBF*, 9:479; BF to Jonathan Williams, Feb. 12, 1786, *WBF*, 9:486; Hindle, *Pursuit of Science*, 263–271.

48. Guillaume Thomas Raynal, *Histoire philosophique et politique des . . . deux Indes* (Maestricht, 1774), 7:92.

49. Hindle, *Pursuit of Science*, chaps. 14 and 15; APS Charter (1780), APS *Transactions*, 2 (1786), xi–xii.

50. APS Minute Book, June 11, 1784 (on balloons), Aug. 12, 1784 (on Lafayette), Dec. 9, 1784 (on Mesmer report), Feb. 4, 1785 (on Vergennes), APS.

51. APS Minute Book, Sept. 16, 1785, Sept. 27, 1785, APS.

52. Ibid., Sept. 27, 1785, APS.

53. Hindle, *Pursuit of Science*, 271–272; BF diary, *WBF*, 10:346; BF to the "Princess Dashkow," May 7, 1788, *WBF*, 9:649; Pascal Pontremoli, ed., *Mémoires de la Princesse Dashkov* (Paris, 1989).

54. BF to JL, Apr., 18, 1787, *WBF*, 9:572–573.

55. BF to Le Veillard, *WBF*, 9:Mar. 16, 1786, 497; BF to Le Veillard, Apr. 15, 1787, *WBF*, 9:560; BF to JI, Apr. 29, 1785, *WBF*, 9:321.

56. Editorial note, *PBF*, 1:xxi; Richard Bache to BF, July 14, 1778, *PBF*, 27:89–90, 90n.

57. BF to MS, May 6, 1786, *WBF*, 9:512.

58. APS *Transactions* 2 (1786), iii; APS Minute Book, Oct. 21, 1785, Nov. 4, 1785, Jan. 28, 1786, APS.

59. APS *Transactions* 2 (1786), xxvii–xxviii.

60. The letter's recipient was misaddressed as "Alphonsus," a medical Le Roy and no relation. See Le Roy to BF, Oct. 9, [1785/1786], Franklin Papers, APS.

61. BF, "Maritime Observations," 294–296 (on water and wind), 300–306 (on flooding, double hulls, lightning rods), 308–309 (on water jet propulsion), 311–313 (on kite-brake), 319 (on landsmen).

62. Ibid., 318–319 (on Cook, compass), 320–323 (on food, etc.).

63. Ibid., 321, 323.

64. Ibid., 314, 315.

65. Ibid., 315–316.

66. BF to Jonathan Williams Jr., Jan. 19, 1786, *WBF*, 9:480 (see also 398n).

67. BF to JI, Apr. 29, 1785, *WBF*, 9:317.

68. On the Mississippi, see Gerald Stourzh, *Benjamin Franklin and American Foreign Policy* (Chicago, 1954), 145–146, 169–179; BF to Charles Pettit, Oct. 10, 1786, *WBF*, 9:544.

69. Remarkably, Franklin only once used the term *balance of power*, despite the

prevalence of that political concept. And he strongly backed Pennsylvania's experiment, starting in 1776, with a unicameral form of government, thus rejecting a long tradition in Anglo-American politics that stressed balance between political interests, principally the few (the elite) and the many (the people). See Stourzh, *Franklin and American Foreign Policy*, 24–28, 254–256.

70. BF, "Maritime Observations," 314–315.

71. Ibid., fig. facing p. 328.

72. Ibid., 316.

73. Ibid., 329.

74. Thomas Paine to George Washington, May 1, 1790, *The Complete Writings of Thomas Paine*, ed. Philip S. Foner, 2 vols. (New York, 1945), 2:1303; J. B. Hewson, *A History of the Practice of Navigation* (Glasgow, 1951), 240. See also Ellen Cohn, "Benjamin Franklin, Georges-Louis Le Rouge and the Franklin/Folger Chart of the Gulf Stream," *Imago Mundi* 52 (2000), 139.

75. On Franklin pointing and interacting with nonhuman entities, see *BFP*, Illus., 2, 6, 7, 8, 30, 32, 33.

76. A partial collection of Franklin's final philosophic works would appear in 1787, but he would not write any new pieces for it; "Maritime Observations" was the last. See B[enjamin] Franklin, *Philosophical and Miscellaneous Papers* (London, 1787).

77. BF to the Abbé Morellet, Apr. 22, 1787, *WBF*, 9:577.

78. Max Farrand, ed., *The Records of the Federal Convention of 1787*, 4 vols. (New Haven, 1911), 3:91.

79. *SFF*, 238–243.

80. *Autobiography*, 192; BF to Whatley, May 23, 1785, *WBF*, 9:337–338.

81. Andrea Sutcliffe, *Steam: The Untold Story of America's First Great Invention* (New York, 2004), esp. 10, 30, 40–42, 46, 59, 83; Hindle, *Pursuit of Science*, 374–377; *SFF*, 242; BF to Benjamin Vaughan, May 14, 1788, Papers of Benjamin Franklin, Library of Congress; BF to JL, Oct. 25, 1788, *WBF*, 9:679.

82. Robert K. Merton, *On the Shoulders of Giants: A Shandean Postscript* (New York, 1965).

83. Farrand, *Federal Convention*, 1:197–200, 523; Jack N. Rakove, *Original Meanings: Politics and Ideas in the Making of the Constitution* (New York, 1996), chaps. 4 and 8.

84. William M. Fowler Jr., *Rebels under Sail: The American Navy during the Revolution* (New York, 1976), 284; Farrand, *Federal Convention*, 2:208; Rakove, *Original Meanings*, 225.

85. Franklin's Sept. 17, 1789, speech at the Constitutional Convention, in *The Autobiography and Other Writings on Politics, Economics, and Virtue*, ed. Alan Houston (Cambridge, 2004), 362.

86. Ibid.

87. [BF], "An Address to the Public," *WBF*, 10:67, 68. Franklin would never meet excellent proof of the power of education, African-American mathematician Benjamin Banneker, whose first almanac appeared in 1791, one year after Franklin's death.

88. Thomas Walpole to Edward Bancroft (extract), [July 14, 1778], *PBF*, 27:86; BF to Vaughan, July 26, 1784, *WBF*, 9:247.

89. BF to Samuel Elbert, Dec. 16, 1787, *WBF*, 9:625.

90. *Autobiography*, 198–199.

91. BF to Morellet, Dec. 10, 1788, *WBF*, 9:691.

92. Ibid.; *Autobiography*, 161, 240–246.

93. *Autobiography,* 256–257.

94. [BF], "To the Editor of the Federal Gazette," Mar. 23, 1790, *WBF,* 10:88–89.

95. BF to Jane Mecom, Aug. 3, 1789, *WBF,* 10:33; BF to Mecom, Mar. 24, 1790, *WBF,* 10:91–92.

96. BF to Thomas Jefferson, Apr. 8, 1790, *WBF,* 10:92–93.

97. Aldridge, *Franklin and His French Contemporaries,* 151.

98. Adams cited in Joseph J. Ellis, *Passionate Sage* (New York, 1993), 66.

99. Epitaph, 1728, *PBF,* 2:111; BF will and testament, [June 22, 1750], *PBF,* 3:482.

Chapter 10

1. Alfred Owen Aldridge, *Franklin and His French Contemporaries* (New York, 1957), 221.

2. On Franklin will and codicil, see *WBF,* 10:493, 506–508.

3. Ibid., 493–494, 499, 503–508.

4. Ibid., 495–499, 508, 509; Richard Bache to BF, Oct. 17, 1779, *PBF,* 30:551 (on Lewis Bache).

5. Richard Price to BF, Apr. 3, 1769, *PBF,* 16:107; Samuel Fayerweather to BF, Dec. 5, 1768, *PBF,* 15:283–284, 285.

6. BF to Joseph Banks, July 27, 1783, *WBF,* 9:74–75; BF to John Lathrop, May 31, 1788, *WBF,* 9:651.

7. BF to Samuel Danforth, July 25, 1773, *PBF,* 20:324; BF to JB, [end of Apr.? 1773], *PBF,* 20:190 ("d'être entonné avec quelques amis dans des muids de Madere . . . pour être alors rendu à la vie par la chaleur du soleil de ma chere patrie").

8. BF to George Whatley, May 23, 1785, *WBF,* 9:334; BF to CC, Oct. 16, 1746, *PBF,* 3:92; Joseph Kastner, *A Species of Eternity* (New York, 1977), 66, 106, 318. Luckily, the Bartrams cultivated the tree, which has not been seen in the wild since 1803.

9. BF to George Whatley, May 23, 1785, *WBF,* 9:333–334.

10. Roger Hahn, *The Anatomy of a Scientific Institution: The Paris Academy of Sciences, 1666–1803* (Berkeley, 1971), chap. 6.

11. Aldridge, *Franklin and His French Contemporaries,* 212–215.

12. Durand Echeverria, *Mirage in the West: A History of the French Image of American Society to 1815* (Princeton, 1968), 170–171; Albert Henry Smyth, "The Life of Benjamin Franklin," *WBF,* 10:493.

13. Aldridge, *Franklin and His French Contemporaries,* 225, 228.

14. Hahn, *Anatomy of a Scientific Institution,* 150–151, chaps. 7 and 8; Henry Guerlac, *Antoine-Laurent Lavoisier: Chemist and Revolutionary* (New York, 1975), 124–131.

15. Zoltán Haraszti, *John Adams and the Prophets of Progress: A Study in the Intellectual and Political History of the Eighteenth Century* (New York, 1964), chap. 12; Aldridge, *Franklin and His French Contemporaries,* 13.

16. Aldridge, *Franklin and His French Contemporaries,* 130.

17. M. H. Abrams, *The Mirror and the Lamp: Romantic Theory and the Critical Tradition* (New York, 1953), 303–312; cf. David Knight, "Romanticism and the Sciences," in *Romanticism and the Sciences,* ed. Andrew Cunningham and Nicholas Jardine (Cambridge, 1990), 13–24; William Wordsworth, *The Prelude,* bk. 3 (London, 1850); Sergio Perosa, "Franklin to Frankenstein: A Note on Lightning and Novels," in *Science and Imagination in Eighteenth-Century British Culture* (*Scienza e immaginazione della cultura Inglese del settecento*), ed. Sergio Rossi (Milan, 1987), 321–328.

18. Smyth, "Life of BF," 489–490; Charles Coulston Gillispie, *Science and Polity in France at the End of the Old Regime* (Princeton, 1980), 144.

19. Steven C. Bullock, *Revolutionary Brotherhood: Freemasonry and the Transformation of the American Social Order, 1730–1840* (Chapel Hill, N.C., 1996), 85–86.

20. Nian-Sheng Huang, *Benjamin Franklin in American Thought and Culture, 1790–1990* (Philadelphia, 1994), 26–30.

21. John Adams to Benjamin Rush, Apr. 4, 1790, cited in David G. McCullough, *John Adams* (New York, 2001), 420.

22. Richard Hofstadter, *Anti-intellectualism in American Life* (New York, 1963), esp. chaps. 2 and 6, quotations on p. 147; Haraszti, *John Adams and the Prophets of Progress*, chaps. 2 and 3.

23. John C. Greene, *American Science in the Age of Jefferson* (Ames, Iowa, 1984), chap. 1; Joyce E. Chaplin, "Nature and Nation: Natural History in Context," APS *Transactions* 93 (2003), 75–95.

24. Carla Mulford, "Figuring Benjamin Franklin in American Cultural Memory," *NEQ* 72 (1999), 419–421.

25. Ibid., 421–425; Huang, *Benjamin Franklin in American Thought and Culture*, chap. 2; *Proceedings of the Right Worshipful Grand Lodge . . . at Its Celebration of the Bicentenary of . . . Brother Benjamin Franklin* (Philadelphia, 1906), 10, 35.

26. Mulford, "Figuring Benjamin Franklin," 428–434; Huang, *Benjamin Franklin in American Thought and Culture*, chap. 2.

27. Mulford, "Figuring Benjamin Franklin," 428–434, 441.

28. [BF], *Journal of Paris*, Apr. 26, 1784.

29. *BFS*, 12–13; Charles Tanford, *Ben Franklin Stilled the Waves . . .* (Durham, N.C., 1989), chap. 8.

30. Most published scholarship on Humboldt is in German or Spanish. But see Douglas Botting, *Humboldt and the Cosmos* (New York, 1975).

31. Thomas Truxtun, *Remarks, Instructions, and Examples . . .* (Philadelphia, 1794), "Explanation of Chart," n.p.; Margaret Deacon, *Scientists and the Sea, 1650–1900: A Study of Marine Science* (London, 1971), 203–204.

32. Jonathan Williams, *Thermometrical Navigation . . . Through the Gulf Stream . . .* (Philadelphia, 1799), iii–ix, 1–10, 13–15.

33. Anita McConnell, "Six's Thermometer: A Century of Use in Oceanography," in *Oceanography: The Past,* ed. Mary Sears and Daniel Merriman (New York, 1980), 252–265; Deacon, *Scientists and the Sea,* 208–210, 222–223.

34. Helen M. Rozwadowski, *Fathoming the Ocean: The Discovery and Exploration of the Deep Sea* (Cambridge, Mass., 2005).

35. A. D. Bache, "Lecture on the Gulf Stream," *American Journal of Science and Arts* 30 (1860), 1–17; Deacon, *Scientists and the Sea,* 291; Hugh Richard Slotten, *Patronage, Practice, and the Culture of American Science: Alexander Dallas Bache and the United States Coast Survey*, chaps. 4 and 5, quotations on pp. 72, 162.

36. Deacon, *Scientists and the Sea,* 291, 293–295; Frances Leigh Williams, *Matthew Fontaine Maury, Scientist of the Sea* (New Brunswick, N.J., 1963), 150–157, 178–195, 258–268, quotations on pp. 260, 261; *Oxford English Dictionary*, s.v., "oceanography."

37. Greg Dening, *Mr Bligh's Bad Language: Passion, Power and Theatre on the Bounty* (Cambridge, 1992), 326.

38. Greene, *American Science*, chaps. 1, 10, 11.

39. Editorial note, *PBF,* 14:25–28; BF to George Croghan, Aug. 5, 1767, *PBF,* 14:222 (on Franklin's belief that fossils were signs of climate change, not extinc-

tion); Rhoda Rappaport, "The Earth Sciences," *CHS*, 419–435; Paul Semonin, *American Monster: How the Nation's First Prehistoric Creature Became a Symbol of National Independence* (New York, 2000); Erasmus Darwin to BF, July 18, 1772, *PBF*, 19:210–212; Robert Waring Darwin to BF (Paris), Franklin Papers, APS.

40. Conway Zirkle, "Natural Selection before the *Origin of Species*," APS *Proceedings* 84 (1941), 71–123; Zirkle, "Benjamin Franklin, Thomas Malthus and the United States Census," *Isis* 48 (1957), esp. 59–60, 60n.

41. Mary Jo Nye, *Before Big Science: The Pursuit of Modern Chemistry and Physics, 1800–1940* (Cambridge, Mass., 1996), chaps. 1–4.

42. Gordon John Steele, *A Thread across the Ocean: The Heroic Story of the Transatlantic Cable* (New York, 2002); Williams, *Matthew Fontaine Maury*, 225–257, quotations on p. 250; Mulford, "Figuring Benjamin Franklin," 431.

43. Peter Louis Galison, *Einstein's Clocks, Poincaré's Maps: Empires of Time* (New York, 2003).

44. Nye, *Before Big Science*, chap. 6, 201–211; Daniel J. Kevles, *The Physicists: The History of a Scientific Community in Modern America* (Cambridge, Mass., 1987), chaps. 11 and 15.

45. Alan J. Friedman and Carol C. Donley, *Einstein as Myth and Muse* (Cambridge, 1985), chaps. 1 and 4.

46. Kevles, *Physicists*, chaps. 8–10, 19–21; Peter Galison and Bruce Hevly, eds., *Big Science: The Growth of Large-Scale Research* (Palo Alto, Calif., 1992); Richard Rhodes, *The Making of the Atomic Bomb* (New York, 1986).

47. Robert Jungk, *Brighter Than a Thousand Suns*, trans. James Cleugh (New York, 1958), esp. 178–179, 184–186, 203–205, 233–235; Friedman and Donley, *Einstein as Myth and Muse*, 168–178.

48. Deacon, *Scientists and the Sea*, 342, 356–357, 375–376, 382; Gary E. Weir, "Fashioning Naval Oceanography: Columbus O'Donnell Iselin and American Preparation for War, 1940–1941," in *The Machine in Neptune's Garden: Historical Perspectives on Technology and the Marine Environment*, ed. Helen M. Rozwadowski and David K. van Keuren (Sagamore Beach, Mass., 2004), 65–95.

49. Edward Wenk Jr., *The Politics of the Ocean* (Seattle, 1972).

50. Kevles, *Physicists*, 391.

51. Friedman and Donley, *Einstein as Myth and Muse*, esp. chaps. 4 and 6.

52. National Science Foundation, *Science and Engineering Indicators 2000*, available at http://www.nsf.gov/statistics/seindoo and the 2004 update at www.nsf.gov/statistics/seindo4, accessed on Dec. 21, 2005.

53. W. S. Broecker, "Thermohaline Circulation, the Achilles' Heel of Our Climate System: Will Man-Made CO_2 Upset the Current Balance," *Science* 278, no. 5343 (1997), 1582–1588; B. Dickson et al., "Rapid Freshening of the Deep North Atlantic Ocean over the Past Four Decades," *Nature* 416 (2002), 832–837; Brian Fagan, *The Little Ice Age: How Climate Made History, 1300–1850* (New York, 2000), pt. 4; Rachel Carson, *The Sea around Us*, special ed. (New York, 1989), 167–184.

54. Timothy Ferris, *Seeing in the Dark: How Backyard Stargazers Are Probing Deep Space and Guarding Earth from Interplanetary Peril* (New York, 2002).

55. Roderick Cave and Geoffrey Wakeman, *Typographia Naturalis* (Wymondham, UK, 1967), 12–14; Eric P. Newman, "Nature Printing on Colonial and Continental Currency," *Numismatist* 77 (1964), 147–154.

56. Newman, "Nature Printing," 299–306, 457–465, 613–623; Colden cited in *PBF*, 2:386n; Cave and Wakeman, *Typographia Naturalis*, 14.

ACKNOWLEDGMENTS

"I should be ungrateful," wrote Poor Richard (alias Benjamin Franklin) in 1735, "if I did not take every Opportunity of expressing my Gratitude; for *ingratum si dixeris, omnia dixeris.*" And so I give "my most humble and hearty Thanks" to the following organizations and individuals:

For access to archives and help with research there, the American Philosophical Society (particularly Roy Goodman and Valerie-Anne Lutz); the Papers of Benjamin Franklin, Yale University (especially Ellen Cohn, *the* expert); the National Maritime Museum, Greenwich, England; the National Archives, London; the Post Office Archives, London; and the Houghton Library and Map Collection, Harvard University.

For providing critical venues at which I presented parts of this project, the Forum on European Expansion and Global Interaction, the Massachusetts Historical Society, the International Society for Intellectual History, the Johns Hopkins University, and the McNeil Center for Early American Studies.

For their superb work as research assistants, Joseph Adelman, Nathan Perl-Rosenthal, and James Fichter.

For giving me the incredible opportunity to see the Gulf Stream the way Franklin did—from a tall ship—the Sea Education Association of Woods Hole, Massachusetts.

For her faith that an inchoate idea about Franklin could be turned into a book manuscript, Zoe Pagnamenta.

For her careful guidance, which made a manuscript on Franklin into a book about him, Lara Heimert.

For their patient assistance with the many technicalities that now go into making a book, Eddie Lee and Christine Marra.

For their valuable help, encouragement, and advice, Alice Walters, Sally Hadden, Norman Fiering, Stella Fitzthomas, Mordechai Feingold, Charles Rosenberg, and Laurel Ulrich.

For reading portions of the manuscript, James Delbourgo, Darrin McMahon, Nathan Perl-Rosenthal, Fredrika Teute, and Matthew Underwood.

For reading the whole manuscript, David Armitage, Bernard Bailyn, Clint Chaplin, Steven Shapin, and Kara Swanson.

For 1,001 pieces of wisdom, David Armitage.

For waiting decades for me to write a book on a topic he was really interested in, Clint Chaplin.

Index

Page numbers in **bold** indicate figures.